BANGKOK
May 2010

The **Institute of Southeast Asian Studies (ISEAS)** was established as an autonomous organization in 1968. It is a regional research centre dedicated to the study of socio-political, security and economic trends and developments in Southeast Asia and its wider geostrategic and economic environment. The Institute's research programmes are the Regional Economic Studies (RES, including ASEAN and APEC), Regional Strategic and Political Studies (RSPS), and Regional Social and Cultural Studies (RSCS).

ISEAS Publishing, an established academic press, has issued more than 2,000 books and journals. It is the largest scholarly publisher of research about Southeast Asia from within the region. ISEAS Publishing works with many other academic and trade publishers and distributors to disseminate important research and analyses from and about Southeast Asia to the rest of the world.

BANGKOK May 2010

Perspectives on a Divided Thailand

Edited by
Michael J. Montesano
Pavin Chachavalpongpun
Aekapol Chongvilaivan

ISEAS
INSTITUTE OF SOUTHEAST ASIAN STUDIES
SINGAPORE

First published in Singapore in 2012 by
ISEAS Publishing
Institute of Southeast Asian Studies
30 Heng Mui Keng Terrace
Pasir Panjang
Singapore 119614
E-mail: publish@iseas.edu.sg
Website: <http://bookshop.iseas.edu.sg>

ISEAS Library Cataloguing-in-Publication Data

Bangkok, May 2010: perspectives on a divided Thailand / edited by Michael J. Montesano, Pavin Chachavalpongpun and Aekapol Chongvilaivan.
1. Thailand—Politics and government—21st century.
2. Monarchy—Thailand.
3. Political violence—Thailand.
I. Montesano, Michael J.
II. Pavin Chachavalpongpun.
III. Aekapol Chongvilaivan.
DS586 B211 2012

ISBN 978-981-4345-35-4 (soft cover)
ISBN 978-981-4345-34-7 (E-book PDF)

(Cover photo: Thai fire-fighters douse the Central World shopping mall building that was set on fire by anti-government "Red Shirt" protestors in central Bangkok, 21 May 2010. Source: REUTERS/Chaiwat Subprasom)

Typeset by International Typesetters Pte Ltd
Printed in Singapore by Seng Lee Press Pte Ltd

CONTENTS

Contributors ix

1. Introduction: Seeking Perspective on a Slow-Burn Civil War 1
Michael J. Montesano

2. The Culture of the Army, *Matichon* Weekly, 28 May 2010 10
Nidhi Eoseewong

3. Thoughts on Thailand's Turmoil, 11 June 2010 15
James Stent

4. Truth and Justice When Fear and Repression Remain: An Open Letter to Dr Kanit Na Nakorn, 16 July 2010 42
Tyrell Haberkorn

5. The Impact of the Red Shirt Rallies on the Thai Economy 55
Aekapol Chongvilaivan

6. The Socio-Economic Bases of the Red/Yellow Divide: A Statistical Analysis 64
Ammar Siamwalla and Somchai Jitsuchon

7. The Ineffable Rightness of Conspiracy: Thailand's Democrat-ministered State and the Negation of Red Shirt Politics 72
Marc Askew

8. A New Politics of Desire and Disintegration in Thailand 87
Chairat Charoensin-o-larn

9. Notes towards an Understanding of Thai Liberalism 97
Michael K. Connors

10. Thailand's Classless Conflict 108
Shawn W. Crispin

11. The Grand Bargain: Making "Reconciliation" Mean Something 120
Federico Ferrara

12. Changing Thailand, an Awakening of Popular Political Consciousness for Rights? 131
David Fullbrook

13. Class, Inequality, and Politics 141
Kevin Hewison

14. Thailand's Rocky Path towards a Full-Fledged Democracy 161
Kasit Piromya

15. The Color of Politics: Thailand's Deep Crisis of Authority 171
Charles Keyes

16. Two Cheers for Rally Politics 190
Duncan McCargo

17. Thai Foreign Policy in Crisis: From Partner to Problem 199
Ann Marie Murphy

18. Thailand in Trouble: Revolt of the Downtrodden or Conflict among Elites? 214
Pasuk Phongpaichit and Chris Baker

19. From Red to Red: An Auto-ethnography of Economic and Political Transitions in a Northeastern Thai Village 230
Pattana Kitiarsa

20. The Rich, the Powerful and the Banana Man: The United States' Position in the Thai Crisis 248
Pavin Chachavalpongpun

21. The Social Bases of Autocratic Rule in Thailand 267
Craig J. Reynolds

22. The Strategy of the United Front for Democracy against Dictatorship on "Double Standards": A Grand Gesture to History, Justice, and Accountability 274
David Streckfuss

23. No Way Forward but Back? Re-emergent Thai Falangism, Democracy, and the New "Red Shirt" Social Movement 287
Jim Taylor

24. Flying Blind 313
Danny Unger

25. The Political Economy of Thailand's Middle-Income Peasants 323
Andrew Walker

26. Royal Succession and the Evolution of Thai Democracy 333
Andrew Walker

Index 339

CONTRIBUTORS

Aekapol Chongvilaivan is Fellow in and Coordinator of the Regional Economic Studies Programme of the Institute of Southeast Asian Studies and editor, most recently, of *Curbing the Global Economic Downturn: Southeast Asian Macroeconomic Policy* (2010).

Ammar Siamwalla is Distinguished Scholar at and former President of the Thailand Development Research Institute. He is the dean of Thai economists, and a scholar with longstanding interests in Thailand's agricultural economy, rural sector, and political economy.

Marc Askew is Associate Professor in the Regional Studies Program at Walailak University. He is, most recently, editor of *Legitimacy Crisis in Thailand* (2010) and author of a series of major articles on the conflict in Thailand's far South.

Chris Baker is an independent scholar. With Pasuk Phongpaichit, he has co-authored numerous volumes and articles treating Thai history, Thai politics, and the Thai economy. Most recently, the pair have translated *The Tale of Khun Chang Khun Phaen* (2010) into English.

Chairat Charoensin-o-larn is Associate Professor of Political Science at Thammasat University. His research and publications concern such modern French critical theorists as Michel Foucault, Roland Barthes, Jacques Derrida, Gilles Deleuze, and Jacques Rancière and include a project on the aesthetics of contemporary Thai politics.

Michael Connors teaches politics in the School of Social Sciences, La Trobe University. He is author of *Democracy and National Identity in Thailand* (2003; revised edition, 2007) and of "Thailand's Emergency State: Struggles and Transformations", *Southeast Asian Affairs 2011*. He is at work on a manuscript entitled "Contemporary Thailand: Politics, Culture, Rights".

Shawn Crispin is Southeast Asia Editor of *Asia Times Online* <http://www.atimes.com> and Senior Southeast Asia Representative of the Committee to Protect Journalists. He is a former Bangkok bureau chief for both the *Far Eastern Economic Review* and *Wall Street Journal*.

Federico Ferrara is Assistant Professor in the Department of Asian and International Studies of the City University of Hong Kong. He is the author of *Thailand Unhinged: The Death of Thai-Style Democracy* (2011) and numerous articles on electoral and party systems.

David Fullbrook is an independent researcher with interests in agri-business, conflict, development, energy, the environment and food security. His expertise lies in China, Laos, the Mekong River, Thailand, and Southeast Asia in general. He has worked with intergovernmental organizations, bilateral development agencies, and corporations, and contributed frequently to newspapers and magazines in the United Kingdom and East Asia.

Tyrell Haberkorn is Research Fellow in the Department of Political and Social Change of College of Asia and the Pacific of the Australian National University. She is the author of *Revolution Interrupted: Farmers, Students, Law, and Violence in Northern Thailand* (2011).

Kevin Hewison is Director of the Carolina Asia Center, and Professor in the Department of Asian Studies of the University of North Carolina at Chapel Hill. He has published extensively for nearly three decades on globalization and social change in Southeast Asia, especially Thailand; democratization; and labour issues.

Kasit Piromya was the Minister of Foreign Affairs of the Kingdom of Thailand from 2008 to 2011. During thirty-seven years as a career diplomat, his posts included those of Thai ambassador to Russia, Indonesia, Germany, Japan, and the United States.

Charles Keyes is Professor Emeritus of Anthropology and International Studies at the University of Washington. He has continuously conducted field-work in Thailand for five decades and published numerous books and articles on issues of religious, social, and economic change in Thailand. His monograph *Isan: Regionalism in Northeastern Thailand* (1967) ranks among the most influential works ever published on Thailand's Northeast. It appeared in Thai translation in 2009.

Duncan McCargo is Professor of Southeast Asian Politics at the University of Leeds and author of *Tearing Apart the Land: Islam and Legitimacy in Southern Thailand* (2008) and numerous other agenda-setting works on Thai politics.

Michael J. Montesano is a Visiting Research Fellow at the Institute of Southeast Asian Studies and a historian. He is the book review editor for the blog New Mandala, and a regular columnist on Southeast Asian affairs for the *Wall Street Journal Asia*.

Ann Marie Murphy is Associate Professor in the Whitehead School of Diplomacy and International Relations at Seton Hall University and Fellow of the National Asia Research Program. Her research, both academic and policy-oriented, concerns political development in Southeast Asia, American policy towards the region, and the international relations of Asia. She is co-editor of *Legacy of Engagement in Southeast Asia* (2008).

Nidhi Eoseewong is one of Thailand's most prominent living historians. He was for many years Professor in the Department of History, Chiang Mai University. A volume of his selected essays in translation, *Pen & Sail: Literature and History in Early Bangkok,* was published in 2005. A prolific columnist, he writes regularly for *Matichon* weekly magazine and in the Monday edition of *Matichon* daily newspaper. In July 2010 he was appointed to the National Reform Committee chaired by Anan Panyarachun.

Pasuk Phongpaichit is Professor of Economics at Chulalongkorn University. In addition to numerous volumes and articles on Thai history and politics and on the Thai economy, she and Chris Baker are, most recently, the translators and editors of *The Tale of Khun Chang Khun Phaen* (2010).

Pattana Kitiarsa is Assistant Professor in the Department of Southeast Asian Studies of the Faculty of Arts and Social Sciences of the National University of Singapore. He has published in both Thai and English in the fields of Thai popular Buddhism, transnational labour migration, boxing, and film. He is the editor of *Religious Commodifications in Asia: Marketing Gods* (2008).

Pavin Chachavalpongpun is Fellow in the Regional Strategic and Political Studies Programme at the Institute of Southeast Asian Studies and Lead Researcher for Political and Strategic Affairs in the Institute's ASEAN Studies Centre. He is a frequent commentator on Thai politics and foreign policy in a wide range of newspapers and author, most recently, of *Reinventing Thailand: Thaksin Shinawatra and His Foreign Policy* (2010).

Craig Reynolds is a Professor affiliated with the School of Culture, History and Language in the College of Asia and the Pacific of the Australian National University. He is the author of *Seditious Histories: Contesting Thai and Southeast Asian Pasts* (2006) and "Behind the Thai Crisis" at Inside Story, 29 April 2010 <http://inside.org.au/behind-the-thai-crisis/>.

Somchai Jitsuchon is Research Director for Macroeconomic Development and Income Distribution in the Macroeconomic Policy Program of the Thailand Development Research Institute.

James Stent served for two decades as a senior executive and director of the Bank of Asia. He is a former director of the Thai Rating and Information Services credit-rating agency, a former council member and Honorary Treasurer of the Siam Society, and a current director of the Beijing Cultural Heritage Protection Research Center.

David Streckfuss is an independent writer and scholar who lives in Khon Kaen, northeastern Thailand. He is the author of *Truth on Trial in Thailand: Defamation, Treason, and Lèse-Majesté* (2010). He is an occasional contributor to such publications as the *Bangkok Post* and *Wall Street Journal Asia*.

Jim Taylor is Senior Lecturer in Anthropology at the University of Adelaide. He is the author of *Buddhism and Postmodern Imaginings in Thailand (2008)* and *Forest Monks and the Nation-State: An Anthropological and Historical Study in Northeastern Thailand* (1993). His interests include critical theory, rural social transformation and cultural change, anthropology and the discourse of development, ethno-ecology, and Thai Buddhism.

Danny Unger is Associate Professor in the Department of Political Science of Northern Illinois University and a scholar of comparative political economy, civil society, and international relations. His books include *Building Social Capital in Thailand: Fibers, Finance and Infrastructure* (1998) and, with Alasdair Bowie, *The Politics of Open Economies: Indonesia, Malaysia, the Philippines and Thailand* (1997).

Andrew Walker is an anthropologist in the College of Asia and the Pacific of the Australian National University. He is co-founder of the blog New Mandala (<http://asiapacific.anu.edu.au/newmandala>), which provides anecdote, analysis, and new perspectives on Mainland Southeast Asia. His new book is *Thailand Political Peasants* (forthcoming).

1

INTRODUCTION
Seeking Perspective on a Slow-Burn Civil War

Michael J. Montesano

History's eventual consensus on the intractable conflict that has scarred Thailand's early twenty-first century is impossible to foretell. That conflict may take its place as but one chapter in a larger story of liberal democracy in retreat, both in an increasingly Sinocentric Greater East Asia and in other parts of the world too. It may come to represent a sad example of rival social and economic elites' selfishly tearing a society apart and in the process dooming a country to long-term decline. It may come to be understood as the inevitable outcome of the post-1960 public policy failings of Thailand and its Southeast Asian neighbours, above all in such areas as education, failings that contrast so markedly with to the successes of such Northeast Asian states as the Republic of Korea.

Scholars may treat the ongoing conflict between Red and Yellow as Asia's first major violent revolution — whether triumphant or extinguished — of the young century. They may see it as the sad end to a royal reign that looked so successful for so long. Or they may determine that it was due to the greed, cynicism, and evil of Thaksin Shinawatra alone.

More hopefully, these years may one day be seen as a time during which Thailand came to grips with its changing nature and worked out — if fitfully and with all too much bitterness and loss of life — a social, political, and economic order that reflected its great fundamental strengths and its enduring potential for pluralism and tolerance. Or these years may remain the subject of ongoing, unresolved, and even violent contention among the historians of the future, Thai and foreign alike.

The uncertainty about ultimate understandings of the post-2005 period in Thai history notwithstanding, the events of recent years have made a number of realities very clear.

First, in a post-Asian Financial Crisis age of increasing income skews and burgeoning finance capitalism, many residents of Bangkok have lost all awareness of and interest in that great primate city's hinterland. The "development era" launched by Field Marshal Sarit Thanarat in exemplary partnership with King Bhumibol Adulyadej in the late 1950s is all but forgotten in the Thailand of 2011. And this is to say nothing of the ethnological studies of Phraya Anuman Ratchathon, the sustained campaign of Prince Sitthiphon Kridikon against the "rice premium" and the urban bias in Thai fiscal policy, and the socio-political vision that motivated Bunchu Rotchanasathian during his tenure as Kukrit Pramoj's finance minister. After all, what value could knowledge of these have, when Kinokuniya at the Siam Paragon or Emporium shopping malls has all the English-language management texts and life-style magazines that the globalized reader might ever need?

Second, concern over the role and future of the Thai monarchy ranks as one of factors that account for Thailand's deep ongoing crisis. Strikingly, as the crisis enters its sixth year, fewer and fewer observers and participants, regardless of their leaning or persuasion, attempt to deny this reality. Even cursory examination of the contributions to this volume makes evident how much and how quickly times have changed in the study and analysis of Thai politics. That study long avoided rigorous consideration of the role of the country's monarchy in its political life. As the basis of scholarship that offered reasonably convincing interpretations of political change in Thailand, focus on other, safer, topics seemed to suffice. No longer. In a certain sense, there is justice in the abrupt recognition that analyses that steer clear of the Thai monarchy and its active role in politics over many years are no longer credible. For the astonishing revival of monarchy during the ninth Chakri reign was central to Thailand's image, at home and abroad, as a successful and exceptional place in the decades after 1960. But there is, as they say, no such thing as a free lunch: the pre-eminence of Thailand's royal institution, its emphasis on entrusting "good men" with influence and authority rather than on fostering the development of other institutions, has had consequences.

Third, on a related note and with Michael Connors's immensely significant contribution to the present volume very much in mind, one finds that the years since Sonthi Limthongkun first launched his campaign to oust Thaksin Shinawatra from the Thai premiership in 2005 have forced Thailand's well born, well educated, well compensated and otherwise fortunate to confront an unprecedented fork in the trail. Elitism and liberalism, which for so long seemed plausibly to follow the same path in Thailand, have parted ways. This development is manifest in examples of many sorts, but two examples serve to illustrate it with particular clarity. The first is the unconcealed bigotry of many Bangkokians towards their rural compatriots, and indeed towards their rural-born neighbours in the Thai capital itself. The second is the accelerating use of the inherently illiberal law of *lèse majesté* to defend an order and an institution long regarded by many as progressive and admirable, if inherently inegalitarian.

The slow-burn civil war that has engulfed Thailand for almost six years has brought many exciting, discouraging, and memorable events. As a number of the contributions to this book indicate, the putsch that saw tanks roll out onto the streets of Bangkok on 19 September 2006 had considerable impact on many observers' understandings of this period. But earlier episodes in the conflict continue to merit attention. Among these are the still poorly understood acquisition of Shin Corporation by Temasek Holdings in January 2006 and the Thai king's portentous remarks to two groups of judges on 25 April of the same year.[1] Among later events, the failure of the putschists of 2006, and of those in league with them, to secure the results that they tried to arrange in the parliamentary elections of 23 December 2007,[2] the ferocious violence of the Yellow Shirts of the People's Alliance for Democracy (PAD) towards the police at Government House during the first week of October 2008, and the same group's occupation of Bangkok's Suvarnabhumi Airport in late November and early December 2008 have also given shape to the ongoing conflict. So have the disruption of the ASEAN Plus Three and East Asia Summits at Pattaya on the part of the Red Shirts of the National United Front for Democracy against Dictatorship on 11 April 2009 and the violence that that same group brought to Bangkok in the days immediately afterward.

Despite this run of dramatic and significant precedents, the events that unfolded on the streets of Bangkok during 14–19 May 2010 were still able to shock and disturb Thailand and the world. Those events followed both a night of chaos and loss of life in the general area of the Thai capital's Democracy Monument on 10 April and the drawn-out occupation of the city's Ratchaprasong shopping precinct by Red Shirt protestors for more than a month thereafter. As time passed, violence — much still poorly understood — began to punctuate that occupation with increasing frequency. Following action by the Thai military to cordon the protest area off on 14 March and several days of pitched battles in districts bordering Ratchaprasong, the protests came to an end in the surrender of the Red Shirt leadership and a horrifying orgy of arson on 19 May. The graphic images of those battles and of that arson that circulated internationally, the reports of the murders of people taking shelter in Wat Pathumwanaram temple, and a cumulative death toll in April and May 2010 that exceeded those of even the long-remembered, epoch-making Thai tragedies of 14 October 1973 and 6 October 1976 gave what happened in Bangkok in mid-May of 2010 an impact and an importance to which this book seeks to speak.

The first three contributions to the volume reflect reactions to and offer perspectives on the shocking and disturbing events of 14–19 May 2010 that date from the days and weeks directly following those events. Nidhi Eoseewong's piece first appeared, in Thai, in *Matichon* weekly magazine less than a fortnight after the violence and arson at Ratchaprasong. James Stent's essay dates from just a week or two later. It was originally circulated in soft copy and appears in published form for the first time here. Each of these contributions to the book both draws on its author's eminence as observer of and participant in Thai society. Each also reflects its author's conviction that the events that had just occurred needed to be put into perspective, regardless of how much grimmer his perspective would make those events appear. Like the Nidhi and Stent pieces, Tyrell

Haberkorn's contribution to the volume, in the form of an open letter to Kanit Na Nakorn dated 16 July 2010, represents an invaluable reminder of the period after 19 May 2010.

This is a period that many on the Yellow side of Thailand's political divide and indeed in the government fronted by Abhisit Vejjajiva would rather see forgotten. They would see it scrubbed from of our memories just as vigorously as, early in that same period, groups of Bangkokians scrubbed the streets of Ratchaprasong of the untidy and unpleasant reminders of the defeated Red Shirts who had occupied those streets for so many weeks. For it was a period that brought not only never fulfilled official promises of "reconciliation" but also an utterly discordant official anti-Red Shirt "witch hunt"[3] both in Bangkok and in provincial Thailand.

It was also the period that motivated the preparation of this volume, whose purpose is to ask, quite simply, "What did the events of mid-May 2010 in Bangkok mean?" As the volume makes clear, observers and students of contemporary Thailand with a range of orientations running from deep "red" to bright "yellow" refuse to forget the urgency that that question assumed during the weeks following 19 May.

To answer the question, the volume's editors commissioned what were envisioned as lightly foot-noted extended op-ed pieces to complement the first three pieces in the book. In the event, some contributors responded with more extended and less lightly cited pieces than others. But all contributors responded in a common spirit of reflection, in a shared recognition of the need to achieve and to share perspective on the events, the loss of life, and the destruction of 14–19 May 2010. Some, maybe most, of the contributions to this volume have interpretive or political agendas. Rather fewer, perhaps, are clearly "yellow" in their point of view than are unabashedly "red". Without naming names, it is nevertheless worth noting that the generally "red" tendencies of foreign and Thai scholars mean that the "yellow" contributions to the volume — each argued with vigour, subtlety, and insight — have disproportionate value to any effort to gain perspective.

Rather than impose thematic or topical organization on the contributions to the book, its editors have opted to present those that follow the first three in alphabetical order of contributors' names. The previous scholarship and commentary of a number of the contributors to the volume will in many cases give their views on the events in Bangkok during mid-May 2010 inherent interest to readers. And the liberty to chart his or her own path through this collection ought allow each reader to focus initially on those dimensions of the conflict currently dividing Thailand that most interest him or her, and to work out for him- or herself how the perspectives advanced in this collection relate to one another, and which perspectives are most compelling. This approach to organizing the volume notwithstanding, it is still useful to call attention to some of the commonalities among the diverse contributions that follow.

Shawn Crispin, Kasit Piromya, and Pasuk Phongpaichit and Chris Baker offer broad interpretations of the dramatic events and underlying developments that culminated in the incidents of mid-May 2010 in Bangkok. In their essays on social inequality and political disenfranchisement and on the Red Shirts and their enemies, David Fullbrook and Jim Taylor also place those events in broad perspective.

The contributions to the volume both of Ammar Siamwalla and Somchai Jitsuchon and of Kevin Hewison submit the matter of inequality as it informs Thailand's Red/Yellow divide to careful scrutiny. Hewison's essay illuminates the troubling realities that characterize Thailand's post-1997 "economic recovery". Aekapol Chongvilaivan analyses the economic consequences of the protests of March–May 2010 and the policy measures that might have addressed those consequences.

The collection benefits from a number of particularly well informed considerations of the patterns of social change in rural Thailand that have been the backdrop to the country's long, deep crisis. These considerations come above all in the contributions of Charles Keyes, Pattana Kitiarsa, and Andrew Walker. Each of these contributions makes very clear how little relevance long-prevalent understandings of rural Thai society have to efforts to think about Thailand's current afflictions and future prospects.

Assessment of those prospects depends on unflinching examination of some of the fundamental, though rarely discussed, features of contemporary Thai politics. The contributions to this volume of Marc Askew, Michael Connors, Duncan McCargo, and David Streckfuss offer such examination. They are joined by Andrew Walker's essay on the looming royal succession and by Danny Unger's path-breaking consideration of the quality of political information in Thailand. Chairat Charoensin-o-larn and Craig Reynolds complement the implicit culturalism of Unger's approach with their own examinations of the most basic foundations of the Thai political order. Finally, in his concrete consideration of the requisite features of lasting reconciliation, Federico Ferrara also turns his attention to Thailand's future.

Over many decades, Thailand's positive international image has served to buttress its domestic social order. It remains too early to know how the country's long post-2005 crisis, the events of May 2010, and the end of the current reign will alter Thailand's international image and thus kick away one of the props on which stubborn, obsolescent understandings of that social order have depended. It is not too early, however, to examine the interface between Thailand's domestic political travails and its international relations. The contributions to this volume of Ann Marie Murphy and Pavin Chachavalpongpun bring just such examinations to the volume.

As the first anniversary of the events that provoked preparation of this volume came and went, it had become clear that the "road map to national reconciliation" that the government fronted by Democrat Party leader Abhisit Vejjajiva had pledged to follow in the aftermath of those events had led Thailand nowhere close to its promised destination. Instead, the Yellow government and its Yellow institutional allies had brought surface quiescence to the Thai political scene; Marc Askew was not alone in recalling Tacitus's well known comment on "wastelands" and "peace" at this time. The government's increasingly frequent references to the possibility of elections in mid-2011 signalled nothing so much as its own and its backers' conviction that they had toughed out the crisis of the preceding year. That conviction brought with it an apparent determination to apply the formulae of messy coalition government, supported by the occasional suasion and coercion of Army and palace, that had characterized the Thai political order during the last twenty years of the twentieth century. In short, Thailand's government after the 2011 election was to look very much like its government in the two years preceding those polls, and very much like the governments led by Prem Tinsulanon during the 1980s and Chuan Leekphai during the 1990s. Of course, some tweaking — relating not least to an older sovereign and increased welfare spending — of the old formulae would be necessary. In the main, however, any fundamental impact of Thaksin Shinawatra on the Thai political order was denied by the Yellow forces in the ascendant until the polls of 3 July put paid to their remarkable illusions.

Parliamentarians on the Red side of Thailand's political divide understood clearly what was afoot. They recognized that powerful interests in Thailand opposed the formation of a Red- or Thaksinite-leaning government after the elections. These Reds Shirt politicians insisted, however, that the presence of representatives of "democratic forces" in the Thai parliament would in itself send a powerful message about Thailand's potential to enjoy a better future. It would make clear that, despite the state of denial into which many on the Yellow side of today's divided Thailand talked themselves, this is not over yet. In an important sense, these Red politicians' perspective made them the great optimists of the moment. For, among foreign observers and members of Thailand's old-time liberal elites, that state of denial — along with the deep division that Prime Minister Abhisit and his confederates failed meaningfully to address after coming to power in December 2008, after surviving the violence of April 2009, and after cracking down on the Red Shirt movement in May 2010 — had led to the conclusion that the Thai political system is in a state of collapse.

The editors of this volume thank the contributors to the volume, both for providing such a stimulating range of perspectives on Thailand's civil conflict and for showing such patience with the lead editor as he worked so slowly on the book. Special acknowledgement is due to Craig Reynolds for translating Nidhi Eoseewong's contribution to this book, and indeed to Professor Nidhi for allowing the inclusion of his piece in the volume. We thank Nick Nostitz for making available the photographs that enrich the book. We are also grateful to Charnvit Kasetsiri for his counsel during the preparation of the volume and to the leadership of the Institute of Southeast Asian Studies for the opportunity to pursue our research on Thailand's politics, economy, and history in such a stimulating and congenial setting. At the same time, we stress that the views expressed in their contributions are the contributors' own, rather than those of the institutions with which they are affiliated or of ISEAS. Finally, we take pleasure in expressing appreciation, yet again, for the efforts of our colleagues in the ISEAS Publications Unit, above all Rahilah Yusuf, to bring this book to press.

Notes

1. A brief review of the events of 2006 is available in Michael J. Montesano, "Thailand: A Reckoning with History Begins", *Southeast Asian Affairs 2007* (Singapore: Institute of Southeast Asian Studies, 2007), pp. 311–39. For subsequent years, see Duncan McCargo, "Thailand: State of Anxiety". *Southeast Asian Affairs 2008* (Singapore: Institute of Southeast Asian Studies,2008), pp. 333–59; James Ockey, "Thailand in 2008: Democracy and Street Politics", *Southeast Asian Affairs 2009* (Singapore: Institute of Southeast Asian Studies, 2009), pp. 315–33; Chairat Charoensin-olarn, "Thailand in 2009: Unusual Politics Becomes Usual", *Southeast Asian Affairs 2010* (Singapore: Institute of Southeast Asian Studies, 2010), pp. 303–32; and Michael K. Connors, "Thailand's Emergency State: Struggles and Transformations", *Southeast Asian Affairs 2011* (Singapore: Institute of Southeast Asian Studies, 2011), pp. 287–305.
2. Those polls are the subject of a superb recent study, Pasuk Phongpaichit and Chris Baker, "The Mask-play Election: Generals, Politicians, and Voters at Thailand's 2007 Poll", Asia Research Institute Working Paper No. 144, National University of Singapore, September 2010, available at <www.ari.nus.edu.sg/publication_details.asp?pubtypeid=WP&pubid=1667> (accessed 26 February 2011).
3. Thitinan Pongsudhirak called attention to the risk of such a witch hunt in comments quoted in the *Washington Post*. See "Thailand tries to go after financial backers of 'red shirts'", *Washington Post*, 28 May 2010 <http://www.washingtonpost.com/wp-dyn/content/article/2010/05/27/AR2010052705708.html> (accessed 5 March 2011).

2

THE CULTURE OF THE ARMY *Matichon* Weekly, 28 May 2010

Nidhi Eoseewong

Say what you'd like, but I've thought for a long time that being a soldier in today's regular Army is a very odd occupation. This is because the soldier is willing to risk life itself to kill a stranger for absolutely nothing. Moreover, you have as much of a chance of being killed as of killing someone else.

Human society created the soldier a long time ago, but soldiers in various societies constituted a caste in the sense that they were born into a lineage of soldiers, for example, the knights in medieval Europe or the samurai during the Edo period in Japan. These people enjoyed many special economic, social, and political privileges and were also feared and respected by the population at large.

Soldiers were willing to risk their lives in battle in order to protect their privileges, or they fought duels to defend their own honour and dignity and to instil fear and respect in others. They did all this entirely

---

This piece originally appeared in *Matichon* weekly magazine, issue 30, 1554 (28 May–3 June 2010), under the title "*Watthanatham kongthap*". It appears here with the permission of the author, in English translation by Craig J. Reynolds.

for their personal benefit, which is little different from the hired gunman nowadays who is willing to kill for a fee.

But soldiers in the regular armies of today gain nothing by risking their lives in that way. They are required to go into battle if ordered to do so by their superiors with the full understanding that they may face the most terrifying dangers. In the midst of a hail of bullets from enemy machine-gun fire causing their mates in battle to be cut down before their very eyes, or shrapnel from artillery fire all the time blasting people into pieces, and so on and so forth, their commanding officers order them to move forward to attack the enemy. In those extremely dangerous conditions there is a real person in uniform who might react according to ordinary human instinct by looking for a way to escape from the danger and return home to his wife and family.

Thus the enormous challenge that all modern armies have to confront: how are they going to retain soldiers in such conditions of extreme danger and keep them from deserting and returning to civilian life? If this cannot be managed, they cannot possibly engage the enemy in battle even for an instant. Soldiers will all break ranks, scatter, and run back to bury their heads in the bosoms of their wives and mothers.

Some readers may object and say that soldiers give their lives to defend their country, so the ideology of nationalism is more than enough to keep an army fighting forever. These nationalist feelings have been instilled in us from an early age, and military training arouses these feelings in soldiers even more intensely. Yet regular armies in modern times know full well that love for the nation alone is not powerful enough nowadays to keep soldiers from running away from the dangers of the battlefield. Do not forget that the nation is something in the imagination that cannot be compared to the concrete realities of peoples' lives. The nation is not like wives and children who are real and who affect a person's life in a concrete way.

Therefore, all regular armies in modern times must rely on two methods that will induce human beings to overcome concern for their own lives and be bloodthirsty enough to perform the cruellest acts in battle.

One method is to make the enemy into a devil (Eng. "demonization"). We can talk about this in a way that Thais today understand very well, namely, that the enemy must be dehumanized. Why is it that the Centre for the Resolution of the Emergency Situation found it necessary to release information about the plan to overthrow the monarchy (*lom jao*) many weeks before it set about dispersing the crowds? This was to demonize "the enemy" first.

In addition to the notion of loyalty to "the royals", the institution of the monarchy in Thai society has become the centre of the universe for everyone's well-being. People in every occupation, including soldiers, are able to imagine a future for themselves in which they gradually advance to this or that goal. At the very least, they aspire to a degree of security, even if it is only to hold on to the security they already enjoy. Today they are privates, tomorrow they are sergeants, and perhaps before retirement they may even reach second lieutenant. Therefore, the real meaning of "overthrow the monarchy" is the cessation of this state of well-being as well as the career prospects that soldiers have come to expect. This would have an inescapable impact on each and every soldier as well as his wife and children.

Thai soldiers were sent off to the battlefields of World War I and told to fight "a righteous war." They fought in the Korean and Vietnamese Wars, and in the war against the Communist Party of Thailand to oppose the devils called communists. Those who seek the overthrow of the monarchy are thus equivalent to devils who must be exterminated, or at the very least they must not be allowed to rise up again.

According to the testimony of a member of the volunteer medical rescue team working at Wat Pathumwanaram at the very end of the crackdown, in the midst of the hail of bullets from Army sharp-shooters that indiscriminately struck those who had taken refuge, people in the temple had called out, "Why are you shooting?" The soldiers had shouted back, "You bastards are nothing but dirt. We will kill you all. You've created havoc."

Note the cruelty of these words, but then the solders are actually talking to the terrible devils rather like the way in which an exorcist disposes of malevolent spirits by drowning them, or by plunging them screaming into rice grains over which he has cast a spell.

Making one's opponent into a terrifying devil leaves the soldier with no choice but to fight to the death. At the very end of the Great East Asian War, the Japanese soldiers were told that the American troops who were creeping up on them would take no prisoners; they would murder all who surrendered. So the Japanese soldiers fought to the death, because if they did not die in battle, they would die in defeat.

The second method on which armies rely involves the creation of a new kind of deep bonding. Let me illustrate with an example from the American military that will make the point clear. All new recruits are trained to have a mate (Eng. "buddy") in the squadrons or platoons that engage in military missions together. War then becomes a fight to preserve life, not only one's own life, but that of one's mate as well. Whether they are reacting to a fatal shot or to a serious injury, soldiers see red not for love of nation, but because they are outraged on behalf of their mates and see it as their duty to avenge them even if they die in the act.

I believe that the Thai Army does not employ the code of mateship. Instead, the Thai Army introduced a new kind of bonding among soldiers in the squadrons, platoons, and fighting cohorts. Seeing a friend fatally injured arouses in a soldier intense feelings of revenge which overwhelms any impulse to retreat.

An officer in the volunteer medical rescue unit, who was working at the Sam Yan intersection, reported that soldiers shot into a civilian crowd and dispersed it, leaving only his own team which had taken cover in the ambulance that was clearly marked. A group of seven or eight armed soldiers approached, and demanded, "You bastards as well?" So the door opened and a member of the rescue team said, "We're not involved — this is an ambulance." That person was shot in the left arm and didn't get a chance to finish speaking. One of the soldiers had already kneeled to take aim. After the chaos of taking care of the injured and being shot as well, when the ambulance was finally able to make its way from the Hotel Miracle, the team passed another group of soldiers who began shooting at them. They yelled out, "Why are you shooting at us? This is an ambulance." The soldiers replied, "You bastards threw something at us."

Don't bother to ask why such a trivial incident should provoke gunfire — it's beside the point. The point is the new self that the Army has created in the squadrons, platoons, and fighting units when they are under attack. Whether or not the person who fired had been hit by something is irrelevant. The act had to be avenged.

All of the material cited above comes from *Prachatai On-line* and appears on many other websites as well, but no accounts of these incidents ever appeared in the so-called mainstream media.

As of 21 May 2010, the number of casualties announced by the Ministry of Public Health is now 85 dead and 1,813 wounded, calculated from the beginning of the protests in March. Almost certainly the death toll is higher, because witnesses have seen soldiers placing bodies in a vehicle (at least four bodies at the Sala Daeng intersection on 19 May). These casualties are the highest in any crackdown since 14 October 1973.

The decision to use armed force to disperse a crowd, even taking into consideration that some of these people had weapons, was a grievous error, not because the Army lacked the equipment to disperse the crowd. The equipment could easily have been purchased. It is well known that the Army is not made to deal with crowds in terms of its psychology. Leave aside the fact that the throng contained their own Thai brothers and sisters, and that this was a crowd in the very country that the Army protected. History has shown that regular armies employ one method only to disperse crowds: a hail of bullets. In other words, the culture of the regular Army makes it impossible to disperse a crowd peacefully.

Thai prime ministers, nevertheless, have used soldiers to disperse crowds many times. The prime minister has always escaped scot-free, at the very most by spending a short time abroad. This includes Mr Thaksin Shinawatra, who ruthlessly dispersed the crowd at Tak Bai with the most inhumane methods. If Thailand allows the current prime minister to escape scot-free on this occasion with such a loss of life, we are sure to experience crackdowns like this again in the future. And don't think next time you won't be a victim.

At the same time, I do not think we should allow those giving the orders to accuse soldiers who have committed these cruel acts of acting wrongly, because soldiers operate within a culture that those giving the orders know full well leaves troops in the regular Army little choice but to conduct themselves in this way.

3

THOUGHTS ON THAILAND'S TURMOIL 11 June 2010

James Stent

BACKGROUND

In the latter part of the 1990s, after the financial crisis of 1997, but before the ascent of Thaksin, I was occasionally asked to speak to groups of foreign investment analysts visiting Thailand. I set forth the gist of what I used to say to these analysts, as it gives context to my thoughts on the present turmoil:

> Thailand is a country characterized by a high degree of ideological homogeneity, with broad consensus at all levels of society on the core

---

This essay was originally written on 11 June of 2010 as a private document to be read by overseas friends inquiring into the events of the previous weeks in Thailand. It subsequently received considerable exposure on the Internet, and the author has now revised it for inclusion in this collection. In the revisions that the author has made, he is indebted to Paul Wedel and to several others who provided excellent feedback and suggestions, from which the final version has benefited. Notwithstanding this, all of the contents of this essay remain the author's sole responsibility and reflect his personal point of view.

values of Thailand and on what it means to be a Thai. This consensus includes veneration of the king, a leading role for the Buddhist religion, adherence to a free market economic system, support for a hierarchical society that emphasizes respect for superiors and seniors, provides an elevated position in society for Army, civil servants and police, and by implication leaves control of the nation in the hands of an establishment that sits at the top levels of the social pyramid. Over the decades, this establishment has instilled this view of the nation throughout all levels of society, with inculcation starting in the schools and reinforced continually through media, portraits of the royal family, etc. To dissent from the main elements of this consensus is to be "Un-Thai". In fact, there have been few dissenters, and those that have bucked the consensus are marginalized, either through social pressure, or through police action. This consensus has made for a stable society in which people generally accept their place in life, but which also allows for sufficient social mobility to accommodate the bright and ambitious. Considerable economic development has occurred under this consensus and stability, and as a result the lot of poor villagers has improved substantially over the past half-century. The fears of many that communism would engulf the nation, as it had China and Indochina, have proven unwarranted.

This stable consensus has benefited the elite levels of society, a few thousand members of which control what happens in the country. This elite occupies the key positions in the bureaucracy, the military, police, business establishment (particularly banks), and clergy, in both Bangkok and in provincial cities. None of them seeks change in the social, political and economic structure that provides them with such a comfortable way of life and position in society, and which has also led to satisfactory growth of the economy and improvement in the lives of the mass of the population.

Political parties in this system do not have significantly different agendas, much less ideologies, because the people that control the parties all share in the benefits of the system. Thai politics has been about dividing up the pie among the elite, with a certain amount of benefits trickling down to the grass roots. The few people, such as Kukrit Pramoj and Bunchu Rotchanasathian, who tried to change the nature of politics to be more responsive to social and economic justice issues, did not have much impact, and civil society was tolerated provided that it did not push radical reform of the system. A man like Banharn Silpa-archa could rise from humble origins through this structure to

> become prime minister, but he did it through playing within the system brilliantly, rather than challenging the system.
>
> The growing middle class accepted this consensus and accompanying political model, as their lives were appreciably improving; the broad mass of farmers and factory workers accepted it as reflecting the nature of the world, and anyway their lot was demonstrably improving over the years, as the cash economy transformed subsistence villages, road networks and electricity reached the farthest corners of the kingdom, and new job opportunities opened up in the cities as outlets for excess rural labour. Besides that, given the unity of the establishment and its grip on the levers of power, how were farmers and labourers going to change the system even if they had wanted to?
>
> But, if this system of elite governance is to continue to dominate Thailand, then Thailand will never fully realize its development potential as a nation, because the majority of the population is not fully involved in the mainstream of society. Those Asian countries that have forged ahead — Japan, Korea, Taiwan, Singapore, Hong Kong, and to a certain extent Malaysia — have brought the majority of their populations into the middle class, providing them with good education, land reform, social welfare, relatively equitable distribution of wealth and power, etc. Thailand does not seem to have that sort of inclusive vision. In fact, in the mid-1990s, when Amnuay Virawan was deputy prime minister and "Economic Czar", it appeared that labor costs were rising to a level that would reduce the profits of labour-intensive factory owners. Rather than encouraging such factories to improve productivity so that they could afford to pay laborers more, Amnuay's answer to the "problem" was to allow the factories to employ immigrant labor from neighboring Cambodia, Burma, and elsewhere, thereby undercutting Thai wages and forcing them back down. If the broad masses of Thais were brought to the levels of their counterparts in Korea and Taiwan, the comfortable hierarchical social structure would be jeopardized. And that might undermine the privileged position of the elite, resulting in a more meritocratic social structure.

Those were my thoughts on Thailand during the latter half of the 1990s. I recall once giving that discourse informally to a *farang* friend. When I had finished, he said, "Well, you may be right, Jim, but if you are right, then I certainly hope it never changes, because I like it just the way it is." That was a very honest statement, because indeed we *farang* have generally also benefited from the way the system works, and as a result have found Thailand a most enchanting place to live (and the United States, as part of its anti-communist efforts in the Indochina region from the 1950s through the 1970s, played a role in fostering this consensus and supported elite control of the country). I reassured my friend that he need not worry, as I saw very little evidence that anything would happen to change the system much in the next few years — the elite had the country under control, the system was well entrenched, and the honest Thai people of the countryside were discouraged from doing much about it. After all, from primary school onwards they had been taught that asking too many impertinent questions was counter-cultural.

Today, I believe that my analysis of the system that prevailed in Thailand was correct, but I was completely wrong about nothing arising to challenge it. A man named Thaksin Shinawatra burst on the scene, and Thailand has never been the same since. From being a country of ideological homogeneity, in the space of a few years it became a country deeply divided. Thaksin astutely recognized that the majority of voters were resident in the countryside, and that they had, over the preceding decades of steady economic development, become a sleeping but nonetheless restless giant that was just waiting to be awakened. Once awakened, that rural electorate has not returned to sleep.

It is well to remember that when Thaksin was first campaigning, he was not only supported by the rural masses, but also by a number of forward-thinking and responsible intellectuals in Bangkok, who saw in him a new type of politician who might bring about some of the changes in Thailand that they knew were needed if Thailand were to be a modern nation and competitive in the twenty-first century. This is significant, as it indicates that a decade ago, a portion of the intelligentsia of Thailand was aware of the need for change in the country, and, despairing of people like former Democrat Prime Minister Chuan Leekphai to bring a new vision to the governance of the country, they placed their hopes in Thaksin as an agent of change.

The tragedy is that Thaksin proved to be a false prophet — a venal and egotistical demagogue who had recognized the potential power of the rural voting masses, but did not use this insight genuinely to reform the nature of Thai society. His motivations seem to me to have been a complex mixture of genuine interest in promoting the good of the nation and greed for power and wealth for himself. I see him in shades of grey — neither the messiah that his rural followers take him for even today, nor the devil incarnate that the Bangkok elite see him as being. Whatever his true nature, he did implement several good policies, such as health care for the poor and the "One *Tambon*, One Product" (OTOP) programme, but he became increasingly corrupt, intolerant, and dictatorial in his governing style. The press was gradually intimidated, the judiciary and other independent parts of the government were subverted, and human rights violations became increasingly blatant.

Yet, in the elections of 2005, Thaksin's party was returned to power with the largest mandate ever awarded by the electorate to a Thai political leader. The Democrat Party, effectively the only organized parliamentary opposition that remained, proved from the time of Thaksin's election in 2001 unable to rethink its approach and image, or to present rural voters with any sort of credible alternative to Thaksin. The educated middle and upper classes of Bangkok seethed with resentment against Thaksin and were genuinely fearful of the power that he might accumulate in the future and the implications of that concentration of power for Thai democracy. But my own feeling at the time was that they would either have to put up some viable political alternative to Thaksin, or else accept that they would have to live under the man for some time to come, as this was the price to be paid for having failed to develop an inclusive national reform vision that reached out to and fully involved the poorer majority of voters who had now turned to Thaksin as their political idol.

Bangkok friends retorted that Thaksin was elected only because of the power of his wealth, and that the voters were bribed. From my own experience in the village of Ban Ton Thi in Chiang Rai, I knew that Thaksin's Thai Rak Thai party was indeed alleged to have paid 500 baht to each villager to secure votes, but in my conversations with the villagers, it was apparent that they genuinely liked what Thaksin was doing for them, and that they felt that he was the first Thai politician who talked to them about their own welfare, and who delivered on his promises. It is a measure of the power of Thaksin's public relations machine that, among the villagers, all good things that were happening in the kingdom were attributed to Thaksin. When I asked the villagers if it were not true that Thaksin was very corrupt, the amused response invariably was "Of course, he is corrupt — all politicians are corrupt, but this is the first corrupt politician who has done something for us." To this day, the corruption, abuses, and personal wealth of Thaksin are glossed over by his rural supporters — not denied, just treated as irrelevant.

THE PRESENT CONFLICT

The tumultuous events that have occurred since the Thai Rak Thai Party's victory in 2005, and the recent conflict in which scores of civilians died and hundreds were wounded, are well known and do not require recounting. The first result of these events has been a breakdown of the social consensus that had existed in Thailand prior to Thaksin's rise to power. The second result is that politics, which earlier I described as a game played between different factions of the power elite of society, has now become a mass preoccupation which the average man on the street treats with deadly seriousness. The majority of the population has been politically awakened, has been made aware that the outcome of elections and other aspects of government have a direct impact on their lives, and has come to believe that it is not without ability to influence the outcome of those elections. But equally, rural voters believe that the military coup that overthrew Thaksin in September of 2006, the two court decisions that successively brought down the Samak Sundaravej government in 2008 (for Samak's accepting payment for an appearance on a cooking show on television), and the Somchai Wongsawat government later in the same year (his People's Power Party, successor to the banned Thai Rak Thai Party was banned for electoral violations), and the cobbling together of a new government under the Democrats, led by Abhisit Vejjajiva, in December of 2008, all effectively denied them their political rights, and cancelled out their votes. In an earlier era, they would probably have simply accepted that this was the way the world worked in a hierarchical society, and that there was nothing they could do about it.

But times have changed. As Bill Klausner has written extensively, the confined worlds of rural Thai villages that he knew in the 1950s, where spirits and officials were to be appeased and a traditional subsistence way of life was passed on from generation to generation with little change, has radically changed. Now the socio-economic conditions of villagers have improved and broadened dramatically: villagers are plugged into the rest of the world via television, mobile phones, pick-up trucks, and family members spending time working at wage-earning jobs in Bangkok. As many taxi drivers, all hailing from countryside villages in the northeast of Thailand, have told me, "We really aren't as stupid as the city people think we are. We used to be stupid, but no longer." They have concluded that the institutions of government were all being mobilized against them, to protect the interests of the establishment (now called the *ammat* in Thai): the Army, which launched the coup against Thaksin, and which sat by idly in 2008 while the Yellow Shirts occupied the international airports and took over Government House, but later sent the troops in to suppress the Red Shirt demonstrations in 2010; the new constitution, more or less foisted on the country under the period of military control in 2007 and designed to change the political game to favour the *ammat*; the court decisions in the political sphere that always seem to favour the *ammat* and take little account of the interests of the common man; and the back-room dealing conducted by the military that in December of 2008 brought the Democrats into power in unlikely coalition with one of Thailand's more unsavoury politicians, Newin Chidchob, As the vicious attacks on Privy Council President Prem Tinsulanon indicate, even elements of the palace have come under suspicion of partiality.

Despite the changed socio-economic circumstances of Thai villagers, it was not inevitable that they would begin to flex their political muscle and demand a greater political voice at that particular time in history. The enthusiasm with which they have embraced Thaksin indicates that their grievances and aspirations had been smouldering for some time, but this should not detract from Thaksin's political achievement in recognizing the political potential that those grievances and aspirations presented, and in embodying that potential in his Thai Rak Thai Party and in himself. It was the combination of a countryside ripe for political mobilization with his own political "marketing" abilities that led to the explosive events of the first decade of the twenty-first century.

As mentioned above, there has been impressive economic development in Thailand over recent decades, which has caused the lives of villagers to change immensely, giving them a sense of potential empowerment and a clearer sense of their rights and interests. Thailand is no longer a poor country, and Bangkok has become a wealthy and cosmopolitan city. But, despite some useful administrative reforms, such as the creation of various independent regulatory commissions at the national level and the increasing empowerment of sub-district- or *tambon*-level government at the grass-roots level, the evolution of political institutions of the country has not kept up with the country's rapid economic and social progress. Since the revolution of 1932, which changed the country from an absolute monarchy to a constitutional monarchy, the political history of Thailand has been a history of gradual swings of the pendulum, with dictatorial conservatism, generally backed by the Army, alternating with more democratic rule. When a period of democratic rule results in excesses, it is replaced by military rule, always with a promise to restore democratic rule at the right time. The pendulum has swung back and forth between the two, but with each swing of the pendulum in the democratic direction, access to political power has broadened, so that by the 1990s the new urban middle class was fully engaged in the political process and was generally quite happy with the direction in which the country was moving.

But, as already noted, economic growth and social modernization greatly outpaced the evolution of political institutions. Thaksin recognized this and used it to his advantage to become the most successful politician that Thailand has ever seen. Despite his authoritarian ways and demagogic style, he was opening the political sphere to the prospect of full participation of the lower classes of society, both in the countryside and in the city. Partially because this threatened the control of the Bangkok *ammat* and its allies in the urban middle class, and partially because of Thaksin's excesses, the *ammat* struck back, first with the anachronistic coup of 2006, and then with a series of actions designed to thwart the parties that were supported by the majority of the electorate. The establishment could not accept the political implications of the changed social and economic conditions of the country, and has tried to turn back the clock, restoring the *status quo ante* — in other words the comfortable world that they had controlled and enjoyed before the advent of Thaksin, and which I have described at the beginning of this essay.

The Bangkok middle classes, who saw their interests as largely tied to those of the *ammat*, were also motivated in their opposition to Thaksin by genuine concern over the cynical fashion in which he had undone many of the checks and balances so carefully implanted in the 1997 constitution, and so they joined in the protests against Thaksin feeling that this was the best way to secure a democratic future for the country. They did not anticipate the unfortunate uncontrolled unraveling of events that was to transpire over the next four years.

Looking at examples from history around the world over the last two centuries, once the middle class becomes entitled, as has happened in Thailand, then eventually the lower classes demand just treatment and a fair stake in society, economy, and polity. In some countries, the elites and middle classes acceded, and the incorporation of the majority of citizens fully into the mainstream has occurred peacefully, resulting in stability, prosperity and buy-in to the system by everyone. Most Western European nations followed this path, as did the United States with the New Deal, Fair Deal, and Great Society. In other countries, such as Russia and China, change only occurred with a violent revolution and radical social transformation. But in either case, change happened. (One easily forgets the dire poverty that existed in large parts of America in the 1920s and 1930s. As recently as 1964, when I first studied economics in university in the United States, a major issue considered in our studies was how to lift the bottom 20 per cent of American society out of abject poverty, with readings such as Michael Harrington's *The Other America*.[1])

Many of the elite of Thailand, believing in Thai particularism (of which more later), does not reflect on the implications of these historical processes in other countries. Thousands of Thais, mostly drawn from the elite and middle classes, were willing to devote their time and money to the illegal occupation of Government House and Bangkok's two international airports in 2008. They felt that they "know better" what is good for the country, and that therefore an illegal coup and illegal take-over of public property were justified in the cause of preventing Thaksin and his supporters or nominees from ruling the country. When I suggested to some of these people that they were attempting through force to repudiate the results of a properly elected and constituted government, they would retort, "But, Jim, those voters are uneducated," implying that one cannot leave decisions on who should run the country up to uneducated farmers and labourers. Of course, being uneducated does not equate to being stupid, nor does it mean that one is not capable of recognizing where one's interests lie. Moreover, if the majority of the country is uneducated, it makes one wonder what the government of the country had been doing over the previous half century if, in the course of economic development, it had neglected to direct sufficient resources properly to educate the majority of the country's citizens. When pressed, these Yellow Shirt supporters would finally say to me, "Well, if democracy means that the majority of the people elect the government, then I am not in favour of that sort of democracy in Thailand." At least that statement has the virtue of being candid, and it is exactly what the most right-wing faction of the Yellow Shirts, the People's Alliance for Democracy (PAD), favours — curtailment of the political rights of the majority in favour of democracy guided by the elite. After all, this was arguably what had worked reasonably well over the half-century prior to Thaksin's rise, and probably was most successful under the leadership of Prime Mininster Prem in the 1980s, when the country was peaceful, stable, and everyone was optimistic about the future of the country and in agreement on the direction of development under capable technocrats.

However, having described the major historical forces that seem to be at work in these protests and made a case for the legitimacy of many of the protestors' grievances, one must take account of the significant level of violence that occurred in Songkran of 2009, on 10 April 2010, and on the afternoon of arson on 19 May 2010, within hours after the Red Shirt leaders had surrendered. Aside from the violence, there is of course the fact that occupying and closing down the commercial heart of Bangkok for several weeks is clearly an illegal act that had massive negative consequences for the Thai economy and for the lives of the many Thai employees who worked in the hotels and stores that were closed down. Four comments on these issues:

1. The precedent of civil disobedience by illegally occupying public space was set in 2008 by the Yellow Shirts when they dispossessed the prime minister of his offices at Government House for several months, and subsequently closed down for a few days Suvarnabhumi and Don Mueang airports, damaging both Thailand's international reputation and the Thai economy. They did not consider that the other side could copy their tactics.
2. As Thongbai Thongbao has written in the *Bangkok Post*, if the Red Shirts were to have peacefully occupied a public park somewhere

in Bangkok where they did not inconvenience the public or disrupt the economy, the government would have paid them scant heed, and eventually they would have wilted under the dry-season tropical sun and failed to accomplish anything. If you are protesting against an entrenched and intransigent establishment, then you need to do something that will force it to pay attention to you. Otherwise, your efforts are in vain.

3. The arson on the final afternoon was clearly planned in advance by the Red Shirt leaders, and went beyond what can be justified as legitimate civil disobedience. The same can be said of sniper and grenade attacks, at least some of which came from the Red Shirts (such as the attack on the Dusit Thani Hotel).
4. Some commentators have written that the arson and other violence with assault weapons deprived the entire Red Shirt movement of legitimacy. I do not agree with that. One is not condoning the mindless mayhem by noting that the overwhelming majority of protestors were, as mentioned below, peaceful, orderly, and committed.

One final point related to violence. The Army resisted being called into the fight for many weeks, insisting that political problems should be sorted out by political means. When Army Commander Anuphong Paochinda finally acceded to Abhisit's request to clear the protestors, many tens of people were killed and many more wounded, almost all of whom were civilians. Allegations that the use of force was excessive and brutal are given weight by the unwillingness of either the military or the government to permit independent full investigation of the military's actions, particularly the deaths of several people within the compound of Wat Pathumwanaram. In any event, it seems to me that the final responsibility for the ninety deaths and hundreds of wounded rests with the political leadership that chose to exercise a military solution during March–May 2010, and not just with the military that carried out the orders

THE RED SHIRTS

In all the emotion-charged debate over Thailand's political travails, perhaps nothing is more confusing, or raises more controversy, than the nature, composition and leadership of the Red Shirts. At one pole are those who say that the protestors are paid to attend rallies, and are heavily infiltrated by well armed "terrorists" under the direction and control of extremists taking their orders from Thaksin. While allowing that many of the protestors are decent farmers from the North and the Northeast, this school of thought maintains that they have been "brainwashed" or at least misled by Thaksin's disciples through community radio and the endless speeches at Ratchaprasong, and that they do not have the educational qualifications to be able to see through Thaksin's propaganda. In other words, they were manipulated pawns in a cynical game. Since the protest was obviously well organized and financed, and since violent acts were perpetrated by some members of the protest group, this school of thought cannot be dismissed as entirely false. On the other side of the debate are those who would paint the protestors as entirely peaceful, which is obviously not true. The truth probably lies somewhere between these two poles.

To get a better sense of the situation, on Sunday, 9 May 2010, prior to the military blockade commencing, I strolled through the Red Shirt encampment, speaking with protestors. With the exception of the black-uniformed security guards, they were friendly, polite, and extremely committed to their cause. The level of organizational competence that was required to have supplied and looked after thousands of protestors encamped on the streets of Bangkok was impressive.

As for the motivations of the genuine protestors, there appear to be three main explanations offered:

1. They were paid to attend. Although many were subsidized, I do not believe that financial compensation would induce those farmers to live for two months camped on the street in Bangkok's sweltering summer, much less risk life and limb. So I rule out financial compensation as the significant motivating factor for most of them. Some of the urban workers may have joined in part because of financial inducements, or been simply drawn in by the lure of excitement, but there is no reason to doubt that they were also supporters of the cause.
2. They were motivated by desire to improve their economic lot in life — hoping that a change in government would bring about an improvement in their circumstances. Some Western commentators have quoted international statistics to demonstrate that Thai farmers are much better off than many of their counterparts in other parts

of the world, that absolute poverty among Thai farmers is quite low, and that the level of inequality in Thailand is unexceptional by international standards. Absolute poverty may be low among Thais, but Chris Baker and Pasuk Phongpaichit have pointed out that the income gap in Thailand between the richest 20 per cent and the poorest 20 per cent is 13–15 times, and the wealth gap is 70 times. Clearly, there are major income distribution and wealth inequality problems in Thailand, but the Red Shirts with whom I spoke did not seem to me to be desperately impoverished.

3. They were motivated to seek a more just political system and to gain respect — to end the political control of the *ammat* and the double standard in Thailand, whereby the rich and powerful can get away with anything and the poor have little recourse for redress of grievances or full exercise of their political rights.

Contrary to Yellow Shirt claims that the Red Shirts are uneducated and manipulated, in my conversations with farmers, innumerable taxi drivers (almost all of whom come from villages in the Northeast), my Bangkok housekeeper (every foreigner's favourite source of insight into Red Shirt political thinking!), and a variety of other interlocutors, I find that the Red Shirts and their sympathizers are articulate and have clear ideas as to what is wrong with the country and with the Democrat Party government led by Abhisit. While discussing to a certain extent economic issues (my village in Chiang Rai is fixated on crop prices, and feels that Thaksin would be aware of these issues in a way that Abhisit is not), most of them dwell primarily on resentment of the *ammat*, on double standards, and on the fact that their vote has been nullified by military coup, court decisions, and political backroom dealing. Despite their slogans, they do not necessarily have a sophisticated understanding of democracy, but they do have a keen sense of exactly how their political rights as citizens have been trampled upon, resulting in the favouring of the rich and powerful by government.

Their articulateness on these issues stems, I believe, to a great extent from community radio, which could be found throughout the country, in both rural and urban areas. Perhaps this is the "brainwashing" that the Yellow Shirts refer to, but it offers a challenge to the "consensus" which has been inculcated into all Thais from an early age. It has changed many rural Thai people from being politically passive to highly politically conscious. Whether that is a good or a bad thing depends on your perspective and where your interests lie. Over the previous half century, the government had brilliantly inculcated the "consensus" described above, but over the past two years the Red Shirts have done an impressive job of organizing political resistance at the grass-roots level in the North and Northeast and raising questions about the consensus in the minds of people at the grass-roots level. The establishment, of course, has always been happy to have rural people politically inert and docile, and now resents the fact that farmers should think that they deserve a real voice in the running of the country.

But the Red Shirt movement is no longer exclusively composed of farmers and urban labourers. It also begins to attract a portion of the urban middle class, including some Sino-Thai shopkeepers, and a few members of the elite as well. These new supporters remain adamantly opposed to Thaksin, and also decry the violent methods that were employed by some Red Shirts on the final day of the protest at Ratchaprasong, and the ill-considered searching of Chulalongkorn Hospital. But the protests have caused them to think deeply about what is wrong with their country, to become receptive to the idea that major changes are necessary, and to be willing to consider that the Red Shirt protests may have arisen out of legitimate grievances, even if they do not approve of the Red Shirts' methods or respect many of their leaders.

One point worth mentioning is the presence in the Red Shirt leadership of some individuals who had been members of the communist resistance of the late 1970s — the so-called October 1976 generation. These idealists, as students faced with military brutality, had literally fled to the hills to join the small hard-core communist insurgency for a few years. A combination of disillusionment with the communists and the generous amnesty engineered by Kriangsak Chomanan and Prem Tinsulanon caused them to return to normal lives in the cities, some to become bankers and brokers, some to channel their idealism into the "rural doctors" movement to serve the health needs of the rural poor, and some to join politics. But their experiences in the 1970s were formative, and some who are in the forefront of the Red Shirt movement today have the emotional scars and bitterness left over from that earlier era of right-wing repression.

If the movement contains idealists, it also contains some shadowy hardcore militants, about whom little is known, but who appear willing to use methods that do fit the definition of "terrorist acts". So the leadership and composition of the Red Shirts is complicated and obscure, with splits between factions. How this will evolve in future months remains to be seen.

A reasonable amount of ink has been spilt over the question of whether the turmoil has been a form of class warfare, of whether it can be classified as urban-rural conflict, or Bangkok versus the rest of the country. There has been criticism of foreigners who (like me in this paper) have talked about the "Red Shirt–Yellow Shirt" conflict, saying that this just shows how little foreigners can understand the complexities of what is going on in Thailand. Indeed, the situation is very complicated and confusing, and every generalization that one makes will prove to have exceptions and to be somewhat misleading — there are some elite supporting the Red Shirts; there are poor people in Bangkok, not just in the provinces; and not everyone easily fits into the Red Shirt and Yellow Shirt categories. Nonetheless, one must employ categorizations and generalizations in order to understand what is going on, and surely it is true that the Red Shirts' principal base of support is in the provinces, among farmers; if it is not class warfare, then at least most of the protestors are less well off than the *ammat* that they attack; and Red Shirt versus Yellow Shirt is short-hand commonly used by most Thais as well as foreigners to describe the two main camps in this complicated strife. And there are some who have cavilled with the very use of the words "class" and "elite" in Thailand, saying that contemporary Thai society has considerable mobility and anyone can rise to the top, and that the term "elite" is too vague and loose a term. But "class" and "mobility" are not contradictory concepts, Thailand is not a "classless society" and we can all agree that Thailand is a nation with both a class structure and class mobility, and that at the top of the heap sit the elite, however defined. So I believe that it is not worth engaging in semantic quibbling over what to call the strife, or the precise nature of Thailand's class structure

Another issue worth mentioning is that the turmoil facing Thailand is described by many as unprecedented. No less eminent an authority on Thai society than Charles Keyes has said that recent events require him to reexamine how he has viewed Thai rural society in the past. Clearly the levels of direct confrontation and the use of highly inflammatory language and reluctance to compromise appear counter to the generally accepted view of Thai society. But I would suggest that it is not entirely unprecedented, and that there is a strain of violence and intolerance lurking beneath the surface in Thai society. One must recall that during the late 1960s and early 1970s, there was a high level of conflict and violence in some parts of rural Thailand, with Red Gaurs and other right-wing groups ruthlessly murdering those whom they suspected of communism; the incitements of the anti-communist monk Kittiwutho to kill communists, in clear violation of the tenets of Buddhism; and of course the massacre of the students at Thammasat in 1976. It is also worth recalling how in the short space of a few years, under the leadership of Generals Kriangsak and Prem, the bitter wounds of the 1970s were healed, and the extreme solutions that had been favored by Prime Minister Thanin Kraiwichian were generally discredited.

How does Thaksin fit into the equation today? Clearly he continues to play a major role behind the scenes, and most of the Red Shirts continue to express their support for him, despite revelations of his corruption and the criminal convictions against him. Nonetheless, the movement that he started now seems to be increasingly taking on a life independent of Thaksin, and Thaksin's goals and the Red Shirt movement's goals are diverging. Thaksin appears primarily concerned to recover his sequestered assets, to clear his personal legal issues, and to be willing to sacrifice everything (and anybody) to achieve these goals. Perhaps this is one reason that the Red Shirt leaders were unwilling to accept Abhisit's proposed compromise, with promise of elections on 14 November 2010. Elections would not further Thaksin's personal agenda; he preferred a violent showdown with no compromise, and may have given Red Shirt leadership orders to scuttle the negotiations.

I believe that history will judge Thaksin to have left a mixed legacy. On the positive side, he brought the majority of Thai people into politics, so that the old clique-filled world of political games that was played among the elite no longer goes unchallenged. And he introduced several policies aimed at improving the lot of the poorer people of the country. He will, however, also be judged for his dictatorial style, for his maltreatment of Muslims in southern Thailand, for his extra-judicial killings of suspected drug dealers, and for his willingness to sacrifice the lives of others to achieve his objectives. Perhaps most tragically, he failed to seize the opportunity presented to him to bring a new breed of politician into government, instead largely satisfying himself with relying on co-opting some of the old power brokers such as Chavalit Yongchaiyut and Newin Chidchob.

But the government and Yellow Shirts have demonized Thaksin. The Abhisit government has spent a tremendous amount of time and effort attacking him, culminating in the recent charges that he is a "terrorist". I recall that in 2009, when Thaksin accepted an appointment as advisor to the Hun Sen government, the Thai government thought that this act would discredit him in the eyes of his followers. I was at my farm in Chiang Rai at the time, and was sceptical of this view, and so when I boarded a flight from Chiang Rai back to Bangkok, I asked the middle-aged, middle-class Thai lady seated next to me (a Chiang Rai resident) what she thought about Thaksin's Cambodian appointment. She sighed, and said "Doesn't this government have anything better to do than to go after Thaksin. You would think that they should be spending their time running the country well to win people over to supporting them."

Many people make the mistake of thinking that, if only Thaksin could be neutralized, then the Red Shirt movement would collapse and everything would go back to the simpler times prior to Thaksin. But the genie is out of the bottle, and there is no putting it back in again. The *status quo ante* will not be restored, even if Thaksin were to genuinely renounce politics and retire to enjoy the secluded pleasures of his seaside home in Montenegro. The more the government demonizes Thaksin, the more Thaksin serves as a potent symbol for the discontent of the Red Shirts. One wonders what Abhisit will do if Montenegro actually decides to extradite Thaksin to Thailand, as requested by the Thai government. The trial would become the focal point for renewed demonstrations and protests.

One problem that the Red Shirts face is leadership. Aside from Thaksin, who is too divisive and morally compromised to lead the nation again, the Red Shirts are not offering up leaders who show promise of being able effectively to lead the nation, even though some of them showed considerable tactical skill in organizing and leading the protests. Nor do the Red Shirt leaders show any greater potential for projecting a new national vision or achieving reconciliation than does Abhisit (discussed below). This became apparent in the post-protest debates in parliament, which were a very unedifying blame game between the two sides. The prospect of Red Shirts taking control of the government inspires no more confidence or enthusiasm than does the present leadership.

THE YELLOW SHIRTS

The composition of the Yellow Shirts is as complicated as that of the Red Shirts. Most of the elite is Yellow, and probably a large majority of the Bangkok middle class is as well. The upcountry middle class appears to be split between Red and Yellow (except for the South, which is more Yellow than other parts of the country). And a small portion of villagers and urban labourers are Yellow, following ingrained instincts of loyalty to traditional institutions.

But the core of the Yellow Shirt movement lies in the Bangkok aristocracy, senior business community, and upper levels of the bureaucracy. Many of these members of the elite are extraordinarily intolerant of the Red Shirts, do not distinguish the legitimate grievances of the protestors from the interests of Thaksin, and are dismissive of the protestors as a ragged bunch of paid hooligans with whom it is useless to negotiate. Most have rarely had interaction with villagers or workers, so do not know what they think. They have not even had the opportunity to hear the opinions of taxi drivers, as they do not ride taxis. Their intransigence seems to me to be the largest obstacle to reconciliation in the country.

THE ABHISIT GOVERNMENT

The first point to consider is whether or not the Abhisit government was legally constituted. Strictly speaking, it is fatuous to say that the government was not legally constituted. In the early days of the Abhisit government, even a BBC journalist in Thailand commented that the government was not legally constituted, as it was not elected by the people. The BBC should understand very well that Thailand has a parliamentary system of government under which the electorate votes into office the members of parliament, who are then legally free to select any person who meets the legal requirements to be the prime minister. That is exactly what happened in the United Kingdom recently with the formation of the Cameron/Clegg government, which was not elected by the voters, but put together by the party chieftains after the election.

The same legal process took place when Abhisit formed a coalition government with the support of Newin and others from the Bhumjaithai, Phuea Phaendin, and other parties in December of 2008.

But at a deeper level, many Red Shirts do not accept the legitimacy of the Abhisit government, and do not feel that it represents them. The last election was held in late 2007, under a constitution that was designed to limit the ability of the successors to Thaksin's Thai Rak Thai Party to win elections. But the People's Power Party, successor to the banned Thai Rak Thai, nonetheless received the largest number of votes, and was able to put together a coalition government. The establishment struck back, using the court system to first declare Prime Minister Samak ineligible to be prime minister, and then banning the entire People's Power Party at the end of 2008. This court ruling, combined with months of protests and illegal occupation of Government House and then of Bangkok's airports, brought to an end the Thaksin nominee government of Samak's successor, Somchai. Reportedly under the guidance of Army Commander Anuphong, during a series of back-room negotiations allegedly held on a military base, Newin, who had been banned from elections but was the power behind the Bhumjaithai Party, was induced to desert Thaksin and join a coalition government led by Democrat Party leader Abhisit.

One can thus understand the feelings of rural people who feel that the judicial system, which has double standards in its application of the law, and the military have thrown out the government that they voted for, and installed in its place a government led by Abhisit, whom most of the rural electorate do not support. They feel that Thaksin was first overthrown by a military coup, which is of course illegal, but was *post factum* legitimated by the new constitution passed in a referendum under somewhat suspect circumstances; that then the Thaksin nominees, for whom they had voted, were manoeuvred out of power, again by military intervention, albeit through secret negotiations rather than through elections.

The way to resolve this issue of legitimacy would be to submit the Democrat-led government to a new election. This Abhisit has been reluctant to do, presumably because he fears that his party would not fare well at the polls, although he has come up with a variety of other reasons for not calling elections. If, when he took office in 2008, he had backed up his reconciliation rhetoric with an amnesty for the 111 banned politicians who were followers of Thaksin, invited the best and the brightest of the Red Shirt leaders to participate in a government of national unity, announced that in one year a new election would be held, and taken steps to end double standards in application of the law, particularly with regard to the leaders of the PAD who had seized the international airport, then the events of the past eighteen months might have unfolded differently.

After Abhisit missed the opportunity to undertake genuine reconciliation upon assuming office, one would have thought that the events of Songkran 2009 would have been a wake-up call, and would have prompted Abhisit to focus his government on the country's most fundamental issues, which are reconciliation of the Yellow-Red divisions, and of the conflict with the Muslims of the far South of the country.

But Abhisit governed as if the times were normal. Instead of focusing on domestic reconciliation and winning over the majority of voters to support the Democrats, he remained aloof, and spent considerable time on trips to major foreign capitals and conferences, which did nothing for his domestic standing. In fairness, he and Finance Minister Korn Chatikawanit have shown reasonable competence in governing, seem to understand that policies must be put in place to reduce wealth and income inequality in the country, and are willing to adopt well considered measures to accomplish that. Despite the political turmoil, their economic policies are bearing fruit, with the economy on track to rebound from contraction in 2009 to 6 per cent growth in 2010.

Unfortunately, however, some of Abhisit's and Korn's policies, such as the 2,000 baht per head hand-out, while perhaps justified as an emergency stimulus measure, appeared to be politically motivated attempts to compete with Thaksin's legacy in the area of populist measures. If so, they were unsuccessful. There is no lack of ideas circulating within the academic community, among NGOs, and elsewhere on what needs to be done to improve economic opportunity for the poorer segments of society. These need to be packaged in clearly understandable ways, and then implemented. Presumably property and inheritance taxes should be priorities.

But passion, fast action, and boldness of vision are also required. That is what Thaksin offered. But Abhisit is unable to travel safely in major areas of the North and Northeast of the country, and when the protests of 2010 began, he took up residence in a Bangkok military base. To the Red Shirts, this only confirmed the view that his government rested entirely on the support of the Army. Apparently the symbolism of moving into an Army base did not bother Abhisit.

Why has a well educated, well spoken, honest and hard-working man like Abhisit failed to understand what the times demanded? Why has he been so intransigent in dealing with the Red Shirts, and why has he turned up the heat rather than lowering it, failing to show tolerance and reach out to the other side? Why has he been unable to communicate effectively with the mass of Thai voters? A few possibilities suggest themselves.

1. He is temperamentally unable to empathize with people who do not share his ordered and rational way of looking at the world. Many Thai voters of the lower economic echelons instinctively sense this, and do not identify with him, even if what he is saying makes sense. A foreign journalist who was given a private interview with Abhisit told me that when she asked Abhisit what was his favourite book, he responded with the title of his favourite economics text. This anecdote gives a clue to the psychological make-up of the man.
2. He is an intensely private and self-controlled man, whose only soul-mate has been his wife.
3. He has never been exposed to people with different backgrounds from his own "Sukhumvit-Eton-Oxford" background. I wonder how many Thai villagers he has ever spent time with, or how often he has had real conversations with ordinary working folk, listened to what they said, and pondered what he could learn from them? He appears to have massive self-confidence in his own rectitude and not feel the need for input from ordinary citizens.
4. The attempt on his life during the Songkran riots of 2009, and the smearing of blood on the gate of his house may have deeply embittered him, rendering him inflexible.

He is an enigma — so smart and attractive, so effective in parliamentary debate, so cool in the midst of crisis, yet seeming unable to show emotion about the tragedy he has dealt with, unable to reach out to the victims in a personal way, and temperamentally averse to patiently finding compromise and negotiated solutions. To compound the problem, he has surrounded himself with advisors and aides who do not compensate for his weaknesses in these areas, and are unable to fill in for him in communicating with the other side. One has the feeling that the Abhisit government has in fact attempted to put forward some useful, progressive policies, such as the property tax that Finance Minister Korn advocates, but the measures have been poorly packaged and presented. Whether for or against Thaksin, one could always immediately name the initiatives that Thaksin was undertaking when he was prime minister, conveying a sense of energy being applied to resolve national problems.

It has been apparent that Abhisit has always been more comfortable rubbing shoulders with international political and business leaders than he has been chatting with his fellow-countrymen in the provinces, and he certainly undertook a large number of trips abroad to wave the Thai flag in his first eighteen months in office. A small but revealing news item appeared in the 4 June 2010 edition of the *Bangkok Post*. The paper reported that Prime Minister Abhisit would fly to Vietnam on 6 June "to attend a two-day World Economic Forum on East Asia" and went on to say that the prime minister "said the priority for government was to restore confidence among the international community since political problems impede economic development". The blood was barely dry on the streets of Rachaprasong, but Abhisit's priority was speaking with international investors? The priority should be 100 per cent on reconciling domestic divisions and restoring harmony to the country. If progress on this is made, the international business community and tourists will regain faith in Thailand without Abhisit attending international conferences.

Unfortunately for Thailand, Abhisit lacks the skills and personality to lead a genuine reconciliation, or to project a bold vision for the future development of the country that would have a chance of uniting most of the country behind him. He, almost as much as Thaksin, has made himself a divisive rather than harmonizing leader.

THAI PARTICULARISM

During April and May of 2010, members of some of Thailand's most prominent families fired off e-mail messages to their friends around the world, bitterly complaining of the biased (pro-Red Shirt) reporting of the foreign press, particularly CNN and the BBC. While some foreign press reporting was inaccurate, selective and uninformed, much of the mainstream reporting was, in my opinion, substantive, balanced, and nuanced, particularly considering the complexity of the situation. The foreign media had some stupid reporting, but so did the Thai media. My housekeeper, glued to the television every day during the crisis, despaired of getting balanced credible reporting — so it depends on your own biases as much as it does on the biases of the reporters, be they foreign or local.

The complaints fit into a pattern of belief on the part of members of the Thai elite that Thailand has a unique and special culture, not easily understood by foreigners. They have used this special culture as an argument for defending their own special class status in a hierarchical society, and this allows them to dismiss any negative foreign commentary on Thailand as uninformed. Thais who argue that too much is made of the "uniqueness of Thailand" are immediately dismissed as "too Westernized".

Of course, the culture of every country has unique aspects, but there are also commonalities and universal patterns as well, and it is possible for foreigners to make informed comments about other cultures, as Tocqueville proved with his writings about America.

When examining the critiques of these prominent Thais more closely, it is apparent that they see only one side of the present conflict, and regard any favourable reporting concerning the Red Shirts as unacceptable.

An unfortunate aspect of this sense of Thai particularism is that it leads to limited interest in examining other national models of development for relevant lessons, or in viewing their own society with a sufficient degree of dispassionate objectivity. This is in contrast to China, which, as described by David Shambaugh in his recent book *China's Communist Party: Atrophy and Adaptation*,[2] has for the last twenty years been assiduously studying examples from all over the world in an enormous range of subjects for relevant models that it can adopt and adapt for use in China, and has also continuously subjected itself to self-examination to determine how it can improve its performance. China, of course, faces a multitude of enormous problems, but one of the reasons for its success is the forthrightness of the leadership in identifying these problems, and systematically but quickly developing appropriate policies to deal with them, often drawing on experience that they have studied from other countries.

Several other nations offer excellent examples of successful coping with the problems that Thailand has been facing. Spain over the past thirty years has dealt with considerable success with many of these issues. It has been very creative in coming up with new ways of dealing with sensitive issues, ranging from the role of the military in the state to decentralization of powers from Madrid to regions and provinces, thereby defusing tensions and actually strengthening the fibre of the nation. South Africa is a model of how to deal with deep societal divisions through tolerance and patience rather than force. Indonesia's resolution of its Aceh separatist issue and movement from military-dominated politics to real democracy is worth studying. In the United States during the 1960s, the violence that arose in Watts and Detroit was perhaps even more mindless and shocking than what has recently happened in Thailand, but it did cause the United States to reflect deeply on the underlying issues that gave rise to such rioting, and ultimately to attempt to address those issues. And there are a host of other examples for Thailand to examine.

RECONCILIATION

If nothing else, it seems to me that the turmoil of April and May 2010, and the deep social divisions and political dysfunction that this turmoil reveals, should provoke deep consideration on the part of the entire nation as to how the Thai state should be constituted in the twenty-first century. One hopes that the elite establishment will recognize that the old consensus on the nature of Thailand has broken down, and that constructive thinking is needed to build a new basis for moving forward in the challenging decades ahead. The elite will be well advised to work cooperatively with Red Shirt leaders in seeking solutions, lest they be excluded in the future from playing a role in the development of a new national model. Thus far, however, I see more recrimination than reconciliation, more short-sighted defensiveness than long-term creative, constructive thinking.

Unfortunately, at this point animosities between the two sides are running high, making reconciliation more difficult than ever to achieve. Preliminary indications in the wake of the events of May 2010 were that Abhisit planned to continue to govern as he had over the previous year and a half, and that over the period prior to new elections he would suppress Red Shirt activity rather than engage with Red Shirts. He would then hope that improving economic conditions and the passage of some sound economic and social reform measures would improve the chances of the Democrats to be voted back into office. Even if this strategy brought electoral success, I do not think that it is the best course for the country, as it would leave behind a legacy of bitterness, and would not resolve some of the fundamental issues of the country that need to be addressed. And, of course, if he does not think that the Democrats will win the election, it is not inconceivable that Abhisit would find excuses to postpone elections beyond the constitutionally mandated date.

What should be done? I would suggest the following as a few of the things that Abhisit should do, but no doubt others can suggest many other steps that should be taken to really achieve the reconciliation goal:

1. Address some of the immediate, glaring double-standard issues, most particularly the failure to move forward with prosecution of the leaders of the Yellow Shirt illegal activities in 2008. That is a minimum requirement for any expression of sincerity towards the Red Shirts, and would send a signal that the law henceforth is to be enforced equally on one and all. It will send a powerful positive signal that will be understood at the grass-roots level of the Red Shirt opposition. Such a measure will require courage on the part of Abhisit, as it will be opposed by powerful interests, but he should make it an issue over which he is prepared to resign if need be. If he does not do this, then his calls for enforcement of law and order are hypocrisy.
2. Another double standard issue that needs to be addressed forthwith is censorship and blockage of opposition radio stations, websites, and other forms of media. This censorship is in stark contrast with the democratic values that the Abhisit government claims to be upholding, and is a blatant example of double standards, since the equivalent Yellow Shirt outlets are not blocked or censored.
3. Give maximum cooperation to the independent commission investigating the violence of April and May 2010, especially the six deaths in Wat Pathumwanaram temple, ensure that it is genuinely independent, and accept its conclusions with good grace. The risk is all too great that the facts may never be fully known.
4. Reach out in a high profile manner to certain of the more responsible Red Shirt leaders, and to respected experts in a range of fields, to work together on proposals for social, political, and economic reform. Demonstrate openness to suggestions, and work in bipartisan fashion to implement as many as possible.

5. Take a serious look at what other nations confronted by similar divisions have done to achieve reconciliation. As mentioned above, Spain, South Africa and Indonesia come to mind as excellent models, but no doubt there are others.
6. The Democrats need to work hard on communicating effectively with voters — package their programmes better, and choose spokesmen who will be credible with the man in the street.
7. Ignore Thaksin — stop making him into a martyr.
8. Call elections within a reasonable time-frame — announce a date, without a lot of conditions, stick to it, and stop offering excuses on why the election has to be postponed. Much more is at stake than just trying to win this election — if the Democrats lose, then they can compete for the next election.

I am not optimistic that Abhisit will wholeheartedly opt for the sort of programme that I outline above. Nothing in his nationwide reconciliation address in the evening of 10 June 2010 would indicate that he has such an agenda in mind.

No one is foolish enough to predict how events will unfold over the next years in this complicated and volatile solution, but I will hazard a few thoughts that are relatively optimistic:

1. The good sense of the Thai people will prevent Thailand from drifting into failed state status, will keep civil war from breaking out, and will steer Thailand away from reversion to anachronistic military strongman rule.
2. Barring unexpected breakthrough, the reconciliation process will take several years, with intermittent turmoil, sometimes violent.
3. Gradually reform will be implemented, the older generation Yellow Shirt die-hards will fade away to be replaced by a younger, more broad-minded elite, and the authoritarian traditions of Thai politics will give way to more stable democracy, as the political structure is brought into line with economic and social development, and tolerance for double standards decreases at all levels of society.

In conclusion, I am in the short and medium term very concerned about how reconciliation can be achieved and I lack confidence in the leadership abilities of Abhisit to heal the wounds of the nation, but in the longer term I am confident that Thailand will find its way again, as it always has in the past, and that the turmoil of the past few years will, in the longer view of history, prove to have been a painful but necessary transition for the country from an increasingly outdated and dysfunctional political structure to a structure adapted to the needs of the majority of the Thai people — a structure that will equip Thailand to meet the challenges of the twenty-first century. Returning to the thoughts that I had been expressing in the 1990s and that I outlined at the beginning of this paper, Thailand is now facing up to the internal obstacles and inequities that have thus far constrained the Thai people from fulfilling their full potential as a nation. Just imagine a future Thailand in which the charm and subtlety of the culture and the innate capabilities of Thais as individuals were joined with the dynamism of a fully engaged and empowered citizenry! That should be a vision that unites all Thais in searching for solutions to the problems that bedevil the nation today. But perhaps it will take some time and a new generation to rise to the challenge and take the reins of leadership.

Notes

1. Michael Harrington, *The Other America: Poverty in the United States* (New York: Macmillan, 1962).
2. David Shambaugh, *China's Communist Party: Atrophy and Adaptation* (Berkeley and Los Angeles: University of California Press, 2008).

4

TRUTH AND JUSTICE WHEN FEAR AND REPRESSION REMAIN
An Open Letter to Dr Kanit Na Nakorn, 16 July 2010

Tyrell Haberkorn

> How to heal a country that has been traumatized by repression if the fear to speak out is still omnipresent everywhere? And how do you reach the truth if lying has become a habit? How do we keep the past alive without becoming its prisoner? How do we forget it without risking its repetition in the future? Is it legitimate to sacrifice the truth to ensure peace? And what are the consequences of suppressing that past and the truth it is whispering or howling to us? Are people free to search for justice and equality if the threat of a military intervention haunts them? And given these circumstances, can violence be avoided?
>
> — Ariel Dorfman, Afterword, *Death and the Maiden*

The events, failed attempts at mediation between the government of Prime Minister Abhisit Vejjajiva and the red-shirted members of the National United Front for Democracy against Dictatorship (UDD), and the violence in which they culminated during April and May 2010 have now become well known globally. The UDD began demonstrating in the Ratchaprasong area of central Bangkok in March, calling for the dissolution of Thailand's parliament and for new elections. It viewed Prime Minister Abhisit Vejjajiva's leadership as illegitimate and his actions as a continuation of the double standards in Thai politics, in which certain groups of people are held to account for their transgressions and others not.

The UDD presence in Ratchaprasong provoked anger among some sectors of the government and some Bangkok residents, and on 7 April 2010 Prime Minister Abhisit put the Emergency Decree in place in Bangkok and in other provinces with a strong UDD presence. The Emergency Decree provides for wide powers of censorship, arrest, and detention, including the use of violence by state actors when deemed necessary to carry out their duties. In this case, the Emergency Decree signalled the possibility of violent state repression, a possibility that came to fruition.

Once the Emergency Decree was in place, the UDD protests became technically illegal, as gatherings of more than five people were not allowed, and any actions taken by state forces to end the protest became technically legal. On 10 April, the Thai Army launched attacks against UDD protestors using tear gas, rubber bullets, and live ammunition. Despite significant numbers of dead and injured, the attacks failed to end the protests, and the UDD vowed to remain in Bangkok until its demands were granted. In the following weeks, the UDD and the Army found themselves locked in a tense stand-off in Bangkok. Other groups, including members of the yellow-shirted People's Alliance for Democracy (PAD) and the multi-coloured shirts, who were also in opposition to the UDD, entered the conflict. On 14 May, units of the Army launched a sustained crackdown aimed at decisively evicting the UDD from the streets of Bangkok. By the time the violence ended on 19 May, the total death toll from April and May 2010 was 90, and the total number of people injured was nearly 2,000.[1] While the available evidence indicates that the UDD as well as state actors used violence, preliminary information suggests that the state used a disproportionate amount of deadly force against the protestors. A report released by the Santi Prachatham Network in mid-June 2010 cast this issue in a particularly salient frame: "It is true that some of the red-shirted protestors had weapons. But it was only a minority. The question here is this: if they were only a few people, was the use of more than 50,000 heavily armed soldiers to end the protests on 19 May appropriate or not? Was it an excessive use of power and force or not?"[2]

Two months after the May crackdown brought an end to the UDD protests, Prime Minister Abhisit remained in power and the Emergency Decree remained in force in Bangkok and eighteen other provinces. According to information released by the National Police Office, at least 417 people were initially arrested in connection with participation in the UDD protests or the fires and rioting that followed the end of the protests — some under the Criminal Code and others under the terms of the Emergency Decree, which allows for thirty days of arbitrary detention before official charges need to be brought against a suspect. In an open letter to Prime Minister Abhisit, Human Rights Watch (HRW) expressed concern over the use of the terms of detention specified in the Emergency Decree by the Center for the Resolution of the Emergency Situation (CRES), a temporary state agency created to deal with the protests and related events, and other state entities to detain a range of actors. Unlike the Criminal Code, which provides a range of safeguards for suspects, the Emergency Decree strips detainees of important protections, including habeas corpus, and also allows for detention at irregular and unknown sites of incarceration. HRW noted that, while the release of the list of 417 detained individuals was a significant step by state authorities, there was evidence to indicate that people were being held in non-standard sites of detention, including Border Patrol Police and Army camps.[3] Arrests widened to target a broad range of actors, including one case in which an activist who attempted to mourn the loss of life of UDD members at the Ratchaprasong intersection was arrested while attempting to tie a red ribbon around a pole in the area.[4] In addition to the detentions in the aftermath of the April–May 2010 protests and crackdown, increasing censorship and control of the media reflected the growing constriction of the circulation of ideas that differed from those of the government.[5]

Despite this context of official repression, and parallel fragmentation and polarization among different sectors in society, the Abhisit government launched a process of national reconciliation comprised of numerous panels. While Dr Prawet Wasi and former Prime Minister Anan Panyarachun were tasked with chairing a panel on national reform, broadly conceived, Dr Kanit Na Nakorn was asked to lead the Independent Truth and Reconciliation Commission (ITRC) (คณะกรรมการอิสระเพื่อตรวจสอบและค้นหาความจริงเพื่อความปรองดองแห่งชาติ). While I began this essay by noting that the series of events that led to the contention and violence in the streets of Bangkok in April–May 2010 are well known, many of the details of those events, and their contexts, remain unknown. Who precisely used violence, under whose orders, and for what reasons, for example, remain largely obscured.

The mandate of the ITRC is threefold; it includes truth-seeking, conflict prevention, and restoration. Dr Kanit has defined truth-seeking as follows:

> This would be to uncover and establish the truth and facts especially with regard to political violence, violations of human rights, loss of lives, physical and psychological injuries, and property and other damages, which occurred during April–May 2010, including the underlying roots causes of the conflict and violence during the past several years, so that all these issues could be clearly identified and common understanding on them achieved.[6]

Given the uncertain nature of what is known about April–May 2010, as well as the importance of finding the truth, or I would argue, *truths*, for conflict prevention and restoration, how the committee carries out its work will be of crucial importance.

Over a period of two years, the ITRC will attempt to clarify what remains unknown. Dr Kanit named the members of his commission in early July, and the group of eight members includes a range of actors, including those from the legal, human rights, and media fields.[7] This means that by July 2012, the events and violence of April–May 2010 will, one hopes, become clearer, with fewer unknowns, and a more just future in prospect. Yet many factors, in particular the fact that the ITRC is meant to examine a conflict that remains unresolved, may complicate its work. The task of the ITRC, in the words of Prime Minister Abhisit, is "to uncover the truth, which would be an important basis for reform and reconciliation", even though many of the conditions which made the violence of April–May 2010 possible, including pervasive polarization in society, the constriction of political space for dissent, and the repressive Emergency Decree, persist.[8] Depending on how the ITRC engages the recent past, and its present outcome, it may either contribute to creating the space for justice — the righting of what is wrong — in Thai society, or further contribute to its foreclosure.

As it would be premature to critique the ITRC before its work has fully begun, I present the remainder of my concerns in the form of an open letter to Dr Kanit Na Nakorn. The letter is intended to be in the spirit of conversation and debate, and I have written it as a scholar who believes that scholars' critiques should, indeed must, attempt to influence the decisions and actions that affect those who experience violence and repression.

* * *

16 July 2010

Dr Kanit Na Nakorn
Chair, Independent Truth and Reconciliation Committee
c/o Government House, Phitsanulok Road
Dusit District, Bangkok 10300, Thailand

Dear Dr Kanit,

It is with great interest that I have followed the establishment of the Independent Truth and Reconciliation Committee, and I look forward to following your work and the Committee's actions over the next two years. What is at stake in the search for truth, or more accurately, truths, about the recent violence is the very status of justice — the righting of that which is wrong — in Thailand. Yet, as you are well aware, the form of the conflict at hand as well as its continuing nature, presents specific challenges to your work. In the remainder of this letter, I outline some of these challenges and query how you might address them. I write to you as both a scholar of histories of state violence in Thailand, and as a North American who has spent over half of the years since 1997 living, studying, and working in Chiang Mai and Bangkok and who cares deeply about the recent past, present, and future of justice in Thailand.

1. *The Emergency Decree and State Actors:* The use of the Emergency Decree during the state crack-down on UDD protestors in April–May 2010 makes ambiguous the accountability of state actors for violent acts that they may have

committed. Section 17 of the Decree reads: "A competent official and a person having identical powers and duties as a competent official under this Emergency Decree shall not be subject to civil, criminal or disciplinary liabilities arising from the performance of functions for the termination or prevention of an illegal act, provided that such act is performed in good faith, is non-discriminatory, and is not unreasonable in the circumstances exceeding the extent of necessity, but does not preclude the right of a victim to seek compensation from a government agency under the law on liability for wrongful acts of officials."[9] One reading of this section is that there is space for state actors who may have used violence to evade responsibility, or at least to evade being held to account; the paying of compensation does not necessarily equal the acceptance of wrongdoing and responsibility. Yet one of Prime Minister Abhisit's statements indicates that this might not be true in practice. He commented that "the Government would lend support to this independent committee and would respect its findings, as it was a matter of principle that the Government was under the law and stood ready to be held accountable for unjustifiable actions."[10] How will the ITRC approach this situation of ambiguity? Where will the "truth" be located with respect to the actions of the state? Will the actions of state actors be viewed as violence in need of investigation, or as the justified actions of those carrying out their necessary duties?

2. *Protection of Those Who Share Information*: In the aftermath of the violence of April–May 2010, the atmosphere in much of Thailand remains tense, and those in the UDD remain fearful of accusations of wrongdoing, arbitrary detention, or even death. Many stories of intimidation and killing following the crackdown in Bangkok and the return of UDD members to their home provinces have circulated. In addition, in recent years posting information or ideas deemed to be anti-monarchical or dissident in other ways has led to the interrogation, and in some cases the arrest and prosecution, of activists and writers. When asked by a reporter if victims who came to speak to the ITRC would be safe, Mr Somchai

Homlaor, one of the members of the Commission, commented that although the ITRC cannot provide amnesty for those who come to provide information (as did the Truth and Reconciliation Commission in South Africa), those who came forward would be safe. He explained that the ITRC would protect the information shared with it, and if those who came forward did not want their names or titles to be used, they would not be used. When asked if villagers might be afraid to provide information, given that the Emergency Decree was still in force, Mr Somchai commented that the Decree cannot be used to harm anyone who comes forward to give information to the ITRC. If someone comes to give information and is then arrested under the Emergency Decree, he promised personally to go to the court to oppose it, unless the person had an already existing criminal arrest warrant.[11] Mr Somchai's assurance of the protection of those who come forward is significant. Yet there is another register in which fear and safety may operate: that of an individual even deciding to come forward to provide information to the ITRC. While it may be unrealistic to expect the ITRC to address widespread fear and mistrust of the state, and of anyone at all connected to the state, by some members of Thai society, the ITRC should consider what this fear might mean for the search for truths about the events of April–May 2010. Who will be afraid to come forward, and what will these lacunae mean for the truths that the ITRC can use in the service of reconciliation?

3. *Allow for Many Truths:* Throughout this letter, I have used the awkward plural "truths", rather than the singular "truth". While the title "Independent Truths and Reconciliations Commission" does not roll off the tongue as effortlessly as the singular version, the plural form is necessary here. One of the persistent characteristics of both the violence of April–May 2010 and the contention in the months and years leading up to it was the deep polarization between different sectors of society. The divisions have been so grave that those who stand on opposite sides view one another in such a

way as not even to recognize these divisions. For example, the red-shirted members of the UDD view their struggle as one for democracy and greater social access, while some of their opponents, including some actors within the state, view them as part of a plot to overthrow the monarchy. Given this state of affairs, how will the ITRC identify the truth? Perhaps the solution is to work and act with many truths, and to recognize the existence of many truths as both evidence and methodology. One strategy for accessing the range of truths, and perhaps addressing the issue of including the experiences of people who may not feel comfortable sharing their stories with a body with some relation, however distant, to the state, is for the ITRC to make use of the reports of the various civil society, media, and human rights groups that have collected stories and testimonies. These resources include the mid-June report of the Santi Prachatham Network,[12] the ongoing work of *Prachatai* online newspaper,[13] and the work of the Human Rights and Legal Assistance Center for those affected from Political Turmoil (HLAC).[14] Each of these entities may have recorded truths from different kinds of survivors and witnesses of the violence of April–May 2010, and the inclusion of these multiple accounts will make the ITRC's work more comprehensive and wide-ranging. The inclusion of many truths will also mean that the work of the ITRC may not end contention or disagreement, but the recognition of many truths is crucial to any form of reconciliation.

The work of the Independent Truth and Reconciliation Commission is particularly significant at this moment in Thai history. It is true that, as you and the other members of the ITRC have repeatedly pointed out, it is not within your mandate to name the perpetrators of violence or to punish anyone. You yourself commented that "our main duty and goal is not punishment but restoration of peace".[15] But you cannot deny that the manner in which the ITRC conducts its work, and in which the judiciary and government act on its recommendations, will have profound implications for the future of impunity in Thailand.

I urge you and the other members of the ITRC to struggle to allow for the many truths about the events of April–May 2010 to be brought into the open, to use your work to hold accountable those who committed violent acts, no matter what side they were on, and to contribute to building a less violent and more just Thai society. I have included what may initially seem like an unusual enclosure to an open letter: a play. The play, *Death and the Maiden*, by Ariel Dorfman, is an account of how citizens search for truth in the aftermath of violence and terror. Dorfman served as a cultural advisor to the democratically elected Chilean socialist President Salvador Allende's chief of staff. He fled his country under fear of detention and death shortly after the 11 September 1973 coup that inaugurated the military dictatorship of General Augusto Pinochet.[16] While precise figures about the number of people targeted during the sixteen years of the Pinochet regime remain elusive, conservative estimates indicate that there were approximately 1,200 torture centres scattered throughout the country, 29,000 people who were tortured, and 3,000 people who were killed.[17]

Written in 1990, shortly after Dorfman and his family returned to Chile after a long period of exile, *Death and the Maiden* is about an unexpected encounter between a torture survivor and a man she believes to have been her torturer. Paulina Salas, the torture survivor, is waiting at home for her husband, Gerardo Escobar, who is late because his car has a flat tire; he receives assistance for his flat tire from a man named Roberto Miranda. A few hours after Gerardo arrives home, Roberto stops by their house to return the spare tire, and Gerardo invites him in, first for a drink and then to stay the night, as it has grown late. Roberto's turns-of-phrase, smell, and manner trigger Paulina's memory. She recalls him as her former torturer and rapist. In the middle of the night, she wakes Roberto, binds his hands and feet, and begins interrogating him about his actions during the former regime. Over the next day, she demands his confession. On the basis of her judgement of the confession — its veracity or falsity — Paulina will claim or spare Roberto's life.

As Dorfman and his characters were struggling with the thorny questions of how to search for justice when victims and perpetrators continue to live side-by-side, how to mediate among and with multiple forms of truth, and how to act when fear of possible repression continues to circulate in the aftermath of violence, a Chilean state and a Chilean society to which democracy had been newly restored were attempting to do so as well. One of President Patricio Aylwin's first actions when in 1990 he became the first elected leader to succeed General Pinochet was to establish a body to investigate the state violence of the previous sixteen years. The National Commission for Truth and Reconciliation, also known as the Rettig Commission after the name of its chair Raúl Rettig, was tasked with documenting human rights abuses that had resulted in death or disappearance during the years of military rule. Torture and other forms of violence that did not result in death were excluded from the Commission's work.[18] In total, the Rettig Commission examined the cases of 3,428 individuals. Of these cases, 2,920 were found to be within its mandate, while 508 were excluded. Ultimately, 2,279 individuals were found to be victims of human rights violations; in 641 cases, the Commission "could not come to conviction". In addition, there were 449 cases in which the Commission was only given a name without additional information and was therefore unable to conduct further investigation. Although victims were named in the report of the Rettig Commission, perpetrators were not.[19]

Dorfman's play, which is set in the present and in "a country that is probably Chile but could be any country that has given itself a democratic government just after a long period of dictatorship", unsettles the work of the Rettig Commission and other similar bodies by outlining the impossibility of justice in the aftermath of a sustained period of state violence and terror.[20] Most powerfully, when there are two competing and diametrically opposed accounts of an event, can truth be located? And if so, where and how? In the play, Paulina named Roberto as her torturer, and he insisted that he was not. Their assertions came in the context both of her status as a former dissident and his as a former accomplice of the state. When the play ends, the readers do not know definitively if Roberto tortured Paulina during the prior regime, or if Paulina murdered Roberto in the present of the play. Truth, and justice, are deferred.

Even though justice may be impossible, the attempted search for justice in the aftermath of ruptural violence is necessary. While it would be politically and intellectually irresponsible to say that the events of April–May 2010 in Thailand are comparable to the sixteen years of terror in Chile during the Pinochet regime, the broad questions raised by Dorfman's play may be useful in your work.

Sincerely,
For justice,
Tyrell Haberkorn

Enclosure: *Death and the Maiden*, by Ariel Dorfman.

Notes

1. See International Crisis Group, "Bridging Thailand's Deep Divide", Asia Report No. 192, 5 July 2010, available at <http://www.crisisgroup.org/en/regions/asia/south-east-asia/thailand/192-bridging-thailands-deep-divide.aspx> (accessed 7 March 2011). Two journalists numbered among those killed and injured during these events; see Reporters Without Borders, "Thailand: Licence to Kill", July 2010, available at <http://en.rsf.org/IMG/pdf/REPORT_RSF_THAILAND_Eng.pdf> (accessed 7 March 2011).
2. Author's translation; Santi Prachatham Network, "Social Science Perspectives on State Violence" [Lak mummong thang sangkhomsat to khwamrunraeng doi rat], Thammasat University, 19–20 June 2010, p. 1.
3. The list of 417 detainees can be found in Thai on the website of the Thai National Police Office <http://www.saranitet.police.go.th/pdf/news09062553.pdf> (accessed 7 March 2011) and in English on that of *Prachatai* Online <http://www.prachatai3.info/english/node/1885> (accessed 7 March 2011).
4. Sombat Bunngamanong was detained for holding a memorial for victims of the violence at Ratchaprasong on 26 June 2010. He was released on 13 July 2010. For more information on the conditions of his arrest, see the Asian Human Rights Commission (AHRC) urgent appeal on his case: AHRC, "UPDATE (Thailand): Release Sombat Boonngamanong and all detainees under Emergency Decree, 6 July 2010". <http://www.ahrchk.net/ua/mainfile.php/2010/3497/> (accessed 7 March 2011).

5. See Santi Prachatham Network, "Social Science Perspectives on State Violence", and Reporters Without Borders, "Thailand: Licence to Kill", for analyses of the atmosphere of censorship that prevailed after 19 May 2010.
6. Royal Thai Embassy, Tokyo, "Independent Fact-finding Commission for Reconciliation holds first press conference after formal establishment", 12 July 2010, available at <http://www.thaiembassy.jp/rte2/index.php?option=com_content&view=article&id=249:independent-fact-finding-commission-for-reconciliation-holds-first-press-conference-after-formal-establishment&catid=46:press-release&Itemid=92> (accessed 7 March 2010).
7. The seven commissioners, in addition to Dr Kanit, were Kittiphong Kittiyarak, Permanent Secretary of the Ministry of Justice; Dr Jutharat Uea-amnoey, lecturer in the Faculty of Political Science, Chulalongkorn University; Dr Decha Sangkhawan, Dean of the Faculty of Social Administration, Thammasat University; Manit Suksomchitra, President of the Thai Press Development Foundation; Dr Ronnachai Kongsakon, Deputy Dean of the Faculty of Medicine, Ramathibodi Hospital; Somchai Homlaor, Chair of the Campaign Committee for Human Rights; and Dr Surasak Likhasitwatanakun, Dean of the Faculty of Law, Thammasat University.
8. Royal Thai Embassy, Singapore, "Independent committees to steer national reform process established to move reconciliation forward", 30 June 2010, available at <http://www.thaiembassy.sg/press_media/news-highlights/independent-committees-to-steer-national-reform-process-establishal-to-m> (accessed 7 March 2011).
9. "Emergency Decree on Government Administration in States of Emergency", B.E. 2548. The English translation, which I have used here, and the original Thai version are available at <http://thailand.ahrchk.net/edecree/index.php> (accessed 7 March 2011).
10. Royal Thai Embassy, Tokyo, "PM clarifies Government's intention regarding reconciliation process", 16 June 2010, available at <http://www.thaiembassy.jp/rte2/index.php?option=com_content&view=article&id=234:pm-clarifies-governments-intention-regarding-reconciliation-process&catid=46:press-release&Itemid=92> (accessed 7 March 2011).
11. "Senator Accuses DSI Director General of Serving Adminisration" [So. wo. cha athibodi di es ai rapchai fai borihan], *Khao sot*, 13 July 2010, available at <http://www.khaosod.co.th/view_news.php?newsid=TUROd01ERXdOekV6TURjMU13PT0%3D&sectionid=TURNd01RPT0%3D&day=TWpBeE1DMHdOeTB4TXc9PQ%3D%3D> (accessed 7 March 2011).
12. Santi Prachatham Network, "Social Science Perspectives on State Violence".

13. *Prachatai* Online collected information about people who died, were injured, disappeared, were arrested, or have otherwise experienced injustice. For more information, see <http://prachatai.com/affected-center-special>.
14. The HRLAC collected testimonies first from an office at the 14 October 1973 memorial, and continued to do so at the offices of the Cross Cultural Foundation. For more information, see <http://www.naksit.org/content/view.php?id=350>.
15. "We're here for answers, not a witchhunt", *Bangkok Post*, 8 July 2010.
16. Danny Postel, "Interview with Ariel Dorfman," *The Progressive*, December 1998 (available at <http://www.progressive.org/mag_intv_dorfman> (accessed 7 March 2011).
17. Monte Reel and J.Y. Smith, "A Chilean Dictator's Dark Legacy", *Washington Post*, 11 December 2006, available at <http://www.washingtonpost.com/wp-dyn/content/article/2006/12/10/AR2006121000302.html> (accessed 7 March 2011).
18. The Rettig Commission report is available on the website of the United States Institute for Peace <http://www.usip.org/resources/truth-commission-chile-90> (accessed 7 March 2011).
19. In early 2004, the Valech Report, which documented the work of the National Commission on Political Imprisonment and Torture (chaired by Bishop Sergio Valech), released further information about the nearly 29,000 cases of torture that did not result in death. These cases were excluded from the Rettig Commission's inquiry, in the service of speed and reconciliation. The Valech Report is available on the website of United States Institute for Peace <http://www.usip.org/resources/commission-inquiry-chile-03> (accessed 7 March 2011).
20. Ariel Dorfman, *Death and the Maiden* (New York: Penguin Books, 1992), front matter.

5

THE IMPACT OF THE RED SHIRT RALLIES ON THE THAI ECONOMY

Aekapol Chongvilaivan

INTRODUCTION

Early expectations for Thailand's economic performance in 2010 were cheery, as its 2009 performance coupled with upbeat business confidence around the globe in the last quarter of the same year painted a fabulous picture of the Thai economy reaching a GDP growth rate of 4.5 to 6 per cent in 2010. All major sectors — manufactures, tourism, finance, and trade — exhibited positive growth figures during the country's strong recovery from the global economic downturn. By June, however, the country appeared to be on the verge of losing all gains from the global economic turnaround, as the Red Shirt army had jeopardized livelihoods in the Ratchaprasong district — the hub of business activities in Thailand.

This essay aims to provide a realistic assessment of the impacts of Thailand's never-ending political pandemonium. The analysis of several

---

This essay is an extended version of Aekapol Chongvilaivan, "Economy and Jobs Are Also Victims", *Straits Times*, 24 May 2010..

economic indicators reveals that economic hardship in the aftermath of the Red blockade will prove transitory and limited only to a plunge in GDP growth by 1 to 2 per cent as business confidence bounced sharply back to its pre-crackdown level and as the manufacturing sector — a key driver of Thailand's economy — continued to enjoy the global economic recovery and a surge in export demand from emerging Asia. However, closer examination at the sectoral level reveals that Thailand's generally resilient economic condition conceals the excruciating pain felt by the labour force. The Red uproar pushed millions of workers, especially those employed in the service and the wholesale and retail trade sectors, into unemployment. Several policy responses to shield the economy against weakening sentiment and the physical damage done during the protests are proposed. These measures include tax relief, provision of liquidity to businesses in the erstwhile no-go zone, direct subsidies for those affected by the crackdown, and long-term economic policies to bridge Thailand's income gap.

The organization of this essay is as follows. The second section reviews developments in the Thai economy leading up to the 2010 crackdown. The third section assesses the economic impacts of the Red strife on the economy. The fourth section concludes and discusses several policy measures intended to revive economic sentiment and shield the most vulnerable against the knock-on effects of the country's political conflict.

ECONOMIC OUTLOOK LEADING UP TO THE 2010 CRACKDOWN

The Thai economy was hit hard by the global economic downturn and domestic political turbulence in 2009. The economy entered its worst post-1997 recession with a contraction in GDP of 2.3 per cent. Demand from Thailand's major trading partners plunged by 13.9 per cent, and de-leveraging in the global financial hubs of New York and London triggered a massive reversal in FDI inflows, amounting to US$1.2 billion. Poor consumer and business confidence led to cutbacks in domestic consumption and investment, as durable goods consumption and investment in new projects were deferred.

Table 5.1 paints a clear picture of deteriorating economic performance in Thailand against a backdrop of the economic catastrophe of 2009.

Table 5.1
Thailand's Economic Performance in 2009

	% Change year on year		*Contribution to GDP Growth*	
	2008	*2009*	*2008*	*2009*
Consumption	3.0	–0.1	1.8	0.0
Private	2.7	–1.1	1.4	–0.6
Public	4.6	5.8	0.4	0.5
Investment	1.2	–9.0	0.3	–2.0
Private	3.2	–12.8	0.5	–2.1
Public	–4.6	2.7	–0.3	0.1
Domestic Demand	2.5	–2.4	2.1	–2.0
Exports	5.1	–12.7	3.6	–9.2
Imports	8.5	–21.8	4.6	–12.6
GDP Growth	**2.5**	**–2.3**	**2.5**	**–2.3**

Source: Bank of Thailand.

Even though several stimulus pushes, such as health and infrastructure investment and public transfers, were implemented to mitigate the adverse effects of the downturn, the drastic fall in private consumption and investment fuelled a remarkable drop in the domestic demand of 2.4 per cent. Domestic political unrest worsened the sombre outlook for the Thai economy, as many countries issued travel warnings for Thailand. In the first half of 2009, Thailand experienced a sharp plunge in the number of tourist arrivals of 16.1 per cent. The global economic crisis and political uncertainties likewise severely deterred private investment, which exhibited an exponential decline of 12.8 per cent

Thailand's external trade picture was equally bleak. Export and import volumes declined by 12.7 and 21.8 per cent, respectively. The deglobalization trend observed in 2009 made itself felt via proliferating production networks connecting the Southeast Asian economies into a nexus of vertically related production. Therefore, the economic slump in economic powerhouses like the United States and the European Union (EU) led to collapses in trade throughout the region.

However, the first quarter of 2010 witnessed a turnaround for the Thai economy, thanks to strong export demand from emerging markets, and on top of accommodative monetary and fiscal policies that revived producer and consumer confidence and shored up economic activity. Private consumption started to exhibit positive growth, favouring the agricultural and tourism sectors as well as employment. The manufacturing sector, particularly the electronics industry, was among the very first economic sectors to manifest strong recovery, owing to buoyant economic conditions in China and other Asian countries and to rising domestic demand resulting from the government's macroeconomic stimuli. External stability remained exceptionally resilient as the country continued to run current account surpluses and to maintain a high level of foreign reserves. As of December 2009, Thailand's international reserves amounted to US$138.4 billion, compared to US$111.0 billion in 2008.

In the period leading up to the political crackdown of April–May 2010, economic conditions in Thailand remained sound. The economy had recovered from the global and domestic upheaval that inflicted deep pain during the first half of 2009. The robust revival was due to significant rises in export demand in addition to the expansion of private consumption and investment.

RED BLOCKADE HITS THAI ECONOMY HARD

The aftermath of the unfolding stampede nevertheless reversed the trend towards Thailand's economic recovery. The barbaric protests of the United Front for Democracy against Dictatorship (UDD) bogged the economy down in yet another round of chronic unrest. The two-month closure of the Ratchaprasong area brought an end to the country's good economic fortunes.

Trends in consumer and business confidence in the first half of 2010 perhaps best reflect the short-term impacts of the Red Shirt rallies on the Thai economy. Table 5.2 portrays the Business Sentiment Index (BSI) by economic sector.[1] As shown in this table, political violence slashed business confidence from a level of 55.7 in April to merely 46.0 in May, below the threshold level of economic stability (BSI = 50). The clashes between the Thai government and the Red Shirts seemed to inflict deep pain on all major economic sectors — especially manufacturing, construction, trade, and services — as their BSIs significantly declined to a critical level. It should also be highlighted that deteriorating business sentiment against a backdrop of political crackdown tends to be short-lived. Indeed, the figures presented here reveal a prompt recovery in the

Table 5.2
Business Sentiment Index (BSI) by Sectors

	Jan 2010	*Feb 2010*	*Mar 2010*	*Apr 2010*	*May 2010*	*Jun 2010*
BSI	50.4	51.3	55.7	46.0	49.9	52.1
Manufacturing	50.4	51.7	57.1	47.1	51.6	53.2
Infrastructure	60.6	55.3	61.0	59.8	57.4	54.8
Construction	47.9	54.1	54.3	44.8	48.1	48.1
Trade	47.7	47.6	49.9	41.6	44.6	49.8
Transportation	54.9	62.0	59.0	54.7	55.1	55.3
Finance	57.0	53.3	63.8	52.9	55.7	58.5
Service	51.5	48.2	52.2	30.7	37.3	37.2

Source: Bank of Thailand.

BSI across a wide range of economic sectors. This recovery does not, however, mean that the long-term effects of the unceasing political turmoil are trivial. Underlying political uncertainty will exert pressure on Thailand's economic performance and competitiveness in the global marketplace.

The detrimental impacts of the Red Shirt rallies on the Thai economy proved uneven across sectors. Worst hit by the Red siege was tourism. The Tourism Council of Thailand projected a sharp plunge in the number of foreign arrivals from 14.14 million in 2009 to no more than 13 million visitors in 2010, as Bangkok and other tourist attractions became unsafe. Monthly figures for foreign tourist arrivals in Figure 5.1 further reveal that the Red rallies were a crucial threat to the tourism sector. Arrival figures declined persistently from a peak of 1.49 million people in February 2010 to merely 0.94 million in May 2010. This drastic fall in the number of foreign tourists meant losses of billions dollars for hotels, restaurants, transportation businesses, and shopping centres. Other non-manufacturing sectors, such as wholesale and retail trade, construction, and financial intermediaries, felt equally excruciating pain. Fear and distress arising from bloodshed wiped out consumer spending. Companies likewise postponed and even cancelled investment projects.

Economists seemed to reach a consensus that the impacts of the Red Shirt protests on the overall Thai economy were limited to a drop in the annual GDP growth of 1 to 2 per cent. Figure 5.2 presents Thailand's prospects of economic growth in 2010. Prior to the political crisis,

Figure 5.1
Number of Foreign Tourists (persons)

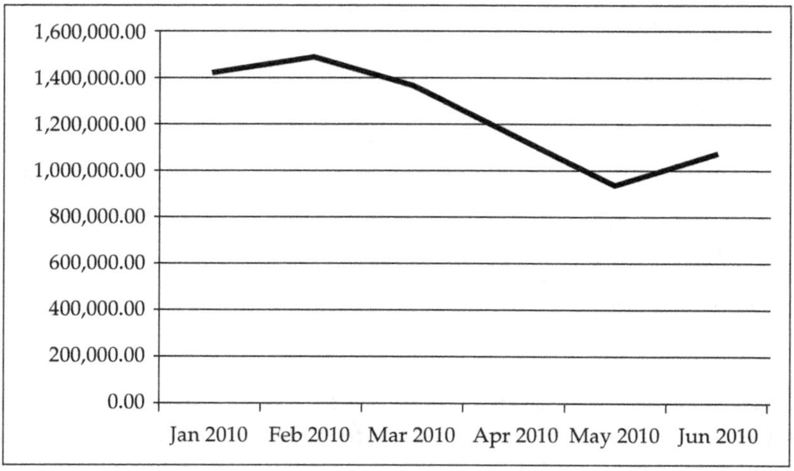

Source: Tourism Authority of Thailand.

Figure 5.2
Thailand's Quarterly GDP Growth

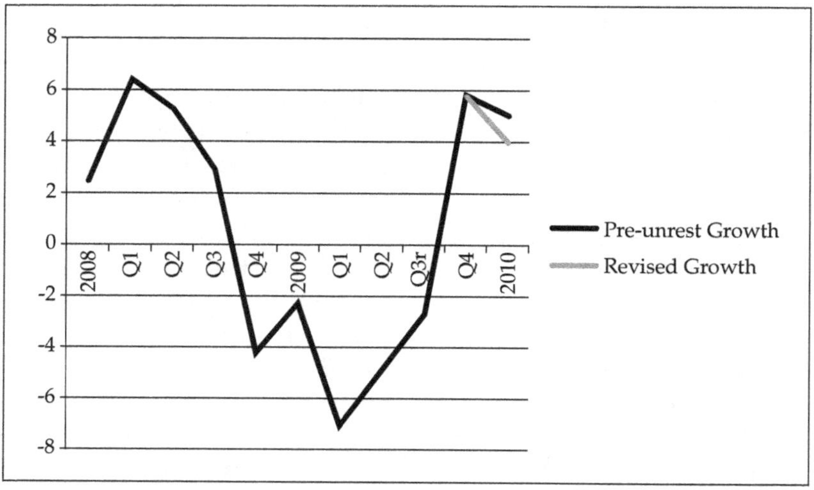

Source: Bank of Thailand.

Table 5.3
Structure of the Thai Economy in 2009–10

Sector	*GDP by Sector (%)*	*Labour Force by Sector (%)*
Agriculture	8.9	38.2
Manufacturing	39.0	14.0
Wholesale and Retail Trade	13.7	15.7
Construction and Mining	4.5	6.1
Services	37.2	31.3

Source: Bank of Thailand.

the Thai economy was expected to attain 4.5 to 6 per cent growth in 2010, as the surge in export demand from emerging Asia enabled the country to bounce back strongly from the economic slump of 2009. However, at mid-year the unceasing political instability that adversely affected a wide array of economic activities forced government authorities to revise economic growth predictions for 2010 downward to at most 4 per cent.

There are at least two main considerations that explain why Thailand's economic prospects in the aftermath of the Red Shirt protests remained rather promising. First, the collapse in business confidence appeared to be provisional. Table 5.2 demonstrates the swift recovery of the overall BSI in May–June 2010, during the period in which the Red Shirts gave up and the UDD's leaders surrendered. The instantaneous revival of business confidence was observed among affected sectors, particularly manufacturing, construction, trade, transportation, finance, and services. An influx of foreign visitors in June 2010 confirmed the recouped confidence. As portrayed in Figure 5.1, the number of foreign tourists hit 1.07 million visitors in June 2010 and was expected to return to the pre-crackdown level in the following months. In addition, manufacturing production accounts for 39 per cent of Thailand's GDP and is thus a driving force of economic growth (see Table 5.3). In the first and second quarters of 2010, the manufacturing sector continued to benefit from the growing global demand for exports, which boosted its production as well as performance.

This picture can nevertheless lead to unwarranted optimism. Expectations of macroeconomic resilience do not reflect the sharp contraction of the country's labour market. Table 5.3 demonstrates this point by highlighting the fact that Thailand's manufacturing sector, though big in size, can absorb only 14 per cent of the labour force, while the same service sector (including finance, hotels, restaurants, and others) that suffered greatest losses during the protests contributes 31.3 per cent of total employment. The prolonged collapse in trade also threatened the 15.7 per cent of the labour force employed in the wholesale and retail trade sectors.

CONCLUSIONS AND RECOMMENDATIONS

The Red Shirt rallies brought Thailand's upbeat economic performance, achieved in the context of global economic recovery and rising export demand from emerging Asia, to a halt. Although the April–May cataclysm contributed partly to a slowdown in GDP growth by 1 to 2 per cent in 2010, the inherent political uncertainties inflicted deep pain on a wide range of economic sectors, particularly tourism, hotels, restaurants, and wholesale and retail trade. Thailand's unending political chaos may in the end cost many of its people their jobs.

While the Thai economy stood to tap the rapid revival of economic activity after May 2010, several stimulus measures targeted at the victims of the Red uproar and intended to allow the Thai economy to participate in Asia's economic growth needed to be undertaken.

First, tax relief packages had the potential to revive spending on consumption and business confidence, especially in the Ratchaprasong and Silom districts, where hundreds of shopping malls, hotels, restaurants, financial firms, and other businesses shouldered the damage done during the Red protests. These tax incentives could have been be given in terms of Goods and Services Tax (GST) exemptions, income tax deferrals, and property tax waivers.

Second, the government needed to make sufficient liquidity available for entrepreneurs in dire need of cash to perk up their businesses, particularly in the no-go zone most affected by the Red Shirt protests. This could have been done through financial measures such as deferred interest payments, additional loan packages, and lower interest rates.

Third, hundred thousands of workers in the central business district, especially those engaged in temporary jobs and the self-employed, were running out of money after the slowdown in business activity.

The government needed to undertake initiatives to bail out those susceptible to the political tide by providing direct subsidies or income tax exemptions.

Lastly, it is undeniable that one of the root causes of the unremitting political conflict in Thailand is the income inequality between people in the cities and those in rural areas who depend on a traditional agricultural sector that has faded away and been replaced by modern manufacturing industries. Long-term economic development policies must focus on enriching the livelihoods of people in the agricultural sectors through social security programmes and education.

The gun-fire stopped on 19 May 2010, but the damage still remained. While millions of Thais feel the ripple effects of the Red rallies on the economy, no concrete remedy measures were put in place. As Thailand's political unrest is chronic, the government must resort to fiscal and monetary measures to help those suffering from the fallout of the future clashes.

Note

1. The interpretation of the Business Sentiment Index (BSI) is as follows: a BSI figure of 50 implies that business sentiment remains stable, a figure of greater than 50 indicates that business sentiment has improved, and a figure of less than 50 that it has worsened.

6

THE SOCIO-ECONOMIC BASES OF THE RED/YELLOW DIVIDE
A Statistical Analysis

Ammar Siamwalla and Somchai Jitsuchon

The political conflict in Thailand during the past six years, involving increasingly large numbers of participants outside the usual elite, has elicited a great deal of speculation on the background of the Red Shirts and the Yellow Shirts. Foreign journalists, relying on interviews with the red-shirted demonstrators, have tended, for example, to conclude that most of these demonstrators are rural, poor, and primarily from the Northeast. Yellow Shirts, insofar as they have been able to attract interest from these journalists at all other than as the group that closed down Suvarnabhumi Airport, are said to be supporters of the "elite". These views nicely complement each other and simplify matters for their audience.

Matters are a little more complicated, as was pointed out in a presentation made by one of us during the 2009 Year-End Conference of the Thailand Development Research Institute.[1] Based on an extensive survey, that presentation came to the preliminary conclusion that there is no substantial difference in the social backgrounds of people who support the Red and Yellow points of view. It is important to bear in mind that, in both that presentation as well as in what follows, we are *not* studying the demonstrators themselves, who are only about 1 or 2 per cent of the population, but the much more numerous people who support the points of views expressed in the demonstrations.

This paper uses the same data as the earlier presentation, but it substantially refines that presentation's preliminary finding by using what we believe to be a more thorough and objective method to classify respondents into Reds and Yellows and then to find out what socio-economic backgrounds appear to make people choose to lean towards the Reds, the Yellows, or neither. The paper is somewhat unusually ordered: the next section describes the data source used and proceeds directly to the results of the analysis. We leave to the end the technical details of how we proceed from the data to the results.

THE DATA

The data used both in the earlier presentation and in this paper come from a survey of political attitudes conducted by the National Statistical Office (NSO), using a questionnaire prepared by the Thailand Development Research Institute (TDRI). The objective of the survey was to answer broad questions relating to economic inequality to the political divide that affects Thai society. This questionnaire was appended to the usual Socio-Economic Survey (SES) conducted by the NSO every year. It was administered to a sub-sample of SES respondents, numbering 4,097 households, in August and September 2009. This period was some months after the bloody Songkran of 2009, and half a year before the March–May 2010 demonstrations. From this sub-sample, we find data from 3,655 households usable. This combination of SES data and data from the appended questionnaire allows us to link the responses to questions in the latter to the very rich data on the household socio-economic characteristics in the former, larger survey. In the appended attitude survey of political attitudes, we use responses to the question, "What are the causes of the current political conflict in Thailand?" as the major input in a classification of respondents into three groups: "Reds", "Yellows", and "Neither".

Note that while the response to political attitude questions and the consequent political affiliation pertain mostly to the individuals chosen by households to respond to the survey, many of the socio-economic variables used in the analysis below refer to the entire household.

RESULTS

The statistical analysis detailed in the final section of the paper shows the following socio-economic variables to have some impact on the probability of an individual acquiring the political tag of Red, Yellow, or Neither.

Age: Older people tend to be neither Red nor Yellow, with a slight tendency of younger people to be Yellow. Red support appears to come from all age groups.

Economic Well-Being — Level: There is a clear tendency for better-off people to be Yellow. Thus Bangkok people (across all income classes) are more likely to be Yellow, while outside of Bangkok the better off are more likely to be Yellow. Poorer people in general are less likely to be either Red or Yellow. Surprisingly, Red support appears to bear no relation to income — rich or poor are equally likely (or equally unlikely) to be Red.

Economic Well-Being — Change: We also ask in the appended survey whether the respondent feels that he or she or his or her family has experienced a change in economic well-being compared to ten or twenty years ago. There are five possible answers to this question: much improved, improved, unchanged, worse, and much worse. There is some evidence that a *change* in economic status affects respondents' support for the Red cause. Those who feel that their conditions have much improved have a lower probability to support the Reds, while those whose conditions have worsened are more likely to support them. Strangely enough, people whose economic conditions have worsened much are more likely to support the Yellows.

Occupational and Labour Status: Try as we might, we find that occupational status — whether, for example, the respondent is self-employed, or a business owner or employee — has no effect on whether he or she is Red or Yellow. Members of one occupational group, housewives, do tend to be pronouncedly Red, for reasons for which we have no explanation. We tried testing the effect of gender across the sample, but none was found.

Regions: Except for Bangkokians, who tend to favour the Yellows and who would be less likely to be uncommitted, there is very little specifically regional support for the Reds or the Yellows.

The results of the statistical analysis are mostly negative. In particular, the identification of the Reds with the poor is a myth. In general, few socio-economic variables are unequivocally decisive in determining political affiliation, at least between Red and Yellow, in Thailand today. Paradoxically, the group to whom we have pinned the label "Neither" shows a much stronger socio-economic basis. They are older, poorer, and less likely to be Bangkokians.

OBTAINING THE RESULTS FROM THE DATA

1. Identifying the Reds and the Yellows

Among the questions asked in the political attitude survey, we ask people to respond to the open-ended question: "What are the causes of the current political conflict in Thailand?" Each respondent is asked to give three answers. The responses are assigned by the enumerator to one among sixteen possible answers; see Table 6.1 for a list of the possible answers and for counts of all the responses in the sample. For each respondent, there are thus three answers, ranked according to the order of response. These answers are the variables which may be used to classify the respondents into three different political groups: Red, Yellow, and Neither. The earlier Somchai-Viroj paper looks only at the first reply of each respondent, and if it belongs to a pre-defined set of responses, called the Red or the Yellow or the Neither "discourse", the respondent is assigned to the relevant group. In this manner, each household is slotted into one of three groups.

This method is unsatisfactory, first of all because such a procedure ignores the second and third answers, which may be relevant in defining a "discourse". By focusing on only the first response, we lose the valuable information in second and third responses. More importantly, there could be considerable disagreement over exactly which response belongs to a particular "discourse". In this paper, we employ a statistical technique called cluster analysis[2] to find out how the data on responses cluster themselves and the combination of responses within each cluster. From the characteristic combination within each cluster, we then assign the households within the cluster their political colouring.

Recall that each respondent could give three of the sixteen possible responses. We represent this set of responses as a sixteen-dimensional vector, each element of which represents a possible response. If the respondent does not choose a particular answer, then the value of the corresponding element of the vector is zero. If he or she chooses to give a particular answer as the first response, we assign the value of 3 to the corresponding element of the vector. Similarly we assign the values of 2 and 1 to his or her second and third answers, respectively. Now, imagine each household's response as a point in sixteen-dimensional space. A cluster is then a set of points that are "close together". The closeness of the points represents the similarity in the grouping of the answers by each respondent.

The software programme allows us some freedom to choose the number of clusters. After a number of tries, we find it best to settle on four clusters, rather than three for the three groups. Table 6.2 shows the distribution of the answers by cluster. The answers are weighted 3, 2 and 1 according to whether they are responded first, second or third, when asked. The sum across households of these weighted scores is shown on the left-hand side of the table. Next we have to make a judgement on which of these four clusters represents which political group. To make that judgement we have to highlight the relative emphasis of each cluster on particular answers or groups of answers. To gauge that emphasis, we calculate the odds ratio for each cell, shown on the right-hand side of the table. For each cell, the odds ratio is the ratio between the proportion of the number of respondents in the cell in the row total and the proportion of the corresponding column total to the overall total. For example, for the top left-hand corner cell, take the proportion 1,924 of its row total, and divide it by the proportion of the proportion of 7,918 to the overall total 20,467. In this particular case, the odds ratio turns out to be 0.9616. This means that the choice of response 1 for Cluster 1 is not out of the ordinary, because the ratio is close to unity. On the other hand, the choice of the same response for Cluster 3 is striking, with the odds ratio at 2.0305, meaning that the choice of response 1 for Cluster 3 has more than double the probability of every other cluster.

From the odds ratios in Table 6.1, it is not very hard to pick out Cluster 2 as primarily indicating Red households. We next decide to judge Cluster 1 as indicating the Neither category. The cluster's main emphasis is on the second response, with the odds ratio standing at 2.3. This is almost a non-response. "Polarization and inability to compromise" is almost a definition of political conflict, and thus seems a safe answer for people who have not opted for the Reds or the Yellows whose demands and grievances are more specific. The tricky choice is for Clusters 3 and 4. The combination of responses favoured by respondents in each of those two clusters could equally represent the Yellow discourse, in that they lean towards an anti-"old"-politics view of the world. We have therefore chosen to combine the two clusters as representing the Yellow view of the world.

2. Choosing to be Red or Yellow or Neither

Having assigned households in all the clusters to the corresponding political groupings: Red (Cluster 2), Yellow (Cluster 3 and Cluster 4) and Neither (Cluster 1), we next find out the social and economic backgrounds that determine their affiliations. We employ multinomial logit analysis. This type of analysis is used when individuals make a choice among a set number of political affiliations. The technique allows us to calculate the probability of a person choosing each of the affiliations, given information on the variables of his or her household's or his or her own social and economic characteristics.

Table 6.2 reports on the results of this analysis. It does not show the probabilities directly, but the marginal effects on the probabilities of a particular variable *relative* to the base variable shown in the last column, holding all other variables constant. Thus, the figure –0.14 on the third line in the Yellow column of the table means that a person aged 25 to 34 is 14 per cent less likely than a person aged 15 to 24 (the base) to be a Yellow. He is at the same time 3 per cent more likely to be a Red. The 14 per cent greater likelihood to be a Yellow is statistically significant while the likelihood of being Red is insignificant. We draw upon Table 6.2 to draw the conclusions reported earlier in the paper.

Observe that every row sum of these marginal effects is zero; the probabilities of any individual being Red, Yellow or Neither have to sum up to unity. To conserve this quality of the probabilities, any *change* in

Table 6.1
Distribution of Responses by Clusters and Odds Ratios

		Total points					*Odds Ratio*			
No.	*Response*	*Cluster 1*	*Cluster 2*	*Cluster 3*	*Cluster 4*	*Total*	*Cluster 1*	*Cluster 2*	*Cluster 3*	*Cluster 4*
1	Politicians unable to divide up the cake	1,924	51	2,936	261	5,172	0.96	0.06	2.03	0.31
2	People are polarized, unwilling to compromise	3,626	190	102	153	4,071	2.30	0.27	0.09	0.23
3	Governments and politicians are too corrupt	393	65	728	1,575	2,761	0.37	0.14	0.94	3.54
4	Some are unwilling to accept election results	315	536	222	189	1,262	0.65	2.46	0.63	0.93
5	Protestors do not respect the law	328	363	264	166	1,121	0.76	1.87	0.84	0.92
6	People are unequally treated. Double standards	250	429	275	145	1,099	0.59	2.26	0.90	0.82
7	Unequal understanding of politics	209	439	226	125	999	0.54	2.54	0.81	0.78
8	People sell votes, politician buy votes	263	313	217	188	981	0.69	1.85	0.79	1.19
9	Parliamentary dictatorship, politicians grab all pork	101	233	221	155	710	0.37	1.90	1.11	1.35
10	Gap between rich and poor, urban and rural	189	222	136	117	664	0.74	1.93	0.73	1.09
11	Military coup and intervention in politics	90	190	111	55	446	0.52	2.47	0.89	0.76
12	Media do not perform adequately and are biased	90	201	66	55	412	0.56	2.82	0.57	0.83
13	Loopholes in the Constitution	67	166	107	55	395	0.44	2.43	0.97	0.86
14	Independent agencies fail to do their duties	46	72	55	38	211	0.56	1.97	0.93	1.12
15	Others	20	23	34	6	83	0.62	1.60	1.47	0.45
16	Too much judicial intervention in politics	6	42	19	13	80	0.19	3.04	0.85	1.01

Source: Raw data from National Statistical Office/TDRI Survey.

Table 6.2
Marginal Effects of Social and Economic Characteristics on the Probabilities of Being Red, Yellow and Neither

	Marginal Effect			
Variable	*Yellow*	*Red*	*Neither*	*Base*
Age 25–34	–0.10	0.004	0.10	Age 15-24
Age 35–44	–0.11	–0.02	0.12*	Age 15-24
Age 45–54	–0.14**	0.03	0.10	Age 15-24
Age 55–64	–0.10	–0.05	0.14**	Age 15-24
Age > 64	–0.13*	–0.03	0.15**	Age 15-24
Bangkok (Bkk)	0.12**	0.007	–0.13**	Other Regions
Housewife	–0.01	0.08**	–0.07	Other Occupation
"Income" Quintile 2*non–Bkk1	0.09**	–0.007	–0.08**	"Income"Quintile1*nonBkk1
"Income" Quintile 3*non–Bkk1	0.04	0.03	–0.08*	"Income"Quintile1*nonBkk1
"Income" Quintile 4*non–Bkk1	0.08*	–0.00	–0.08*	"Income"Quintile1*nonBkk1
"Income" Quintile 5*non–Bkk1	0.11**	0.018	–0.12**	"Income"Quintile1*nonBkk1
Much Improved in 10–20 yrs.	0.15	–0.06*	–0.09	Improved in 10-20 yrs.
Not much changed in 10–20 yrs.	0.08**	–0.01	–0.06**	Improved in 10-20 yrs.
Worsened in 10–20 yrs.	0.002	0.05*	–0.06	Improved in 10-20 yrs.
Much worsened in 10–20 yrs.	0.19*	–0.02	–0.17*	Improved in 10-20 yrs.

Notes:
[1] "Income" is measured by per capita total expenditures.
*Significant at 10% level.
**Significant at 5% level.
Source: Raw data from NSO/TDRI Survey.

the factors affecting any one of the probabilities will have to change the other probabilities in an offsetting fashion, so that the sum remains one. Thus the sum of marginal effects is zero.

Notes

1. See Somchai Jitsuchon and Viroj Na Ranong, "Survey Results of People's Views about Politics and Social Welfare to Create Social Justice" [*Phon kansamruat thatsana prachachon to kanmueang lae sawatdikan sangkhom phuea sang khwampentham thangsangkhom*], "Report of the 2009 Year-end Conference on 'Economic Reforms for Social Justice'" (on CD-ROM) (Bangkok: Thailand Development Research Institute, 2009).
2. Maurice Kendall, A. Stuart and J. Keith Ord, *The Advanced Theory of Statistics, Volume I: Design and Analysis, and Time Series* (London: Charles Griffin, 1983), pp. 403–418.

7

THE INEFFABLE RIGHTNESS OF CONSPIRACY

Thailand's Democrat-ministered State and the Negation of Red Shirt Politics

Marc Askew

Thailand's Democrat Party-led administration under the leadership of Prime Minister Abhisit Vejjajiva emerged victorious following the dramatic and ultimately bloody confrontations with the Red Shirt movement during March-May 2010. But this victory was achieved at the expense of persistent, in fact exacerbated, political polarization. This is so because the Red Shirts' second messianic attempt to force political change by mass action was suppressed not simply by legally sanctioned military power — the state's reaction was legitimized by the application of two potent conspiracy discourses, namely "terrorism" and the overthrow of the monarchy. The former is newly devised, but the latter is old; I describe it here as Thailand's "Primary Conspiracy Theory". There is not the space here to elaborate at length on the historical genesis and various mutations of the Primary Conspiracy Theory and its formal and informal institutional supports (the former exemplified in the manipulation of Thailand's *lesè majesté* law). Suffice it to say that the increasingly hysterical claim since late 2005 that the "monarchy is in danger" from evil plotters is a vital dimension of hyper-royalist Thai popular nationalism and an institutionalized discourse embraced and deployed by key palace-aligned conservative actors (notably Privy Council President Prem Tinsulanon), the now dominant Queen's Guard faction of the military and the Democrat Party. This trend has certainly not been discouraged by the palace, exemplified by the queen's attendance of and utterances at funerals of members of the People's Alliance for Democracy (PAD) in 2008. Deployed by the PAD as a vital weapon to mobilize popular middle-class opposition to then Prime Minister Thaksin Shinawatra and by the military command as a crucial justification for the 2006 coup against him, the imperative to "protect the monarchy" has become the key pre-emptive ideological buttress for conservative rule in the name of "Democracy with the King as Head of State." The Primary Conspiracy Theory has long lurked in Thai conservative discourse, both as a central anxiety and a political weapon, reflecting the revival (and re-sacralization) of the monarchy in post-1945 Thailand. At times of system strain, such as the Cold War period, and currently in the anxious closing years of the ninth reign, it has been openly deployed as a mechanism to silence dissent and critique. Viewed from a historical perspective, Democrat leaders' pious declarations in April 2010 that the Red Shirt movement was intent on toppling the monarchy (officially recognizing long-standing PAD accusations and popular gossip) underlined the widely recognized techniques of a party that undermined political enemies by spreading scandal and rumour — famously exemplified in 1946 in the claims by Democrat Party members that their political arch-enemy Prime Minister Pridi Phanomyong was behind the death of the young King Ananda Mahidol.

The symbolic overkill harnessed by the Democrat administration in April–May 2010 was an indicator of just how threatening the Red Shirt challenge had become. Directed principally at the Red Shirt leadership and former Prime Minister Thaksin, these demonizing efforts assumed somehow that ordinary Red Shirt followers would not also take them to heart as a negation of their political ideals and identity by an intransigent establishment. But the stoking of moral panic and condemnation only managed to convince those Thais who were already opposed to the Red Shirt movement and Thaksin, leaving Red Shirt supporters and many others alienated from Thailand's increasingly repressive post-2006 political dispensation.

Following the convergence of unprecedented numbers of protestors on Bangkok from 12 March 2010, the government struggled to manoeuvre for political space against the Red Shirt demand for the unconditional dissolution of parliament. As the demonstrations proceeded with no let-up during March and into April (interspersed with mysterious bombing attacks), Abhisit's government faced the challenge of managing the meaning of events as they unfolded before both a domestic and an international audience. It was imperative in the international arena, as it was domestically, for the government to affirm its legitimacy as an administration with a legal and moral mandate to preserve that version of constrained parliamentary democracy endorsed by the coup of 2006 and enshrined in the 2007 constitution. Eventually, it was Red Shirt disorganization and mismanagement in an environment of uncontrollable violence, notably from 10 April, that gave the government the pretexts to authorize the use of military force and to justify these actions as a legitimate defence against "terrorism" and a comprehensive plot against the Thai monarchy. Though these paranoid discourses have been contested within the country, the fact that the government was willing to endorse and then sustain them in its anti-Red Shirt effort, and even in the aftermath of 19 May, highlights the emergence of an increasingly reactionary state ideology, one which will stymie genuine political change towards fuller electoral democracy in the future.

A little over a week following the 10 April violence in Thailand's capital, I wrote an essay describing the intensification of symbolic confrontation between, on the one side, the Red Shirt leadership and, on the other, both the Democrat-led government and the emerging support among middle-class Bangkokians for a decisive official crackdown on the protests. That piece, on which this essay also draws, concluded by highlighting the growing importance of the government-sanctioned anti-monarchical conspiracy theory.[1] Developments since that time have confirmed this trend, exposing the centrality of chronic paranoia in Thailand's contemporary conservative political culture, exemplified in the Democrat Party and its support base in Thailand's Upper South and in even more extreme form in the middle-class based PAD. The alleged treasonous intent of the red Shirt movement was certainly not the only discourse generated to symbolically delegitimize the protestors and their leaders, but it was the most powerful and insidious.[2] Critical Red Shirt mistakes and deficiencies gave the conservative Democrats and their coalition allies an ideal opportunity publicly to unleash the theory of a plot to topple the monarchy. The charge of *"lom chao"* (anti-monarchical, literally "toppling the lords") was a critical domestic smear campaign mobilized to negate Red Shirt demands for popular electoral democracy. But it had little impact on the vitally important audience of foreign government observers, whom the Democrat-led government needed to keep on-side and at a distance from the Red Shirts. For this purpose, the quasi-legal terminology of "terrorism" was cranked up to reinforce the taint of criminality against Thaksin and the Red Shirt leadership.

The crushing of the Red Shirt movement's demonstrations in May 2010 and its repressive aftermath were a sequel, or rather a completion, of the government's defence against the Red Shirt assault of a year earlier, during which time the Red Shirts' National United Front for Democracy against Dictatorship (UDD) was officially categorized as a "security threat" in the broadest sense. This categorization served as a pretext for wide-ranging censorship which targeted not only Thaksin-supporting zealots, but also intellectuals and political commentators deemed to be critical of the monarchy because of their critiques of Thailand's power structure in general. Of course, the Primary Conspiracy Theory was already well-established by late 2008, when the Democrat-led coalition assumed power at the behest of the military and proclaimed its determination to ensure "protection of the monarchical institution" as its main policy objective. Cultivated for decades by political opportunists, the Primary Conspiracy Theory re-emerged into public life from late 2005, during the anti-Thaksin campaign of the PAD. The events of April–May 2010 brought about the official institutionalization of the theory, which requires no proof for its demonstration; its very utterance is hedged by sacredness and buttressed by powerful formal and informal sanctions. Though many government bureaucrats, military and police privately express disapproval, and even embarrassment, at the government-sanctioned invocation of the Primary Conspiracy Theory, they remain publicly silent because of its intimidatory power. Much has already been written about the government-endorsed crackdowns on websites and chat rooms on both security grounds and on suspicion of *lesè majesté* prior to, during, and after the confrontations of last year. Since April–May 2010 the Democrat Party has presided over an ever-more paranoid state apparatus. It is able, too, to rely on powerful extra-parliamentary forces, not least in the guise of the PAD, even though this group has proved to be a volatile political bedfellow for the Democrat-led administration.

What seemingly began as a festival of popular democracy among crowds of Red Shirt supporters demanding the dissolution of parliament and new elections turned into a bloody confrontation on 10 April, as troops attempted to clear the core rally area around the Phan Fa Bridge and the Democracy Monument in central Bangkok. A predictable blame game escalated between Red Shirt leaders and the Democrat-led government, centring on the question of responsibility for the targeted killings that occurred that night. The April carnage was the prelude to the later escalation of violence. As with all crowd-government confrontations since 2008, the threat and the reality of violence were a critical ingredient in both the power-play and the discourse. As with the clashes of October 2008 and April 2009, too, the party that was demonstrated to be the instigator would lose all political capital. Put more bluntly, though culpability has been contested in every instance of crowd-government confrontation since October 2008, the party that can project innocence to both the international world — in simple terms, the United States Department of State — and the Bangkok middle class wins the symbolic legitimacy game. This time, the Red Shirt leadership and its supporters affirmed their commitment to peaceful protest, but such commitment was compromised from the beginning by a string of bombings on military installations and other public places. As in April 2009, the Red Shirt leadership claimed that its peaceful protests were being discredited by a "third hand". For its part, the government and the military could not locate the culprits behind these bombings, despite the finger being pointed at the maverick pro-Thaksin general Khattiya "Se Daeng" Sawatdiphon. While the Abhisit government stuck with its mantra of upholding the law, the inability of the authorities convincingly to identify and apprehend culprits in attacks that occurred well before the 10 April clash raised questions about both the capacity of the authorities and the unity of the Thai Army itself.

As with all previous clashes, controlling the narrative of culprits and victims was imperative. The government began its effort to assert such control when it declared a state of emergency (under the Emergency Decree of 2005) on 7 April, after Red Shirts broke into the parliament compound[3] to demand an explanation for the alleged presence of explosives at the Ratchaprasong rally site. Armed with the extraordinary powers granted by the Emergency Decree, the government cut the signal of the Red Shirt cable TV channel, People Channel, on the grounds that it was disseminating distorted information. Dozens of news websites reporting on the Red Shirts or critical of the government were blocked. By conspicuous contrast, all television channels explicitly critical of the Red Shirts, including the Yellow Shirt PAD station ASTV, remained untouched, and fervently anti-Thaksin, anti-Red Shirt websites were allowed free rein. The government's main TV channel, NBT, stepped up its condemnation of the Red Shirts, most stridently in its talk shows, which were hosted by such ardent enemies of Thaksin Shinawatra as Chirmsak Pinthong and featured sympathetic interviews with PAD leaders. Abhisit presented himself in the state media as a calm, almost therapeutic national leader. Spokesmen for the Centre for the Resolution of the Emergency Situation (CRES) were clinical and measured in their delivery. But Abhisit deliberately permitted a chorus of emotional condemnation from numerous sources in the public arena, including the Democrat Party, to savage the Red Shirts.

On the afternoon of 10 April, troops moved into the Ratchadamnoen Avenue area to pressure protestors. By dusk, the scene was one of mayhem; confusing accounts reported the shooting of both Red Shirts and soldiers — including senior officers — as well as the death of a Japanese photographer. Video footage that appeared the following day revealed shadowy black-clad figures firing weapons of war. Other clips indicated that gun-fire also came from upper floors or roof-tops of surrounding buildings. The identity of these figures was unclear, but the government quickly cast them as "terrorists" connected to elements of the Red Shirt movement and bent on creating chaos. This narrative failed to account for the large number of Red Shirt deaths. The official assertion that soldiers played no role in shootings aroused great scepticism. A change in the CRES's military spokesman's information from an initial statement (on 11 April) that soldiers had only fired live rounds in the air to an admission (on 13 April) that soldiers had fired live rounds in self-defence seemed to justify that scepticism. A number of possible scenarios might explain the shootings and clarify the identity of perpetrators, including the involvement of serving military personnel engaged in their own covert conflict with superiors. Over the whole period of the Red Shirt demonstrations, the Thai military showed a singular lack of capacity in identifying and apprehending those responsible for violent attacks. This failure allowed room for rumour and speculation about clandestine military involvement in sparking the violence. For its part, the Red Shirt leadership blamed the military for fomenting the shootings of 10 April. Both sides periodically displayed captured weaponry to condemn their opponents as the originators of the violence. It was a ritual that continued throughout the period.

The 10 April events gave the government the opportunity to undercut the legitimacy of the demonstrations by introducing, and quickly making routine, the label of "terrorist" in its proclamations and other announcements, slipping between legal and moral condemnation. Though in his own formal pronouncements Abhisit made an effort to separate ordinary Red Shirt demonstrators from unprincipled terrorist gunmen, other government figures were more hysterical in using "terrorist" as a comprehensive smear against the movement. Thus, while Suthep Thueaksuban — deputy prime minister in charge of security and head of the CRES — branded the black-clad gunmen explicitly as "terrorists" to be sought and arrested on specific charges, he also made the broader claim that Red Shirt leaders knowingly supported the gunmen's violence in an effort to overthrow a duly constituted government. Visiting the United States, the fiery Minister for Foreign Affairs Kasit Piromya linked the 10 April violence directly to Thaksin. Without a shred of evidence to demonstrate the former prime minister's culpability, Foreign Minister Kasit denounced Thaksin as a "bloody terrorist", taking the opportunity to slam foreign countries for not assisting in his arrest and extradition to Thailand. In an announcement linking the UDD leaders to the "*ai mong*" (hooded men), Deputy Prime Minister Suthep reinforced the state's emerging terrorist conspiracy narrative with the charge that the Red Shirt movement "wanted to change the country's system", anticipating the later CRES announcement of an anti-monarchical plot among UDD leaders.[4] This charge served to besmirch the Red Shirt movement and its membership as a whole. Ordinary Red Shirt supporters were advised to quit the site of the rally, now consolidated at the Ratchaprasong intersection, for their own "safety". This attempt to split Red Shirt followers from the leadership proved a dismal failure. The "terrorist" slur backfired and pushed the Red Shirts further into their own paranoid political reality of a government and military conspiring to massacre them.

Even before the violent clashes of 10 April, the paranoid discourse of "the nation and monarchy in danger" was encouraged to flourish in anti-Thaksin media outlets, completely unrestrained by the government. On 8 April, a regular political chat show on the English-language TAN cable TV station, an outlet in the Yellow Shirt ASTV conglomerate, featured *Nation* newspaper journalist Sophon Ongkara lambasting the government for doing too little, too late. He condemned Red Shirt protestors as "just a bunch of thugs ... working for Thaksin's agenda to get rid of the monarchy." On the very evening of the 10 April clashes, a major gathering of the PAD's New Politics Party was held in Krabi Province and televised by the ASTV "e-san Discovery Channel". With no sense of the irony of his pronouncements Chamlong Srimuang condemned the Red Shirts for breaking the law. He sought to vindicate the PAD's own previous illegal efforts in invading Government House and the country's airports by claiming that these had been undertaken for the higher good of saving the country and monarchy. This purpose contrasted with the motivations of the Red Shirts, who acted as minions of Thaksin. Chamlong and others slammed both the government and the Army for their weakness, promising that the Yellow Shirts would step in if the government did not act.

From 16 April, several political networks claiming that they represented non-aligned citizens, with some led by noted Yellow Shirts, demonstrated in front of the headquarters of the 11th Infantry Regiment, from which both the CRES and Prime Minister Abhisit operated. They opposed the dissolution of parliament and urged the government to apply sterner measures, under a declaration of martial law, against protestors. This development was significant; it contrasted with the government's recruitment of a "blue shirt" militia openly to oppose the Red Shirts in 2009. This time, the Red Shirts' opponents were supposedly ordinary, non-aligned citizens. Nevertheless, the slogans of many of these people betrayed their long-held conservative Yellow Shirt ideology, which branded the Red Shirt movement a traitorous plot to destroy the Thai monarchy. In the southern province of Satun, a Democrat Party stronghold, a demonstration of a so called "many-coloured" group displayed banners that both urged the government not to dissolve parliament and proclaimed that all Thais must protect the royal institution. One banner read "Overthrowing the Monarchy — just to think about it is to be in error."[5]

At a PAD meeting on 19 April, the organization's leadership announced a seven-day deadline for the government to arrest UDD "terrorists" and to end Red Shirt activity, or it would "step in." Such criticisms ultimately aided the government by providing the public endorsement that it needed to force the military to act strongly against demonstrators and "terrorist" elements. This hard-line orientation was already evident in the military's announcement that units preparing to protect the Silom Road area of Bangkok from Red Shirt demonstrators would use live rounds in self-defence. Young middle-class Bangkokian Facebook groups also joined the growing numbers of Thais aggressively denouncing the Red Shirt demonstrators as uneducated rural dupes polluting the metropolis. Concerned observers compared the emerging atmosphere of conservative backlash to the paranoia that accompanied the massacre of protesting students at Thammasat University in October 1976.

The mobilization of anti-Red Shirt groups in Bangkok was a critical prelude to the ramping up of violence, providing an opportune moment for the government to unveil its ultimate propaganda trump card of an anti-monarchical *"lom chao"* conspiracy. On 22 April, during a demonstration of a "many coloured" group against Red Shirt protestors in the Silom area, grenades were fired from Lumpini Park into the crowd, killing three and injuring seventy-five people. No Red Shirts were injured, a point which implicated UDD-affiliated armed groups as culprits.[6] In the light of the Silom violence, the government now branded the "real" UDD goal as a treasonous insurrection. On 25 April, Abhisit solemnly announced in an official TV broadcast that the aim of the Red Shirt movement was not the dissolution of parliament, but actually the creation of a new Thai state. His assertion echoed the bogus Red Shirt stickers placed around the Silom area at the time, pronouncing Thaksin the "Head of a New State".[7] Three days later, the CRES publicized a chart on state-run television purporting to represent a comprehensive plot to topple the monarchy. Allegedly based on "intelligence", the names in the chart included the usual suspects such as Thaksin, Red Shirt leaders and business supporters, but the list also extended to newspaper and journal editors and to intellectuals suspected of *lèse majesté*. Arrows linking the boxes on the chart implied a functional chain of relationships among people and groups: this claim was not demonstrable, but the paranoid logic of the conspiracy theory did not require detailed information.[8]

Provincial governors from the North and Northeast were summoned to Bangkok to be officially informed of the *"lom chao"* plot and of the presence of suspected members of the conspiracy in their areas of responsibility.[9] Evidence for the involvement of and relationships among many individuals was partial, even on the admission of the military spokesman for the CRES, but the sinister and self-confirming status of the list was reinforced when that spokesman blandly stated that suspects who objected to their presence in the chart could simply sue the authorities to "demonstrate their innocence".[10] At the beginning of May the Kafkaesque scenario took a menacing, inquisitorial turn when the first cases of individuals named in the *"lom chao"* plot were passed to the Department of Special Investigation (DSI) for the processing of arrest warrants. Bizarrely, on the same day, 3 May 2010, Abhisit announced his five-point "compromise" (*prongdong*) plan, which set out the conditions for a national election for 14 November.[11] A bludgeon had accompanied an olive branch.

Both the Red Shirts and the government sought to cultivate the support of foreigners, who were important actors in this unfolding drama, whether in the guise of governments, the media, expatriate residents of Thailand or tourists. The Red Shirts sought to encourage outside intervention after the 10 April debacle and to deflect the "terrorism" slur, and the government to persuade the international community to accept the government's version of events — together with Thaksin's alleged culpability — and the reasonableness of Abhisit's evolving responses. Tourism dollars and investment were at stake. The *"lom chao"* theme cut no ice as a measure to de-legitimize the Red Shirts in foreign eyes; instead, Abhisit and his officials focused on pinning the roots of the escalating violence on the Red Shirts and Thaksin, and showing that the government was adhering to international standards of crowd dispersal and due process. Criticism of "ignorant" and "romantic" foreign Red Shirt sympathizers was common in blogs and newspapers alike.

But foreign reporters and commentators were not as naïve as some criticism of foreign media reporting claimed. During March–May, the small number of adventurous Thai journalists willing to risk the sanctions of their senior editors and anti-Red Shirt colleagues, along with members of the Western press corps, discovered that Red Shirts had genuine grievances connected to the distribution of power in their country. Further, if foreigners' video clips had exposed the black-clad gunmen of 10 April to the benefit of the government, during the final military crackdown following 14 May, foreigners also exposed — and directly experienced — pre-emptive and targeted firing on unarmed civilian protestors by troops.

A year earlier, Abhisit's government had made much of the American State Department's public disapproval of Red Shirt violence. This time it was more difficult to gain unequivocal U.S. support. In fact, a senior American diplomat showed an embarrassing interest in exploring the reasons for Red Shirt discontent. This would not do. In early May, Assistant Secretary of State Kurt Campbell had breakfast with a group of prominent Red Shirt supporters, including former Thai Rak Thai Party executive and Deputy Prime Minister Chaturon Chaisaeng. Prominent Democrat Party members were also invited to this event, but declined. Campbell was subsequently upbraided by Foreign Minister Kasit for allegedly interfering in Thailand's affairs. This criticism came despite Campbell's praise for Abhisit's road map to national reconciliation.[12] Other foreign officials pushed for both sides to end the standoff, but the government could not tolerate the representation of Thailand's crisis that this approach implied: that would entail recognizing that the establishment-backed Democrat government was one of the proximate causes of the problem. In the weeks following the messy end of the demonstrations, state media played up American approval of Abhisit's road map while clouding foreign governments' real concerns about the crackdown. Though global approbation of the government's measures was not evident, it was nevertheless selectively constructed for a domestic audience.[13]

Following the arson in Bangkok and the provinces that followed the end of the Red Shirt demonstration on 19 May, the government pushed home its "terrorist" claims against Red Shirt leaders, both those under arrest and those who remained at large, and against Thaksin himself. The Emergency Decree allowed for initial arrest and detention and the subsequent filing of charges. Some charges were announced prior to arrest and detention, but others were not.[14] The net was broad, as befitting the state's view of a comprehensive threat posed by a wide range of traitorous anti-monarchical plotters, provocateurs of violence, organizers and sympathizers alike. "Terrorism" was easily enough applied as general delegitimizing smear in state propaganda. But in the aftermath of the demonstrations the government seemed oblivious to the contradiction represented by its simultaneous promotion of a reconciliation plan and the comprehensive stigmatization of the Red Shirt movement. This latter effort was driven home by state media's flood of arson images paired with clips of Red Shirt leaders' inflammatory statements, many selectively extracted from speeches given in 2008 and early 2009. Mainstream newspapers played their part, particularly after an arrest warrant was issued for Thaksin on terrorism charges on 25 May. The newspaper *Daily News*, for example, ran a lurid cartoon juxtaposing a portrait of Thaksin with an evil-looking caricature of Osama Bin Laden.[15]

In legal terms there were difficulties with the terrorism charges, despite the government's aim to use them finally to decapitate the Red Shirt movement and to apply pressure on the international community at last to bring Thaksin to heel. Successful prosecution on charges of terrorist acts under the Thai penal code (section 135, ironically introduced by the Thaksin government) required that such acts, or support for those acts, be proven to be the results not simply of intentions to cause property damage, injury or death, but the outcomes of broader intentions to "(a) cause general public fear and disorder; and/or (b) cause pressure to bear against the Thai government, any foreign government or any group/organisation, to take some action or refrain from taking some action being demanded."[16] Existence of these intentions distinguishes general spontaneous rioting and violence from coordinated and purposeful terrorism. After the arson of 19 May, terrorism charges were extended from three existing suspects to important Red Shirt leaders, and to Thaksin himself. The number of people facing this charge totalled thirty-nine by June. The group included Phuea Thai Party politicians. Government claims sounded ominous and impressive, but their actual veracity was dubious and likely to be unprovable. For Thaksin, officials claimed that they had enough evidence to prove that he was the mastermind of the disorder, claiming that he had funded the demonstrations to the tune of 1.5 million baht per day and organized the smuggling of arms and fighters from Cambodia.[17] At the end of July the formal terrorism charges against Thaksin were sent to prosecutors by the DSI, which hoped to use them to gain a breakthrough in efforts to extradite him. These charges drew on information obtained from Red Shirts who had allegedly seen the errors of their ways while in detention, no doubt providing or fabricating information under pressure of interrogation and assurances of lenient treatment. The great irony of the terrorist label — rapidly cemented in both government and PAD discourse about the Red Shirt leadership — was that it had also been applied legally to Yellow Shirt PAD leaders and supporters for the disruption and damage caused by their protests of 2008, which presaged the installation of the Democrat-led coalition government. Of the accused, Foreign Minister Kasit, then the Democrat party's shadow foreign minister as well as a PAD supporter, proved the most righteous in protesting the "terrorist" label. The charges against and public branding of the PAD had after December 2008 been conveniently dropped, just as the court cases against the PAD leadership had been conveniently slowed.

On 9 June, the government's NBT television ran a programme reviewing the March–May events, laying the blame for the violence squarely on Red Shirt conspirators and Thaksin. At the end of the show, the two female hosts happily promoted two pocket books about the *"lom chao"* conspiracy. In the same month, Abhisit's *"prongdong"* programme was launched with a fanfare of piously worded commitments to re-engineer the social and constitutional structure of the country in order to reduce conditions for political instability. In reality, the programme was virtually identical to the government's compromised and lacklustre "reform" programme announced in early 2009. From the beginning, the whole process of reaching rapprochement with ordinary Red Shirt supporters and other government critics had been fatally compromised: not only by the operation of concrete legal restrictions and censorship, but by the continued symbolic defilement institutionalized by the officially endorsed twin conspiracies of terrorism and traitorous plotting against the monarchy. As it did during the crisis, the Abhisit government generally tolerated continued smears against the Red Shirts from numerous quarters — from Facebook groups to the PAD and the Democrat Party spokesman (though not without some embarrassment in the latter case over his unsubstantiated claims about Red Shirt guerrilla training camps).[18]

Following the fatally botched Red Shirt assault on the government, and under the shadow of persistent and paranoid propaganda, Thailand under the Democrats had moved further right. Their pious rhetoric of "*prongdong*" masked fundamental contradictions. The events of March–May 2011 may have allowed Thailand's post-coup establishment to move closer towards eliminating its primary *bête noire* (Thaksin), but, to paraphrase Tacitus, "they created a wasteland and called it peace".

Notes

1. Marc Askew, "Thai style chaos and the right wing backlash", *New Mandala*, 20 April 2010 <http://asiapacific.anu.edu.au/newmandala/2010/04/20/thai-style-chaos-and-the-right-wing-backlash/> (accessed 7 March 2011).
2. On the representation of the Red Shirt protestors as a polluting presence in the Thai metropolis, see Thongchai Winichakul, "The 'germs': the reds' infection of the Thai political body," *New Mandala*, 3 May 2011 <http://asiapacific.anu.edu.au/newmandala/2010/05/03/thongchai-winichakul-on-the-red-germs/> (accessed 7 March 2011).
3. A few of the protestors did manage to enter the building itself. But the vast majority of media reports on this event misrepresented it by confusing the grounds of parliament with the parliament building itself. Most claimed that "parliament" was "stormed", thus wittingly or unwittingly supporting the Abhisit government's pretext for the declaration of emergency.
4. "Hunt is on for armed terrorists: Suthep", *The Nation*, 14 April 2010.
5. In Thai, "*Lom sathaban khae khit ko phit laew*". See *Deli niu*, 22 April 2010.
6. "Why the Red Shirts never targetted for grenade attacks?", *The Nation*, 24 April 2010.
7. These stickers were condemned by UDD leaders and Thaksin alike, though the term "New State" had been used in Red Shirt publications previously to refer to eliminating the political influence of non-elected influential figures such as Privy Council President Prem Tinsulanon.
8. Sources close to the CRES highlighted that, though the chart was compiled by military personnel attached to the Internal Security Operations Command, the naming of the chart itself was the doing of Deputy Prime Minister Suthep.
9. "The provincial governors were informed that the objective of the demonstration of Red Shirts was not simply for the dissolving of parliament but for destroying the institution." See *Thai rat*, 28 April 2010.
10. "CRES challenges people on the list who think they are innocent to sue",

Thai rat, 30 April 2010.

11. The points of the road map were: 1. Respect for the monarchy; 2. Efforts to address social and economic injustice through national reform; 3. Ensuring free but responsible media; 4. A probe into incidents resulting in the loss of life or affecting the public's sentiment; and 5. Amendment of the constitution to render it fairer to all parties.
12. "US involvement in Thai politics", *The Bangkok Post*, 10 May 2010.
13. For a perceptive treatment of the Abhisit government's schizoid attitude towards the foreign media and foreign observers, see Thitinan Pongsudhirak, "The widening battle over foreign perceptions," *The Bangkok Post*, 2 July 2010.
14. See, for example, Achara Ashayagachat, "Govt accused of dubious arrest", *Bangkok Post*, 25 May 2010.
15. *Deli niu*, 14 June 2010.
16. Thai Civil Code, Section 135/1–3.
17. "Thai court orders Thaksin arrested on terrorism charges", Reuters, 25 May 2010 <http://www.reuters.com/article/idUSTRE64C0L620100525> (accessed 7 March 2011).
18. See, for example, "Army denies reds training as guerrillas", *The Bangkok Post*, 10 July 2010.

8

A NEW POLITICS OF DESIRE AND DISINTEGRATION IN THAILAND

Chairat Charoensin-o-larn

I

For those who are not familiar with the history of modern Thai society and politics, the images of the Thai military's brutal dispersal of the Red Shirt protestors in the heart of Bangkok's business district on 19 May 2010 — resulting in scores dead, nearly 2,000 injured, further scores of missing persons, and general unrest in the city as a consequence of such a disgraceful action — might appear shocking and unthinkable, to say the least. However, May 2010 was not the first time that a civilian government asked the Thai armed forces to suppress the Red Shirt protestors. A similar incident took place a year earlier, in the bloody events of April 2009, when the military also moved in to crush the Red Shirt demonstrators, though with fewer fatalities than during the riots of the following year.[1]

Thailand's armed forces have long been known for their brutal suppression of dissidents, be they communist instigators during the Cold War years, student activists in the 1970s, demonstrators for democracy in the 1990s, or southern separatists[2] and Red Shirts in the most recent period. Furthermore, the military's role in staging countless *coups d'état* to usurp power from civilian governments represents a hallmark in the historical record of modern Thai politics. What is so different about the most recent rounds of events in Thailand is the changing role and image of the Thai military from yesterday's usurper of power to today's force for stability, a force necessary for the survival of a sitting civilian government. The role of the military in Thai politics has, then, become increasingly sophisticated. The military is now much more effective in accomplishing its aims. These circumstances leave the future of Thai democracy overshadowed by a cloud of doom.[3]

The suppression of the Thai people's desire for democracy, equality, and justice — whether in the form of violent military crackdowns, of legal threats including charges of *lèse majesté* or involvement in the alleged current "anti-monarchy movement,"[4] or of vigorous and misguided campaigns on behalf of a distorted ideology of national unity[5] — has long been a prominent feature of the activity of Thailand's ruling elites. Violent crackdowns on the Red Shirt demonstrators in April 2009 and May 2010 are just two recent manifestations of an old-style politics of desire. What has been suppressed, that is, is not the protestors but rather their desire for equality and justice — or, in the Red Shirts' own jargon, for the abolition of "double standards" in Thai society and politics.[6]

These two recent episodes of suppression have transformed the Red Shirt protestors' desire for equality with and justice from Thailand's ruling elites into a desire for revenge and disintegration. The reasons for this transformation lie in the lack of words of consolation or apology from the authorities, particularly the military, for the deaths of Red Shirt protestors. Furthermore, the images of Red Shirt detainees with chains on their legs when they appear outside of the prison are not only sore to the eyes but also inflict pain in the hearts of their supporters. This lack of consolation or apology and these images stand in contrast to measures undertaken to raise the spirits of the people of Bangkok whose lives of luxury were disrupted by Red Shirt "invaders" in March, April, and May of 2010. These measures included a campaign to clean up the streets of Bangkok made dirty by the Red Shirts and the closing of Silom Road on two consecutive weekends to permit a shopping spree by the people of the city.[7] They made unmistakable an urban bias against the grass-roots Red Shirts. They left members of the Red Shirts movement feeling like less than citizens of the wider community and less than genuine human beings.

Far worse were the alleged murders of people linked to the Red Shirt leadership, either as guards or as organizers recruiting demonstrators to take part in the 2010 rally in Bangkok. These killings began to occur in the wake of 19 May crackdown.[8] A large number of Red Shirt leaders and protestors were also detained. This group included several activists connected to the Red Shirt movement whom the government held under the Emergency Decree in order to prevent them from organizing political rallies. A smear campaign to discredit the Red Shirts also began. It accused them of being terrorists and anti-monarchists. Stories of the Red Shirts setting up bases in Bangkok and the provinces to train their followers in the use of weapons to fight against the government were also spread. Eighty-three individuals and businesses were accused of funding the Red Shirt protests of the March–May 2010 period; the government froze their assets pending further investigation. It thus became clear that a violent purge to eradicate the Red Shirt movement was in the making. This purge could only hinder the major national reconciliation and reform package proposed by Prime Minister Abhisit shortly after the turmoil of May 2010.[9]

What I am arguing here is that two kinds of politics of desire coexist in Thai society: the old politics of desire for suppression on the part of Thailand's ruling elites and the new politics of desire for the creation of new ideals on the part of the Red Shirts and other lovers of democracy. Thai politics at this juncture is the interplay between the "desiring machine" of the Red Shirts and other supporters of democracy and the repressive desire of ruling elites.

II

Understanding this new politics of desire in recent Thai politics requires a brief theoretical digression on the notion of desire itself. Desire here is used in the Deleuzeo-Guattarian sense as propounded in two much-acclaimed volumes on capitalism and schizophrenia.[10] According to Deleuze, "desire only exists when assembled or machined."[11] Outside this assemblage, we cannot find desire. Desire thus involves an incessant effort to create or produce a connection or plane of immanence. Desire in Deleuze's hands is no longer *a lack* that needs to be suppressed like libidinal/sexual desire or the Oedipus complex in psychoanalysis. In this regard, Deleuze's entire intellectual project sets itself against lack and negation. In other words, desire in the Deleuzian sense is a space of connection which makes possible all kinds of production and creation. Desire in this sense is a matter of effectuation rather than satisfaction. Therefore, desire for Deleuze is expressed in the form of a desiring machine that is ready to connect and be connected. Desire for Deleuze is thus like a factory. With this desiring machine, the unconscious is no longer suppressed inside us. Rather, it can produce and create all kinds of connections. The goal of Deleuze's politics of desire is to change society through a change in the social unconscious.[12] In any society, various forms of power are present to suppress the desire for creation and connection. They permit the suppression of majority.

Hence, Deleuze and Guattari think in terms of connection, transversal, and addition. They have created several terms to characterize their mode of thought, terms such as rhizome, assemblage, deterritorialization, multiplicity and nomadology. They propose schizo-analysis as a means to accommodate such a mode of thought. Deleuze was once quoted as saying "a schizophrenic out for a walk is a better model than a neurotic lying on the analyst's couch."[13] The whole idea of this mode of thought is to create a smooth space by deterritorializing existing codes. In a smooth space, everything can be connected. Likewise, flow and flight are the two main features of this kind of space. Nomadic thought is thus thought that lies outside and beyond the existing frames of reference in a society; its purpose is to arrive at another mode of thought. Deleuze himself puts it this way: "the nomadic adventure begins when they seek to stay in the same place by escaping the codes."[14] Thus, what desire brings about is not a disruption but a line of flight or of escape from the existing codes. Deleuze's notion of desire points to the creative or productive side of the unconscious.

III

The new politics of desire for a smooth space presents a sharp contrast with the old politics of desire for striated space. The logic of the old politics of desire is built around the notions of consensus, reconciliation, normalcy, unity and integration, while the logic of the new politics of desire is based on the notions of transgression, disagreement and disintegration. The former suppresses difference, while the latter restages the space for difference, which will finally lead to equality, which is in turn another name for democracy. If capitalism reduces all desire to market-oriented relations with an emphasis on consumerism as a means to fulfill desire, then the old politics of desire of Thailand's ruling elites subsumes all desire of the Thai people into the royalist-*cum*-nationalist discourse. It thus leads to the worship of unity and stability at the expense of singularity and difference. Thailand's ruling elites have never hesitated to use force to restore "national unity". The use of force against the Red Shirts with the stated objectives of "reclaiming the space" and "compressing the space" are two obvious recent examples.

In contemporary Thailand, unity and national reconciliation constitute what Lyotard has aptly termed a "meta-narrative".[15] The function of the meta-narrative is to suppress a variety of minor narratives. In addition to violence, Thailand's ruling elites have resorted to ideological measures to curb the rising desire of the Thai people. The most notable example of such measures in recent years is the implementation of the sufficiency economy philosophy of His Majesty the King. As its main thrust, this measure applies ethics rather than economics to help alleviate the plight of the rural and urban poor. This philosophy asks the Thai people to be good and to act accordingly despite their poverty and ignorance. Indeed, "sufficiency" or *khwamphophiang* in this philosophy simply means to know and to stick closely to one's present position regardless of the suffering one has endured. As long as one is a good (read "happy for what one has or is") person, then the entire nation will be happy and prosper. Put another way, Thailand's ruling elites perceive that all of the country's problems are rooted in the lack of morality and ethics among the Thai people. To make good this lack will put the whole nation right on track again. The form of power that Thailand's ruling elites use is thus similar to what Foucault has called "biopower" — the power to regulate and control the lives of the people in a certain way.[16]

The economy of sufficiency has then been transformed into what Andrew Walker calls "sufficiency democracy"[17] or what was previously known as "Thai-style democracy". The essence of this sufficiency democracy is a strategy to delegitimize parliamentary democracy through a critical discourse that stresses vote buying in order to discredit both the rural electorate and elected politicians.[18] This discourse takes the Thai rural electorate as prey to the vote-buying practice of politicians, or as the victims of fugitive former Prime Minister Thaksin Shinawatra's populist politics. The logic is straightforward. The less trustworthy elected politicians, political parties and rural voters are, the greater the legitimacy and credibility of the ruling elites to rule from behind the scenes. Therefore, sufficiency economy coupled with sufficiency democracy serves as the ruling elites' main ideological mechanism for suppressing the recent, growing desire for equality and justice among the Thai rural masses and the urban poor. Seen in this light, the Red Shirt protests can clearly be perceived as an attempt to form what Deleuze and Guattari call "a line of flight" to escape Thai elites' suppression of those latter groups' desire. Prior to the promotion of the sufficiency economy philosophy, Thailand's ruling elites deployed the allegedly Buddhist concept of the law of *karma* to freeze the desire of the Thai people for a greater say in the political life of their country. As Thai society becomes more complex, it requires a new ideological device to suppress that growing desire.

A variety of measures to shut down the desire for equality and justice among the Thai rural masses and urban poor all seem to have failed miserably: the coup of September 2006, the dissolution of the Thaksinite Thai Rak Thai (TRT) and People's Power Parties, the royalist campaign of the Yellow Shirt People's Alliance for Democracy (PAD), the installation of the Abhisit-led government and its rule through the invocation and extension of the Emergency Decree starting in April 2010, in addition to all sorts of schemes to effect "national reconciliation". The rise to power of Thaksin and his implementation of highly popular populist policies made possible the realization of the desiring machine of the rural masses and the urban poor. They learned that "one man, one vote" has real power, that it can lead to public policy that tangibly affects their daily lives. The universal health-care scheme is the most obvious example of such policy consequences of the popular vote for the TRT party.

The desire for a better life and fair treatment from the state has now been connected to Thaksin's populist policies and platforms; this connection makes possible the desiring machine of the rural masses and the urban poor. Once this desiring machine starts working, it is extremely difficult for Thailand's ruling elites to shut it down. Attempts by those elites to turn the clock back to the good old days of the politics of desire that obtained before the rise of the TRT have met strong resistance. The unrest of May 2010 was a manifestation of the simmering new politics of desire of unprivileged Thais, and Thailand's ruling elites ought to pay close attention. However, the prime minister at the time — a man whose name itself means "privilege" — appeared to lack an understanding of the new politics of desire of the unprivileged.

IV

The current political divide in Thailand has caused the old fabric of society to begin to crumble rapidly. One cannot today criticize the Red Shirts without being branded a Yellow Shirt or *ammat* supporter. At the same time, one cannot comment on the Yellow Shirts or on the government without being called red or anti-monarchy. The Thai people have become what Althusser terms the "ideological state apparatus".[19] They must police one another to ensure that people on the other side of the divide hold the "right" idea. For example, a contestant in the popular reality TV show *Academy Fantasia* expressed a view on Twitter that faulted Prime Minister Abhisit for neither resigning nor dissolving the House of Representatives because of the violence of May 2010. This contestant found himself subjected to all sorts of abusive language and pressured to withdraw from the contest. Finally, his mother had to make a teary-eyed apology on behalf of her son, while withdrawing him from the contest.[20] This example is just one of many cases in which the ideological police have put pressure on those holding different political opinions.[21] Moreover, mention of the monarchy in any way other than one that follows the official line results in the accusation of involvement in the movement against the monarchy. This accusation represents the newest tactic adopted to suppress the desire of the Thai people to be different. Not only has the tolerance for different views diminished, but "free speech" has been supplanted in Thai society by "right speech" or, to use a phrase popular in the West, by "politically correct" speech.[22]

In sum, a strong reaction from the old politics of desire of Thailand's ruling elites has met the emergence of the new politics of desire for equality and justice in contemporary Thai society. Those elites have employed both violent and ideological means to suppress the rising desire of the Red Shirts, whose members come mainly from the rural masses and the urban poor that benefited so greatly from Thaksin's populist politics. The freedom and liberty of the Thai people have succumbed to ruling elites' desire to suppress the rising desire of the country's rural masses and urban poor for greater political space in society. However, the Red Shirts have successfully planted the desire for equality and justice among people long accustomed to the hierarchical Thai social structure. They have challenged the meta-narrative of unity by paving the way for a heretofore minor narrative to emerge as a narrative of major importance. Their goal is to create a smooth space in which this new desire can be materialized.

Notes

1. For an analysis of the Red Shirt movement, see Chairat Charoensin-o-larn, "Redrawing the Thai Political Space: The Red Shirt Movement", paper presented at the workshop on "Rural-Urban Networks and Transitions in Asia: Re-spatializing Cultural and Political Imaginaries", jointly organized by the Asian Urbanism Cluster of the Asia Research Institute and the Cities Cluster of the Faculty of Art and Social Sciences, National University of Singapore, 25–26 February 2010.
2. Reports of the deaths of Muslim suspects while in military custody in the South are widespread. See, for example, "Detainee's death stirs fury in the South", *Bangkok Post*, 6 July 2010. However, the most notorious recent violence of the military against Muslims in southern Thailand remains the excessive use of force at the Krue Se mosque and the Tak Bai incident, both in 2004.
3. Citing American President Barack Obama's dismissal of his top commander in Afghanistan, General Stanley McChrystal, after the latter's criticism of his policy, a *Bangkok Post* columnist pointed out how unprofessional the Thai military has been; see "More a professional farce than force that we have here", *Bangkok Post*, 1 July 2010.
4. King-oua Laohong, "Anti-monarchy movement in DSI's sights", *Bangkok Post*, 9 July 2010, and "DSI sets up force to tackle anti-monarchy movement", *The Nation*, 9 July 2010.
5. See, for example, Pavin Chachavalpongpun, "'Unity' As A Discourse in Thailand's Polarized Politics", *Southeast Asian Affairs 2010* (Singapore: Institute of Southeast Asian Studies, 2010), pp. 332–42. A campaign of this kind was the Abhisit government's "6 Days, 63 Million Opinions" phone-in to gauge public opinion, which was nothing but a political ploy to get the prime minister on the national news. See "Ring-a-ding ting-tong", *Bangkok Post*, 6 July 2010.

6. For the meaning of "double standards" in the Thai context, see Chang Noi (pseud.), "Talk about double standards", *The Nation*, 8 February 2010.
7. It is interesting to note that the announced purpose of the *Bangkok Post* Minimarathonm held on 1 August 2010 was to bring smiles back to Bangkok and especially to the Ratchaprasong area in which the Red Shirts staged their protests and demonstrations. Meanwhile, on 25 July 2010, the first bomb after the May crackdown exploded in front of the Big C Superstore near the site of the Red Shirt rallies two month earlier, killing one and wounding at least ten.
8. For details, see Piyaporn Wongruang, "Red shirts fear the worst", *Bangkok Post*, 11 July 2010.
9. At least six committees were set up to undertake the task. These included two national reform committees, as well as committees on media reform, police reform, truth and reconciliation, and constitutional amendment.
10. For more details, see Gilles Deleuze and Félix Guattari, *Anti-Oedipus: Capitalism & Schizophrenia*, translated by Robert Hurley, Mark Seem, and Helen R. Lane (London: The Athlone Press, 1983), and Gilles Deleuze and Félix Guattari, *A Thousand Plateaus: Capitalism and Schizophrenia*, translated by Brian Massumi (Minneapolis: University of Minnesota Press, 1987).
11. Gilles Deleuze and Claire Parnet, *Dialogue II*, translated by Hugh Tomlinson and Barbara Habberjam (New York: Columbia University Press, 1987), p. 96.
12. Philip Goodchild, *Deleuze and Guattari: An Introduction to the Politics of Desire* (London: Sage Publications, 1996).
13. Quoted by Mark Seem, "Introduction", in Deleuze and Guattari, *Anti-Oedipus*, p. vxii
14. Gilles Deleuze, *Desert Islands and Other Texts 1953–1974*, translated by Michael Taormina (Los Angeles: Semiotext(e), 2004), p. 260.
15. Jean-François Lyotard, *The Postmodern Condition: A Report on Knowledge*, translated by Geoff Bennington and Brian Massumi (Minneapolis: University of Minnesota Press, 1984).
16. Michel Foucault, *The History of Sexuality Volume 1: An Introduction*, translated by Robert Hurley (New York: Vintage Book, 1980).
17. Interview with Andrew Walker, "*Setthakit phophiang prachathippatai pho phiang lae ratthamanoon chaoban*" [Sufficiency economy, sufficiency democracy, and the rural constitution], *Fa diaokan* 6, no. 2 (April–June 2008): 58–69.
18. A discussion of this discourse can be found in William A. Callahan, "The Discourse of Vote Buying and Political Reform in Thailand", *Pacific Affairs* 78 (Spring 2005): 95–113.

19. Louis Althusser, "Ideology and Ideological State Apparatuses", in *Essays on Ideology* (London: Verso, 1976), pp. 1–60.
20. See "AF's Mark pulled from concert for criticizing PM," *The Bangkok Post* 1, 1 July 2010.
21. For more of these cases, see Voranai Vanijaka, "Sense & decency", *Bangkok Post*, 11 July 2010, and Mae Moo, "Unjust Accusations, Bad Boy Calling, Naked Truth", *Bangkok Post*, 25 July 2010.
22. An awkward rationale for this distinction is provided by Thanong Khanthong, "A case of free speech and right speech", *The Nation*, 9 July 2010.

9

NOTES TOWARDS AN UNDERSTANDING OF THAI LIBERALISM

Michael K. Connors

It is easy to understand the plausibility of the case that the principal struggle unfolding in Thailand today pits democracy against authoritarianism. The events of the past five years seem to speak for themselves: the 2006 coup against the "pro-poor" Thaksin government, the manipulated pro-military constitutional referendum of 2007, the judicial dissolution of the Thai Rak Thai (2007) and its successor People's Power (2008) parties, and the subsequent military-supported installation of a Democrat-led coalition government in late 2008. Then of course comes the spilling of blood that feeds the democracy-authoritarianism narrative: the bloody crackdown in April–May 2010 against Red Shirt protestors

Part of this article appeared as "Why Thai Politics is No Longer Normal", *The Age*, 19 May 2010. Several sections have also appeared on the author's blog "Sovereign Myth" <http://sovereignmyth.blogspot.com/>.

and the imposition of a draconian state of emergency, human rights violations, and the suspension of due process for hundreds of political detainees.

The "democratic versus authoritarian" narrative, connected to the idea of a popular struggle against a rich establishment, has captured international attention. It is also at the heart of the self-presentation of the National United Front for Democracy against Dictatorship (UDD), so brilliantly exemplified by the etching of the word *phrai* (commoner, bondsman) onto red tee-shirts. There are elements of truth in this formulation. But the same general tension — democracy versus authoritarianism — could just as easily substitute for a short history of human society, with one problem: it explains everything generally, but nothing particularly. In recent times the formulation has led to skewed analysis of Thailand's crisis, and to a cheer-squad mentality that fails to capture intra-class/intra-state conflict and inter-class/inter-state-agency cooperation. It obscures the nature of Thailand's recent past and its likely future trajectory. Moving beyond such a simplistic analysis makes possible a more serious probing of the specific nature of the conflict and of the possibilities for its resolution. Early-twentieth-century Marxist Antonio Gramsci offers the best argument against simplistic representation: "A given socio-historical moment is never homogeneous; on the contrary, it is rich in contradictions."[1] To understand Thailand's rich contradictions, it is better to drop the catch-all explanation and to come to grips with the specificity of the crisis at hand.

These notes towards an understanding of Thai liberalism are, I suppose, an uncomfortable call for observers to stand at some intellectual distance from the daily malaise of democracy in Thailand and to seek more sensitive lenses through which to examine both the interests and ideologies behind the competing claims of now fundamentally antagonistic elites, and the popular bases with which these interests and ideologies are articulated.

While rich in contradiction, the Thai context nevertheless has a dominant dynamic. That dynamic includes the largely *unexplained* pacting during 2005 and 2006 of statist conservatives and elite liberals against the emergent and competitive authoritarianism represented by Thaksin Shinawatra.[2] It also includes the re-pacting of those same elements upon the emergence of the Red Shirt movement (itself composed of some liberal elements).[3]

I say "unexplained" because, for the most part, political liberalism in Thailand is not taken seriously by analysts. It is seen as rhetorical and mealy-mouthed. When it is recognized, it is viewed as having been eclipsed by the instrumental politics of competing networks. There is thus nothing to explain. Scratch a political liberal in Thailand, and underneath is a snivelling courtier ready to serve monarchy, military and bureaucracy, or any paymaster — or so it is claimed. This view of Thai elites holds that ideas and social projects do not matter; only venal interests are deemed relevant. The view also broadly endorses a conspiratorial understanding of politics. This understanding has it that a monolithic elite self-consciously acts as the puppet master in all matters. This view does not recognize the fragmented and hostile relations between liberals and conservatives, because it takes Thai liberals and conservatives to be, fundamentally, one and the same.

At another level, a number of non-governmental organizations, activists and public intellectuals have taken a non-antagonistic, if not sympathetic, position to the anti-Thaksin side. Arguably, this position makes these groups and individuals distantly complicit in the authoritarian resolution to the crisis.[4] But, just as differences between liberals and statists are elided in the conventional narrative, so too are those between elite liberalism and the social liberalism espoused by Thailand's NGOs. NGOs' failure to rally to the Red Shirts leads critics to bundle them together as part of the *ammat* (the bureaucratic-aristocratic establishment), as if those who have struggled for social justice over the last generation have suddenly become concerned only with their own interests and those of Thai elites. By the force of this logic, those who do not side with the Red Shirts are merely morally defective and opportunistic.

A morally charged critique based on the allegedly defective character of those with whom one disagrees does not advance understanding of different strategic positions. Rather, it leaves one in the realm of puppet play, of good and evil, and of caricature. It results in accounts lacking in explanatory power, their rhetorical force notwithstanding.[5]

Illumination of the contradiction of Thai liberalism's pact with statist conservatism, only one of many pacts now in operation, requires an answer to one crucial question: why was Thaksin deposed? The answer is clear: Thaksin threatened a tentative liberal-conservative pact, one that emerged in the 1990s, on sharing power. The pact put Thailand on a trajectory towards a more liberal-democratic polity. A variety of social forces, their interests differentially entangled in that project, mobilized against Thaksin. This mobilization culminated in the September 2006 *coup d'état*. Subsequent developments have certainly transformed the nature of the struggle from an intra-elite contest into a broader societal conflict. Confronting the transformation of the pro-Thaksin side into a messily conjoined quasi-popular/counter-elite movement advancing egalitarian positions, the liberal-conservative pact has hardened. The "soft coup" of 2006 has become a distant memory.

In a moment of profound structural crisis, Prime Minister Abhisit Vejjajiva symbolized the liberal pact with statist conservatives.[6] His government's maintenance throughout 2010 of the Emergency Decree invoked in April 2010 subsequent to the crushing of the Red Shirt rebellion revealed the foundations of sovereign power in force. But this was not naked power, even if it was abusive. Its purported aim was to prepare the ground for the realization of liberalism's preferred state form in the post-crisis period. Such is Thai liberalism's current internal logic and public message: *judge us not by situational logic and actions, but by our long-term project*, to which we now turn.

After the February 1991 coup — an attempt by statists and conservatives to roll back the emergence of a more open and democratic society — a politically liberal reform movement emerged in Thailand. Elites recognized that the semi-democracy of the 1980s was the creature of an age gone by. This movement resulted in the celebrated 1997 "People's Constitution", which formally enshrined liberal doctrine at the heart of the Thai state. Henceforth, executive power (rooted in a democratic mandate) would be subject to a variety of liberal checks and balances. An electoral commission and constitutional and administrative courts would scrutinize the exercise of that power.[7] No one expected a smooth path to liberal democracy in Thailand. The military's corporate interests remained. Networks around the monarchy continued to wield power. Corruption was pervasive. The liberal project was understood to be gradual and generational.

Then the project came unstuck. While in government during the Asian economic crisis of 1997–2000, the liberally oriented Democrat Party failed to offer anything except implementation of an International Monetary Fund austerity programme and the creation of a social-welfare safety valve in the form of the Social Investment Fund. Such liberal feebleness paved the way for Thaksin and his brand of authoritarian populism and 'pro-poor' policies.[8]

During his term as prime minister (2001–06), Thaksin tore up the aspirational liberal settlement. His disregard for human rights and for the institutions intended to subject executive power to checks and balances is well documented. So, too, is the level of electoral support that he enjoyed, which won him power in 2001 and 2005. [9] His project was a modernized and globalized Thai capitalism whose midwife would be elected authoritarianism. Liberalism, such as it was, and democracy, such as it could be, parted ways.

The Yellow Shirt movement against Thaksin that arose in 2005–06 brought together liberal middle-class elements, members of the rural poor and unionists opposed to privatization programmes. It also included elite conservative elements fearful that Thaksin was pushing them out of their traditional roles as power brokers. These elements viewed Thaksin as a threat to the social order and, importantly, to the monarchy.[10]

Since 2006, Thai liberals have joined with conservative elements in the state, and with the Yellow Shirts, to try to defeat Thaksin and his supporters. Together, they played a role in bringing down the elected pro-Thaksin governments in late 2008. They were and are driven by a flawed logic of gradually returning Thailand to something like the liberal-conservative settlement of 1997, with all of its compromises and more besides. Liberalism's dependence on its erstwhile statist competitors in the military and bureaucracy make those additional compromises necessary.

FROM LIBERAL-CONSERVATIVE PACT TO LIBERAL AUTHORITARIANISM

Two compelling fears drive Thailand's now-transformed liberal authoritarianism, by which I mean the use of authoritarian means to return Thailand to its elitist liberal trajectory.

The first is fear that an alternative modernizing network of politicians, statists, and business, under the leadership of Thaksin, and possibly with support of a new monarch, will block a return to the circumscribed but pluralistic competition for power that characterized the emergent liberal-conservative period of the 1990s to early 2000s.[11] Corporate interest also drives those who would stand to lose from the end of that regime of circumscribed competition. And when self-interest finds justification in pious commitment to a visibly threatened social order brutal action unremarkably follows. Thaksin's modernizing authoritarianism was antagonistic to an established historical bloc whose members believed that, all things being equal, it was edging Thailand in the right direction. That bloc is not intent on establishing a Burmese-style junta, or on returning to policies of benign neglect of the poor. Should it succeed in its goals, the most likely outcome will be a partially reformed (for survival requires some degree of reform) but nevertheless elite-controlled order. Evidence for these likely goals is to be found in the way in which the Abhisit government sought to accelerate land reform and to address other socio-economic grievances whilst simultaneously trying to bring political contestation under control.

A new logic is now also present, one that transcends earlier fears of populism. The roots of this second fear lie in apprehensiveness over the unleashed expectations of Thailand's less powerful classes coupled with a relentless organizational drive to return to power by Thaksin. It is also rooted in concern over those classes' new-found fury at the bare-faced authoritarian posture of the Abhisit government and its hardline backers in the Thai military. The very existence of armed elements in the Red Shirt camp (incredulously denied by Red Shirt sympathizers or explained away as a desperate strategy) fuelled this contingent authoritarianism, and forced it to reveal itself.

In this post-coup phase, in which might is doubly right, situational logics and political choices have brought into being a reactionary societal current that gave partisan legitimacy to the Abhist government. Relief that the Red Shirts had been "dealt with" gave rise to exaltation of the "handlers". Take as one example the adulation of Centre for Resolution of Emergency Situation (CRES) spokesperson Colonel Sansern Kaewkamnerd, as in *The Nation*'s 30 May 2010 article "Saluting the kingdom's coolest colonel". It was a legitimacy that rested on portraying the Red threat as criminal and terroristic, and therefore not worthy of political engagement.

The threat of social upheaval, of a world turned upside down, brought all sorts of pathologies to the surface: witch-hunts, educational ostracism, dehumanizing portrayals of those who disagree, bloodcurdling snobbery and a recapturing of the City of Angels by sovereign consumers speedily spending the country out of crisis. Unsettled by the emergence of a rival state in the heartland of Bangkok during April and May of

2010, as exemplified by the imposition of Red Shirt control on street corners and influence on sections of the state's police and armed forces, people began to howl in mid-2010 for a political cleansing as malignantly intended as it would be destructive. Liberalism looks at itself in the mirror and wonders how it got to this state.

THINKING ABOUT LIBERALISM AS A PROBLEMATIC, NOT AS A DOCTRINE

The question arises, does what we are discussing have anything to do with liberalism? In reply, I would note that it is best to think of liberalism in general, and in the Thai case in particular, not simply as a philosophy of the conditions for individual autonomy, but as a response to the problems of governance in complex societies in which modern state structures emerge, power centres are plural, and conflict and public interest require regulation and adjudication to preserve defined liberties.[12] At a minimum, liberal aspiration accords with the division and accountability of power. I am speaking more of a political than individually centred philosophical liberalism. Liberalism, in its own way, asks, *What is to be done*?

What is to be done with an electorate — judged in part to be dependent and lacking in capacity because of the nature of information flows — that keeps returning to office (in 2005, 2008 and 2011) a political class that will move Thailand away from the liberal-conservative settlement of 1997? Thai liberalism is no different from historic forms of liberalism that feared the "tyranny of the majority" and the egalitarian impulse of democracy. Many liberals are disposed to support or at least condone aristocratic tutelage over citizens who need to be "developed" before they can be sovereign. It took several generations in many countries for liberalism to settle into democratic realities. It still does not quite fit, and liberals the world over must constantly deal with the populist underside of democracy and the illiberal nature of big business and the security state.

What is to be done with a political class that is highly corrupt and money-driven? Classic liberal themes of public interest, of conflict of interest, and of virtue come into play. Everywhere, liberals rally against the decline of virtue. But in its present moment, elite liberalism makes compromises and is articulated with corrupt or conservative elements "on the right side". Its pragmatic side is a reflection of politics as the art of the possible. Think of the pragmatic alliance between the Democrat Party and its coalition partners during 2008–11. Presumably, virtue's day will come.

What is to be done with the statist and conservative institutions of monarchy, military and bureaucracy, and with the networks that permeate them? Precisely because this problem is deemed less serious than the Thaksinite threat, it is momentarily put aside. Should the Thaksinite and populist threats be neutralized, one may expect a return of the ongoing contest between liberal and statist conservative elements. That the peak statist element of "the network monarchy" is a gerontocracy gives the advantage to the elite liberal network.[13]

One particular way in which liberals have sought to engage and gradually transform the monarchy is by embedding what I have called "royal liberalism".[14] In doing so they are reenacting liberalism's historical flirtation (in France and England) with monarchy as a guardian centre above "politics", what leading Thai legal scholar Bowonsak Uwanno describes as the "the supreme ombudsman". [15] In that role, the crown supposedly acts as the liberal regulator, ensuring the division of power and protecting the public interest. Aside from its legitimating function, the idea of "royal liberalism" is a reforming, indeed disciplining discourse directed *at* the Thai monarchy and at those who mobilize the institution for illiberal purposes. It is a claim on the monarchy as a public institution. The aspiration for liberal monarchy is challenged by the reputed relationship between Thaksin and the crown prince. That relationship would raise the spectre of a weakened "ombudsman", and a directly politicized monarchy. Of course, the status of the current "ombudsman" is not up for discussion among Thai liberals. This is one limit, among many others, of Thai liberalism.

What is to be done to bring future stability and to secure a political settlement? Here the liberal impulse is strongly evident in the habitual selection of two prominent royalists, Anan Panyarachun and Prawet Wasi, to head government-sponsored reform and reconciliation committees following the events of May 2010. The re-emergence of organic intellectuals of the emergent liberal state of the 1990s, after several years of effective silence, to spearhead the Abhisit government's reconciliation plan came just when liberalism's pact with state authority was at its apex and there existed a supra-state of exception. Nevertheless, and to repeat, while some predicted a lurch towards a Burma-like scenario and military ascendancy, the evidence suggests a return at some point to the elite liberal politics of the 1990s accompanied and diminished by strengthened military corporatism. Such permutations are the stuff of history.

I am suggesting that, despite the rupture of the 2006 coup, a great deal of continuity links 1992 to 2010 — something evident in the content of the 2007 constitution, notwithstanding its roll-back in some important areas. It was easy to label politics immediately after May 2010 as laden with fascist intent and practice, but the charge hardly makes sense if one considers historic forms of fascism. Moreover, sloganeering and misdiagnosis preclude the development of a progressive strategy to take advantage of the opportunities provided by the existing contradictory situation.

It is necessary to come to terms with Thailand's liberal tendencies, however unhandsomely Thai liberalism enters into pacts with authoritarianism in moments of crisis and with conservative social traditions as part of its commitment to nation-building. The contention that the post-December 2008 authoritarian phase in Bangkok's politics made liberalism all but redundant betrays an unfamiliarity with liberalism as a problem-solving orientation as much as a series of principles, and with its history of siding with order over disorder. It is a history that has involved, for example, a certain fondness for Bismarck, a recognition of monarchy, and an aristocratic disposition masquerading as virtuous citizenship. Liberal problematics and discourses are not simply an iterance of settled doctrine. Rather, they are unique expressions of an endeavour for openness in the prevailing power relations specific to a given society at a given time. Thai elite liberalism resonates with historical forms of what Alan Kahan calls "aristocratic liberalism".[16]

Thai liberalism may be wrong in its strategic readings of the balance of power, opportunistic in its pacting, and elitist in its assumption of guardianship. But it *is* in its stated ambition a form of liberalism, however diminished and enfeebled. When Abhisit proclaims himself a political liberal, I believe him.

Prerogative rule by the executive in extraordinary times is not a concept alien to the liberal tradition. But such rule does bring an obligation for authoritarian liberalism to make clear how, if at all, its actions will return politics to a liberal democratic pathway. At the moment of writing, this was the paramount problematic facing the Abhisit government.

Notes

1. Antonio Gramsci, *A Gramsci Reader — Selected Writings 1916–193*, edited by David Forgacs (London: Lawrence & Wishart, 1988), p. 393.
2. On competitive authoritarianism, see Thitanan Pongsudhirak, "Thaksin: Competitive Authoritarian and Flawed Dissident", in *Dissident Democrats: The Challenge of Democratic Leadership in Asia*, edited by John Kane, Haig Patapan and Benjamin Wong (New York: Palgrave Macmillan, 2008), pp. 67–84.
3. See Michael Kelly Connors, "'Liberalism, Authoritarianism and the Politics of Decisionism in Thailand", *Pacific Review* 22, no. 3 (July 2009): 355–73.
4. Significant critiques of the Thai NGO and people's sector appear in Kengkij Kitirianglarp and Kevin Hewison, "Social Movements and Political Opposition in Contemporary Thailand", *Pacific Review* 22, no. 4 (September 2009): 451–77, and Jim Glassman and Bae-gyoon Park, "Failed Internationalism and Social Movement Decline", *Critical Asian Studies* 40, no. 3 (September 2008): 339–72.
5. Demonstrated by the wide support that such views hold among those who post comments on New Mandala, the influential blog on Mainland Southeast Asia <http://asiapacific.anu.edu.au/newmandala>.
6. On the historical nature of the crisis, see Michael J. Montesano, "Contextualizing the Pattaya Summit Debacle: Four April Days, Four Thai Pathologies", *Contemporary Southeast Asia* 31, no. 2 (August 2009): 217–48.
7. Michael K. Connors, "Political Reform and the State in Thailand", *Journal of Contemporary Asia* 29, no. 2 (1999): 202–26.
8. Kevin Hewison, "Crafting Thailand's New Social Contract", *Pacific Review* 17, no. 4 (December 2004): 503–22.
9. See Duncan McCargo and Ukrist Pathamanand, *The Thaksinization of Thailand* (Copenhagen: NIAS Press, 2005); Pasuk Phongpaichit and Chris Baker, *Thaksin*, 2nd ed. (Silkworm Books: Chiang Mai, 2009) for important treatments of the period.
10. Michael K. Connors, "Article of Faith: The Failure of Royal Liberalism in Thailand", *Journal of Contemporary Asia* 38, no. 1 (February 2008): 143–65.
11. See Michael K. Connors, "'Liberalism, Authoritarianism and the Politics of Decisionism".

12. For a view of liberalism through a historical lens, see Andreas Kalyvas and Ira Katznelson, *Liberal Beginnings: Making a Republic for the Moderns* (Cambridge: Cambridge University Press, 2008). I also attempt a historical reading of Thai liberalism in Michael K. Connors *Democracy and National Identity in Thailand* (London and Copenhagen: Routledge and NIAS Press, 2003 and 2007).
13. Duncan McCargo, "Network Monarchy and Legitimacy Crises in Thailand", *Pacific Review* 18, no. 4 (December 2005): 499–519.
14. Connors, *Democracy and National Identity in Thailand.*
15. Bowonsak Uwanno, *Kotmai kap thanglueak khong sangkhom thai* [Law and Alternatives for Thai Society] (Bangkok: Nitthitham Press, 1994).
16. See Alan Kahan, *Aristocratic Liberalism: The Social and Political Thought of Jacob Burckhardt, John Stuart Mill and Alexis de Tocqueville* (Oxford: Oxford University Press, 1992).

10

THAILAND'S CLASSLESS CONFLICT

Shawn W. Crispin

On 26 February 2010, Thailand's Supreme Court handed down a landmark decision against former Prime Minister Thaksin Shinawatra. It ruled that the businessman-*cum*-politician had abused his power by enacting policies during his six-year tenure of office (2001–06) that directly benefited his family-owned communications companies at the state's expense. The verdict called for the seizure of US$1.4 billion of the US$2.3 billion worth of Thaksin's and his family's assets frozen after the military toppled his government in a 2006 coup. Thaksin reacted to the decision by calling it "unfair";[1] he later claimed that it was a reflection of the "double standards" in Thai society that favour the rich over the poor.

Two weeks later, Thaksin's affiliated pressure group, the red-shirt-garbed National United Front for Democracy against Dictatorship (UDD), mobilized over 100,000 protestors, mainly from the country's northern and northeastern provinces, in Bangkok to protest the court decision and call upon Prime Minister Abhisit Vejjajiva to dissolve parliament and hold new elections. Within four days, the numbers at the UDD's protest site had fallen off significantly, dipping on March 16 to around 20,000, including hundreds of red-shirt-wearing street vendors.[2] Thaksin was quoted in the local media imploring politicians in the Thaksinite Phuea Thai Party to boost protestor numbers. He claimed that the government had "bribed"[3] UDD demonstrators to quit the rally.

Protestor numbers, first at the UDD's original Phan Fa bridge site and later at the heart of the Ratchaprasong luxury shopping district, waxed and waned dramatically, depending on the time of day and on planned protest activities. By late April, there were frequently fewer than 2,000 people milling around the largely vacant protest site in the mornings and early afternoons.[4] That ebb and flow raised important questions about whether the protest was populated in the main by politically awakened poor rural farmers, who in their economic plight often slept on the streets of the protest site, or instead by the middle classes, who had the means to stay in hotels or the option of returning home after attending rallies after work on weekdays or on the weekends. The fluctuating and often low numbers also gave the lie to the notion that the UDD was an organic social movement rooted in rural Thailand, as popularly portrayed in the mass media and by the UDD itself. It is more likely that the UDD was in the main a manipulated mass, mobilized from above and bank-rolled at the grass-roots level by Thaksin and his elite supporters for their own narrow and opportunistic political purposes.

Thailand's escalating political conflict has often been crudely reduced to a good-versus-evil battle for democracy. It has been represented as a morality play pitting an entrenched urban and bureaucratic elite that favours an inequitable status quo against a marginalized rural countryside awakened by the September 2006 coup that ousted Thaksin to demand true democracy, more social justice, and a larger slice of the national economic pie. A more complex interpretation is that Thailand's power struggle is at its core one between two competing elites, each capable of mobilizing disruptive crowds of their colour-coded supporters, and neither particularly democratic in its history or outlook. Each camp is vigorously, and sometimes violently, jockeying for position ahead of an uncertain royal succession. The two camps hold competing views on the appropriate role of the monarchy and monarchical institutions in Thai society after the ailing King Bhumibol Adulyadej passes from the scene.

There is potentially much at stake: the royally affiliated Crown Property Bureau controls more than 40 per cent of all property in

Bangkok's central business district, and a faction of the UDD has called privately for those lands to be confiscated and redistributed. *Forbes* magazine recently estimated King Bhumibol's personal fortune, including Crown Property Bureau lands, at US$30 billion. It has consistently ranked him as the world's wealthiest royal. The old elite's power derives largely from its extensive land holdings, bureaucratic position and privilege, and association with the royal palace. Its members are known to share a more insular view of the country's future and to favour a measure of protection against foreign capital. Thailand's competing *nouveaux riches*, on the other hand, have more recently built their fortunes in business and industry. They generally, though not universally, advocate the country's greater integration into the global economy.[5]

Thaksin, who initially straddled the line between the new and the old, built up a billion-dollar private telecommunications empire through state-granted virtual monopoly concessions over mobile telephone and satellite services. In 2001, he rose to political power through a populist campaign in which he vowed to prioritize local over foreign interests. His message resonated widely at a time when the International Monetary Fund had imposed austerity and market-opening measures as conditions for bailing Thailand out after the 1997–98 Asian Financial Crisis. Thaksin made good on many of his promises to both old and new elites, including through the creation of a state-run financial bail-out firm. That firm rehabilitated hundreds of Thai entrepreneurs' crisis-induced debts at sharp discounts to their original loan obligations to banks at the state's expense, while largely keeping circling foreign investors at bay. He also padded old elite interests through a sizeable expansion of the bureaucracy, including the creation of several new ministries, which he dressed up as bureaucratic "reform".

However, Thaksin's perceived co-optation of royal images and symbols to win over rural constituencies to his populist programmes sparked suspicions among the royalist establishment, including the influential royal advisors on the Privy Council. These suspicions led to concern that the ambitious politician had designs on filling the power vacuum that would open upon King Bhumibol's eventual passing with his own brand of benevolent strongman leadership. The People's Alliance for Democracy (PAD) protest group, known for their royalist Yellow Shirts, first took to the streets in reaction to the potent charges that Thaksin had shown disloyalty to the throne — an allegation that he has consistently denied. First aired on national television in September 2005 by media mogul and eventual PAD co-leader Sonthi Limthongkun, those charges captured the imagination of Bangkok's middle class and galvanized a street movement focused mainly on themes relating to defence of the monarchy.

The PAD's street rallies, clearly backed by members of the old elite, paved the way for Thaksin's military ouster. The coup-makers justified their action by stressing his corruption, anti-democratic tendencies, and disloyalty to the crown. In 2008, after the country was returned to rule by an elected government, but with a less democratic constitution, the PAD paralysed the workings of two Thaksin-affiliated administrations by laying siege to Government House and occupying Bangkok's two international airports. While the PAD, like the UDD, claimed to be fighting for democracy, its calls selectively to roll back universal suffrage and its extra-constitutional urging of royal and military intervention in politics frequently laid bare its underlying reactionary agenda. Those anti-democratic leanings turned Western media opinion against the PAD and arguably influenced the comparatively sympathetic press coverage and academic treatment accorded to the UDD despite that latter group's own violent and illiberal tendencies.

UDD leaders claimed throughout the nine-week protest of March–May 2010 to be engaged in a non-violent struggle for democracy and social justice against an illiberal aristocracy and bureaucratic elite fronted by Prime Minister Abhisit's government. That message was made clear to foreign observers and reporters through the centrally produced English-language signboards posted and strategically held by demonstrators at the front of the protest's main stage. To reinforce their movement's rich-versus-poor propaganda, UDD organizers produced and distributed red tee-shirts emblazoned with the Thai word *phrai*, which translates loosely to "slave" or "serf" in English, among their followers.[6]

Those good-versus-evil rally cries, however, conveniently overlooked Thaksin's own authoritarian record, blotched by his well documented efforts to bypass parliamentary processes, undermine checking and balancing institutions, and suppress the free press. They also turned a blind eye to Thaksin's own propensity for violence — witnessed in his brutal 2003 "war on drugs" campaign, which led to the extrajudicial killing of over 2,200 drug suspects — and his heavy-handed policies towards Malay Muslims, which played a large role in reigniting what had been a dormant insurgency in the country's three southernmost provinces.

While the PAD's anti-democratic pronouncements and airport seizures were widely and critically analysed, fewer journalists and academics saw fit to probe Thaksin's ties to rogue military officials and the clearly strategic use of violence during the UDD's protest campaign. In a wave that coincided with the start of the UDD's March–May 2010 protests, more than fifty bomb attacks were launched against the stated enemies of Thaksin and the group.[7] In the run-up to the highly anticipated court decision on Thaksin's assets, a bomb laden with C–4 explosive material was discovered and defused in front of Thailand's Supreme Court. A rogue Thai Army officer allied to Thaksin, Major General Khattiya Sawatdiphon, alias "Se Daeng", made veiled threats through the media before the announcement of the verdict in that case, suggesting that judges and officials handling the case were at risk of assassination. After the guilty verdict, Khattiya cryptically predicted that a bombing campaign could erupt across Bangkok. Subsequent grenade attacks against private companies, government offices and military installations bore his prognostication out.

Khattiya, Thaksin, and the UDD leadership[8] denied responsibility for the attacks. They claimed that the Thai military and the Abhisit government had orchestrated the attacks to discredit their "peaceful" protest movement. However, several Western diplomats in Bangkok who tracked the attacks believed they were the violent manifestation of Thaksin's frequent, vague references to "iron fist in a velvet glove" tactics. Those tactics later became more openly apparent with the emergence of the heavily armed "men-in-black", who embedded themselves with the UDD and fired on government security forces during the later phases of the March–May 2010 protests. This record raises important questions about why so many journalists and academics continued to subscribe to the UDD's narrative of non-violent class struggle and to its claims that its protest was about something bigger than Thaksin's own interests. The exiled former premier perpetuated those claims of non-violence during the later stages of the protests, presumably to escape personal culpability for the group's turn to violence.

In a now-famous exchange between the exiled Marxist academic Ji Ungpakon and freelance journalist Philip Cunningham, the two veteran observers of Thailand jousted over whether the UDD's uprising should be considered a genuine or sham revolution.[9] Ji argued that, in the absence of a functioning political left, tycoon Thaksin had been able to exploit and mobilize around divisions between rich and poor in Thai society. He was thus able to launch a genuine pro-democracy movement that transcended his money and influence, Ji contended. Cunningham retorted that members of Thailand's long disenfranchised political left had been duped by Thaksin and the UDD into seeing a "false dawn". He argued that Thaksin and the UDD had hijacked the genuine grievances of the poor to serve their own narrow interests, including the restoration of Thaksin's wealth.

While in power Thaksin's unique brand of populism was widely deconstructed. Certain left-leaning academics who had overestimated the political significance of rural organizations such as the Assembly of the Poor[10] bought into the demonstrably false notion that Thakin's was the first Thai government ever to dedicate significant material resources and policy attention to the countryside. Thaksin effectively marketed his populist offerings — including a cheap universal health-care scheme, debt moratoria for cash-strapped farmers, and "village development funds" — through his dominance and manipulation of the state media. But all such policies combined never amounted to more than 80 billion baht per year, a trifling budgetary sum on a per capita basis, especially next to the 1.2 trillion baht that Thaksin earmarked to rehabilitate a small group of indebted industrialists and property developers flattened by the Asian Financial Crisis of the late 1990s.

Under Thaksin's direction, the state broadcast media, from which some academic estimates suggest that more than 90 per cent of the population until recently received its news, hammered home nightly the notion that his government was the first to make helping the rural poor a policy priority. Through the blunt force of repetition, this message became political truth to many rural Thais. To be sure, free-wheeling capitalism has contributed to a wide wealth gap in Thailand. As in other capitalist developing countries, economic activity and financial wealth are still disproportionately concentrated in and around the national capital.[11] But the broader economic reality is that successive Thai governments have pushed development into rural areas since the 1970s and have during the same period achieved exceptional results in poverty reduction. That rural push is evident in some of the region's best rural roads, electric power in nearly 95 per cent of Thai households, and extensive, if underfinanced and poorly staffed, educational and health-care infrastructure. Estimates attribute to Thailand the second largest pick-up truck market in the world, trailing only the United States. The size of this market underscores the Thai rural sector's spending power and access to credit, which are considerable in comparison to those of many of its less developed regional neighbours.

As is common among populist leaders, Thaksin's pro-poor claims were often more rhetoric than reality. Emory University academic Richard Doner, an expert on Thailand's political economy, has contended that the conflict is more political than economic. Discounting the prevailing discourse of class struggle, he notes that Thaksin's story jibes neatly with the academic literature on other populist leaders, including cases from Latin America. In that comparative context, Thailand's is one more case of aspiring elites aiming to tap popular discontent to gain dominance over old elites. Doner argues that Thaksin and the UDD have preyed in particular upon rising insecurity in the Thai workforce, including insecurity resulting from the growing use of contract labour to beat down costs and maintain export competitiveness during an era of globalization. Thaksin and the UDD have thus sought to score points against opposing elites.[12] This analysis would explain the UDD's wholesale failure to propose new redistributive or social welfare programmes during its nine-week, purportedly pro-poor, protests. The group's message was instead confined to the urgent need to dissolve parliament and hold new elections, and reinforced by *ad hominem* attacks against the prime minister, his top deputies, and other perceived political enemies in the media and military — as well as occasional calumny and slight directed towards homosexuals and foreigners.

The backgrounds of the UDD's leaders were largely spared critical assessment. It is notable that the UDD's top leadership included no downtrodden farmers or representatives of other disadvantaged groups from the country's poor northern and northeastern regions, where Thaksin's grass-roots support runs strongest. Instead, the protest group was spearheaded by former mainstream politicians and provincial power brokers from either the country's more prosperous and ethnically distinct southern region or Bangkok. Veteran journalist Bertil Lintner called attention to the service of top UDD leader and Phuea Thai Party politician Jatuporn Phomphan as secretary to the minister of natural resources and environment in Thaksin's first government. In this capacity, Jatuporn in 2003 dispatched more than 1,000 policemen to retake through force a large tract of land occupied by poor farmers who claimed that officials had leased the tract to large-scale palm oil producers rather than honour promises to redistribute it to them. He defended the conduct of the police in the ensuing scuffle, claiming that the farmers were "armed" and "broke the law" — ironically, the same charges that the Abhisit government lodged against his UDD.[13] Similarly, UDD secretary-general Weera Musikaphong, a former mainstream politician and erstwhile member of the conservative Democrat Party, also lacks genuine pro-poor credentials. He allied himself with Thaksin after apparently hitting a dead end in his political career. Underscoring his elite credentials, Weera was a close friend to the Vejjajiva family in the 1970s, when — Abhisit's father, former deputy public health minister Atthasit Vejjajiva recalls — he frequently accompanied young Abhisit to local parks and shopping malls.[14]

Natthawut Saikuea, the UDD co-leader who perhaps spoke most forcefully about social inequality during the protests of March–May 2010, is the wealthy owner of a massive rubber plantation and the co-owner of a high-end resort in the southern province of Nakorn Si Thammarat. While the upstart politician was advocating class warfare and criticizing an anti-democratic "aristocracy" on the UDD's protest stage in May 2010, his wife gave birth to a child at Bangkok's elite, five-star Bamrungrad Hospital rather than at a state hospital at which Thaksin's 30 baht health care program for the poor would have applied.

Thailand's politics has always been driven more by personality than ideology, and Jatuporn's, Weera's, and Natthawut's elite backgrounds are consistent with that analysis. Duncan McCargo, perhaps the most astute contemporary academic observer of Thailand's politics, wrote in a recent article that the international media coverage of the UDD protests was "woefully simplistic".[15] McCargo argued that the Red Shirts were "not all poor farmers" and that "[t]heir demonstrations are not spontaneous out-pourings of resentment against the Thai aristocracy."

McCargo revealed the UDD as a set of "loose, relatively autonomous networks, mainly but not entirely rurally based" and found that many local UDD leaders doubled as "vote-canvassers", or members of rural elites. He also argued that the UDD consisted mainly of

> elected members of sub-district administrative organizations, self-employed and semi-skilled workers, low-ranking members of the security services, and farmers holding sub-contracts to produce crops for agribusiness. In other words, these are mostly lower-middle-class people, not those living at the margins of Thai society.[16]

Taking McCargo's analysis forward would seem to indicate that the PAD and the UDD, both organized and bankrolled by elites, are more similar than different despite their divergent portrayals in the media. Indeed, the UDD was created after a careful study of the PAD's tactics and strategies, including its use of inflammatory rhetoric to rouse crowds and a 24-hour satellite news television to broadcast protests to galvanize and sustain support outside of Bangkok, according to UDD co-organizer Jakrapob Penkair. Sitting in its sprawling studio atop a Bangkok shopping mall, he told this writer in mid-2007 that it intended to model the protest group's partisan television station on Fox News in the United States.[17] The UDD's soon-to-be top leaders — including Weera, Jatuporn, and Natthawut — had already been hand-picked by Thaksin. They gathered at the new station's headquarters long before the UDD pitched itself as an "organic" social movement.

Perhaps the biggest foil to the class struggle narrative is the regional dimension of the crisis. While Thaksin holds popular sway in much of the country's poor northern and northeastern regions, the Democrats dominate the South and usually carry Bangkok. Thaksinite political parties have consistently played up their pro-poor credentials to win votes, but their candidates have repeatedly failed to make headway in the Democrats' southern stronghold, despite the region's stubborn pockets of poverty, particularly among Muslim communities. Nor does the class struggle construct adequately explain why the Democrats and Thaksin-aligned People's Power Party split the December 2007 vote nearly evenly on the Central Plains, a rice-growing region home to many poor farmers. Academics specializing on the country's southern politics and elites, including one of the editors of this volume, have so far largely failed to shine light on this significant and no doubt complex geographical component to the crisis.

A more incisive and perhaps relevant analysis would steer clear of outmoded Marxist discourses and instead aim to deconstruct the UDD's activities — including its tilt towards violence and mobilization of symbols and themes of class struggle — as part of a complex negotiation between Thaksin and the old elites aligned against him. This negotiation directly concerns the eventual post-Bhumibol Thai order. It was accelerated with the help of international mediators in the wake of the violence and crackdown of May 2010. The crucial early role of a Swedish parliamentarian, who has maintained close communications with Thaksin and attempted to mediate the conflict from behind the scenes, has — like the more recent efforts of a mediation organization headquartered in Switzerland — gone entirely unstudied. Understanding of these mediated discussions between competing elites could provide important insight into the motivation and psychology behind the events that culminated in the crackdown and arson attacks of 19 May 2010 and also explain the subsequent accommodation that saw tensions cool significantly in the latter part of 2010. So, too, could a study of the hidden masterminds behind the UDD's strategy and propaganda, including former journalist and chief Thaksin policy advisor Phansak Winyarat and Phrommin Lertsuridet, both of whom played critical roles in shaping the group's messaging and media strategies.[18]

All of these under-researched areas point to the pressing need for revisionist interpretations of Thailand's ongoing conflict. These interpretations must transcend the simplistic and misleading discourse of class struggle that has been advanced by Thaksin's operatives for propaganda purposes and uncritically perpetuated by many foreign academics. For instance, new research that builds on the UDD's experience could provide fresh perspectives on the make-shift village that supposed poor and aggrieved farmers maintained for months on end outside of then Prime Minister Chuan Leekphai's offices but dismantled within days of Thaksin's election in January 2001. A deeper view of the dynamics and personalities behind the country's increasingly debilitating rally politics would shine light on aspects of the conflict that have for various reasons been intentionally kept in the dark. Such research could include fresh analysis of the 1992 pro-democracy movement, stripped of its post-Cold War, Third-Wave democracy context and now viewed more clearly in the light of the personalities involved. For the same protagonists who then fought for democracy against the Thai military have now split into Red and Yellow camps, each claiming a commitment to democracy.

The UDD and its March–May 2010 protest clearly represented different things to different people, including those among the protest group's fragmented and opportunistic leadership. Its split personality has no doubt contributed to the wide-ranging interpretations of the UDD and of its significance in the contemporary Thai context. For all the romantic portrayals of a rich-versus-poor class struggle, Thailand's political battle boils down to a fight between competing elites who, for all their pretensions of fighting for democracy and social justice, are in actuality illiberal mirror images of one another.

Notes

1. "Thaksin to cope with 'unfair' decision", *Bangkok Post*, 26 February 2010.
2. Also see <http://2bangkok.com/10/RedProtests1003.shtml> (accessed 7 March 2011) for images of the diminished numbers of protestors on 16 March 2010.
3. "Thaksin draws comparison between Abhisit and Hitler", Thai-Asean News Network, 17 March 2010.
4. Author's observation, Ratchaprasong, Bangkok, 20 April 2010.
5. See Shawn W. Crispin, "Dueling Elites: Thailand's Political Standoff", *Global Asia* 4, no. 2 (Summer 2009): 78–83.
6. See the bilingual "Questions and Answers: United Front for Democracy Against Dictatorship (UDD) — Red in the Land", a six-point, 22-page pamphlet dated 28 April 2010. This piece of propaganda literature briefly outlines the UDD's aims, relations with Thaksin, and position on the monarchy.
7. See Shawn W. Crispin, "Bombs away in Thailand", *Asia Times Online*, 2 April 2010.
8. See Shawn W. Crispin, "Bloody desperation for Thailand's reds", *Asia Times Online*, 17 March 2010.
9. This exchange is available in "Debating the Crisis in Thailand: Is Red Shirt Movement a Genuine Grass Roots Struggle, or Front for Ousted Ex-PM, Billionaire Tycoon", *Democracy Now!*, 18 May 2010 <http://www.democracynow.org/2010/5/18/debating_the_crisis_in_thailand_is> (accessed 7 March 2011).
10. See Chris Baker, "Assembly of the Poor: The New drama of Village, City and State", paper presented at the Seventh International Conference on Thai Studies, University of Amsterdam, 5–8 July 1999. Baker took issue with this author's seminal reference to Thaksin as a "populist" (in "Thailand Incorporated", *Far Eastern Economic Review*, 18 January 2001) in Pasuk Phongpaichit and Chris Baker, "Pluto-Populism: Thaksin, Business and Popular Politics in Post-Crisis Thailand" (available at <http://pioneer.chula.

ac.th/~ppasuk/plutopopulism.pdf>), but his analysis has come around to that assessment.

11. For the crucial work on Thailand's rural-urban divide, see Anek Laothamatas, "A Tale of Two Democracies: Conflicting Perceptions of Elections and Democracy in Thailand", in *The Politics of Elections in Southeast Asia*, edited R. H. Taylor (Cambridge, New York, and Melbourne: Woodrow Wilson Center Press and Cambridge University Press, 1996), pp. 201–23.
12. For an overview of Thailand's historical policy responses to vulnerability pressures, see Richard F. Doner, *The Politics of Uneven Development: Thailand's Economic Growth in Comparative Perspective* (Cambridge: Cambridge University Press, 2009), pp. 95–141.
13. See Bertil Lintner, "Thai turmoil was no 'class war,'" *Sydney Morning Herald*, 7 June 2010. For a more in-depth treatment, see Lintner's "The Battle for Thailand", *Foreign Affairs* 88, no. 4 (July/August 2009): 108–118.
14. Atthasit Vejjajiva, conversation with author, Bangkok, April 2010.
15. See Duncan McCargo, "Thailand's twin fires", *Survival* 52, no. 4 (21 June 2010): 5–12.
16. Ibid., p. 9.
17. Jakrapob Penkair, interview with the author, Lad Phrao, Bangkok, 21 June 2007.
18. Sean Boonracong, UDD international spokesman, in an October 2009 phone conversation with the author said that he received frequent instructions from Phansak Winyarat concerning "strategic management" of the UDD's communications, including instructions to "discredit" this author's journalism on the UDD's Facebook page.

11

THE GRAND BARGAIN
Making "Reconciliation" Mean Something

Federico Ferrara

Not five decades ago, political scientist David Wilson described Thai society in terms that offer a window into the socio-economic roots of the political crisis that has enveloped the country since 2006. Back then, Wilson observed "a clear distinction between those who are involved in politics and those who are not" — adding that "the overwhelming majority of the adult population is not." He went on to say:

> The peasantry as the basic productive force constitutes more than 80 percent of the population and is the foundation of the social structure. But its inarticulate acquiescence to the central government and indifference to national politics are fundamental to the political system. A tolerable economic situation which provides a stable subsistence without encouraging any great hope for quick improvement is no doubt the background of this political inaction.[1]

Writing on the heels of Field Marshal Sarit Thanarat's 1958 conservative revolution, David Wilson was correct to identify in the "acquiescence" and "indifference" of the vast majority of the public the fundamental basis of "Thai-Style Democracy" — a system of government that, notwithstanding the appropriation of some of the trappings of democracy, has since largely preserved the right of men of high birth, status, education, and wealth to run the country.

Indeed, it was in the interest of building this system of government that Sarit had insisted that the rural population be forever content to eke out a simple existence upcountry — the refusal of many to embrace their station in life portending the "deterioration" of Thai society.[2] It was in the interest of preserving this system of government that the Thai people have more recently been urged to walk "backwards into a *khlong*" and renounce progress in favour of a simpler existence.[3] And it was in the interest of reiterating what this system of government once expected of them that Prime Minister Abhisit Vejjajiva promised in March 2010 that everything will be fine in Thailand, so long as the Thai people continue to "do their jobs lawfully".[4] In a "Sufficiency Democracy", as Andrew Walker calls it, a good citizen is not just satisfied with whatever life has given him; equally important, he accepts a political role commensurate to the size of his *barami*. [5]

"Thai-Style Democracy" was not destroyed in one day. Despite increasingly desperate pleas to be content with what they have, over time the people of Thailand have had enough of a "stable subsistence" and have flocked to Bangkok to fulfill dreams that their leaders said they should not dare harbour. Economic growth and modernization gave rise to hopes that a "quick" and decisive "improvement" in their material condition would soon be within their grasp. Confronted with the refusal of the country's ruling class to grant them a fair share of the country's newfound prosperity — reliably built on the backs of the people — they shed their "indifference" and began to vote, *en masse*, for those who at least bothered to pay some lip service to their empowerment. And when their will was overturned, not once but three times over the four years from 2006 to 2010, for many among them "acquiescence" was quite simply no longer an option. *"Mai pen rai"* has turned into *"mai yom rap"*.

For a variety of reasons — not the least of which is the arrogance of its guardians — "Thai-Style (Sufficiency) Democracy" has been in failing health for almost two decades. It finally died some time between 12 March and 14 March 2010, overpowered by the tens of thousands of people who marched on Bangkok to demand equality, justice, and "real" democracy. On March 20, its corpse was paraded through the city in a festive, fifty-kilometre-long procession attended by hundreds of thousands — what amounted to an unmistakably Thai rendition of a New Orleans jazz funeral.

The Red Shirts could never hope to bring a million people to Bangkok, given the monumental logistical challenges that that task would have presented under the best of circumstances. At the end of the day, their numbers were depressed further by the fact that these were not the best of circumstances. Thanks, in part, to the complicity of their own most dim-witted leaders, in advance of their "final battle against dictatorship" the Red Shirts were successfully portrayed as barbarian "rural hordes" — most of them paid, some of them brainwashed, many among them not really Thai — determined to lay waste to the capital city in a last-ditch effort to rescue the dwindling fortunes of one man. Just in case the widely anticipated prospects of violence and chaos (periodically revitalized by well timed police raids and mysterious bomb attacks) had failed to scare enough people into staying home, hundreds of trip-wires were laid in the form of checkpoints extending deep into the Isan countryside. Then, just at the opportune time, the government pressed the panic button when it imposed the Internal Security Act on 11 March and began speaking openly about the possibility of invoking the Emergency Decree — what would later amount, in practice, to an *autogolpe*.

And yet they came — not in large enough numbers to inaugurate a new system of government, to be sure, but in numbers certainly large enough to trample the old one to death. Some argued, with merit, that their motives remained diverse, their demands inarticulate, their strategy underdeveloped, and their leadership coarse, homophobic, and hopelessly divided against itself. Still, the death of the old system required no clear vision, no unanimity of motive, no strategic acumen, and no enlightened leader; indeed, it did not even require the physical removal of Prime Minister Abhisit's puppet regime. What definitively snuffed the life out of "Thai-Style Democracy" was that its foundation of indifference and sheepish acquiescence had been thoroughly dismantled. "Thai-Style Democracy" could no longer endure once its founding ideology was exposed as an especially ignoble adaptation of Plato's "Noble Lie". It was merely by standing up to say "enough" that hundreds of thousands of people, many belonging to constituencies whose right to participate in the country's government had never before been acknowledged, accomplished what previous democratic movements could not — put the old system to death.

In the wake of what was, at least by the official estimates, the deadliest episode of repression of pro-democracy demonstrators in the history of Thailand, Prime Minister Abhisit promised "reconciliation". Just in case the details of the prime minister's "road map" had not made it perfectly clear, the actions that his government took following the dispersal of the Red Shirt rallies on May 19 erased any doubts that what Mr Abhisit meant by "reconciliation" was neither accountability nor the resolution of substantive differences by way of compromise. In the government's usage, "reconciliation" meant "restoration" — the restoration of "Thai-Style Democracy", the restoration of the Thai people's lost acquiescence, the restoration of their innocence from the taint of foreign ideas like "democracy", "equality", and "progress".

The call to "protect the monarchy", in particular, was in keeping with the old Saritian tradition of borrowing the government's legitimacy from the throne, while the witch-hunt to root out a phantom conspiracy to overthrow the monarchy underscored its determination to perpetuate the five-decades-old habit of branding the government's enemies as closet republicans. The promise to address some of the economic grievances put forth by the Red Shirts, while ignoring their political demands, reflected the government's conviction that a few handouts might just be enough to bribe Red Shirt sympathizers into abandoning the fight for their civil and political rights. The commitment to making the media into a "constructive tool" — presumably by censoring news outlets reporting less "constructive" facts as well as by educating the public to make "correct use" of new media[6] — was evidence of the same "father knows best" arrogance exhibited by each of Thailand's past military regimes. Finally, if Mr Abhisit's attempt to whitewash just the latest episode of state violence in Thailand aimed to extend to himself and his colleagues the cover of impunity enjoyed by those who carried out similar massacres in 1973, 1976, and 1992, his campaign to disguise the cover-up as an "independent investigation" exposed his government's unfailing contempt for the intelligence of its citizens.

Perhaps the best evidence of the government's reactionary designs was offered by the extreme repression with which it felt necessary to complement its "road map for reconciliation". Mr Abhisit could not stay on without inviting the military to stage a coup on his behalf (or accepting the *fait accompli*) — that is, without claiming dictatorial powers for himself and the newly instituted Centre for the Resolution of the Emergency Situation (CRES). Mr Abhisit's administration oversaw the most heavy-handed, most systematic attempt to silence voices of dissent since the days of Prime Minister Thanin Kraiwichian in 1976–1977; those media outlets not censored were enlisted in a massive propaganda campaign to prop up the government and destroy the opposition. Mr Abhisit presided over the killing of ninety people, just to recapture a few square kilometres of prime real estate in central Bangkok from largely unarmed protestors. Following the dispersal of the rallies, Mr Abhisit pursued the Red Shirts relentlessly. Over four hundred were arrested — some held without charge, others tried and convicted at lightning speed, still others subjected to trumped up terrorism charges leading to possible death sentences.

These measures suggested that Mr Abhisit's government had neither the authority nor the ambition to bring about meaningful "reconciliation". But if the idea that reconciliation would be achieved on a foundation of repression and impunity was chimerical, the government's "road map for restoration" — to re-educate the sceptical, terrorize the reticent, and crush the undaunted — might turn out to be no less fanciful.

Over the course of its half-century life span, "Thai-Style Democracy" adapted successfully in response to at least two major disruptions comparable to the one constituted by the assertion of Thai Rak Thai's electoral dominance, and that of its successor parties, from 2001 onward. In both prior instances, successful adaptation was preceded by attempts at restoration whose failure offers valuable clues about the prospects faced by the effort that followed May 2010.

The 1976 coup that installed Thanin's despotic regime, following the gruesome massacre of dozens of students at Thammasat University, marked an attempt to restore Thailand to the days of Field Marshals Thanom Kittikhachon and Praphat Charusathian, if not of Sarit, after the chaotic period of "real" democracy ushered in by the protests of 1973. Even the extreme repression unleashed by Thanin, however, could not bring back "Thai-Style Democracy" in its original, Saritian form — a form devoid of meaningful political rights and representative institutions. Failed restoration gave way to adaptation. The solution was "Premocracy", a hybridized form of government that combined elements of democracy (increasingly powerful elected representatives) with features of the old system (the 1980–1988 premiership of unelected Prime Minister Prem Tinsulanon, whose position did not hinge on the composition of the elected legislature).

Similarly, General Suchinda Kraprayun's 1991 coup marked an attempt to restore Thailand to the days of Premocracy after Chatchai Choonhavan's two-and-a-half-year tenure as prime minister — an attempt to turn back the clock to a time when an unelected military man could rule Thailand, legitimized by the existence of a functioning parliament but not meaningfully encumbered by any changes that elections might bring to its composition. That restoration failed, too, when tens of thousands of people rose up against Suchinda in May 1992. Once again, Suchinda's brutality could not bring back that which had been already confined to the history books. The solution was a new adaptation that both satisfied the Thai people's wish to elect their premiers and also preserved the influence of unelected institutions to impose national policy through the manipulation of elected governments notorious for their weakness, fragmentation, and corruption.[7]

The failure of these two prior instances of restoration did not bode well for Mr Abhisit in the aftermath of 19 May 2010. The lesson is that no amount of repression in the short term can restore the long-term stability of a social contract whose enforcement has outlasted the people's availability to honor it. The solution is either adaptation or more repression. But while the former is complicated by the fact that "Thai-Style Democracy" has arguably run out of room to adapt, the latter is made unthinkable by the fact that what little popular legitimacy the government's authoritarian measures were provisionally accorded was soon just an increasingly faint heartbeat away from vanishing entirely.

By the second half of 2010, it was difficult to tell whether, as Thitinan Pongsudhirak had earlier argued, Mr Abhisit really saw himself as the "savior of the throne".[8] It was even more difficult to determine the extent to which he was in control of his own government, in view of the increased prominence of the CRES and the party dissolution cases that hung over his head like a sword of Damocles until December. Certainly, some scepticism appeared warranted; Mr Abhisit was smart enough to know that the most dangerous threat that the monarchy faces today is the continued misuse of the imperative to defend it as the pretext for extrajudicial executions, illegal detentions, political persecution, and military dictatorship. In the long run, the March–May 2010 Red Shirt demonstrations may well be remembered as merely the first ripple in what is a possible tsunami headed in the direction of Thailand's establishment. The question as 2011 began was whether the Thai ruling class was prepared to fight to the death, or whether it was open to eventually cutting a deal.

Beyond the value that achieving a measure of "real" reconciliation sooner rather than later might have for the country as a whole, there were good reasons why Thailand's ruling class might want to cut sooner rather than later. Simply stated, Mr Abhisit's backers had an opportunity to get a better deal in late 2010 and early 2011 than they are likely ever to get in the future. First, the establishment temporarily weakened the old Thai Rak Thai's coalition that Thaksin put together in both the legislature and in the electorate — preventing a new social contract from being imposed on Thaksin's terms.[9] But the star of its big-time players is fading fast, while its bench is not especially deep on charisma, competence, and legitimacy. Second, the government's repression successfully disrupted the Red Shirt organization, giving the establishment a chance to co-opt enough of the movement's political agenda to defuse the more radical ambitions that it ascribed to the Red Shirts. But for the reasons mentioned above, this level of repression is unlikely to be sustainable in the long run. Finally, the arson attacks that took place on 19 May provided the government — and Thailand's eagerly compliant media — with just the sort of apocalyptic images that it needed to substantiate, retroactively, its case for massacring the Red Shirts. But the support for the government could only go downhill from there, as the deluge of lies and repressive measures that the administration used to keep its story straight proved increasingly unpopular, and its "road map for reconciliation" revealed itself as nothing other than a futile, clumsy attempt to shove the toothpaste back into the tube.

In short, what Thailand's predicament called for in late 2010 and early 2011 was not the small-time partisan hackery that the Abhisit-led government offered, but rather the sort of "Grand Bargain" that results from a comprehensive renegotiation of the social compact between the old ruling class and the old subordinate classes. While the details of this compact should be open for discussion, it is probably safe to say that only a bargain that recognizes the people's right to govern their own country can offer a chance for stability. The citizens of Thailand, whether or not they sympathize with the Red Shirts, have repeatedly affirmed the eagerness to live in a "real" democracy. The time has come to grant them that right.

During and after the crisis of March–May 2010, such publications such as the *Economist, Wall Street Journal,* and *Washington Post* complemented their criticism of Mr Abhisit's road map with the call for an election. To be sure, holding an election would be preferable to the spectacle of an attempted restoration pursued by a half-civilian, half-military mongrel of an administration. But an election — even one preceded by minor constitutional reforms — could do little to solve the conflict's more structural causes. The problem is neither the constitution nor the composition of the House of Representatives; it is rather that constitutions and representative institutions in Thailand are so readily disposable, whatever their content and composition.

At the very minimum, "reconciliation" requires broad consensus on three foundational principles that form the basis of every stable society free of significant levels of state violence and repression:

(1) Feudal and capitalist elites accept government by representatives chosen by a majority of the population. In return for ceding the right to run Thailand, for abandoning the PAD's fascist fantasies, and for renouncing their power to make and break governments through their control of a rigged judicial system, such elites enjoy the opportunity to exercise the same outsized influence on the political process that men and women of high status and vast means enjoy in every democratic society around the world.

(2) In return for the right to live under governments of their own choosing, the majority agrees not to use its power to trample on the rights of minorities — be they the political opposition that Thaksin's administration sought to muzzle, the small ethno-linguistic groups that Thaksin's administration repressed in its fight against the Muslim insurgency in the South, or the presumed deviants that Thaksin's administration targeted during the "War on Drugs". While the real reasons for the 2006 military coup were others, it is difficult to imagine that the coup would have gone off quite as smoothly without some of the excesses of Thaksin's administration during 2001–2006.

(3) The military is aggressively restructured and perhaps decisively downsized — such that it is rendered inoffensive, placed firmly under civilian control, and transformed into a professional force dedicated to the country's external defence. That defensive mission supplants the military's historic and continuing focus on the maximization of the power and wealth of its chieftains through the systematic suppression of the Thai people's democratic aspirations. Whatever the state of the military at any given time, politicians must agree to kick the habit of relying on the armed forces either to consolidate their power or to regain it after losing elections.

The essence of democracy is choice — a choice offered at regular intervals between competing and often divisive visions, platforms, and philosophies of government. But for these choices to be meaningful and to be made freely, elections must take place in a context of a fundamental agreement on the rules of the game. Thailand is a long way from achieving a consensus on this basic point; what is worse, the constituencies controlling most of the money, guns, and power are especially divided on these issues. Based on the events of the past several years, it is virtually certain that an election held in the post-May 2010 political context could do little to move the country in the direction of "reconciliation". It is rather more likely that the polls would breathe new life into the ongoing attempt by the PAD, the military, and the courts to undermine the country's confidence in democratic institutions and procedures.

"Reconciliation" is less likely to occur as the consequence of an election like that of July 2011 than as the result of a process of comprehensive reform, perhaps overseen by a unity government that includes all major parties represented in parliament. The reform process should aim to produce a new social compact and to enshrine the resulting agreement in a new constitution. The exact composition and selection procedures for the new "Constituent Assembly" or "Constitutional Convention" are important, but they are secondary to ensuring that the process is at least as inclusive and participatory as that which led to the adoption of Thailand's 1997 constitution. As diverse as possible an array of interests must be given not only a stake in the process. They

must also be given enough guarantees so that their interests and goals are best pursued within the newly instituted rules of the game. This is the key to Thailand's future stability, to making democracy "the only game in town".[10] Whereas the process may well fail to bring along the tinfoil hatters who support the PAD, its inclusiveness is likely to reduce the appeal of extremist, "anti-system" forces or otherwise to complicate future efforts to subvert the results that it produces. A unity government, moreover, would offer politicians the best chance to make common front against the assault that the military and other unelected institutions are guaranteed to launch in an attempt to sabotage the process suggested here and to blow up any emerging consensus on the need to diminish their power.

Simple though this reform agenda may be, it is quite possible that this alternative "road map" will require autonomy, courage, statesmanship, and a commitment to genuine reconciliation in measures that exceed the stocks available to both government and opposition in Thailand today. With or without the stewardship of the current set of leaders, there can be no doubt that Thailand will eventually find real reconciliation through real democracy. The lingering questions are when, how, and at the expense of how many more lives.

Notes

1. David Wilson, *Politics in Thailand* (Ithaca: Cornell University Press, 1962).
2. Thak Chaloemtiarana, *Thailand: The Politics of Despotic Paternalism* (Chiang Mai: Silkworm, 2007 [1979]), pp. 105–106 and 122.
3. See Pasuk Phongpaichit, "Developing Social Alternatives: Walking Backwards into a *khlong*", in *Thailand Beyond the Crisis*, edited by Peter Warr (London: Routledge, 2005), p. 161.
4. Wassana Nanuam, "Abhisit calls in media to slam Thaksin", *Bangkok Post*, 20 March 2010.
5. Andrew Walker, "Sufficiency Democracy", New Mandala, 4 October 2006 <http://asiapacific.anu.edu.au/newmandala/2006/10/04/sufficiency-democracy/> (accessed 7 March 2011).
6. Asina Pornwasin, "Govt backed cyber scouts to monitor internet", *The Nation*, 2 July 2010.
7. See Duncan McCargo, "Network Monarchy and Legitimacy Crises in Thailand", *Pacific Review* 18, no. 4 (December 2005): 499–519; see pp. 507–515.

8. Simon Roughneen, "Sunlight Creeping through the Bangkok Gloom", *Irrawaddy*, 4 May 2010 <http://www.irrawaddy.org/article.php?art_id=18376> (accessed 7 March 2011).
9. For a sense of what the "terms" were, see Kevin Hewison, "Crafting Thailand's New Social contract", *Pacific Review* 17, no. 4 (December 2004): 503–22; see pp. 514–18.
10. See Juan Linz and Alfred Stepan, *Problems of Democratic Transition and Consolidation: Southern Europe, South America and Post-Communist Europe* (Baltimore: The Johns Hopkins University Press, 1996), p. 5.

12

CHANGING THAILAND
An Awakening of Popular Political Consciousness for Rights?

David Fullbrook

Streets in downtown Bangkok and the centres of several cities in Isan and Lanna—the Northeast and North of the country — were occupied by protestors from March to May of 2010. As the days went by and tensions grew, fuelled by anger and rhetoric, the odd bombing and assassination, the protests appeared to draw ever greater crowds, especially at weekends. This was the most incongruous act of public political consciousness and uprising in the history of Thailand.

Explanation of the causes and nature of the 2010 protests requires, first, a brief description of the protests and their denouement (informed in this case by direct experience of them) and, second, dismissal of several accounts of the protests that play down their significance and misrepresent their nature. Such explanation clears the way for the central argument of this essay, that the protests were a withdrawal of consent to be governed by people who felt that their rights had been pushed aside by a privileged minority whose members favoured restoring and perpetuating inequality and were willing to use coercion to impose their interests on the country at large.

Protestors began their occupations of the Phan Fa Bridge and Ratchadamnoen Avenue and of Ratchaprasong — a commercial district of glitzy malls, glass skyscrapers and luxury hotels and apartments — in March 2010. The mood was joyous, the atmosphere almost like that of a carnival with hawkers quick to move in to offer all the staples of life usually sold on the streets of Bangkok. Thousands of free meals were dished up daily. Hundreds of speakers and dozens of video screens were erected around the protest sites. Professional film crews broadcast the events. Enthusiastic staff and volunteers managed security, received donations and tried to return lost items to their owners.

By day protestors often numbered only in the hundreds. As night fell people came in their thousands, poor and rich together, sitting and standing, chatting and cheering in streets usually jammed with cars. They listened intently as one orator after another took to the stage, speakers and radio eerily echoing their voices far beyond, to condemn the 19 September 2006 coup, the Army and the government; to speak of injustice, unfairness and double standards; to demand a free and fair election. They spoke with colour and flair. They drew on images from far and wide, among them Robin Hood, Dracula, and ancient Troy besieged by Greek enemies.[1]

Day after day I met protestors, poor, well-off and wealthy alike, who felt that the coup of September 2006 had dealt them a great injustice because it destroyed their right to choose a government through the power and value of their vote. The coup said that the feelings and opinions expressed through votes were worth nothing. The coup was an affront that these protestors felt deeply because of Thailand's history of coups, state violence and absence of justice for the hundreds, at least, killed for protesting for their political rights since the 1950s. Time and again they would share in lively conversation their disgust at the double standards of the powers behind the coup and Abhisit Vejjajiva's Democrat government. Many, but by no means all, expressed pride in and gratitude for the elected governments of Thaksin Shinawatra which implemented policies that they felt had made a difference to their own lives or to family and friends.

The mood changed on 10 April, when the government responded to the withdrawal of consent with coercion. That evening, in a botched effort to end the protest on Ratchadamnoen Avenue, troops shot dead around twenty protestors on a few side streets and around the Democracy Monument. A handful of soldiers were also killed by unknown assailants. As the Army withdrew, abandoning armoured personnel carriers and trucks, protestors and residents filled the streets. They were angry, condemning and cursing the Army. A shrine formed around the brains of a protestor splattered on the tarmac by a shot fired from an armoured personnel carrier a few metres away. Photographs indicate that he was shot for simply holding a flag of the movement. Shrines also took shape at other spots where protestors died. Vehicles abandoned by the Army were soon covered in political graffiti. Most common was "*thorarat*", or "tyrant".

It might be said that the mood of the protests changed. Defiance set in. Anger became hatred. What happened on 10 April was a harbinger of what was to come. The protest at Ratchadamnoen was wound down a few days later. The movement focused on securing and expanding the blocks that it had come to control around Ratchaprasong. The writ of the government stopped at the barricades marking the boundaries, which steadily expanded, of this "liberated" zone, the Bangkok Commune. Grenade attacks and shootings increased in the weeks after 10 April. Sniper fire directed at protestors along Rama IV Road and around the Din Daeng intersection killed and wounded dozens.[2] The night often echoed with explosions of fireworks, drums, and cheers, and occasionally explosions or gunshots.

A few hours after sunrise on 19 May the Army launched Operation Ratchaprasong. On Ratchadamri Road by Chulalongkorn Hospital and Sarasin Road beside Lumphini Park, armoured personnel carriers charged through barricades of tyres, wire, and bamboo pikes that could easily have been breached by a few civilian bulldozers. Troops armed with rifles, shotguns, and grenades followed, watched over from the rooftops of the hospital by snipers. They charged into protestors, who — well aware of the state's history of violence against Thai citizens — were armed with slingshots, sticks, and fireworks. There were among a few thousand protestors left at Ratchaprasong several men in black armed with rifles. Their identities, motives and mission remain the subject of speculation. Gunfire, ricochets and explosions echoed all morning and into the afternoon and evening. Troops killed between forty and fifty protestors.

Weak protestors replied to the state's excess of violence by improvising a weapon out of fire. I watched with disbelief farcical attempts to torch buildings. At Ratchaprasong they only set alight Central World mall, with a few dozen more buildings torched around the city and in the provinces. Fire reportedly ripped through Central World because water supplies had been turned off, leaving the sprinklers dry, and despite the efforts, if any, of armed security guards. Had the protestors actually been prepared for, experienced in, or competent in acts of arson, Bangkok's skyline might have been darkened by many more thick plumes of acrid smoke.

As dusk closed in a few hours later, not far from the burning Central World a middle-aged man in a black jacket crouched behind a concrete traffic barrier around a BTS pillar where Wat Pathumwanaram meets Siam Square. Some thought he was on the Red side, others were not so sure. He was preparing to confront troops with an M-16 rifle. In a place usually crowded with people out to shop, eat, or sell, a lonely gunman ready to battle soldiers was disturbing, an image of civil war.

Early the next morning I returned to his position. There were signs of a gunfight. A few dozen rounds had gouged holes into the concrete. Where the gunman had crouched there were a handful of spent cartridge cases, a couple of dud rounds, and — smeared on the concrete BTS pillar — dark red-brown stains that might have been blood. Who he was, what he was doing, why he was preparing to face deadly odds, and what became of him are, like so much about the events of 2010, unknown.

THE NATURE AND AGENCY OF DISSENT

The protests of 2010 were on a scale and of a character that suggest that they represented the sentiments of more than just a small minority. The protests were organized by the National United Front for Democracy against Dictatorship, or UDD,[3] a mass-member organization that appeared to be growing rapidly. Hundreds of people queued each day to join the UDD, against backdrop banners of prominent members — including Member Number One Thaksin Shinawatra — the popular prime minister deposed by the 2006 coup. The UDD had a collective leadership of social activists, academics, and a couple of respected local politicians. They insisted that the organization was independent of and not influenced by Thaksin.

During the course of spending two months observing the protests and talking with participants, I concluded that the UDD did not account for all the protestors, but was rather a formal embodiment of a much wider sentiment. I came to understand this dissent and resistance against the will and interests of the *ammat*, or aristocratic elite — which perpetrated the 2006 coup and engineered the installation of the Democrat government of Abhisit Vejjajiva — as a social movement. The Red social movement was a state of mind rather than even an informal organization. I considered people to be part of the Red social movement if they opposed the 2006 coup and were in favour of participatory politics through general elections, or "democracy". Views within the movement were not homogenous. From it arose several informal and formal organizations, local and national. The largest and best supported was the UDD. Smaller, but also notable because of its more radical position arguing for armed revolt was *Siam Daeng*, or Red Siam.

The character, feeling and passion of the protests of people identifying with the Red social movement is hard to convey in a few words. However, it is important to address doubts that have been expressed in several oft repeated claims about the origins of the movement, the organizations that it produced, and the motives of protestors.

- *Protestors were mainly poor rural Thais who are too simple and poorly educated to have ideas about politics, democracy or justice.* It was true that by day protests took on a rural hue. Come nightfall, however, the protests swelled with urbanites from shops, factories and offices. They parked hundreds, perhaps thousands, of cars each night along Phetburi Road and Soi Lang Suan, near Ratchaprasong.[4] As for the rural people among protestors, well, rural Thais have never been so well informed or so aware as today, thanks to ubiquitous mobile phones and Internet access. Moreover, it is not unusual in conversation for rural people to offer up clear and penetrating insights and awareness of the problems facing Thailand.
- *The popularity of Thaksin, the elected prime minister deposed by the Army, among the protestors proves that the protests are a plot that he orchestrated to pave the way for his return.* Thaksin was mentioned by speakers on the Ratchaprasong stage, and occasionally he phoned in or tweeted encouragement. Some paraphernalia sold at the protests did bear his image. He was a member of the UDD and may have been influential in its genesis. He was often mentioned in conversation. However, he was frequently but a sub-topic in conversations that revolved above all around rights, inequality and

injustice. Popularity does not automatically translate into control. Speeches from the stage focused on double standards and on principles and ideas for participatory politics and a just society governed by a state that enjoys the consent of the people. Indeed, Thaksin's governments did not live up to many of the high ideals and aspirations expressed on that stage.

- *Thaksin paid the costs of the protests, which may have run into tens of millions of baht.* No evidence has been presented to substantiate this claim. In view of the interest of the state in proving the protests to be a sham, this lack of evidence is telling. At the same time, it cannot be discounted that Thaksin and other major politicians were contributing, perhaps quite significant sums, in support of the protests. Indeed, some local politicians advertised their donations and support. But, again, donations do not necessarily imply control, and control does not necessarily require money. Furthermore, money can buy many things, but among them may not be fervour, pluck, and passion, above all like those demonstrated by protestors running into the smoke and gunfire on 19 May to rescue others wounded by troops.[5] Donations and voluntary efforts by people at the protests and around the country did help sustain the protests; the names of some donors and volunteers were read to the crowds every day. The possibility remains that donations from the public supported the protests to a greater extent than any secret donations by politicians.
- *Thaksin paid people to protest.* Talk was of money concealed underneath the food provided to protestors. I never saw any money in the bowls of food being dished up and often offered to me. It is not inconceivable that some protestors were paid. However, if payments were made the mechanisms were obtuse. If they went on for months and on a large scale, they would not only have been costly but also have brought considerable risks of being revealed through hard evidence. Moreover, if payments were made to facilitate protest by people who could not otherwise afford to exercise their rights and express their opinions by joining protests in Bangkok, then were those payments anything but a reflection of the realities of the structure of power and the inequalities of wealth that impinge on expression and participation

in the political process? Rights that cannot be exercised because of poverty are hardly rights at all. Furthermore, if people did accept money, it does not inhibit their agency freely to think, feel and hope.

The scale of protest and the determination, persistence, and commitment of protestors — and above all else their engagement, enthusiasm, and passion through the searing summer heat and the rain and in the face of the coercion of the state — contrast starkly with unsubstantiated claims that the protests were the ploy of one man. The Red social movement and acts of dissent through protest were genuine, reflecting deeply held concerns and feelings. Claims that deny the agency of common people, presented without solid evidence, avoid considering the unsettling possibility of change and its implications. Directly confronting the doubts raised about the Red social movement opens space to consider people's concerns over inequality, coercion, and consent.

POLITICAL AND ECONOMIC INEQUALITY

If the Red social movement and its protests were genuine, what then were they about? The 2006 coup and the excise of power by the *ammat* to block the will of majority might be a popular explanation. But it highlights the symptoms rather than the causes of dissent and revolt. The will and ability to exercise such power are consequences of unequal rights. Who has rights to what under what circumstances and on what terms determine the balance of equality and inequality that shapes a political system. Thailand, it might be said, is a land of great inequalities, none more obvious than that of wealth. Economic inequality in Thailand is wide and has been widening despite rapid economic growth and industrialization since the 1960s.[6]

Yet this sharp economic inequality, shaping lives and livelihoods for decades in Thailand, did not suddenly strike society to tear a deep gash out of which discontent, disenchantment, and disaffection spilled onto the streets of Bangkok and other cities. The act of violence that gravely wounded society was the 19 September 2006 coup against the elected government of Prime Minister Thaksin. Citizens were relieved at gunpoint of their sovereignty as enshrined in the constitution.

Might overcame rights nakedly to impose the power of a few over the many in a gross display of the arrogance and persistence of political inequality.

So, while great disparities in wealth, and even class envy and conflict, may have been necessary to lay the foundations of dissent, they were not sufficient to spark protest and revolt. The spark was the coup. It tore down efforts to introduce political equality through the right to engage in the participatory politics of one-person, one-vote. It coercively asserted and defended political inequality. The inequality at the heart of the Red social movement, the one most keenly felt, was thus not economic but political. The Red social movement withheld consent from the government installed by the military and demanded the return of its members' rights and of political equality.[7]

Political equality expressed through voting has become more valuable for several reasons. First, experience since 2000 has demonstrated to citizens that their votes can put in place a government that implements policies to attend to their needs and interests. Second, the ability effectively to influence the government through votes has become especially important for rural people because in much of the countryside people have come to depend more on the state for their livelihoods.[8] Third, citizens have become more sophisticated and aware over the last few decades through an expansion of media, work experiences through migration, mobile phones and the Internet.

While economic inequality may be most keenly felt in daily existence, it appears that political equality is the more pressing matter, because it offers some prospect for redressing economic inequality. This consciousness of the value of political equality may be indicative of considerable change in the polity and a herald of what is to come.

COERCION

In the face of widespread dissent the Abhisit government used coercion to suppress challenges to the political inequality with which it had become associated and that it was trying to protect. Coercion was applied through administrative, legal, psychological and violent means. Legal inequalities were used to sustain political inequalities through detentions and prosecutions — including secret trials — that violated human rights.

These are acts of administrative coercion to reinforce the armed coercion of the coup and the violence against protestors.

Legal processes were subverted to the benefit of the government and the *ammat*. For example, in July 2010 one case of electoral impropriety involving a donation in 2005 of 258 million baht to the Democrat Party was inexplicably dropped by the Department of Special Investigations because of insufficient evidence.[9] The Democrat government displayed considerable zeal in detaining and prosecuting Red movement activists and protestors but indifference to bringing pro-government Yellows (including its own foreign minister Kasit Piromya) to trial for occupying Bangkok's airports and injuring and killing opponents on the streets for a week in late 2008. Legal inequality as displayed in these cases echoes with many of the experiences of ordinary people in Thailand. It exemplifies the double standards of which so many in the Red movement spoke in my encounters with them.

The state portrayed protestors as terrorists who presented an existential threat to the country. Such dramatic propaganda and the correspondingly disproportionate violence on the part of the state were employed to stir fear among the public; this amounted to psychological coercion. The state presented itself as the defender of the public against terrorists who had been constructed by state propaganda out of the raw material of civilian protestors. That the state went to such lengths is indicative of its fear of the protests and its consequent need to rally and reinforce what support the regime could find among the Thai public.

In addition to developing a sense of threat and feelings of fear, the state used disproportionate violence as a demonstration of power not simply to disperse the protestors but to exterminate them and their appetite for protest. This intent was evident in the character of the Army's Operation Ratchaprasong on 19 May 2010. Troops were armed for war — equipped to crush and not simply to disperse an essentially peaceful protest, an act of civil disobedience. The operation, with its dramatic scenes of armoured personnel carriers charging barricades of tyres and wire and of troops clambering over the top, was theatre, an act of coercion to impose fear on those who would dissent from and challenge the established order of power and privilege.

While the coercion of May 2010 may have bolstered support for the government among some elements of the public, it almost certainly failed to extinguish the desire for change, the political consciousness, or the antipathy for the Democrat government and the elite interests that it represented. There are several reasons that coercion failed to break the morale of the Red movement. Ordinary people are better educated and are more cosmopolitan than in the past. Less affluent participants in the protests at Ratchaprasong could speak of an astonishing range of experiences of work and travel; this in itself underlines what a changed country Thailand has become. With nearly everybody holding a mobile phone and able to access the Internet, the internal connections of society are stronger; light shines into more corners. The events and experiences of April and May 2010 became instant history, myth, and lore — through videos and photos shared by telephones, social networks, blogs and tweets, DVDs and CDs, newspapers and magazines.

Although citizens and mass movements were able to shape some of the information flow during previous episodes of political confrontation, the state benefited from considerable asymmetry, achieved through its ability to create and control the expensive media resources of the analogue era. In recent events, however, the asymmetry has never been closer to balance. It may even have tilted in favour of mass movements, which had probably never been so national in reach as in the era of mobile phones and the Internet, fast public transport and an economy of migration for employment. To counteract and suppress the resultant ideas, interpretations, and views was beyond the capacity of the state, even with its internal security laws and willingness to disregard human rights.

CONSENT

Millions of Thais withdrew their consent through opposition and protest after prospects for political equality were dashed by the September 2006 coup and subsequent political violence on the part of the state. The deficit of legitimacy resulting from the withdrawal of consent left the government dependent upon coercion to enforce inequality. Coercion cannot, however, restore consent because consent has been withdrawn in protest against the coercion embodied in that coup and in developments thereafter. Disenfranchised voters across social classes, and their elite cheer-leaders and benefactors, have demonstrated the fortitude and courage to resist coercion and demand political equality.

At the same time, Thais who disliked Thaksin and his policies and cheered the coup, the *ammat*, and the Democrat government must also give their consent to be governed. Thaksin's contempt for some of the institutions and ways of democracy, including human rights, remain matters of considerable concern.

A return of political equality in free, fair, and open elections and of all sides' respect for the results is a necessary step towards restoring consent for Thailand's government. But in the long run it has to be accompanied by the development of impartial and effective legal and administrative institutions to enshrine and defend rights, moderate inequality, and tackle injustice. Dissent and protest in Thailand over the last several years may represent a political awakening which will in time lay the foundations for such developments.

Notes

1. For a discussion and examples of the rich, varied and even contradictory symbolism employed by participants in the revolt, see <http://thailandtrouble.blogspot.com/2010/06/symbolic-power.html> (downloaded 18 July 2011).
2. The government announced on several occasions during the later stages of the protests that it had deployed snipers in areas that it had designate free-fire zones. For the renowned photographer Nick Nostitz's vivid account of being pinned down by their fire at Din Daeng on 15 May, see <http://asiapacific.anu.edu.au/newmandala/20 10/05/16/nick-nostitz-in-the-killing-zone/> (downloaded 18 July 2011).
3. The National United Front for Democracy against Dictatorship and *Siam Daeng* emerged from a split within the United Front for Democracy against Dictatorship in 2007.
4. In socio-economic terms, the Red movement is dominated by the rural and urban working class; it thus reflects the numerically dominant social groups in Thailand as a whole. Notably, many middle-class and even wealthy people participated in the 2010 protests in Bangkok, especially on the weekends. Although rural people arguably formed the backbone of the protests, the numbers of urbanites or long-term migrants from countryside to city were significant throughout. The Centre for the Resolution of the Emergency Situation estimated that 70 percent of protestors were from Bangkok and neighbouring provinces; see *Prachatai*, 21 April 2010, "Sansern: red shirts preparing weapons including bamboo rockets to fight aircraft" (http://www.prachatai.com/english/node/1756, downloaded 16 July 2011).

5. The Philippine ambassador to Thailand was taken aback by the nature of the protests, which he felt were genuine and quite unlike paid events that he had witnessed in the Philippines; see "Departure from diplomacy", *Bangkok Post*, 6 June 2010 <http://www.bangkokpost.com/news/investigation/38300/departure-from-diplomacy> (downloaded 15 July 2011).
6. See, for example, Alain Mounier and Voravidh Charoenloet, "New Challenges for Thailand: Labour and Growth after the Crisis", *Journal of Contemporary Asia* XL, no. 1 (February 2010): 123–43 (the author thanks Kevin Hewison for calling his attention to this article); United Nations Development Programme, *Thailand Human Development Report 2009: Human Security, Today and Tomorrow* (Bangkok: United Nations Development Programme 20009); Medhi Krongkaew, "Economic Growth and Social Welfare: Experience of Thailand after the 1997 Economic Crisis", paper presented at the International Seminar on Promoting Growth and Welfare: The Role of Institutions and Structural Change in Asia, organized by Economic Commission for Latin America and the Caribbean, the Institute of Developing Economies, Japan, and the Instituto de Economia, Brazil, in Santiago de Chile, 28–29 April, and Rio de Janiero, 2–3 May 2002, p. 6; and Peter Warr, "Thailand in Crisis — part 5", pod-cast from the Australian National University, Canberra, 24 June 2010 <http://www.youtube.com/watch?v=yJfCoVzXLuM> (downloaded 15 July 2011).
7. Equality, justice, and fairness are the principles underlying the Six Points of the UDD. Its primary goal is not a simple redistribution of wealth, and it favours a capitalist economy; see National United Front for Democracy against Dictatorship-Red in the Land, "Questions and Answers", 28 April 2010 (available at <http://picasaweb.google.co.uk/103657339709676300673/UDDQA28April2010#> downloaded 15 July 2011).
8. Andrew Walker, "Thailand in Crisis — part 3", pod-cast from the Australian National University, 10 June 2010 <http://www.youtube.com/watch?v=eL-jWO8di44> (downloaded 15 July 2011).
9. "DSI drops case against TPI", *Bangkok Post*, 19 July 2010 <http://www.bangkokpost.com/news/politics/186848/case-against-tpi-dropped> (downloaded 15 July 2011).

13

CLASS, INEQUALITY, AND POLITICS

Kevin Hewison

In late March 2010, I made one of several visits to the Phan Fa Bridge, where Red Shirt demonstrators were gathered in large numbers. That evening, my stroll was brought to a halt by a phrase that I had not previously heard from the protestors' stage: "*songkhram chonchan*" or class warfare. It was not a term that I had heard much in public discourse, but it did seem to strike a chord with the assembled protestors.

During the second rising of the Red Shirts, from late 2009, the rhetoric of the leadership increasingly came to focus on broadly conceived issues

The author is indebted to Pasuk Phongpaichit and Chris Baker for providing Figures 13.2 to 13.5 and for drawing Figure 13.6; see Pasuk Phongpaichit and Chris Baker, "The Mask-play Election: Generals, Politicians, and Voters at Thailand's 2007 Poll", Asia Research Institute Working Paper No. 144, National University of Singapore, September 2010, available at <www.ari.nus.edu.sg/publication_details.asp?pubtypeid=WP&pubid=1667> (accessed 26 February 2011). The author is grateful to Parichart Siwaraksa for NESDB incomes data. He also thanks Chris Baker, Andrew Brown, David Fullbrook, Tyrell Haberkorn and Michael Montesano for comments on an earlier draft of this piece.

of status and class. The protestors famously adopted the old word for bonded commoner — *phrai* — to designate their position vis-à-vis the "*ammat*" or ruling "elite". Most of the issues that they raised, from double standards to political power, revolved around deeply felt and easily recognised issues of inequality.

Despite some alarmist claims, including from members of the Abhisit Vejjajiva regime, most notably Foreign Minister Kasit Piromya, the Red Shirt leadership of March–May 2010 was not composed of throwback Marxist-Leninist revolutionary communists.[1] One of the leaders, Weng Tojirakan, had been with the Communist Party of Thailand (CPT), and others had links with people who had once been with the now long-defunct CPT. But the claim that these others were communists because of links such as these falls on the fact that the deeply royalist, yellow-clad People's Alliance for Democracy (PAD) also had many similar links. Even in the darkest days, just before the military crushed the demonstrators on 19 May 2010, a Red Shirt booklet stated, "We want a free capitalist state in which the gap between the rich and the poor is reduced. We want to create more opportunities for the poor."[2] This is hardly the stuff of Marxist revolutionaries bent on establishing a classless society. Nonetheless, the Red Shirt appeal to class and status both angered and frightened many in the camp supporting the government of Prime Minister Abhisit.

One possible reason for these reactions was the remarkable demonstration of solidarity between Red Shirts and Bangkok's service and working people most vividly seen on 20 March 2010. For much of that day, a Red Shirt convoy wound its way around Bangkok receiving overwhelming displays of support from crowds that lined the city's streets. Nothing like this had ever been seen before, not even in the heroic days of the early 1970s, when the student movement built alliances with workers and peasants. For those in government, this display of potential political power must have been traumatizing.

The government and its supporters were even more perturbed when the international media began to describe the Red Shirt protest as a class conflict or as one pitting the poor against the mainly Bangkokian rich and ruling elite, supported by the city's middle class. For example, a Reuters report to the *Washington Post*, under a subheading "Class Warfare", referred to "messages of class warfare and social injustice".[3] The *Sydney Morning Herald* stated that protestors were "[a]ngered by one of Asia's widest income gaps, [and] they say Mr Abhisit embodies a privileged class of military officers, judges, bureaucrats and royal advisers that sits above the law."[4] And the *Irish Times* invoked the image of an Eton- and Oxford-educated "rich kid" Prime Minister Abhisit, facing off against the poor and disadvantaged, noting: "The conflict reflects deep polarisation and class tensions in Thai society ... [M]ost of the red-shirted demonstrators are poor peasants from the country's north or workers from the cities".[5] *The Irrawaddy* magazine said that the Red Shirt demonstrations were an "unprecedent[ed] movement of rural working-class Thais [that] challenges the Bangkok establishment's hold on power".[6] Numerous other media outlets made similar claims.

The government initially countered with rudimentary claims that Red Shirt protestors, being supported by the wealthy former Prime Minister Thaksin Shinawatra, could not possibly represent the class interests of the poor. Abhisit took this line, painting Thaksin as a master manipulator and stating, "Thaksin ... should not speak in a way that could create hatred between rich and poor. Society would be fine as long as people could do their jobs."[7] Another government response was to assert that the Democrat Party-led government had done more for the poor in one year than had the Thaksin administration in the whole of its tenure.[8]

For all the nay-saying and desire to blame Thaksin for the rally from March to May 2010, the argument in this chapter is that the available data lend considerable support to an interpretation of Thailand's political conflict centered on class. There is a rich theoretical and empirical literature on the poor, class and politics. However, because we do not have much reliable or sensible data on the Red Shirts and their organization, this paper does not argue for a *direct* link between class and political mobilization.[9] Rather, the contention is that structural and economic factors provide an important underlay to a rich carpet of political, social and cultural elements of political activism in Thailand.

As Tom Bottomore once observed, the "division of society into classes or strata, which are ranged in a hierarchy of wealth, prestige and power is a prominent and universal feature of social structure".[10] A problem associated with studying class and class conflict in Thailand is that the categories of data collected by official organizations seldom easily translate into class categories. The discussion that follows accepts this problem and focuses on class conflict rather than class war, acknowledging that in each society there are underlying antagonisms born of different and inherently conflicting material positions and, therefore, class interests. In capitalist society, these different material positions are built on exploitation. Rather than engage in debate about class, the initial task of this paper is to detail the data that are available, on poverty, inequality and incomes, before turning to political concerns.

POVERTY

Poverty levels have been studied by the Thai government and Thai and foreign academics for many years and the data are clear. These data show that economic growth since the mid-1950s has had a significant impact on reducing absolute poverty — as measured, however, against absurdly low poverty lines.[11] Table 13.1 shows poverty rates for 1988 and 2004. There have been some bumps along the way — most notably associated with the Asian economic crisis of the late 1990s — but the downward trend is unmistakable. Urban areas have done better than rural areas, but the decline in absolute poverty is marked.

Despite the decline, poverty remains a social issue and a political problem. Depending on the data used, up to seven million Thais still live below the poverty line. Most of those who remain in poverty are rural people, often landless or with small holdings, and having low levels of education. A disproportionate number of these people live in the far South, the North and Northeast of Thailand. According to the UNDP, the highest rates of poverty in 2007 were in Narathiwat, Nan, Buriram, Srisaket and Mae Hong Son Provinces. Significantly, more than 80 per cent of those in poverty in that year were domiciled in the northern and northeastern regions.[12]

Table 13.1
Poverty in Thailand

Year	*Urban*	*Rural*	*Nationwide*
1988	25.2%	52.9%	44.9
2004	4.9%	14.3%	11.3

Source: Peter Warr, "The Economy Under the Thaksin Government: Stalled Recovery", in *Divided Over Thaksin*, edited by John Funston (Singapore: ISEAS, 2009), p. 164.

INCOME

Poverty and income are obviously related, with poverty decreasing in Thailand as incomes have risen. Income data are also readily available, and for a long period, in the regular household surveys undertaken by the National Statistical Office (NSO). Table 13.2 indicates the increases in average monthly household income levels for Thailand as a whole since 1975/76. But national averages hide provincial differences. In 2007, the national average was 18,660 baht, but in Bangkok it was nearly twice this figure at 35,007 baht. In the North and Northeast, it was 13,568 and 12,995 baht, respectively. In other words, in 2007, average incomes in the North and Northeast were roughly one-third of those in Bangkok. In that year, the highest average household income was in Bangkok, with households there earning almost five times more than in the lowest-ranking province, Mae Hong Son in the North.[13] With regard to later data in this chapter, it is worth keeping in mind that average incomes in nine of the 14 southern provinces exceed the national average. Fifteen provinces had average incomes of less than two-thirds of the nation-wide average in 2007: one in the South, five in the North and nine in the Northeast.

But even provincial averages obscure important income differences. The NSO's 2007 household survey reveals that the national average per capita income for the poorest 10 per cent of the population was just 1,001 baht per month. In the North it was 872 baht, and in the Northeast a meagre 797 baht.

Table 13.2
Average Monthly Household Income (in Baht), Selected Years, 1975/76–2007

Year	*Income*
1975/6	1,928
1981	3,378
1986	3,631
1990	5,625
1996	10,779
2000	12,150
2007	18,660

Source: National Statistical Office, Thailand, Household Socio-economic Survey 2000 and 2007.

A crucial and related statistic shows that, since 1960, the trend has been for capital's share of GDP to increase, with a decline for labour's share (with labour defined broadly as non-owners). Generally, this period has also seen increases in labour productivity accrue to capital in the form of increased profits. Since 2000, the average profit rate in Thailand has increased from about 5 per cent to almost 11 per cent. This pattern is true for the manufacturing sector, where productivity increases have been greatest, as it is for the economy as a whole. Economists show that the increase in profit rate is essentially divorced from increases in expenditures on equipment, construction and gross fixed capital formation. Essentially, then, the increase in the profit rate has come from squeezing workers out of their share in income derived from increases in labour productivity. In other words, there has been a redistribution of income from labour to capital.[14]

INEQUALITY

Thailand's record of poverty reduction and rising incomes has not seen inequality reduced, as the already well off have enjoyed greater increases in income than other Thais. That the persistence of inequality is a public-policy problem and a political issue has not always been recognized. In 1999, for example, in the teeth of the Asian economic crisis, John Ravenhill chastised this author for identifying "unequal distribution of income as the major problem threatening Thailand's growth".[15] Ravenhill was remarkably short-sighted. During the 1997–1998 economic crisis, income and wealth inequality were identified in World Bank, United Nations Development Program (UNDP) and other national and international reports as a major drag on Thailand's development.

Inequality is not a new political issue. Even in the heyday of consistent economic growth in the 1970s and 1980s, income inequality increased in Thailand. Figure 13.1 shows an unmistakable trend for the already rich to take an ever larger share of income while the share for the poor is reduced. Some argue that while the income share of the poor has been reduced, incomes have nevertheless risen. This is true. However, as noted above, average per capita income for Thailand's poorest remain abysmally low.

Thailand's Gini coefficient has also worsened, from about 0.4 in the 1960s to 0.5 and above in the period since the mid-1980s. In this period, the ratio of incomes received by the top 20 per cent of earners has been 12–14 times that of the bottom 20 per cent. According to the UNDP, this pattern is inconsistent with regional trends in Southeast Asia.[16]

These patterns are reproduced in other measures of wealth. Figures from official surveys in 2007 show that the top 10 per cent of families controlled 51.32 per cent of wealth, while the bottom 50 per cent only controlled 8.5 per cent. For land, houses and other assets, a similar pattern of inequality is seen. In many parts of the country, big landowners now control significant portions of land. For example, in Bangkok, Phuket, Samut Prakan and Pathum Thani, the biggest fifty landowners control between 10 and 14 per cent of all land.[17]

Amongst the wealthiest landholders is the royal family, or the monarchy. Indeed, it owns what is arguably the largest business conglomerate in the country, with the assets of its Crown Property

Figure 13.1
Income Distribution Trends, Selected Years, 1975/76–2008

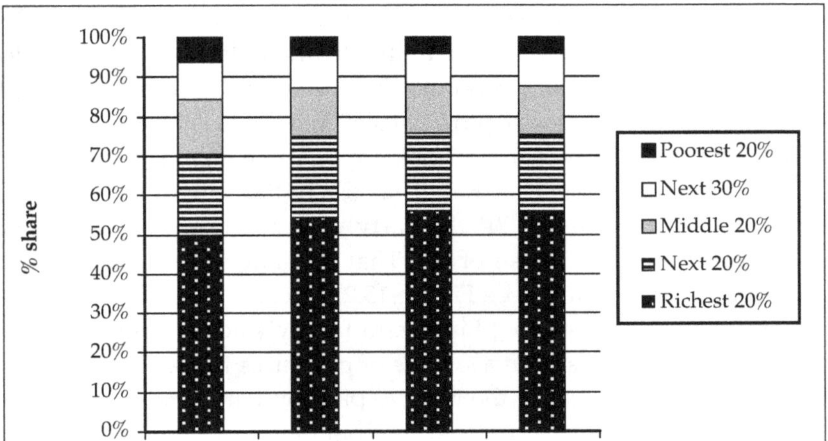

Source: NSO Household Socio-economic Surveys as analyzed by the National Economic and Social Development Board.

Bureau (CPB) alone worth some US$41 billion in 2005. Of that, about US$38 billion was in property, concentrated in Bangkok and surrounding provinces.[18] While it held about $3 billion in shares in 2005, the CPB was not ranked in *Kanngoen thanakhan* magazine's yearly list of the 500 largest shareholding families at the stock exchange. The family ranked highest in 2005 was the Shinawatra family, with just under $1 billion in holdings.[19]

Shareholding and business concentration is important, for in the analysis that the World Bank conducted following the post-1997 economic crisis, it came to the startling conclusion that the source of inequality was to be found in *profits*: "even though non-farm profits ... constitute only 22% of total income, their contribution to overall income inequality is ... 56%".[20] And profits in Thailand have increasingly been monopolized by the largest businesses. In 2000, the largest 20 per cent of firms gained 81 per cent of the income, and this figure rose to 86.3 per cent in 2008.[21]

VOTING PATTERNS

As indicated above, making direct correlations between political mobilization and official economic data is fraught with problems. So I will simply present the available, admittedly blunt, data on recent political events. The manner in which politics has been polarized means that, to determine support for broad "pro-Thaksin" and "anti-Thaksin" coalitions, voting patterns from recent elections are of some significance.

Thaksin formed his Thai Rak Thai (TRT) Party in 1998, and in its first election campaign in 2001 the party very nearly won a majority of the seats in the lower house of the Thai parliament. A spatial pattern in the voting was evident (see Figure 13.2). Clearly, TRT was supported strongly in the North — the Shinawatra family's home base — in most parts of the Northeast and in a swathe of provinces in the Central Plains. The post-election merger of the New Aspiration Party and several other small parties with TRT meant that its dominance in the Northeast was soon extended. It should not be forgotten that TRT received strong support in Bangkok. The lack of support in the South, except in the southernmost provinces, is explained by the long dominance of the Democrat Party apparatus in that region.

Figure 13.2
Voting Patterns, by Party, 2001

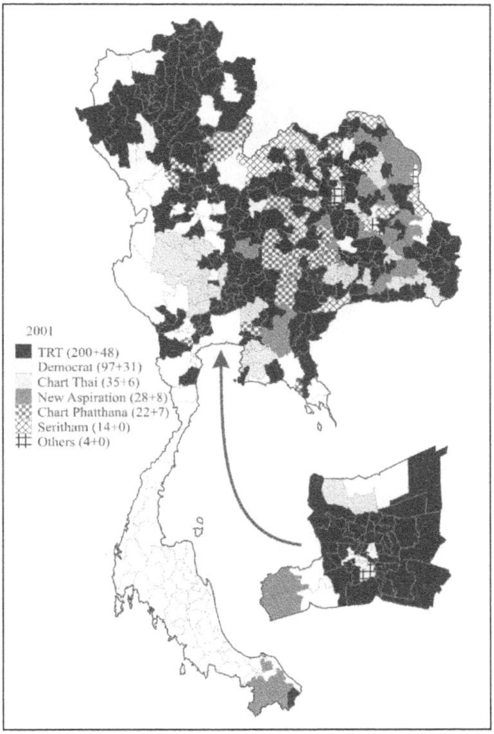

By the time of the 2005 election, the TRT government had been in power for a full term and had set its signature policies in place. These were widely popular, and the result was that the TRT won a landslide, taking 377 of the 500 seats in the lower house of parliament. The next largest party, the Democrat Party, took 97 seats. In the North, TRT gained 71 of 76 seats. In the Northeast, it took 126 of 136 seats, 80 of the 97 contests in the Central Plains, and 32 of 37 in Bangkok. The lack of support in the South continued; TRT took just one of the 54 seats in that region. That the 2005 polls were such a landslide means that their results do not show a spatial pattern, except for the most obvious split between places south of Bangkok and those north and east of the capital (see Figure 13.3).

Figure 13.3
Voting Patterns, by Party, 2005

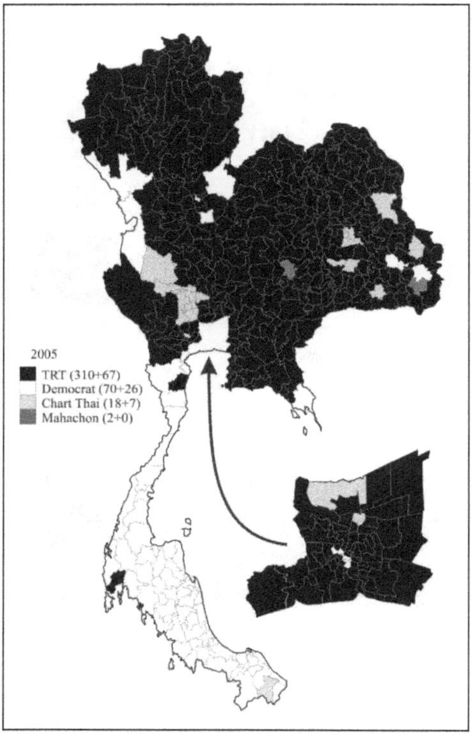

Of course, in September 2006, Thaksin was ousted in a military coup that followed the snap poll that he called in April 2006. As the Democrat Party and several other parties boycotted the election, we can skip those results. The next voting opportunity came when the military-appointed government held a referendum on its new constitution in 2007. The use of government and military resources to promote a "yes" vote was enormous, and the repression of those opposed to the military's constitution significant. Even so, because there was opposition, the spatial pattern of voting gives further evidence of political division.

In Figure 13.4, it is the lighter colours that indicate support for the "no" campaign. It has to be added that some who opposed the draft charter voted for it on the basis of repeated military and government

Figure 13.4
Voting Patterns, Constitutional Referendum, 2007

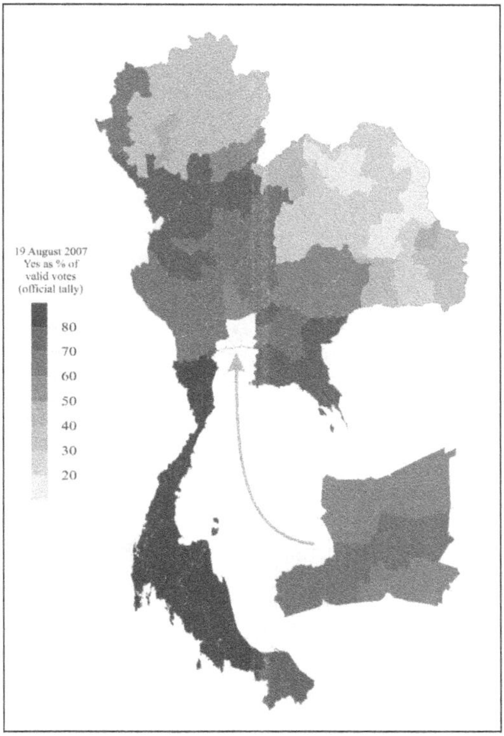

statements that accepting the draft would mean an early election and that the elected government could amend the constitution.

It is evident that those who were prepared to challenge the military and its government were overwhelmingly in the North and Northeast. The strongest support for the military's constitution was in the Democrat Party-dominated South.

The next opportunity to vote was in the 2007 election. By this time, Thaksin faced multiple criminal and corruption investigations and charges, 111 members of the TRT had been banned from politics, TRT had been dissolved by court order, and the power of the military and its appointed government was ranged against the pro-Thaksin proxy People's Power Party (PPP).

Figure 13.5
Voting Patterns, 2007 Election

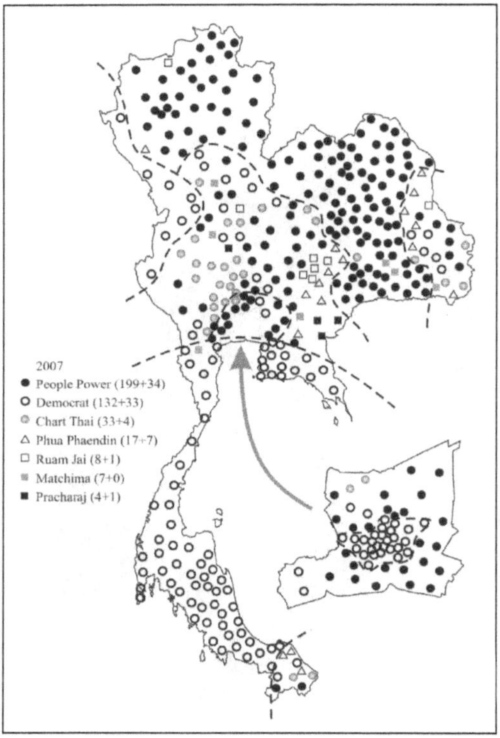

Figure 13.5 indicates the results of those polls, which saw the PPP emerge as the party with the highest number of seats. Despite considerable interference and manoeuvring by its opponents, PPP was able to form a coalition government. Figure 13.5 is different from those for 2001 and 2005, as provinces were clustered into different regional groupings and the voting system had changed under the junta's constitution. Nonetheless, the regional pattern remains clear.

PPP was supported strongly in the North and Northeast, and the Democrat Party was strongly supported in the South (except the deep South). PPP also had a number of constituencies supporting it in the Central Plains, while Bangkok was ringed by PPP seats. The commercial heart of the city voted overwhelmingly for the Democrat Party. This

Figure 13.6
Provinces Under Emergency Rule, May 2010

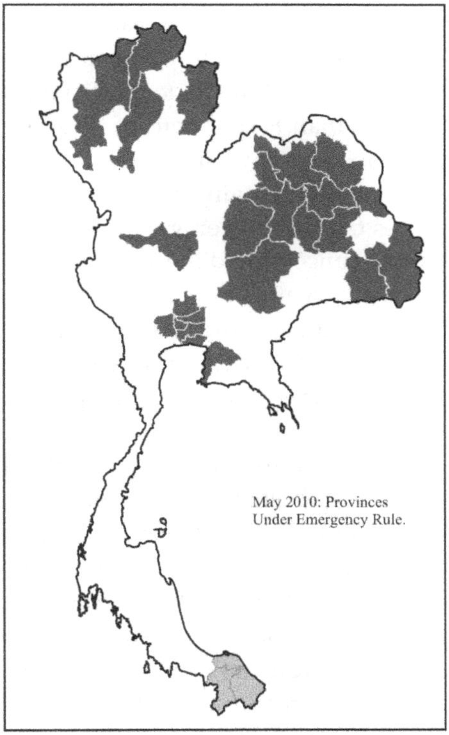

ringing corresponds with the pattern of factory development and working class dormitory suburbs that surround central Bangkok.

For the period from 2001 to 2007, the voting patterns are clear and an underlying spatial pattern apparent: there was (and remains) strong and sustained support for the "pro-Thaksin" group of parties in the North, the Northeast, a string of Central Plains provinces and the outer suburbs of Bangkok. Just to make the point even clearer, Figure 13.6 shows the provinces put under emergency rule by the Abhisit government following the crackdown on Red Shirts on 19 May 2010. Bangkok and surrounding provinces, the Northeast and the North again figure prominently. (The far southern provinces have been under emergency rule since 2005).

CLASS AND POLITICS?

This paper has so far presented data on incomes, poverty, inequality and voting patterns with a focus on those at the bottom levels of Thai society. To summarize: *absolute poverty* has been greatly reduced. Up to seven million people still live below the low official poverty line, mostly in rural areas, with more than 80 per cent of these in the northern and northeastern regions. Incomes have increased, but average incomes in the North and the Northeast remain only about one-third of those in Bangkok. The provinces that have average incomes of just two-thirds the national average are also concentrated in the same regions. Inequality has generally worsened, has been attributed to the distribution of profit; it is seen in incomes, wealth and land and asset ownership. Voting patterns show sustained support for the broad "pro-Thaksin" group of parties in the North, the Northeast, some Central Plains provinces and the outer suburbs of Bangkok.

The spatial overlap on these data is remarkable and is further emphasized by the UNDP data showing that the 2007 average per capita gross provincial product in provinces that voted for the Democrat Party was 221,130 baht per year and the corresponding figure provinces that supported the PPP was just 92,667 baht per year.[22]

This overlap of economic indicators with voting patterns does not mean that there is also political mobilization. At the very least, as the UNDP report stated, "it is difficult to contend that inequality is not a contributing background factor" in recent political conflict.[23] More than this, though, low incomes, skewed ownership of assets and the siphoning of income to the already wealthy indicate an embedded pattern of exploitation in Thailand. It is true that there has been income inequality in Thai society over a long period of time. The point, however, is that there appears to have been a worsening of exploitation as inequality has deepened and the pace of income shifts has accelerated.

It is reasonable to assume that those who are economically exploited are aware of their predicament. They have missed out on the gains from growth and have seen their relative shares of income, wealth and land ownership reduced and productivity gains snatched away. This awareness may be expressed in various ways. When voting is permitted, those subject to exploitation may support political parties perceived as having programmes that support their interests. It is a reasonable supposition that rural-based voters in the North, the Northeast, and parts of the Central Plains and workers around Bangkok did this when they repeatedly chose pro-Thaksin parties. Support for the "pro-Thaksin" camp has been strong in the very same areas in which incomes are low and poverty most evident.

At the same time, as Nidhi Eowseewong has recently pointed out, it is equally understandable that those who thought that they were being disadvantaged by those same policies, or who found them politically repugnant, should support the PAD and the 19 September 2006 coup and vote for the Democrat Party.[24]

As Nidhi suggests, linking these economic factors with political mobilization relies mostly on anecdotal evidence. The only data that he can cite shows that PAD protestors were more likely to be within the social security system than Red Shirts, suggesting the former are wealthier. That said, the anecdotal evidence is strong in pointing to major support for the Red Shirt protestors among rural and working class people. Even if that evidence is rejected, the existing data are sufficient to confirm that there is an underlying disparity, based in economic exploitation, that provides an underlay to political mobilization.

Relations of exploitation are maintained through political control. The Democrat Party-led coalition government that came to power in late 2008 and its military-appointed predecessor of 2006–07 engaged in repeated acts to protect the state and "national security" — often meaning the monarchy. While the Democrats were defeated in the elections of 2001, 2005 and 2007, their strongholds are in the South — a relatively wealthy region — and the affluent parts of Bangkok. It also has obvious and strong support from business, the Bangkok middle class and the traditional elite. Defending its government, the state and the symbols of the establishment is portrayed as a response to "terrorism". In fact it is to protect the political and economic status quo through the extensive use of the state's repressive agencies.

Putting all this together, it may be a stretch to refer to the Red Shirt uprising of March–May 2010 as a class war, but the underlying data and the anecdotal evidence suggest that there is good reason to agree with the characterization of Red Shirts across the country as supported by people who have long understood economic disadvantage and exploitation. To deny this reality is to ignore too much. To say that the Red Shirt uprising may not have been a "simple" class struggle is undoubtedly an understatement; this paper has not addressed the issues of status, hierarchy, repression, corruption, double standards, educational disadvantage, ethnicity, and more. These issues can be related to class location, for class inequality has impacts on a range of other inequalities. Even Prime Minister Abhisit's government seems to agree, for the second point in its "reconciliation road map" of 2010 recognized that the "current conflict ... is in fact based on injustices that exist in society and its economic system".[25]

Notes

1. Kasit's claims, also stated in official Ministry of Foreign Affairs releases, are in an interview with Spiegal Online, 15 July 2010 <http://www.spiegel.de/international/world/0,1518,706552,00.html> (accessed 22 July 2010).
2. UDD/No. Pho. Cho., *Kham tham lae kham top rueang no. pho. cho. daeng thang phaendin* [Questions and answers about the UDD-Red in the land] (Bangkok, 28 April 2010); available at <http://picasaweb.google.co.uk/103657339709676300673/UDDQA28April2010#> (accessed 7 March 2011), p. 4.
3. Jason Szep and Ambika Ahuja, "Thai Protesters Hunker Down for Long Battle". *Washington Post,* 2 April 2010 <http://www.washingtonpost.com/wp-dyn/content/article/2010/04/02/AR> (accessed 4 April 2010).
4. Daniel ten Kate, "Thailand's poor irked by a privileged leader", *Sydney Morning Herald,* 10 April 2010.
5. Editorial, "Thailand Needs Fresh Elections", *Irish Times,* 14 April 2010 <http://www.irishtimes.com/newspaper/opinion/2010/0414/12242682979> (accessed 14 April 2010).
6. Aung Zaw, "Chaos in Thailand", *The Irrawaddy,* May 2010 <http://www.irrawaddy.org/print_article.php?art_id=18396> (accessed 7 May 2010).
7. Cited in Banyan, "Bloody Shirts in the City of Angels", *The Economist,* 22 April 2010 <http://www.economist.com/node/15955366> (accessed 1 May 2010). This position later received the support of Nobel Laureate Amartya Sen, who was reported in *The Nation* (21 July 2010, <http://www.nationmultimedia.com/home/apps/print.php?newsid=30134219> (accessed 21 July 2010) as saying: "he did not know enough about Thailand to describe or explain its troubles as a class war. But there must be something more to the conflict when the poor happen to be led by the richest man in the country..." Sen is factually wrong — the richest person in the country is the king. The notion that social movements and class struggles cannot be joined or even led by those with wealth is a fallacy.

8. See S. Crispin, "Fortress Bangkok Targets Business", *Asia Times Online*, 23 April 2010 <http://www.atimes.com/atimes/Southeast_Asia/LD23Ae01.html> (accessed 23 April 2010); and Kraisak Choonhavan, "Thailand: A Class Struggle?" *The Irrawaddy*, 1 May 2010 <http://www.irrawaddy.org/opinion_story.php?art_id=18361> (accessed 4 May 2010).
9. For example, on mobilization, see G. Shatkin, *Collective Action and Urban Poverty Alleviation* (Aldershot: Ashgate, 2007). For one of the attempts to assess political orientation, see the contribution of Ammar Siamwalla and Somchai Jitsuchon to this volume, "The Socio-economic Bases of the Red/Yellow Divide: A Statistical Analysis". This contribution concludes that "there is no substantial difference in the social backgrounds of people who support the Red and Yellow points of view". This conclusion seems incongruous when the authors also state, "There is a clear tendency for better-off people to be Yellow..." Just to confuse readers a little more, the authors add: "... the identification of the Reds with the poor is a myth."
10. T. Bottomore, *Classes in Modern Society* (London: George Allen & Unwin: 1965), p. 11.
11. In 2007, one official poverty line was 1,443 baht per person per month. The minimum wage, variable by province, was about 140 baht per day at the time. Hence, the poverty line was about one-third of the minimum wage.
12. UNDP, *Thailand Human Development Report 2009: Human Security, Today and Tomorrow* (Bangkok: United Nations Development Programme, 2010), pp. 123, 151–52.
13. Ibid., p. 123.
14. See Alain Mounier and Voravidh Charoenloet, "New Challenges for Thailand: Labour and Growth after the Crisis", *Journal of Contemporary Asia* 40, no. 1 (February 2010): 123–43.
15. John Ravenhill, review of *The Political Economy of Southeast Asia: An Introduction*, *The Journal of Economic Literature* 37, no. 3 (September 1999): 1212.
16. TDRI, *Thailand Economic Information Kit* (Bangkok: Thailand Development Research Institute, 2004), p. 20; UNDP, *Thailand Human Development Report 2009*, p. 79.
17. The data are from a draft paper by Duangmanee Laowakun, "*Kan krachuk dua khong khwammangkhang nai sangkhom thai*" [The Concentration of Wealth in Thai Society], presented at a seminar at Chulalongkorn University, 8 March 2010.
18. Porphant Ouyyanont, "The Crown Property Bureau in Thailand and the Crisis of 1997," *Journal of Contemporary Asia* 38, no. 1 (February 2008): 166–89; see pp. 183–84.
19. *Kan ngoen thanakhan* [Money and Banking], December 2009, p. 212.

20. World Bank, *Social Monitor VI: Poverty and Public Policy* (Bangkok: The World Bank Thailand Mission, 2001), p. 30.
21. Nidhi Eoseewong, "*Suea lueang pen khrai lae ok ma thammai*", [Who are the yellow shirts and why did they come out?], *Mathichon* daily, 5 July 2010.
22. UNDP, p. 78.
23. Ibid.
24. Nidhi Eoseewong, "*Suea lueang*".
25. Ministry of Foreign Affairs, Thailand, "PM proposes five-point roadmap for reconciliation towards elections by year-end", 4 May 2010 <http://www.mfa.go.th/internet/news/35058.doc> (accessed 6 July 2010).

14

THAILAND'S ROCKY PATH TOWARDS A FULL-FLEDGED DEMOCRACY

Kasit Piromya

INTRODUCTION

The events on the streets of Bangkok during March–May 2010, or rather during 2006–10, must have made many people, foreigners and Thais alike, wonder what went wrong with Thailand — a country once known in the West as Southeast Asia's "beacon of democracy". It would be naïve to try to answer this using the *coup d'état* that ousted an elected, but highly corrupt, prime minister in 2006 as the starting point of all that has seemingly led Thailand astray, or to argue that only elections could reignite the country's democratic fire.

Most democratic societies around the world have gone through sometimes traumatic democratization processes of their own. Thailand is no exception, as it goes through another tumultuous chapter in the story of its democratic development, a story that began nearly eight decades ago.

MOVING TOWARDS LIBERAL DEMOCRACY

During the latter half of the twentieth century, Thailand had a fair share of intermittent coups, military or authoritarian governments, short-lived yet democratically elected coalition administrations, and revolts against dictatorial regimes. The Black May public uprising in 1992 ushered in a period of serious political reform and led to the 1997 constitution, generally known as the "People's Constitution" because of its drafters' extensive direct engagement with the public.

The 1997 constitution recognized more rights and freedoms than any previous Thai constitution. It was designed to create greater transparency, with a strong system of checks and balances and provisions to open the political process to greater public participation, especially on the part of civil society organizations. Its provisions also aimed at creating stronger political institutions and decentralizing administrative power. They were poised to make far-reaching reforms in the quality of Thailand's democracy, especially by ending the cycle of corrupt politicians' exploitation of the state for personal interests.

With the adoption of the 1997 constitution, Thai society was upbeat, optimistic that liberal democracy had won and that decades of authoritarianism, money politics, and corrupt and unstable coalition governments would be a thing of the past. It witnessed greater political participation on the part of civil society, contributing to the vibrancy of political life, and greater decentralization, following a process that today sees local authorities elected by the people. There was greater openness, and the media could operate with freedom from intimidation. Thailand had really become a "beacon of democracy," despite its economic troubles in the wake of the Asian Financial Crisis.

THE ONSLAUGHT OF ILLIBERAL DEMOCRACY

It was at this juncture that Thaksin Shinawatra, a telecommunications tycoon, came onto the Thai political scene. Indeed, it is not Thaksin but rather what he represents, as made evident through his actions, that really matters and that in fact turned the tide of Thailand's democratization process.

After leading his Thai Rak Thai Party (TRT) to victory in the 2001 elections, it did not take Prime Minister Thaksin long to demonstrate his disdain for the letter and spirit of the 1997 constitution or to set out to change the fundamental structure of Thai politics in the direction of single-party autocracy.

First, Thaksin sought to achieve total dominance over party politics by gobbling up smaller parties into a grand coalition that eventually included a total of 364 of the 480 members of Thailand's House of Representatives. He achieved this end by exploiting constitutional provisions originally designed to enable Thailand to overcome its painful experience of weak civilian governments. The House of Representatives — the lower house of parliament — was thus marginalized, as the opposition's formal actions were blocked, and it became impossible to muster the requisite number of votes to launch a censure motion against the prime minister during the entirety of his administration. In a show of his disregard for parliamentary rule, Thaksin rarely attended parliament except for major occasions, sessions were regularly abandoned for lack of quorum, and the TRT government passed several critical measures by executive decree rather than legislation.

Second, the independence of watch-dog agencies and of Thailand's Senate was greatly undermined. Although the Senate — the upper house of the Thai parliament — was supposed to be a critical part of the 1997 constitution's system of checks and balances, it was packed with the wives, children, and associates of politicians, as well as with a large contingent of former government officials with close ties to the ruling party. The situation grew so dire that journalists denounced the upper house as "an assembly of slaves". The state of the constitutional oversight bodies, including the Election Commission and the National Anti-Corruption Commission, was not much better, for their members were appointed by the pro-government Senate.

Third, criticism was muzzled, as Thaksin set about to control the media through intimidation and financial means. Local NGOs documented a string of cases in which news editors and journalists in both the print and broadcast sectors were dismissed or transferred, or had their work tampered with, to appease the government. Libel suits with astonishingly high damages claims were routinely used to silence critical voices. Corporate and government advertising was misused to reward media outlets that followed the government line and to punish those that dared to criticize Thaksin or his government. Official approval for work permits and visa renewals and threats of deportation became the government's tools for pressuring foreign journalists working in Thailand. Both Thaksin himself and a number of his associates owned or bought major stakes in many of Thailand's media outlets. In 2004, Human Rights Watch concluded that Thaksin had been able to monopolize public opinion to the extent that this enabled him to do "many things that military dictators in the past could only accomplish through brute force".[1]

Never a true believer in democracy, Thaksin once remarked that "Democracy is just a tool, not our goal", and in his speeches during the 2005 electoral campaign, he would often say that the rule of law, democracy and human rights were not important because they often got in the way of "working for the people". He described criticism by the press or the opposition as "destructive" and suggested to his constituents that making him into a powerful executive would deliver them greater benefit.

While it is true that Thaksin generated real popular support with social programmes aimed at the rural poor, his populism was also a cover for corruption, cronyism, and profiteering. During the period of his rule, laws and rules were manipulated to favour his businesses, boosting their market value by three times in four years according to some estimates. On 26 February 2010, the Criminal Division for Political Office-Holders of Thailand's Supreme Court delivered a ruling on the confiscation of Thaksin's assets worth some 46.3 billion baht (US$1.4 billion). It found that he acquired these assets inappropriately, through acts constituting a conflict between personal and public interests.

As authoritarianism, corruption, nepotism, and human rights abuses flourished under Thaksin's rule, and with parliament unable to provide any recourse, the frustrations of large segments of the population reached a boiling point in late 2005. These frustrations subsequently led those groups to take to the streets. The anti-Thaksin movement was huge; hundreds of thousands of people took part in a series of demonstrations in Bangkok and elsewhere, led by a coalition called the People's Alliance for Democracy (PAD). The PAD, at the time, brought together groups that could be described as an urban elite or conservatives and groups made up of social movements, trade unions, and non-governmental organizations with a grass-roots base, such as workers, farmers, teachers, and students.

For the first time during Thaksin's period in government, a mass movement had emerged to articulate different criticisms against him at the same place and time. These criticisms included those related to corruption, massive tax evasion, free trade agreements, efforts to curb freedom of media, disrespect for the monarchy, and violence in the South. A range of ideas for political reform linked to the demands of rural people in such areas as land reform, alternative agriculture, and community-controlled natural resource management was also voiced. Although the unified calls for Thaksin's resignation emanating from various sectors of society had accumulated to a critical mass, it was clear that Thaksin would not bow to popular pressure, and he began to mobilize his own supporters.

As it became increasingly evident that the conflict between rivals and supporters of Thaksin would sink deeper into violence, the Thai Army staged a *coup d'état* on 19 September 2006. Other reasons given by the coup leaders were corruption, the abuse of power, interference with the system of political checks and balances, human rights violations, and destruction of national unity.

After the coup, a new constitution was drafted with the aim of doing away with money politics, promoting good governance, and strengthening democracy where it counts most — in the areas of accountability, the rule of law, respect for human rights, and public participation. Thailand's 2007 constitution encourages ethics and transparency and predictability in policy processes and obviously includes a stringent set of rules against election fraud.

With the constitution approved by a majority of voters on 19 August 2007 in Thailand's first-ever national referendum, general elections were held on 23 December 2007. The People's Power Party (PPP), a successor party of Thaksin's TRT, won the highest number of seats — but fell short of a parliamentary majority. It formed a coalition government, but in the following year the party came under fire when its deputy leader faced charges of electoral fraud. These charges led to the PPP's dissolution by the verdict of the Constitutional Court on 2 December 2008. Subsequently, former PPP members of parliament joined the Phuea Thai Party, which had been established in anticipation of the PPP's dissolution. On 15 December 2008, Thailand's parliament elected Abhisit Vejjajiva the country's new prime minister, after former coalition partners of the PPP decided to support a coalition led by Mr Abhisit's Democrat Party.

PROTESTS-*CUM*-ARMED INSURRECTION

After the Democrats were able to form a government, the National United Front for Democracy against Dictatorship (UDD), commonly known as the Red Shirts, was mobilized to pave the way for Thaksin's return to power and to nullify criminal convictions against him. After their protests in April 2009 failed to bring down the government, the Red Shirts resumed their protests in March 2010, shortly after the Supreme Court ruled against Thaksin in a case that led to the seizure of a considerable share of his long-frozen assets.

As its protests gained momentum, the UDD sought to distance itself from Thaksin; his association with the movement had begun to undermine its legitimacy. Moreover, the objective of bringing back Thaksin had not been well accepted in Thai society. The UDD therefore changed its tactics. Thaksin's phone-ins became less frequent, and the narrative of the protests shifted to a Marxist-Leninist interpretation of Thailand, employing the rhetoric of class conflict. The UDD also drummed up the issue of the legitimacy of the Abhisit government, even though that government had come to power through exactly the same procedures as the previous two UDD-allied administrations.

The rhetoric of class — stressing the ideas of a rich-poor, urban-rural divide in Thai society and of class war — did resonate well with the Red Shirt protestors and their supporters in the media and academia. It gave apparent justification to the UDD's cause, even though it in no way reflected the reality in Thailand. Although social and economic disparities do exist in the country, over the years Thai society has become more urban and egalitarian. It has come to feature a growing middle class. Aristocratic titles were eliminated a long time ago, and there exists a high level of social mobility, as anyone can climb from lower to higher social strata. Indeed, recent Thai prime ministers include men who came from simple, underprivileged backgrounds, such as Mr Banharn Silpa-acha and Mr Chuan Leekphai.

Comparatively, the level of income disparity in Thailand is also no different from that of other developing countries, especially other ASEAN members, as measured by the Gini coefficient and by the ratio of the income or expenditure of the richest 10 per cent to that of the poorest 10 per cent of the population, according to the United Nations Development Programme. In fact, according to the latest statistics, the gap between the richest 10 per cent and the poorest 10 per cent of the population in certain developed countries, such as the United States and the United Kingdom, is greater than that in Thailand.

The most worrying aspect of the UDD protests of April and May 2010 was the presence of professionally trained and well financed armed elements that used lethal weapons, sometimes indiscriminately, against both security personnel and the general public. When the UDD accepted Prime Minister Abhisit's reconciliation plan, which included the offer of elections in November 2010 in exchange for an end to the demonstrations, Thaksin interfered. His interference caused the UDD leadership to back out of its agreement with the premier and continue protesting. The hard-core elements of the UDD had successfully hijacked the movement and were determined to bring down the government through violent means.

While these armed elements were provoking and causing violence, the opposition parties and protest leaders were drawing attention from local and foreign media and the diplomatic corps in an effort to put the blame for the violence on the government and state security forces. Some media allied to the UDD continued to manipulate and incite hatred, violence, and divisions among the people through hate speech and disinformation.

Thaksin remained deeply involved in these activities. He continuously provided the UDD with support, covertly and overtly, manoeuvring from overseas. He had played a similar role during the riots in April 2009. On 25 May 2010, the Criminal Court — having considered evidence and witnesses from both the authorities' and Thaksin's sides — found that there was sufficient evidence to issue an arrest warrant against Thaksin on a charge related to terrorism in accordance with the Thai Criminal Code.

The UDD protests, which ended on 19 May 2010, numbered as one of the two armed insurrections aim at overthrowing a legitimate government that Thailand has confronted in its decades of democratic development. The first insurrection was the struggle of the Communist Party of Thailand (CPT) during the Cold War, between the early 1960s and the mid-1970s. This insurrection was waged in the jungles. Some of the most important UDD leaders, acting as strategists, were former members of the CPT. They have adapted Marxist-Leninist rhetoric and tactics to their current movement. The only major difference between these two events was probably that the battle had moved from the jungles to the streets of Bangkok.

REFORM AND RECONCILIATION

On 19 May 2010 Thailand thus saw the "sea of fire" of which some UDD leaders had spoken on stage at their rallies. The losses and damages that occurred were regrettable and demanded investigation. In this regard, an independent fact-finding commission was set up and started working to uncover the facts about the violent incidents that occurred and the circumstances surrounding the political problems that confronted Thai society so as to provide remedies.

In the aftermath of this tragic episode, Thailand has the opportunity to prove to itself and the world the strength of its national character and its commitment to promoting reconciliation to overcome the deep divisions that exist in its society. These divisions are not about "classes" but rather about perceptions and beliefs. For Thais themselves, this is an opportunity to reflect on what needs to be done and what reforms to undertake to strengthen further the fundamentals of democracy, sustainable development, and social harmony.

The reconciliation plan proposed by Prime Minister Abhisit Vejjajiva was aimed not only at bridging these divides, but also at addressing their underlying causes. These causes include the problem of the revered institution of monarchy being drawn into the political conflict by various groups; the problem of disparities and economic and social injustices that have long plagued the country; the problem of the media being manipulated to incite hatred and violence; the problem of apprehension, which requires that facts be established about the violent events that transpired; and the problem of various political rules which remain highly contested.

The reconciliation process has been underway since the protests ended. Mechanisms or committees driving each of the plan's main components were set up. Thais have been called upon to join and take ownership in moving the process forward, particularly with regard to efforts to address grievances — including economic disparities, poverty and social injustices — that have existed in Thai society for far too long. These grievances partly caused people to take to the streets. This reform process will be an inclusive, participatory, and civil society-driven undertaking. The reform committees are chaired by respected former Prime Minister Anan Panyarachun and by Dr Prawet Wasi, both recipients of the Ramon Magsaysay Award for their service to society. After gathering views from the people, identifying and prioritizing needs, and considering how to resolve these problems, they will recommend both short- and longer-term strategies and plans of action for the government's consideration and implementation over a period of three years — a period extending beyond the term of the Abhisit government.

Another important dimension of reform has to do with the media — a process spearheaded by the media themselves. This process of reform is important because, over the past few years, some media have become tools used to incite violence and hatred. The aim of media reform is to enable the media to serve as a mechanism for constructive communication among Thais and to contribute to healing the divisions in the society while ensuring media freedom.

As for Thailand's democratic development, we have seen that reforms put in place through the 1997 constitution were not continued or consolidated because of the misfortune that the first elections held under that reformist constitution brought in a government that exploited its loopholes to ensure autocratic rule. While there is no doubt that democracy remains important for the Thai people, democracy means different things to different people. Emphasis has at times been focused on the institutional forms of democracy rather than on its substance.

The events of April and May 2010 underlined the need for Thai society at large to try to find ways to ensure, among other things, that different political views can co-exist and that political differences can be resolved through democratic means — not through extra-constitutional means like military intervention or violence; that our system can respond more effectively to the needs of people; and that the Thai populace has a deeper understanding of the ideals and principal values of democracy such as the importance of the rule of law, good governance, accountability, and respect for human rights. It is when we achieve these, rather than simply when we hold elections, that Thailand will truly and sustainably become a beacon of democracy.

CONCLUSION

History has shown that Thai society has always tried to move beyond the scourge both of its authoritarian past and of the money politics that has dominated its political life for far too long. The country has succeeded in overcoming the influence of communism, risen against dictatorship, and thwarted moves towards an elected but autocratic government under single-party rule. Through all these ups and downs, the Thai people have demonstrated that they are committed to democracy, and that the type of democracy to which they aspire is one based on principles of liberal democracy with a multi-party, parliamentary system, and a constitutional monarchy.

The resiliency of Thai society makes me, for one, confident that such a democracy will be achieved, sooner rather than later.

Note

1. International Freedom of Expression Exchange, "ALERT: Libel suit against prime minister's critics deepens assault on the press, says Human Rights Watch", 1 September 2004 <http://www.ifex.org/thailand/2004/09/01/libel_suit_against_prime_minister/> (accessed 11 March 2011).

15

THE COLOUR OF POLITICS
Thailand's Deep Crisis of Authority

Charles Keyes

On 19 May 2010, beginning at about four o'clock in the morning (I know the time because I was already on-line watching the tweets), Thai military forces began to position themselves around the Ratchaprasong/Lumphini/Silom area of central Bangkok, where protestors known as the "Red Shirts" had been rallying since 3 April. As the troops tightened the noose, the leaders of the protestors — who now numbered about 3,000 — decided to surrender in order to limit the loss of lives that they realized would happen. Many of the women and children at the protest site had taken refuge in nearby Wat Pathumwanaram. Six people, including a nurse, were shot at the temple. With these deaths, the total number of those killed in the conflict between 10 April and 19 May was

---

The first version of this paper was presented at a seminar organized by the University of Washington Southeast Asia Center on 7 June 2010. A revised version was presented at a seminar at the University of Lund, Sweden, on 31 August 2010. I am grateful to Jane Keyes and Nicholas Keyes for comments on that version and to those who participated in the seminars for their reactions.

officially pegged at eighty-seven.[1] Of these, eleven were soldiers, and the others were civilians.[2] The total number injured was at least 1,800, the majority of them civilians.

After the military moved to end the protest rally, a number of hard-core followers of the Red Shirts, clearly following advance planning, set fire to buildings in the central business district, with the greatest destruction being at the Central World Plaza of Bangkok, the second largest shopping mall in Southeast Asia. Moreover, Red Shirts mobilized followers up-country to attack and burn provincial office buildings in Udon Thani, Khon Kaen, Mukdahan, and Ubon Ratchathani in northeastern Thailand, from which many of the followers of the Red Shirts come. The toll of dead and injured and the destruction of buildings made this the worst civil violence in Thailand's history.

What I wish to do here is first to talk about who the Red Shirt supporters were (and are) and then to discuss the implications of this intense civil conflict. It is my contention that the strong support for the Red Shirts from among those living in and originating from rural northeastern Thailand is indicative of deep division of Thai society that cannot be overcome by the prosecution of the Red Shirt leaders or government "development" programmes that perpetuate the traditional hierarchical relationship between officials and subjects. Northeastern families today have become increasingly "cosmopolitan" because they are linked to a global labour force, have sophisticated understandings of Bangkok society, and yet still retain long-standing resentment for being looked down on as country bumpkins. The quest by northeastern Thais and their kinsmen in working-class jobs in Bangkok for greater recognition of their voices in political decision-making will, thus, continue. I further maintain that so long as the elite in Bangkok and their urban middle class supporters do not extend such recognition in meaningful ways, there can be no genuine "reconciliation".[3]

WHO ARE THE RED SHIRTS?

A large percentage — perhaps a majority if the shouting on the Thai blogosphere is any indication — of middle class Bangkokians believe that the Red Shirts are ignorant peasants who have been bribed or deluded by Thaksin Shinawatra, the very wealthy entrepreneur who served as Thailand's prime minister from 2001 to 2006. Since Thaksin was removed from office by a coup in 2006, subsequently was found guilty *in absentia* of abuse of office and sentenced to two years in jail, and, in 2010, had a large amount of his wealth confiscated as a consequence of a judicial decision, the assumption is that he is using his wealth to fund the Red Shirt movement in order to regain both his wealth and power. Thaksin has been in exile since 2008, but keeps in touch with his followers by e-mail, phone calls, and satellite links. He often addressed the Red Shirt rally from a satellite link that allowed him to appear on screen from the stage at the front of the rally. Some pro-government media and some officials in the government, such as the deputy prime minister in charge of security, Suthep Thaugsuban have also accused Thaksin of seeking to replace the monarchy with a republican system of government. On 25 May the government of Prime Minister Abhisit Vejjajiva brought charges against Thaksin for "terrorism", on the premise that he was responsible for the Red Shirt protests and, especially, for ordering the burning of buildings that followed.

As I wrote in an op-ed piece published on 26 May 2010 in the *Bangkok Post*, "Thaksin has become in [the] eyes [of many] the devil incarnate — a demon-like figure very comparable to the witches in traditional societies who are seen as the causes of all misfortunes and maladies. If only he could be permanently removed from further involvement in Thai politics, they believe, then Thailand could return to a calm, cohesive society." But, I continued, a focus on Thaksin as the *sole* cause of the conflict would be a strategic mistake and "the path to reconciliation will soon lead to a dead end, and further conflict will ensue".[4]

Because Thaksin is from the northern province of Chiang Mai, he has a strong network of support in that region. Several of the visible leaders of the Red Shirt rally in Bangkok were from southern Thailand.[5] The regional roots of such leaders notwithstanding, most of the Red Shirt followers who congregated at the protests sites in Bangkok were from rural northeastern Thailand. A very large percentage of these people were actually working in Bangkok, however.

A primary reason that those opposed to the Red Shirts cannot see beyond Thaksin is that they have almost no first-hand knowledge of the rural world from which most of the Red Shirts have come. Very few middle class Bangkokians have roots in the Thai countryside; rather, many have ancestors who came from rural southeastern China. When middle class Bangkokians think of rural northeastern Thailand, they tend to draw on images of northeasterners that come from films, television programmes, and the mass media. These images tend to be of peasants (*chao na*) who make their living through agriculture and who have only a limited understanding of the larger world. When they appear in the urban world — as in the recent popular film *Ma Nakhon* (Citizen Dog) — they are either depicted as buffoons or as people mystified by the modernities of Bangkok.[6]

Such images are very much at odds with the reality of northeastern Thailand. I have been engaged in long-term research in rural northeastern Thailand since the early 1960s. I have observed the radical transformation in village life in the Northeast. Even in the 1960s, a significant percentage of village men sought temporary work in Bangkok and its vicinity to generate cash income to supplement the agricultural production of their families. By the 1980s most villagers had come to realize that the only way that cash incomes of families could be substantially increased was through non-farm labour. Young unmarried women, who because of the adoption of birth control methods could postpone child-bearing, joined men in seeking temporary work in factories and other venues in the Bangkok area. An increasing number of men also began also to take up contract labour work outside of Thailand.

That very high numbers of villagers from northeastern Thailand have chosen to work for extended periods — often years — away from their natal villages is a consequence of the marked inequality in standards of living between rural communities and Bangkok. This inequality became even more marked as the Thai economy boomed starting in the mid-1980s. This is clearly demonstrated in the United Nation Development Programme report for Thailand for 2009.[7]

Even though most northeastern villagers have found non-farm jobs in Thailand, large numbers of mainly men have been attracted by overseas work — first in the Middle East and then in Taiwan, Singapore, and Japan[8]. An indication of the significance of this overseas contract work appeared in the Bangkok papers just after the Red Shirt rally began in Bangkok. On 19 March, a worker recruited from Thailand was killed in Israel by a rocket fired from the Gaza strip. *The Nation* reported that the Thai who died was one of 30,000 Thais working in Israel.[9] By the early twenty-first century, well over a million workers, overwhelmingly from rural northeastern Thailand, had spent several years each working overseas. It is safe to surmise that the percentage of northeastern villagers with passports is higher than the percentage of Bangkok middle-class Thai.

By the late twentieth or early twenty-first century most people born in villages in northeastern Thailand were dependent more on cash income from work outside the village or from local enterprises such as shops, rice mills, vehicle repair shops, cafes and food stands that had been started with capital from work outside villages than they were on the sale of agricultural products. As a consequence of work experience in Bangkok, elsewhere in Thailand or abroad, those born in villages in northeastern Thailand have come to see themselves as belonging to much larger worlds than those defined by the perimeters of their home communities. Yet most continue to identify as villagers and even as agriculturalists. I have characterized northeasterners today as "cosmopolitan" villagers — that is, people who remain deeply attached to their natal villages and to the cultural and religious traditions of rural society but who also have sophisticated understandings of the global economy and the society of the nation in which they live and work.[10]

The expansion of the horizons of northeastern villagers is also a consequence of exposure to mass media. Since the 1980s, when much of the rural northeast was electrified, villagers have become avid consumers of mass media. Indeed, television ownership in the Northeast is today probably little different than television ownership among urban households. By watching Thai soap operas as well as news reports, northeastern villagers have become even more conscious of the contrast between their lifestyle and that of the urban middle class. Mass media have thus served to intensify for both sides the sense of difference between villagers and middle class urbanites

The new cosmopolitan villagers are not recognized by most middle-class Bangkokians even though they encounter such people on a daily basis as household servants, service workers, shop salespeople, factory workers, and taxi drivers. Rather, they have continued to think of northeasterners as "stupid buffaloes" (a common pejorative during the crisis).

Whereas most Thai officials and political parties have continued to retain a patronizing view of northeasterners, the Thai Rak Thai party founded by Thaksin Shinawatra cultivated a very different relationship with this segment of the Thai population. Thaksin sought to build a mass political party that was based in part on old-style money politics organized through local operatives and in part on offering supporters, especially in northeastern and northern Thailand, government support for locally administered programmes rather than ones that were handled by the bureaucracy — programmes that would also have palpable benefits for these supporters. As Pasuk and Baker have written in their influential biography of Thaksin, "Under the new TRT system, the central government became the source of village funds, agrarian debt relief, cheap health care, OTOP [sub-district-level production] schemes, cheap computers, and other offerings."[11] As this support began to be implemented, northeasterners, northerners, and some others began to enthusiastically embrace Thaksin and the Thai Rak Thai party.

As I myself witnessed while watching the election of 2005 in a village in northeastern Thailand, large numbers of "villagers" now living in Bangkok returned to the Northeast to vote. The roads of the Northeast in early February 2005 were filled with Bangkok taxis, most of which are owned or driven by northeasterners. They brought many other northeasterners back to their "home" villages to vote. As I wrote in my field notes at the time: "Whatever the long-term consequences of this election may be, it is clearly evident from our conversations with villagers that they are very much involved in the political process. This is a radical change not only from forty years ago, but even twenty years ago, when Thai politics was entirely confined to elite groups in Bangkok."[12] In short, while Thaksin's populism was unquestionably self-serving, it also had the consequence of empowering villagers. They were willing to overlook Thaksin's authorization of extrajudicial killings of presumed drug dealers, control of the media, dismissal of civil society organizations, overweening arrogance, and especially use of his power to enhance the wealth of himself and his family, which had become the source of increasing criticism among the urban middle class, non-governmental organization workers, and academics.

By late 2005 this criticism had become increasingly magnified in protest rallies organized by Sonthi Limthongkun, another media magnate, one-time ally of Thaksin, and his equal in projecting self-importance. Sonthi, together with Chamlong Srimuang — a very controversial former major-general who had had a role in putting down the student movement in 1976, ex-mayor of Bangkok, leader of protests against military rule in 1992, prominent lay leader of the schismatic Buddhist movement Santi Asok, and founder of the short-lived Phalang Tham (Dhammic Power) political party — founded the People's Alliance for

Democracy (PAD). The PAD, which subsequently came to be referred to as the "Yellow Shirts" after followers adopted the colour associated with the birthday of King Bhumibol Adulyadej, was initially organized to force Thaksin to resign as prime minister and then, after the coup in September 2006 that did remove him, was regrouped to ensure that Thaksin could never return to power.

Although the Yellow Shirts drew their primary support from the Bangkok middle class, they also had strong support from many in the NGO movement and in labour unions for workers in government-owned industries, two groups that had suffered under Thaksin. United by their common dislike, even hatred, of Thaksin, the Yellow Shirt supporters do not, in fact, constitute a coherent class segment of Thai society. Moreover, they have been given backing by many in the military and in the old royal and bureaucratic elites.

The images following the September 2006 coup, with people in Bangkok offering flowers and welcoming the military forces, suggested that the coup was widely accepted. In retrospect those welcoming the coup were primarily from among Bangkok's middle class — that is, from among those who had supported the PAD's challenge to Thaksin. What was not evident at the time was the very different view held not only by people in northern and northeastern Thailand but also by the large numbers of people especially from the Northeast who now worked in Bangkok. By the end of 2006, opposition to the coup begin to be organized, most significantly by a group who called themselves the United Front for Democracy against Dictatorship (UDD). The UDD would subsequently become better known as the Red Shirts.

Although the government installed by the coup leaders failed to implement policies to end the insurgency in the Malay-Muslim areas of southern Thailand or to advance the economic interests of the country, it did succeed in instituting legal actions against Thaksin and the Thai Rak Thai Party. Both Thaksin and the leaders of the Thai Rak Thai were banned from participation in politics for five years, thus causing Thai Rak Thai itself to be abolished. As the coup leaders had set aside the constitution of 1997 — the so-called "People's Constitution," which was the most democratic in Thai history — the government arranged for the drafting of a new constitution. This was put to a referendum in August 2007. The referendum passed with 57 per cent of those voting, but it was noteworthy that 44 per cent of the electorate did not vote and, even more significantly that 62 per cent of the votes in northeastern Thailand were against the new constitution. This dissent reflected a very different view of what constituted the basis of political legitimacy on the part of northeasterners from the view of supporters of the new constitution.

In December 2007, a new election was held, and, to the shock of the Yellow Shirts, the junta, and the outgoing government, the People's Power Party (*Phak Phalang Prachachon*) the successor to Thai Rak Thai, won the greatest number of seats and formed a government with Samak Sundravej as prime minister. Such a government was not acceptable to the Yellow Shirts and their backers in the military, bureaucracy and palace. Legal actions led to Samak's being forced to resign. The People's Power Party still commanded sufficient seats to form a government under Somchai Wongsawat. But judicial disestablishment of the People's Power Party meant that this government was allowed to have only a very brief existence. A new successor party to Thai Rak Thai, the Phuea Thai Party, was formed.

Throughout 2008 the Yellow Shirts staged increasingly disruptive protests against what were claimed to be governments headed by Thaksin's surrogates Samak and Somchai. These protests culminated in the PAD takeover of Bangkok's airports on 28 November 2008. Yellow Shirt pressure together with a number of judicial actions paved the way for the Democrat Party, the largest anti-Thaksin party in parliament, to form a new government at the end of 2008. This government, led by Prime Minister Abhisit, has been in office ever since.

There can be no question but that the success of the extra-parliamentary Yellow Shirt protests was a stimulus to the Red Shirt movement. If free elections could be held, the Red Shirt leaders have said, then the people's will would lead to a democratic government organized by the Phuea Thai Party, the successor party to Thai Rak Thai. Arguing that the Abhisit government came to power through non-democratic means, the Red Shirts have since 2009 mobilized to pressure that government to resign and call new elections.

In April 2009 the Red Shirts staged their first major protests, disrupting and then forcing the cancellation of an ASEAN Summit in Pattaya and occupying Government House. The climax came on the day of the Thai New Year (*songkran*), 13 April, when security forces confronted Red Shirt demonstrators near the Victory Monument. Over a hundred demonstrators were injured, and at least one was killed. The show of force persuaded Red Shirt leaders to withdraw. The Abhisit government branded the UDD as "national enemies".[13] The government also moved to place tighter controls on the community radio stations, websites, and satellite broadcasts that were being used by the Red Shirts. The Yellow Shirts, however, were never criticized by Abhisit for their take-over of the airport, and legal action against them has been allowed to drag out. The Red Shirt leaders and their supporters have been strongly critical of the "double standard" that has been detrimental to their movement and supportive of the Yellow Shirts.

After the Songkran 2009 events, the Red Shirts moved to regroup. With probable monetary support from Thaksin, the leaders were able to bring into existence a wide-flung organization with many local leaders not only in villages but also in urban Bangkok. The government and the PAD have made much of Thaksin's financing of the Red Shirt movement, a point again often associated with the accusation that the Red Shirts are simply Thaksin's mercenaries. Such a conclusion ignores the fact that Red Shirt followers have also contributed much money themselves and have given greatly of their time. Given the deaths and injuries suffered by followers, it is patently clear that many, perhaps most, of the rank and file of the Red Shirts have become followers because they truly believe that the movement, if successful, will enhance their status in Thai society.

Despite the strong and often articulate denials by such Abhisit government supporters as Kraisak Choonhavan and even a few Western journalists that there is no fundamental class conflict in Thai society,[14] the fact remains that many Red Shirts do see their struggle in class terms. This is manifest in the way in which Red Shirt leaders have asserted that their followers are *phrai* in opposition to the *ammat*. These terms are derived from terms used in Siam's pre-modern period and refer to bondsmen and aristocrats. This language was chosen to be provocative rather than ideological, but the labels also had powerful resonance for those camped out in one of the wealthiest shopping districts of Bangkok.

The Red Shirt movement has never been fully coherent. Some of the leaders have strong loyalty to Thaksin. At least a few have become true revolutionaries, and some have joined for the thrill of a violent struggle. The majority most probably has joined in the hope that the movement really can lead to a democratic system in which their voices count equally to those of the rest of the citizenry of the country.

THAILAND'S CRISIS OF POWER

The Red Shirt advocacy of democracy has its roots in Thailand's first modern revolution, one that took place in June 1932. That revolution was led by a small group of non-royal bureaucrats and military officers. They succeeded in compelling then King Prajadhipok to agree to the establishment of a constitutional monarchy. I believe that it is very relevant for understanding the present crisis to know that northeastern villagers enthusiastically embraced the new democratic system as shown by their active participation in the first parliamentary elections that occurred after the 1932 revolution.[15] The promise of that revolution soon was denied, first by Plaek Phibunsongkhram, one of the "Promoters" of the 1932 Revolution who became a fascist "leader" and then by military-led governments.

A new order emerged after Field Marshal Sarit Thanarat seized power in 1957. Sarit recognized that the legitimacy of a military-led government was problematic in the eyes of much of the population. He therefore struck an alliance with the then young King Bhumibol.

King Bhumibol became king under inauspicious circumstances. First, as a child he did not live in Thailand but in Switzerland owing to the desire of the Promoters of the 1932 Revolution to keep the royal family out of sight. He was not first in line for the throne after the abdication of King Prajadhipok; instead the Regents — led by one of the Promoters — had chosen his older brother, Ananda Mahidol. After King Ananda, his brother and sister and his mother (his father having died many years earlier), returned to Bangkok in 1946, he died of a still not fully explained gunshot wound while in the palace. After this tragedy the new King Bhumibol's mother soon took him and his sister back to Switzerland. It was not until 1950 that he returned to be crowned.

So long as Field Marshal Phibun was prime minister, the role of the king was significantly constrained, as Phibun did not want him to be a threat to his own power. After Sarit overthrew Phibun, however, he recognized that the king was widely popular and a new system of power evolved, with the military holding effective authority while the monarchy provided legitimacy.

The military element of this political system was challenged in the early 1970s by a student movement whose members came primarily from families who were part of a growing urban middle class. The challenge mounted by this movement was initially successful in 1973 and led, with the king's support, to the reinstitution of an elected parliament as a basic political institution. However, in 1976 the military, also with the support of the palace, which was frightened by the overthrow of the governments of Laos, South Vietnam, and Cambodia, forcibly reinstituted military rule. There were at the same time some in the upper echelon of the military who recognized that, unless the middle class had a larger say in policy formation through a parliament, the Thai economy would suffer. This echelon was also concerned about a growing insurgency led by the Communist Party of Thailand, whose followers came primarily from rural northeastern and northern Thailand.

Generals Kriangsak Chomanan and Prem Tinsulanon, who led governments from 1977 to 1988, implemented an amnesty that led to the end of the insurgency and then allowed for more authority to be vested in an elected parliament. Nonetheless, the basic foundation of the political system — the relationship between the monarchy and the military — remained in place. After a government formed from parliament sought to curtail the role of the military, the military staged another coup in 1991. By this time the urban middle class, which had become much larger because of a significant economic boom, was unwilling to accept the system and in 1992 the first mass protests of urban dwellers took place. Although the military initially sought to suppress the protests by deploying lethal force, they were finally compelled to back off when the king intervened.

Two major changes ensued from the May 1992 confrontation. First, the moral authority of the king grew substantially. Secondly, with the king's blessing political parties were able not only to form parliamentary governments, but they also worked together to shape a new constitution — one that was finally approved in a referendum and promulgated by the king in 1997.

By the beginning of the twenty-first century, it appeared that Thailand had finally developed the democratic system under a constitutional monarchy that had first been envisioned in the 1932 Revolution. Then Thaksin Shinawatra arrived on the scene.

Thaksin was not only able to take advantage of the new constitution to promote his Thai Rak Thai party, but he also was acutely aware of the loopholes in the constitution that obstructed the justice system from exercising any significant check and balance on executive and legislative power. Although Thaksin was assiduous in showing outward deference to the king, he began to act more and more like Phibun — that is, as a leader who could assert his authority without reference to the king because he had a mass following.

The opposition to Thaksin brought together rather strange bedfellows, namely, the old establishment of the military and palace and the recently emergent middle class, whose members thought of parliament as their institution. What these bedfellows did not take into account was that Thaksin had unleashed a tiger in the populist movement that he had helped to create but that was no longer his to command or control.

The crisis has also been exacerbated by the prospect of a change in the monarchy in the not too distant future. King Bhumibol is now 83 years old and has been hospitalized since September 2009. For whatever reason, he has not publicly intervened since the intense confrontation began in March 2010. Any discussion of the succession has been impossible in Thailand because of the draconian application of *lèse majesté* laws. Thus, there is no planning, at least to the knowledge of the public, for what will be a radical transition since Crown Prince Vajiralongkorn does not command the respect that King Bhumibol has. Although there has been some incisive analysis of what the transition might bring by *The Economist*,[16] the Associated Press,[17] the *Financial Times*,[18] *The Independent*,[19] not to mention the incendiary report on the Australian Broadcasting Corporation's programme "Foreign Correspondent",[20] the Thai press has been totally muzzled. Indeed, so dire are the presumed consequences of speaking about the transition in Thailand that in the parliamentary debate about the events of April-May, the leader of the opposition Phuea Thai party even sought to propose that Foreign Minister Kasit Piromya, who had broached the possibility of discussing the succession in public remarks made in Washington, be charged with *lèse majesté*.

The looming succession is also a major factor in Thai politics. There are unquestionably strong pressures from the palace, many military officers, the PAD, and the leadership of the Democrat Party to ensure that Prime Minister Abhisit or, at the very least, a party not descendent from Thai Rak Thai be in power when the succession occurs. There is, thus, a deep political crisis in Thailand because the monarchy, which has been a fundamental pillar of the Thai nation since the country first was transformed from an empire into a modern state and has been particularly significant since the late 1950s, may soon no longer be the major arbiter of political legitimacy.

CONCLUSION

The Abhisit government announced as part of its proposed "road map to reconciliation" that it would promote policies that addressed the issues that motivated many to support the Red Shirts. Whether this would be possible depended of course on how well the government understood the issues facing Thailand.

The crisis in Thailand has overlapped with the global economic crisis that began in 2007. Although the Thai economy as a whole did not suffer a significant decline in 2008 and 2009, despite the PAD's occupation of the airports in late 2008, the impact on those supporting the Red Shirts was much greater.[21] The manufacturing sector dramatically contracted. While middle-class Bangkokians were able to weather the contraction in the economy without much pain, factory and service workers — overwhelmingly from the Northeast — saw significant declines in income and rises in unemployment or underemployment.[22] This was made worse by the decline in jobs outside Thailand that northeasterners might seek. One immediate consequence of unemployment and underemployment has been the growth in the number of young men who no longer can find good non-agricultural jobs and who, at best, would have to turn back to subsistence farming. It is very probable that it is this population of young unemployed or underemployed men from whom the shock troops of the Red Shirts were drawn.

Secondly, the "villagers" of Thailand need to be made to feel that they are recognized as being equal citizens within the Thai nation. Again, I would like to quote from the op-ed piece that I published in the *Bangkok Post* in May 2010:

> Support for the red shirt movement is very strong throughout rural northeastern and northern Thailand in part because villagers and their kinsmen who work in Bangkok and elsewhere are aware of being constantly denigrated by members of the middle class, particularly in Bangkok.

> This denigration has deep historical roots. The people of the Northeast and North were seen by Central Thai as "Lao" when they were first integrated into the new nation-state of Thailand. Although the people of these regions have long since come through participation in mass education and consumption of Bangkok-based media to identify as "Thai" who are also Khon Isan (northeastern Thai) and Khon Muang (northern Thai), older negative images persist of these people being somehow less "Thai" than middle class Bangkokians.
>
> Negative images, especially of northeasterners, have been used often in films and TV dramas. In the past few years, people of these regions have been branded over and over again by commentators on ASTV, the television network of the People's Alliance for Democracy (PAD), in many Bangkok newspapers, and in hundreds of blogs and Facebook pages as being stupid "buffaloes" and even more vulgar characterizations. Somehow those who generate such media depictions seem to believe that "villagers" are uninformed, and unaware of these characterizations. On the contrary, they are very much aware of them, and this constant denigration has become one of the primary drivers of the conflict.

The virulent rhetoric used about the Red Shirts has a counterpart in the hateful language used by some of them against the government and the establishment. Such rhetoric, drawn from a ideology that contrasts with traditional cultural practices that accentuate having a "cool heart" and maintaining harmony, has also been among the most shocking characteristics of the crisis. Again as I said in my op-ed piece: "It is critical that Thais rediscover the true Buddhist value of working to cool passions."

On 23 May 2010, four days after the climax of the confrontation in Bangkok, Apichatphong Weerasethakun, a forty-year old film director from Thailand won the most prestigious prize of the 2010 Cannes Film Festival, the Palme d'Or. That his film, *Uncle Boonmee Who Can Recall His Past Lives*, a film that combines magical realism, history and myth, should have been chosen for this prize was stunning — perhaps most of all to Thai who have not been particularly fond of his previous films. Indeed, there is a serious question as to whether this film, like his most recent previous one, will have to undergo censorship if it is to be shown in Thailand.

Apichatphong is himself a native of northeastern Thailand, the stronghold of supporters of the Red Shirts. And his film is set in the region and "alludes to the troubled history of the Northeast."[23] In his acceptance speech Apichatphong said "I hope the government of Thailand will take notice of [the award]. This is not a political film, but yet we suffer from censorship and restriction from them when it comes to making movies. I hope they see what we can achieve. I think Thailand needs some kind of hope in other ways because we are very depressed about the confrontation of different ideologies right now." [24]

Albeit in a different way than the Red Shirts demonstrators, Apichatphong was also challenging the establishment in Thailand. In his case, he had been engaged with other independent film-makers in protesting against the Ministry of Culture, which had recently chosen to allocate half of a special fund of 200 million baht for support of film producers to Mom Chao (Prince) Chatrichaloem Yukol for the third and fourth instalments of his nationalistic story of the medieval King Naresuan. In a very real way, Apichatphong's confrontation with the Ministry of Culture epitomized the issue that had led to the violent confrontation on the streets of Bangkok.

If the Abhisit government were truly to advance the country along a path towards reconciliation, it needed to sponsor a campaign to guide middle-class Bangkokians and others virulently opposed to the Red Shirts to recognize that they share a national community with those "villagers" who live not only in the rural areas but also in Bangkok itself. As an editorial in the *Bangkok Post* on 23 April 2010 said, as it was becoming apparent that there would be a calamitous outcome to the confrontation at Ratchaprasong: "The reality is, even if such a tragedy happens, we will still have to find a way to live together."[25]

On 25 April 2010 after the first bloody crackdown on 10 April, the *Washington Post* concluded an editorial with these words: "What ought to be clear by now is that anti-democratic tactics, from military intervention to street barricades to convenient court edicts, will not end Thailand's turmoil. The only solution is for both sides to accept that elections should decide who governs Thailand — and that both winners and losers should respect basic political and civil rights."[26] Although Prime Minister Abhisit offered to hold elections in November during negotiations with the Red Shirts, he withdrew this offer when the Red Shirts rejected his "road map" to reconciliation. And after 19 May, he announced that elections could only be held when it was safe to do so. As Chang Noi observed in a column published in *The Nation* on 31 May, "The prime minister is still saying there can be an election only after peace has returned, which of course means never, since an election is needed to establish peace. The Democrats still seem to think they have a duty to remain in power to engineer reconciliation, when in truth the existence of this government is one of the major barriers to reconciliation."[27]

Despite the continuing tensions, including new ones deriving from Thailand's confrontation with Cambodia over the control of territory around an ancient Hindu-Buddhist temple as well as continued demonstrations by the Red Shirts, most of whose leaders remained under arrest, Abhisit and the Democrats finally decided to support a new election. On 9 May 2011 Prime Minister Abhisit announced that the parliament would be dissolved and a new election would be held on 3 July. The strong support for the Phuea Thai party, now led by Yingluck Shinawatra, the younger sister of Thaksin, especially in the Northeast and North, demonstrate that people in these regions still see a democratically elected parliament as the primary vehicle for representing their interests and as the ultimate source of political legitimacy. Whether it will be allowed to fulfill these roles cannot be determined by one election, especially if the results of the July 2011 election are undermined by either military or judicial interventions or by resurgent Yellow shirt protests. It is yet to be seen whether a true reconciliation can be instituted, with the "rural" people of the Northeast and the North, from whom the Red Shirts have emerged, "allowed" to have an accepted role in shaping Thai governments.

Notes

1. This figure came from Erawan Center of the Bangkok Metropolitan Administration (see <http://thainews.prd.go.th/en/news.php?id=255306030055> (accessed 11 March 2011). In the parliamentary debate that took place in early June 2010, the opposition claimed that there were more than 89 deaths, with some having been concealed; see Kinan Suchaovanich, "Thai Leader Defends Self at Censure Debate", *Associated Press*, 1 June 2009. Subsequent accounts have consistently reported ninety-one or ninety-two deaths, but these figures await official confirmation.

2. The number of eleven military casualties comes from Royal Thai Embassy, Washington, "Thailand Update", 8/2010, 27 May 2010, available at <http://www.thaiembdc.org/Ann_Doc/Thailandupdate8_10.pdf> (accessed 11 March 2011).
3. This paper represents one effort to rethink my understanding of Thai society in light of what I was quoted as saying in a *New York Times* article: "My understanding of what I have learned over the years here has really come into question. I question all the things I've learned about this country." See Seth Mydans, "Bangkok Grows Calm, but Social Divisions Remain", *New York Times*, 20 May 2010.
4. Charles Keyes, "Time Out in Thailand: Dealing with 'the Devil', the Reds, and Looking Within", *Bangkok Post*, 26 May 2010, available at <http://www.bangkokpost.com/opinion/opinion/37712/dealing-with-the-devil-the-reds-and-looking-within>. (accessed 11 March 2011).
5. The strong popular support for the Red Shirts in northern Thailand is due to more than Thaksin's status as a native son. In addition, many in the North share long-simmering resentments about the how the Thai state has curtailed the cultural distinctiveness of the region. The southern origin of some of the Red Shirt leaders is, superficially, odd, as the Democrat Party has long had a dominant role in the politics of the non-Malay south. See Marc Askew, *Performing Political Identity: The Democrat Party in Southern Thailand* (Chiang Mai: Silkworm Books, 2008). A comprehensive study of the Red Shirt movement remains to be written.
6. This 2004 film, by the very creative film director Wisit Satsanathiang, has a complex plot and is not in the typical mould of films that depict rural migrants in the city. Nonetheless, it reinforces the image of such migrants as out of place in Bangkok.
7. United Nations Development Program, *Human Security, Today and Tomorrow: Thailand Development Report 2009* (Bangkok: United Nations Development Program, 2010), pp. 78ff. Also see David Feeny, "The Political Economy of Regional Inequality: The Northeast of Thailand 1800–2000", *Crossroads* 17, no. 1 (2003): 29–59; and Pasuk Phongpaichit and Chris Baker, eds., *Thai Capital after the 1997 Crisis* (Chiang Mai: Silkworm Books, 2008).
8. See Jim Glassman, *Thailand at the Margins: Internationalization of the State and the Transformation of Labour* (Oxford and New York: Oxford University Press, 2004).
9. "Thai Killed in Palestinian Rocket Attack", *The Nation*, 19 March 2010 <http://www.nationmultimedia.com/home/2010/03/19/national/Thai-killed-in-Palestinian-rocket-attack-30125044.html> (accessed 15 April 2010).
10. I first proposed this characterization in a paper entitled "From Peasant to Cosmopolitan Villagers: Refiguring the 'Rural' in Northeastern Thailand",

presented at a conference on "Revisiting Agrarian Transformations in Southeast Asia", Chiang Mai, Thailand, May 2010. A revised version of the paper is forthcoming in *South East Asia Research*.

11. Pasuk Phongpaichit and Chris Baker, *Thaksin*, 2nd. ed. (Chiang Mai: Silkworm Books, 2009), pp. 188–89. OTOP is an acronym for "One *Tambon* [sub-district], One Product".
12. Charles Keyes, Unpublished field notes, 5 February 2005.
13. "Sacrificing Democracy Won't End Thailand's Chaos", *The Age* (Melbourne), 15 April 2009.
14. See Kraisak Choonhavan, "Thailand: A Class Struggle?", *The Irrawaddy*, 1 May 2010; Bertil Lintner, "Thai Turmoil Was No 'Class War'", *Sydney Morning Herald* <http://www.smh.com.au/opinion/politics/thai-turmoil-was-no-class-war-20100607-xped.html> (accessed 12 March 2011).
15. See Dararat Mattarikanon, *Kanmueang song fang khong ngan khonkwa wichai radap parinya ek khang chulalongkon mahawithayalai rueang kanruam klum thang kanmueang khong so. so. isan pho. so., 2476–2494* [Politics on the two Sides of the Mekhong: Chulalongkorn University Doctoral Dissertation on the Political Unity of Northeastern Members of Parliament, 1933–1951] (Bangkok: Matichon, 2003).
16. See "As Father Fades, His Children Fight", *The Economist*, 18 March 2010.
17. Denis D. Gray, "As Thai Monarchy's Power Wanes, King Still Revered", Associated Press, 25 May 2010.
18. Tim Johnston, "Thai Royal Taboo under Pressure", *Financial Times*, 14 April 2010.
19. Peter Popham, "King Bhumibol Adulyadej of Thailand: The Monarch Whose Silence Is Deafening", *The Independent*, 22 May 2010.
20. The ABC report by Eric Campbell appeared on 13 April 2010. There is also a rather curious article by William Stevenson, "Thailand's Silent Monarch", *Toronto Star*, 24 May 2010 <http://www.thestar.com/opinion/editorialopinion/article/813032--thailand-s-silent-monarch> (accessed 12 March 2011). Stevenson's biography *The Revolutionary King: The True-Life Sequel to The King and I* (London: Constable, 1999) blends credible accounts of conversations or interviews the king or palace officials with other material clearly based on rumour or even imagination. In his *Toronto Star* article Stevenson takes as given that there is close relationship between the crown prince and Thaksin.
21. On the growth of unemployment in Thailand since the economic crisis began, see Somchai Jitsuchon, "Employment Impacts in Thailand's Trade and Tourism Sectors from the Global Economic Crisis". Working Paper for the Third China-ASEAN Forum on Social Development and Poverty

Reduction, 4th ASEAN+3 High-Level Seminar on Poverty Reduction, and Asia-wide Regional High-level Meeting on the Impact of the Global Economic Slowdown on Poverty and Sustainable Development in Asia and the Pacific, December 2009 <http://www.adb.org/documents/events/2009/Poverty-Social-Development/WG1A-employment-impact-tha-Jitsuchon-paper.pdf> (accessed 15 June 2010); the World Bank's "Thailand Economic Monitor" for April–June 2009 <http://www.worldbank.or.th/WBSITE/EXTERNAL/COUNTRIES/EASTASIAPACIFICEXT/THAILANDEXTN/0,,contentMDK:22241515~menuPK:333302~pagePK:1497618~piPK:217854~theSitePK:333296,00.html> (accessed 12 March 2010).

22. It is very difficult to find good statistical information on underemployment or on the number of unemployed who have stopped looking for work. The analysis here also draws on the author's observations in northeastern Thailand.
23. Kong Rithdee, "Thai Auteur Stuns with Cannes Win", *Bangkok Post*, 25 May 2010.
24. Emma Jones, "Thai Director 'Shocked' over Palme d'Or Win", BBC News online, 24 Mary 2010 <http://news.bbc.co.uk/2/hi/entertainment_and_arts/10146751.stm> (accessed 15 June 2010).
25. "Volatility Could Spark Civil War", *Bangkok Post*, 23 April 2010.
26. "Stopping Thailand's Endless Battle of the Yellows and Reds", *Washington Post*, 15 April 2010.
27. Chang Noi (pseud.), "If I Shout Loud Enough, I Won't Hear You", *Nation*, 31 May 2010.

16

TWO CHEERS FOR RALLY POLITICS

Duncan McCargo

Mass rallies in the capital city have been a regular feature of Thai politics. They date backing to the 1950s[1] but have been most prominent since the 1970s: the two Octobers of 1973 and 1976, the constitutional amendment crisis of 1983, the rallies against General Suchinda Kraprayun of May 1992, the near-annual farmers' protests of the 1990s, the protests of 2005, 2006 and 2009 against former Prime Minister Thaksin Shinawatra, and most recently the Red Shirt rallies of 2009 and 2010. How are we to understand these rallies in a comparative and historical context? The temptation has been to view Bangkok's big rallies as "people power" movements opposing military rule, and linked to processes of liberalization or even democratization. In other words, the primary comparison is with dramatic ousters of authoritarian regimes elsewhere. The aim of this chapter is to problematize idealized views of rally politics, and to suggest that the United Front for Democracy against Dictatorship (UDD) protests of 2010 were more the result of elite mobilization than a spontaneous uprising of popular feeling.

The turbulent events of March–May 2010 bring me back full circle, to the two modes of politics that I discussed in my early work on Chamlong Srimuang.[2] Following the arguments of Bruce Graham, I have suggested that national politics often derives its momentum from one of two sources: party drive, or rally drive. Party drive is the standard operating procedure of most European democracies: representative parties are formed to articulate the demands of interest groups, to contest elections, and operate within parliamentary systems. Rally drive is essentially extra-parliamentary in nature, and it is linked to strong leadership. As Graham noted, "the rally drive is produced by the diffuse anxieties of groups and individuals who look to prominent personalities to accept a form of moral responsibility for the welfare of the community as a whole."[3]

Graham argued that the rally mode was almost a default mode for Indian and French politics, and a recurrent theme of American politics (in presidential campaigns, for example). He was keen to reject any suggestion that the rally drive was inferior to the party drive, arguing after Nehru that rally politics helped preserve a dynamic and vital connection between the elite and the masses. He cited approvingly De Gaulle's declaration in 1942: "in order to seize victory and to rediscover her greatness, France must form a rally".[4] Fieschi, drawing on Graham's work in her discussions of recent rally politics by the French far right, argues that:

> The Fifth Republic did not simply create a political space structured by the duality of the rally and party drives; it created the possibility of a third type of power which can be considered a version — the French version — or the outcome of the dialectical tension between the two drives.[5]

Fieschi suggests that the French have developed an attachment to ideas of "apolitical" political participation that bypass mainstream representative institutions. These ideas are linked to specific features of French republicanism, but essentially exalt the purity of mass participation over mere party politics.

What does any of this have to do with Thailand? In short, it is the same but different. As in France, a kind of synthesis has taken place between the rally drive and the party drive, producing a third realm of power: the place where party politics and mass politics intersect. Like the French, the Thais have a special place for rally-mode politics, which may receive a high degree of popular acceptance — but only so long as the rallies are not too "tainted" by party politics. Rally politics to protest over a popular cause is acceptable, and indeed often proves necessary to move forward the national agenda. But if rally politics is simply a front for party politics, its integrity and credibility are fatally compromised. This is not me talking; it is the script according to the Bangkok elite. The problem, of course, lies in what one considers to be party politics and how you detect its implicit presence in the middle of a messy public demonstration.

Nearly thirty years ago, Chai-anan Samudavanija talked about the "vicious circle" of Thai politics — a sequence that went coup, constitution, election, crisis, and back to coup.[6] Many hoped that this sequence of political boom-and-bust might have been broken during the long spell of post-1992 stability, the first coup-free decade-and-a-half since the end of absolute monarchy. But it was not to be. Not only did the *coup d'état* of 19 September 2006 suggest that such armed seizures of power continue to serve as a safety valve in the cycle. But a phase of "crisis" — often involving mass rallies — also clearly remains integral to the functioning of Thailand's political order. Things had to get worse before they got better — only later to get worse again. If we accept the essence of the "vicious cycle" argument, at least descriptively, then Thailand has developed a "third type" of politics as merry-go-round, a politics that testifies to both a deep scepticism about representative institutions and a deep attachment to the outward forms of party politics.

What I discovered when looking at Chamlong's role in the 1980s and early 1990s was that he came to rely on rally politics as an alternative modus operandi, a way of pursuing his agenda at junctures when party politics was not working — or at least not going the way he and his supporters wanted. Rally mode politics in Thailand is not inherently liberal, progressive, or democratic; it is a particular way of doing political business. We need, that is, to be wary of romanticizing the politics of the rally. In the Philippines, "EDSA" — the mass demonstrations on Manila's Epifanio de los Santos Avenue that preceded the fall of Ferdinand Marcos — in 1986 was all about removing a dictator, whereas the so called "EDSA 2" of 2001 was about removing a democratically elected president in mid-term. Most of the tactics were the same, as were many of the actors. But the goal was entirely different, and far more troubling. Since the early 1990s, rally politics in Thailand has become increasingly disconnected from progressive causes. It has instead become a standard operating procedure, a means of attempting to bring about regime change without recourse either to a coup or to an election. This politics might be termed one of "manufactured crisis", or "mobilized crisis".

If we compare the 2006 and 2008 People's Alliance for Democracy (PAD) rallies and those of the UDD in 2009 and 2010, the similarities are more striking than the differences. Both movements were led by a core group of prominent and politically well-connected individuals. In the case of the PAD, these individuals included two of the seven leaders of Confederation for Democracy (CFD) that led the May 1992 protests (Chamlong and Somsak Kosaisuk), a prominent media mogul who was also an important backer of the May 1992 protests (Sonthi Limthongkun), an NGO leader who had been a member of the rival Campaign for Popular Democracy in 1992 (Phiphop Thongchai), and a Democrat Party member of parliament (Somkiat Phongphaibun). UDD leaders included Phuea Thai MPs and popular entertainers, along with another of the former CFD leaders (Weng Tojirakan). PAD participants were mobilized through a network centred on the ASTV channel; many of them were already consumers of an established brand of political information. UDD participants were mobilized through a network of community radio stations. During the 2008 protests, most PAD supporters were Democrat Party voters or sympathizers, and while the Democrats denied any formal role in orchestrating the protests, local Democrat vote-canvassers, especially from the South, were involved in bringing protestors to Bangkok. During the 2010 protests, many UDD demonstrators were Phuea Thai Party supporters whose participation was arranged by vote canvassers in the North and Northeast.

A crucial element of the rally mode is the way in which it feeds on collective and individual anxieties, with which Thailand has been awash in recent years. On one level, the rise of rally politics from a relatively intermittent mode of activity to a virtual default mode testifies to growing national anxieties about the country's future, centring on the still unresolved issue of the royal succession. Recourse to rally politics has declined recently in countries such as India, where economic growth has boosted collective self-confidence and feelings of well-being. But the Thai case suggests that it may also tend to rise when national nerves become seriously rattled.

The defining feature of rally politics in Thailand is supposed to be its detachment from party politics. A rally may be legitimate only insofar as it is not part of a wider political "game". This in essence means that those behind the rally are not supposed to be motivated by a quest for electoral advantage or a desire to gain high office. But each of the three most important rounds of rallies in recent decades — April–May 1992, August–December 2008, and March–May 2010 — was actually all about challenging electoral or parliamentary outcomes. If you have a powerful political force but are denied entry to Government House through the ballot box (1992, 2008) or by a parliamentary vote (2010), you may take your cause to the streets. In May 1992, Chamlong and New Aspiration Party leader General Chavalit Yongchaiyut, who played an important but less overt role in orchestrating the demonstrations, faced a constant undercurrent of criticism that their protest leadership was motivated by personal political ambition. They succeeded, however, in sticking to the safer ground of constitutionalism by demanding that the prime minister be an elected member of parliament and in protesting against the "continuation of dictatorship" implied in General Suchinda's rapid metamorphosis from coup leader to prime minister.

The credibility of the 1992 protests was greatly enhanced by their passionate proximity to the controversial March elections; no sooner had Suchinda been appointed prime minister than Chalat Worachat began his hunger strike. By contrast, the PAD in 2008 and the UDD in 2010 were rallying months after the original political provocation, suggesting an element of calculation and a more overt mobilization process. While Graham suggests that recourse to rally drive may be a tactic of last resort for a party politician who has run out of options, in Thailand this is a dangerous game to play. It helped in 1992 that the protest movement was relatively diverse and complex, cutting across class barriers and motivated by a range of goals. The NGO-oriented Campaign for Popular Democracy (CPD), which played the leading role in the first phase of the 1992 protests, was not overtly partisan. The CPD saw the demonstrations more as a process of civic education than a tool of regime change.

In 2008, the PAD was able substantially to downplay its partisanship by running an anti-Thaksin rather than a pro-Democrat campaign.[7] The presence of a Democrat member of parliament among the five core leaders was something of a give-away, and at one point party leader Abhisit Vejjajiva blew it slightly by showing up at a PAD funeral. But it helped that both Sonthi and especially Chamlong had impeccable credentials as longtime critics and adversaries of the Democrats. Another irony was the long-standing opposition of the Democrat Party to the use of street politics. Former Democrat leader Chuan Leekphai won the September 1992 elections with the slogans "I believe in the parliamentary system" and "Chaos is not democracy", implicit rebukes to those among his political rivals who had led the rallies of four months before.

As in May 1992, so too in 2008 there was not complete agreement about the aims of the demonstrations. The PAD leadership talked airily of creating a "new politics" that would curb the excesses of majoritarianism, but the real impact of their protests was to undermine a pro-Thaksin government and to help replace it with a Democrat-led administration. The Democrats were thus once again the beneficiaries of a form of politics that they professed to disdain. And what the PAD's protests clearly illustrated was that, sixteen years on, the tactics of May 1992 could be deployed by many of the same leaders for causes that were much less liberal. In 1992, protestors had opposed the military and supported electoral democracy; in 2008, they were supporting the military and criticizing electoral democracy. Paralysing Bangkok's streets was not in itself a progressive act: what mattered was why you were paralysing them. The very same international media that had lionized the May 1992 protestors were highly critical of the PAD in 2008, especially when it briefly closed Bangkok's airports and left tens of thousands of foreign tourists and business travelers stranded.

In 2010, the question of to what degree the UDD was actually a front for former Prime Minister Thaksin Shinawatra became central to establishing the legitimacy of the protests. The prominence of the issue went to the core of what rally politics means. Just as Suchinda attempted to discredit the May 1992 protests by presenting them as an opportunistic move by ambitious political rivals, so the Abhisit government sought to paint the UDD as a wholly owned Thaksin subsidiary. In both cases, the truth of the matter was somewhat complicated. Personal rivalries between Class 5 and Class 7 graduates of the Chulachomklao Military Academy did play some part in the events of May 1992. Chamlong and Chavalit each had reasons for wanting to remove a prime minister who stood in the way of their own ambitions to achieve high office. Some of the protestors had been mobilized through links to opposition political parties. Nevertheless, most of those who joined the May 1992 protests were animated by a genuine belief that the Suchinda government was illegitimate. There was in fact no clear-cut distinction between a "genuine" and a "mobilized" protestor, for all the Thai discourse surrounding *mop rap chang* (demonstrators for hire). Much the same applied to the PAD in 2008. For all their belief in their cause, those who spent weeks or months camped outside Government House were reliant on handouts, including food, tee-shirts and pocket money provided by sympathizers and rally organizers. How otherwise could they have remained in a place where they had no means of earning a living?

The same realities obtained in the case of the UDD's Bangkok protests during March–May 2010. Despite international media caricatures, those who took part were not simply "poor farmers" from the North and Northeast. Many were vote canvassers, elected members of sub-district-level *tambon* administrative organizations, figures involved in community radio, small-scale contract farmers (whose produce is sold directly to agribusiness rather than on the open market), self-employed and semi-skilled workers, and low ranking security officers.[8] Though wearing tee-shirts declaring themselves *"phrai"* (slaves, bondsmen, serfs), most protestors were actual lower-middle-class people with a substantial stake in the political and economic system, not members of groups living at the margins of Thai society. The red-shirted protestors could not be neatly placed into catch-all categories. Some were animated by partisan political motives; many were out-and-out Thaksin loyalists, or had been been recruited by Thaksin's political networks. But others were motivated by idealism, or by pragmatic reasons such as economic frustrations. The UDD was an extremely decentralized movement, over which the supposed core leaders — of whom there were a large number compared with the tight-knit five-man nucleus of the PAD — had relatively little control.

For the Democrat government and much of the Thai media, the usual rules of the Thai rally-politics game applied in 2010. As Ockey concluded on the basis of his study of the "Hyde Park" movement of the 1950s, "leaders are expected to be free of self-interest, and crowds are assumed to be controlled by their leaders, with no genuine interests of their own."[9] By contrast, for most of the international media and for many academic commentators, the presumed agency of the crowd was the key to understanding the protests, which were presented in terms of an ideological or class struggle in which elite mobilization played very little part. Both readings of the Red Shirt rallies were deeply flawed. The crowds had a significant degree of agency, but they had also been mobilized by Thaksin and his network. The much-vaunted distinction between party politics and rally politics, while analytically useful, could too easily be read as a false dichotomy between two modes of activity that were actually intimately linked during March–May 2010.

If we accept that neither the PAD rallies of 2008 nor the Red Shirt rallies of 2010 can be seen as straightforward strivings for liberal democracy, perhaps we ought to pause and think back to other episodes of rally politics, notably the events of May 1992. How far were the May events a struggle against dictatorship, and how far were they a more murky and ambiguous episode of mass participation mingled with political mobilisation? The 2010 Red Shirt protests were troubling events on many levels: for the violence that they engendered, for the violence that they provoked, and for the savage that polarisation that they revealed. But they are also troubling because they lead us to revisit previous episodes of recent Thai political history with a more sceptical and questioning attitude. Does rally politics deserve more than two cheers?

Notes

1. See James Ockey, "Civil society and street politics: lessons from the 1950s", in *Reforming Thai Politics*, edited by Duncan McCargo (Copenhagen: NIAS Press, 2002), pp. 107–23.
2. Duncan McCargo, *Chamlong Srimuang and the New Thai Politics* (London: Hurst 1997), pp. 15–18; Chapter 8 of this book offers detailed discussion of the events of May 1992.
3. B. D. Graham, *Representation and Party Politics: A Comparative Perspective* (Oxford: Blackwell, 1993), p. 84.
4. Ibid., p. 117.
5. Catherine Fieschi, "Rally Politics and Political Organisation: An Institutionalist Perspective on the French Far Right", *Modern and Contemporary France* 8, no. 1 (February 2000): 71–89; see p. 87.
6. Chai-anan Samudavanija, *The Thai Young Turks* (Singapore: Institute of

Southeast Asian Studies, 1982), p. 11.

7. For a discussion of the PAD, see Duncan McCargo, "Thai Politics as Reality TV", *The Journal of Asian Studies*, 68, 1 (February 2010): 7–19.
8. See Naruemon Thabchumphon, "Contested Political Networks: The Study of the Yellow and the Red in Thailand's Politics", paper presented to the International Workshop on Political Networks in Asia", National Graduate Institute for Policy Studies (GRIPS), Tokyo, Japan, 14 May 2010.
9. Ockey, "Civil society", p. 121.

17

THAI FOREIGN POLICY IN CRISIS
From Partner to Problem

Ann Marie Murphy

Thailand has long been famous for its adroit diplomacy. King Chulalongkorn's consummate balancing of European powers is often credited for Thailand's ability to retain its independence while the rest of Southeast Asia succumbed to colonialism. Skillful diplomacy in the immediate post-Second World War era helped Thailand to avoid occupation and the payment of reparations, the fate of other Axis co-belligerents. Following the communist victories in Indochina, Thailand avoided the retribution normally suffered by losing states after their abandonment by a great power ally by forging an entente with its erstwhile adversary, China. At crucial historical junctures, the ability of Thai leaders to discern changing trends in global politics and shift their country's policy accordingly has been crucial to safeguarding the Thai nation.

Today, Thailand's proud foreign policy legacy lies in tatters. The political crisis ongoing since the September 2006 coup against Prime Minister Thaksin Shinawatra has had deleterious effects on the country's relations with the outside world. At the most basic level, images broadcast around the world of massive street demonstrations by colour-coded protestors and the violence associated with their suppression has forced the international community to reassess long-held perceptions of Thailand as a socially stable, economically prosperous destination for foreign investment and tourists. Pivotal events in the crisis directly affected foreigners in a negative way. The take-over of Suvarnabhumi airport by the Yellow Shirts stranded tens of thousands of tourists and the attack on the ASEAN Summit meetings in Pattaya threatened foreign dignitaries. The 2010 Red Shirt demonstrations in central Bangkok forced many embassies to evacuate non-essential staff, to issue travel advisories, and ultimately to close, while the violence associated with the demonstrators' dispersal saw two foreign journalists killed. As its domestic politics spills over into international affairs, Thailand, long viewed as mainland Southeast Asia's pivotal state, has morphed into a problem state.

The crisis has also politicized Thai foreign policy. Thaksin's mobilization of his supporters from exile blurs the lines between foreign and domestic affairs. Clausewitz's dictum that "war is merely the continuation of politics by other means" might aptly be paraphrased as "diplomacy is merely the continuation of politics in foreign arenas" to describe significant aspects of Thai foreign policy today. Foreign policy is increasingly used as a weapon in Thailand's domestic political battle as each side seeks external support and legitimacy to bolster its position.[1]

The polarization of Thai politics and its extension into foreign policy have complicated the task of engaging Thailand for other members of the international community. Thailand's long-standing outward economic orientation and its status as a regional hub for international institutions, non-governmental organizations, and diplomatic missions mean that many foreigners have interests in the country to protect. In a divided polity in which both sides tend to view actions by foreign countries in zero-sum terms, however, maintaining an even-handed approach to Thailand is increasingly difficult. With the Red Shirts having called for international mediation of Thailand's political crisis and the government of Prime Minister Abhisit Vejjajiva adamantly opposed to it, external actors are increasingly dragged into Thailand's political crisis.

This essay discusses in greater detail the impact of Thailand's crisis on its foreign policy and the challenges that the crisis creates for the international community. A concluding section argues that those who hope for an early return of statesmanship to Thai diplomacy are likely to be disappointed. Domestic political and social cohesion provide the basis for a country's statecraft. Until Thailand puts its domestic house in order, Thailand's foreign policy is likely to remain in crisis.

THE IMPACT OF THE CRISIS ON THAI FOREIGN POLICY: NEGLECT, SPILLOVER, AND POLITICIZATION

Neglect and Spillover

The most fundamental impact of the political crisis in Thailand has been a concern with domestic affairs at the expense of foreign policy. This preoccupation has taken a number of forms, each with different effects for Thailand and external actors. The cancellation of foreign trips — such as Prime Minister Abhisit's decision to skip the April 2010 ASEAN Summit in Hanoi, normally a "must" on the diplomatic calendar — has sent a signal to the rest of the world regarding the severity of the crisis. In the case of the Hanoi meeting, it also cost Thailand an opportunity to influence the summit's outcome.

Second, the crisis has made Thailand a relatively inactive player on issues on which the international community would normally expect it to play a prominent role. With the Burmese junta planning to hold elections in 2010, many Western governments and human rights organizations had hoped to cooperate with Thailand on efforts to ensure that these elections were as free and fair as possible and that they moved the country towards national reconciliation. Instead, Thailand's focus on its own national reconciliation has reduced its attention to Burma. At the same time, Thailand's democratic retreat has reduced its credibility in lecturing Burma on military reform, press freedoms, and the need to respect the outcomes of elections.

Thailand's domestic crisis has spilled over into foreign policy in a number of other ways. Most obviously, the rapid turn-over in prime ministers and foreign ministers has had a disruptive impact. Thailand has had six prime ministers and eight foreign ministers since the 2006 coup. The attendant policy shifts — from the commercially driven embrace of the Burmese junta and Cambodia by Thai Rak Thai's successor parties to the reversal of these policies by anti-Thaksin governments — have caused upheavals in regional relations. Thaksin's sale of Shin Corporation to Temasek Holdings, a Singaporean sovereign wealth fund, sent Thailand's relations with Singapore into a downward spiral following the coup. They recovered only when the government of Prime Minister Samak Sundravej took power.

The crisis has also rendered Thailand incapable of carrying out its diplomatic responsibilities, as illustrated by its troubled chairmanship of ASEAN. The ASEAN chair rotates annually and has traditionally been handed over each July. The ASEAN Charter changed the chair's term in office to run for the calendar year. To enable this change, Thailand was given an unprecedented eighteen-month chairmanship, from July 2008 to December 2009, and was set to enjoy the prestige that would come from having the ASEAN Charter signed in Bangkok. ASEAN countries vary greatly in the managerial capacity that they bring to oversight of the organization's affairs. Most ASEAN members were pleased that Thailand would guide the organization during this pivotal transition; they expected that Thailand would use its famed diplomatic skills on the organization's behalf.

The political crisis dashed these expectations. The Yellow Shirt demonstrations during the final months of 2008 forced the postponement of the fourteenth ASEAN Summit, scheduled for December of that year. The ASEAN Charter was signed not by heads of state meeting in Bangkok, ASEAN's birthplace, but by foreign ministers gathered at the ASEAN Secretariat in Jakarta. When the Association's annual meeting was finally rescheduled, a decision was made to split the ASEAN Summit, duly held in February 2009, from the follow-on meetings of the ASEAN Plus Three and East Asia Summits (EAS). Those latter meetings were set for 11 April 2009 in Pattaya, but Red Shirts stormed the meeting venue in that resort town. They forced the meetings' cancellation and the evacuation of heads of state and government and of diplomats in helicopters and small boats, in a chaotic process that often separated them from their spouses and even their BlackBerries.[2] The violent disruption of the conference damaged Thailand's diplomatic reputation and caused ASEAN to lose "major face."[3]

POLITICIZATION

Most critically, Thai foreign policy has been politicized by the crisis. This politicization has taken three distinct forms: the appointment of highly partisan figures to the position of foreign minister; the use of foreign issues to whip up nationalist sentiment for political purposes; and competing attempts by both sides to ensure that the international community interprets the ongoing crisis in a way that legitimizes their respective positions.

The appointment of figures such as Nopphadon Patthama, Thaksin's personal attorney, and Kasit Piromya, a career diplomat and prominent Yellow Shirt supporter, to the position of foreign minister during the Samak and Abhisit governments, respectively, brings Thailand's political divide into the heart of its foreign-relations bureaucracy. Once at the helm of the Ministry of Foreign Affairs, men on both sides of the divide have used the authority of the state as a tool in their political battle. Nopphadon's first act as foreign minister was to restore Thaksin's diplomatic passport, which had been revoked by the government of Prime Minister Surayut Chulanon. In classic tit-for-tat fashion, Kasit revoked it yet again.

With Thaksin mobilizing his supporters openly from abroad through speeches broadcast in Thailand, the Surayut and Abhisit governments pressured foreign governments to clamp down on Thaksin's political activities, arguing that they were an infringement on Thai sovereignty. Thaksin's conviction on corruption charges in October 2008 expanded the foreign-policy tools available to the Abhisit government in its efforts to limit Thakin's travels and constrain his ability to organize and fund the Red Shirt movement. Previously in self-imposed exile, spent largely in Britain, Thaksin's conviction made him a fugitive from justice. The conviction enabled Thailand to request countries having extradition treaties with Thailand to arrest and deport him. This legal threat combined with Britain's revocation of Thaksin's visa, severely curtailed his physical movements and sent him on a quest for new travel documents and the protection afforded by foreign citizenship. Thaksin today claims Montenegrin citizenship. To judge from a reading of the Thai press, Thai diplomats spent an inordinate amount of time in pursuit of Thaksin after December 2008.

The crisis has provided incentives for politicians in both the Red and the Yellow camps to use foreign-policy issues as a way to mobilize nationalist sentiment in support of their cause. Thailand's conflict with Cambodia over the contested Preah Vihear temple, which a 1962 ruling of the International Court of Justice awarded to Cambodia, offers the most vivid illustration of this trend. In 2006 and 2007, Thailand blocked Cambodia's application to UNESCO for designation of the temple as a

World Heritage site, on the grounds that sovereignty of approximately 4.6 square kilometres around the temple remained in dispute. When the Samak government agreed to support Cambodia's application in June 2008, the People's Alliance for Democracy (PAD) and the Democrat Party accused it of selling out Thailand's national interest to Cambodia in exchange for business contracts. In July 2008, Thailand's Constitutional Court ruled that the entire Samak cabinet had violated the Thai constitution when it permitted Foreign Minister Nopphadon to sign an agreement with Cambodia supporting its application to UNESCO. Nopphadon rejected the allegations, claiming "I have not sold the country out." But the nationalist backlash forced him to resign.[4]

Playing the nationalist card, particularly with volatile neighbours, always carries the risk of spiralling out of control. In the wake of UNESCO's July 2008 decision to grant the temple World Heritage status, Cambodians celebrated in the street, Thai nationalists occupied the temple and within weeks heavily armed troops from both sides were facing off along the border. At first, Cambodian Prime Minister Hun Sen took the high road, urging Cambodians to remain calm, appealing to ASEAN for mediation, and calling for the United Nations to take note of the issue after Thailand rejected any role for ASEAN. [5] In the conflict's early days, Hun Sen's restraint stood in stark contrast to the recklessness of PAD and Democrat leaders. Anytime that Hun Sen exhibits greater statesmanship than his Thai counterparts is a sad day for Thai diplomacy.

The temple dispute did eventually escalate because it allowed Hun Sen to use the conflict to play his own nationalist card ahead of Cambodia's 27 July 2008 elections. Military clashes between Thai and Cambodian forces in October 2008 — the height of the Yellow Shirt demonstrations against the government of Prime Minister Somchai Wongsawat — killed one Thai and three Cambodian soldiers. At this time, Kasit, then shadow foreign minister, insulted Hun Sen with a series of derogatory remarks, including calling him a "gangster". Border skirmishes have led the two sides to exchange gunfire periodically since then. The deaths of a handful of Thai and Cambodian soldiers have resulted. Hun Sen abandoned his early restraint and for a time intervened directly in Thai affairs. He provided sanctuary to Red Shirt leaders, appointed Thaskin an economic advisor,[6] and permitted him to travel to Cambodia. Some reports have claimed that the Red Shirts were stockpiling weapons in Cambodia in anticipation of waging an armed insurgency.

In Thailand, both sides continue to use the temple and Thailand's relations with Cambodia as a political football. Upon taking office, Abhisit suggested pressing UNESCO for a review of Cambodia's application. The appointment of Kasit as foreign minister outraged the pro-Thaksin camp and made him the focus of efforts to weaken and delegitimize the government. The opposition used Kasit's remarks about Hun Sen in a March 2009 no-confidence vote to argue that he was unfit for the job of foreign minister because his comments strained relations with neighbours like Cambodia.

That Thailand would succumb to hurling decidedly undiplomatic language across the border and permit the conflict with Cambodia to turn deadly has damaged Thailand's image, and reinforced perceptions that Thailand in crisis is a problem state, particularly for ASEAN. There is no doubt that Cambodian Prime Minister Hun Sen for a time blatantly took sides in Thailand's political standoff, thereby violating ASEAN's bedrock principle of non-interference. The Abhisit government thus had legitimate cause for complaint. But it is precisely in such difficult situations that the external community expects Thailand to display its famed diplomatic skills.

A PROBLEM STATE: THE CHALLENGE OF MAINTAINING PROPER RELATIONS WITH THAILAND

The polarization of Thai foreign policy made it extremely difficult for other countries to avoid being dragged into Thai politics. Maintaining an even-handed position towards the crisis proved difficult when both parties to Thailand's prolonged conflict were lobbying the external community to accept their interpretation of it. Particularly since the violence of May 2010, Thai foreign policy has focused on damage control. The Abhisit government dispatched envoys to important partners to "explain" the situation in Thailand. This task was, however, complicated by the international publicity campaign that Thaksin and the Red Shirts launched to discredit the government's version of events. The war of words between the two sides has placed the international community smack in the middle, a place most would prefer to avoid.

One of the responsibilities of any country's diplomatic corps is to serve as interlocutors with foreign audiences. Thailand's dependence on external investment and the importance of tourism to its economic prosperity mean that efforts to convince foreign governments to lift the travel advisories that keep tourists and investment away are in the country's broad national interests. But the Abhisit government chose to "explain" Thailand's crisis to foreign governments in a manner geared to serve the particular interests of the anti-Thaksin camp.

The Abhisit government painted the crisis as a conflict pitting an ethical government against a ruthless, corrupt billionaire able to manipulate the country's lower classes by exhorting them to revolution in an effort to recapture his personal political standing and economic assets. The Abhisit government argued that it exhibited great restraint towards the Red Shirt demonstrations for a long time, that it negotiated in good faith a reconciliation plan to end the March–May 2010 protests peacefully, and that moderate National United Front for Democracy against Dictatorship (UDD) leaders accepted that plan before hardliners vetoed it at Thaksin's behest. According to the Abhisit government, therefore, blame for the May 2010 crackdown lay squarely with the Red Shirts. Similarly, acts of sabotage by well armed, well trained "black shirt" gunmen illustrated the existence of a terrorist conspiracy orchestrated and funded by Thaksin.

In contrast, the Red Shirt camp portrayed Thaksin as a democratically elected leader who was illegally overthrown by a military coup, a man who was the victim of politically motivated court convictions. In this interpretation of events, the Red Shirts were peacefully demonstrating for their political rights against an elitist government that sought to retain its traditional political and economic privileges through non-democratic means because it cannot win at the ballot box. According to former foreign minister Nopphadon, the Red Shirts are "simple farmers who love democracy and hate double standards". Blame for the death and destruction, according to this view, should be pinned on the Abhisit government's decision to use lethal military force to disperse peaceful protestors.

The problem facing the international community is that each of these narratives contains elements of truth. More critically, the competing narratives have important implications for how foreign governments might respond to the Abhisit government's requests for cooperation in arresting and repatriating former prime minister Thaksin under extradition treaties. Normally, a government's request for extradition is a legal, rather than a political, issue. The underlying assumption is that anyone convicted by an independent, impartial court of law should be required to serve his time. In Thaksin's case, the controversial legal decisions that resulted in the disbanding of the People's Power Party, the barring of Thaksinite politicians from taking part in elections, and the confiscation of much of Thaksin's wealth have raised questions about the independence of Thailand's judiciary. This pattern of legal decisions gave Thaksin grounds to argue that his conviction was politically motivated, and other countries should not be party to his extradition.

The Abhisit government's seemingly legalistic and bureaucratic requests to other countries for Thakin's extradition had, therefore, an inherently political aspect. They forced governments to determine whether Thaksin's corruption conviction resulted from politically driven judicial machinations or from an impartial review of the evidence and application of the law. In short, these extradition requests required the countries that received them to render judgement on the Thai legal system, something that they were loath to do.

The Abhisit government became deeply frustrated by the unwillingness of the international community to assist in its pursuit of Thaksin. Foreign Minister Kasit lamented that Thailand was "not getting any cooperation at all".[7] The May 2010 decision by Thailand's criminal court to issue an arrest warrant for Thaksin on terrorism charges for his role in orchestrating the Red Shirt protests only exacerbated the dilemma facing other countries. According to Prime Minister Abhisit, the arrest warrant would "reduce the obstacles" to international cooperation because it enabled Thailand to request Interpol's assistance in arresting Thaksin. The terrorism charge, however, was even more controversial than Thaksin's corruption conviction: any request by the Abhisit government for international cooperation to arrest Thaksin and repatriate him to stand trial on terrorism charges forced foreign countries to come to conclusions about the burden of culpability for the May 2010 violence in Bangkok. It is difficult to imagine a more overt intervention in the domestic affairs of another country.

As both Thai camps engage in a competition for international public opinion, they have called attention to the fact that Thai actions and attitudes are increasingly out of sync with twenty-first-century norms. In an era that privileges democracy, good governance, human rights protection, freedom of speech, and the peaceful resolution of disputes, events in Thailand since the 2006 coup have bucked international trends.

Thaksin's exhortation to his supporters to foment "revolution" from the safety of exile and the denigration of the Red Shirts as "Marxist-Leninists" by Abhisit's special envoy, Kiat Sitthi-amon, sound to foreign ears like throw-backs to an earlier era that many thought Thailand had put behind it. Thai diplomacy has long been likened to bamboo: it bends with the wind or shifts in line with global trends to ensure that the country is never broken. Today, Thai diplomacy appears to be battling against the wind and on the verge of breaking.

For countries like the United States, those with significant ties to Thailand, the isolation of the functional aspects of relations from the county's domestic political crisis has emerged as a significant priority. On the economic side, interviews with business people suggest that, when it comes to areas such as investment approvals and licensing, Thailand's government has continued to function smoothly. Similarly, American military officials report a similar situation at the operational level. Exercises take place, officers are trained, and the cooperation regarding the movement of men and supplies through Thai bases to the Middle East is good. Nevertheless, the current political situation has made Thailand sensitive to perceived slights. Despite the solid working relationship, Thai military officials expressed deep concern over the U.S. decision to hold its first military exercise, Angkor Sentinel, with Cambodia. They claimed that it was inappropriate for its U.S. ally to enhance ties with Cambodia while the two neighbours remained locked in a face-off along their shared border. American military officials were forced to underscore repeatedly that the Unite States took no sides in the Thai-Cambodian dispute; they wanted the two countries to work peacefully towards its resolution and on other matters as well.[8]

There is a clear perception in Thailand that outside actors have favourites in the country's political standoff. Traditionally close U.S. ties with the Thai military is often cited as evidence for American partiality to the anti-Thaksin camp, while Thaksin's commercial diplomacy, his "Asia for the Asians" mantra, and his close ties with Chinese leaders are presented as evidence of China's preference for the Thaksinite side. The growing competition between the United States and China for influence in Southeast Asia has led some analysts to argue that China's pragmatic diplomacy during the crisis is likely to ensure its own greater future influence in Thailand and the decline of the influence of the United States.[9]

The paramount interest of Thailand's important foreign partners and friends, however, is not in who prevails but rather in the county's ability to find a way out of its crisis. The longer it goes on, the longer critical issues such as the insurgency in the Thai South will fester unresolved and the more difficult it will become for other countries to stay above the fray. Democracies face the greatest challenges in trying to keep their relations with Thailand on an even keel. Most have made the promotion of democracy and respect for political and civil liberties a central foreign policy plank. Further, democracies' open political systems provide opportunities for NGOs and others to influence their foreign policy. All countries have an interest in stability returning to Thailand, but many democratic countries also have an interest in how that stability is achieved. Countries like China can adhere to a strict policy of "non-interference", while countries like the United States have laws and policies compelling them to speak up against things such as the use of violence and restrictions on press freedoms. Resultant statements say less about American preferences regarding who prevails in the Thai crisis and more about the American policy process.

INTERNATIONAL MEDIATION?

If most countries are attempting to avoid taking sides in the Thai crisis, they nevertheless also face the dilemma of whether active intervention — publicly or behind the scenes — will help resolve the crisis and protect their interests. The sheer number of statements from external actors to note their concern and often to call for international mediation to help solve Thailand's crisis offers telling evidence of perceptions of Thailand as a problem state. At the height of the May 2010 violence, United Nations Secretary General Ban Ki Moon expressed his concern over "the rapidly mounting tensions and violence" and called for the resumption of dialogue.[10] The Abhisit government was more restrained in its response to the United Nations than was Thaksin, who once retorted, "the UN is not my father" after it criticized Thailand's human rights situation.[11] But it nevertheless adamantly rejected any international mediation in the crisis.

Thailand's rejection of a legitimate role for external parties is at odds with its earlier support for a similar idea. In the 1990s, Thai Foreign Minister Surin Pitsuwan emerged as the leading proponent of "flexible" engagement, the principle that ASEAN had a legitimate concern with events in one member that had a negative impact on the region. In such cases, Thailand argued then, deviations from ASEAN's norm on non-interference were warranted by concern for the broader regional good.

Some ASEAN members attempted to put flexible engagement into practice. Indonesian President Susilo Bambang Yudhoyono met with representatives of both Thai camps on the sidelines of the G-20 summit, albeit with little impact, and Indonesia among others offered Thailand its good offices to help resolve the crisis. The dilemma for outsiders is that mediation only works when the parties involved desire it. The Abhisit government rejected the idea of external mediation, using ASEAN's commitment to sovereign integrity as justification. In an ironic twist, it was Vietnam, long one of the staunchest opponents of "flexible engagement" that issued a joint ASEAN statement in its capacity as ASEAN chair expressing the organization's concern over the May 2010 violence and its support for the people and government of Thailand "in finding a peaceful resolution to the ongoing challenge in the country through dialogue and in full respect of democratic principles and rule of law".[12]

As prime minister, Thaksin rebuffed all critical comment on Thai domestic affairs on the part of foreign governments. He famously called the United States a "useless friend" when it raised concerns over extra-judicial killings during his war against drug dealers. Today, both Thaksin and the Red Shirts actively seek foreign support. Anticipating the crackdown that was to come, the Red Shirts in late April 2010 called on the EU to send monitors to their encampment and to pressure the Abhisit government to "avert a human rights catastrophe".[13] Two weeks after Abhisit sent Kiat Sitthi-amon to Washington to seek support for the government's reconciliation plan, former foreign minister Nopphadon arrived in the same city to present the Thaksin camp's view. Nopphadon expressed a desire that "the U.S. would become more engaged about the situation in Thailand", while claiming that this "doesn't mean that they interfere in Thai Politics. It just means they give friendly advice to a friend — it's natural".[14] For long-time observers of Thailand, the spectacle of Surin's own Democrat party adamantly rejecting flexible engagement while Thaskin calls for it suggest that the world has turned upside down.

WHITHER THAI FOREIGN POLICY?

Many Thai analysts believe that the current crisis will prove but a brief exception to Thailand's proud tradition of effective and successful foreign policy. Once calm returns, they argue, Thailand will regain the international stature to which it has become accustomed. In support of this argument, they point to Indonesia, which focused almost exclusively on domestic affairs in the early post-Soeharto period but has recently raised its international profile significantly. It has won a seat on the UN Security Council, become a member of the G-20, and reasserted its leadership in ASEAN and broader regional institutions.

It is unlikely, however, that Thailand will be able to make such a triumphant return to the international stage. Indonesia simply looms larger in international affairs than does Thailand. It is the world's fourth most populous country, third largest democracy, and home to the world's largest community of Muslims. Indonesia is also a member of a number of important global communities: it resides physically in Asia but is part of the broader Muslim world, the developing world, and the community of democracies. Indonesia's ability to navigate these diverse constituencies in pursuit of global peace and stability is what makes it such a potentially important international player. Thailand simply lacks Indonesia's weight in global affairs.

The more important Indonesian lesson for Thailand is not that Indonesia regained its international standing, but that the restoration of that standing came only after Indonesia embarked on a series of dramatic reforms. These reforms were designed to redress some of the same problems that face Thailand today. At the time of Soeharto's fall in 1998, Indonesian leaders had to contend with over-centralized state, a military accustomed to playing a large role in politics, insurgencies at opposite ends of the archipelago, and a lack of consensus regarding how to structure the political system. Since then, a decentralization programme has transferred political and fiscal authority to the districts, ameliorating an important source of grievances outside the capital. The military has returned to the barracks, and Jakarta has forged a historic peace deal with the Free Aceh Movement. The country has also made a successful transition to democracy. None of these steps was easy, all were contentious, but Indonesia today is stronger for having taken them.

Indonesia's current rise in the global arena is due not just to its size but also to its hard-won domestic achievements.

Thailand will not regain its international stature until it has resolved its fundamental political differences. Foreign policy is at heart the pursuit of national interests and the projection of values abroad. Thailand today finds itself locked in a bitter battle over whose interests and what values should be reflected in the political system. Until there is some degree of reconciliation between the two sides, and a basic consensus regarding the interests and values that underpin the Thai nation, it is difficult to envision a revival of Thailand's vaunted statecraft.

Notes

1. This point has been made most strongly in Pavin Chachavalpongpun, "Diplomacy Under Siege: Thailand's Political Crisis and the Impact on Foreign Policy", *Contemporary Southeast Asia* 31, no. 3 (December 2009): 447–67.
2. Confidential interviews with diplomats evacuated from Pattaya in April 2009.
3. Donald K. Emmerson, "ASEAN's Pattaya Problem", *Asia Times Online*, 18 April 2009 <http://www.atimes.com/atimes/Southeast_Asia/KD18Ae01.html> (accessed 12 March 2011).
4. "Thai Government in Disarray", AFP, 10 July 2010.
5. Craig Guthrie, "Taking the High Ground at Preah Vihear", *Asia Times Online*, 25 July 2008 <http://www.atimes.com/atimes/Southeast_Asia/JG25Ae02.html> (accessed 12 March 2011).
6. A post that he resigned in August 2010.
7. P. Paramameswaran, "Thai FM Slams International Community Over Crisis", AFP, 12 April 2010.
8. "Thailand Expresses Concerns over US-Cambodian Joint Exercise", *BBC Monitoring Asia Pacific*, 25 June 2010.
9. Shawn W. Crispin, "US Slips, China Glides in Thai Crisis", *Asia Times Online*, 20 July 2010 <http://www.atimes.com/atimes/Southeast_Asia/LG20Ae01.html> (accessed 12 March 2011).
10. Ambika Ahuja and Bill Tarrant, "Thai Violence Spirals as Both Sides Seek Reinforcements", Reuters, 15 May 2010 <http://www.reuters.com/article/idUSTRE64C0L620100515> (accessed 7 July 2010).
11. Kavi Chongkittavorn , "PM Takes Steps to Mend Relations with the UN", *The Nation*, 21 September 2009.

12. "ASEAN's Chairman's Statement on the Situation in Thailand", issued by the Ministry of Foreign Affairs of Viet Nam, 21 May 2010 <http://www.aseansec.org/24718.htm> (accessed 12 March 2010).
13. Nirmal Gosh, "A Day of Rest", *Straits Times*, 30 April 2010.
14. "Thaksin Aide Seeks US Role in Thailand", AFP, 1 July 2010.

18

THAILAND IN TROUBLE
Revolt of the Downtrodden or Conflict among Elites?

Pasuk Phongpaichit and Chris Baker

Among academics, journalists, and other commentators on Thailand, there are two very different views of the conflict that has steadily grown over the last six years. The first argues that this is an uprising of the downtrodden, especially farmers from the poorer Northeast and far North, demanding a better deal, and being fiercely resisted by an elite, jealous of its power and privilege; underlying this uprising is a great division in income, wealth, power, and opportunity in the society. The second interpretation argues that the social division is illusory or unimportant, and that this is a battle among elites, essentially between former Prime Minister Thaksin Shinawatra and his enemies, with ordinary people being used as paid pawns in the struggle.

This paper was prepared while the authors were visiting scholars under the GCOE program at the National Graduate Institute for Policy Studies and was presented at the GRIPS Forum, Tokyo, on 21 June 2010.

We want to argue that it is both — both a real social movement, and a battle between elite figures and groups. These two historical processes are inextricably intertwined, and that is why the resolution is so complex.

The first section discusses the socioeconomic background, and why a social movement of this force should have appeared at this point in history. The second examines how an elite conflict has developed into competitive mass mobilizations, and a fierce ideological debate.

RISING ASPIRATIONS, GATHERING RESENTMENTS

The press has tended to describe the Red Shirts as the "rural poor". While that description has a kernel of truth, it is also quite misleading. Many of the movement's supporters are well off. Even the poorer ones are not as poor as they were a few years ago. Behind the upsurge, there are two forces. One is a revolution of rising aspirations, driven by increasing prosperity. The other is an outbreak of gathering resentment, driven by ever-widening and more obvious inequality in the distribution of income, wealth, power, and public goods.

Figure 18.1 shows Thailand's economic growth since 1950, expressed in terms of real per capita income. This is one of the best records of any country in the world. The 1997 crisis was a setback, but only temporary. Most strikingly, over the past generation, since around 1980, average real per capita income has tripled. Most Thais are much better off than their parents were. Poverty has declined from around 40 per cent in 1980 to 6 per cent today. But growing prosperity has other results. People have more assets to protect, more interests to pursue. They have more aspirations for themselves and their children. They have more education, more access to information. And they have more demands on the state — to provide public goods like education and health, and public services like a working legal system and functioning police.

The Red Shirts who poured into Bangkok in early March 2010 were not the destitute. They had trucks, pick-ups, and motorcycles. They were relatively well dressed. These were the aggrieved with assets.

But the gains of growth have been very unevenly distributed. Of course that is often the case, but in Thailand the bias has been very marked — as a result of the particular pattern of growth.

Figure 18.1
Real GDP per head, 1951–2009

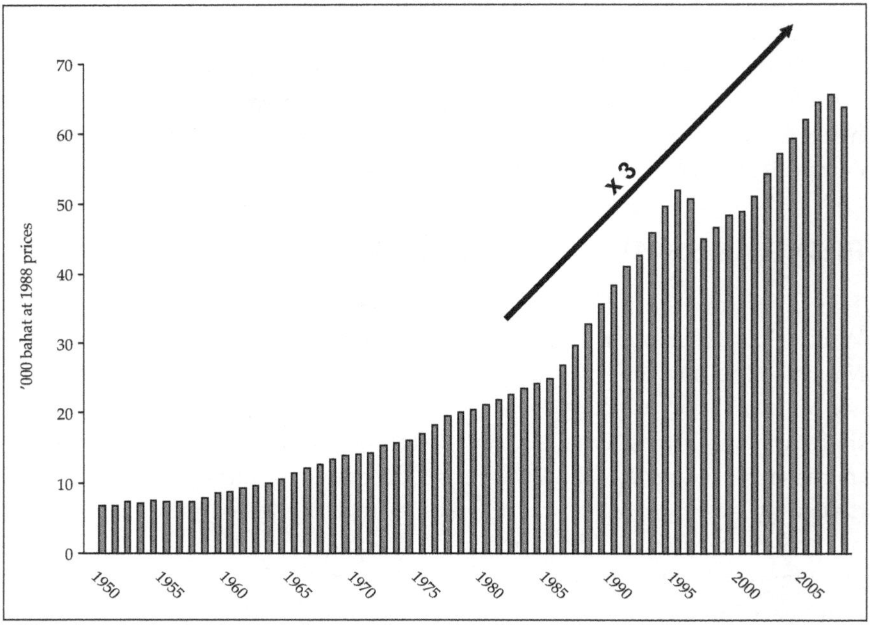

Thailand has aimed for industrialization by relying on borrowed capital and technology, and relying on the world market for demand. This has shaped the workforce in a particular way (see Figure 18.2). Multinational firms use capital-intensive technology, so although manufacturing contributes around 40 per cent of GDP and 90 per cent of exports, it employs only 8 per cent of workers.[1] The government relies on exports for growth and so has no incentive to boost domestic demand. It allows agriculture to decline. Many people are still left in the declining agricultural sector, while others are forced to take refuge in a sprawling urban informal sector of casual labour, vending, and petty services.

Meanwhile, a white-collar middle class has developed, largely to service the multinational-dominated modern economy. Its numbers are rather modest, but their incomes have been boosted close to first-world

Figure 18.2
Labour Force, 2005

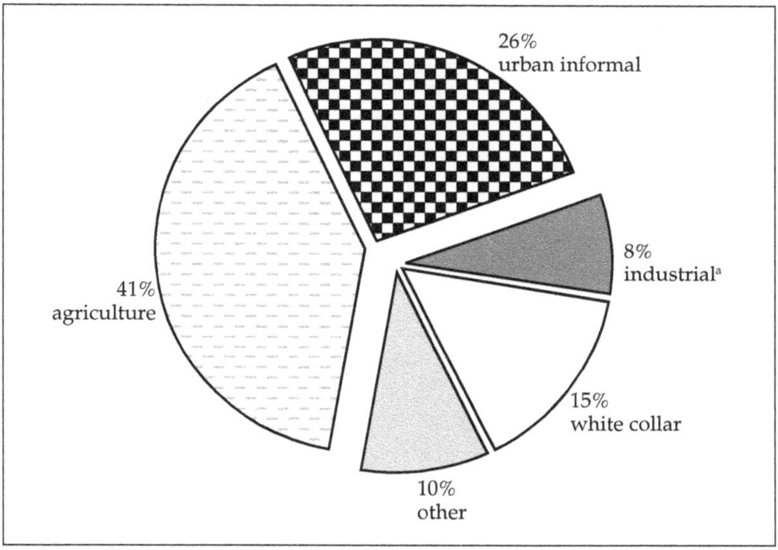

Note: [a]in factories with 10+ workers.

levels. The combination of low numbers and high privilege makes for insecurity.

It is instructive to compare this pattern to that of Japan back in 1970. Then, 34 per cent of Japanese worked in industry, four times the Thai proportion today; only 17 per cent in agriculture, less than half the Thai figure; many more in the white-collar working class, and almost none in the informal sector.

So while Thailand was prospering over the last generation, it was also becoming more unequal. Figure 18.3 shows the Gini coefficient, a measure of income inequality, where higher means more unequal. From 1960 to 1980, inequality gradually worsened, but from the 1980s, when the country launched full-tilt into export-oriented industrialization, it worsened much more steeply. Recently, the trend has flattened but shows no clear sign of improvement.

According to a famous theory advanced by Simon Kuznets, inequality will usually worsen at the early stages of development because only a

Figure 18.3
Gini coefficiet, 1960–2000

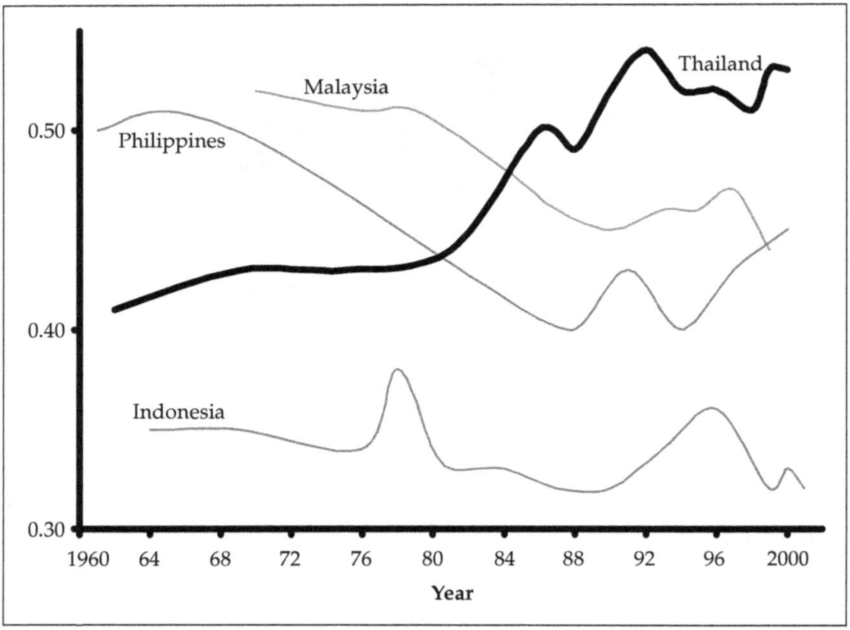

few people benefit, but should then even out as industrialization takes root and more people gain access to opportunities. A Thai economist calculated when Thailand should have reached this turning point, if it followed the pattern found elsewhere. Her answer was 1994.[2] But clearly, the turn never came. Even more striking is the comparison to neighbouring countries. They all have shown improvement, and have now significantly better income distributions than Thailand.

The income gap between the top 20 per cent and the bottom 20 per cent of the population is now about thirteen times. That compares to four times in Japan and Scandinavia, six to eight times in North America and Europe, and ten to twelve times in China and Thailand's Asian neighbours. The countries with income distributions worse than Thailand's tend to be in Latin America, with backgrounds of slavery and plantation economies, and endemic instability.

Recently, there has been the first survey of wealth in Thailand, covering land, housing, and financial assets. It found that the gap between the top and bottom quintiles was a staggering sixty-nine times (see Figure 18.4).

Inequality goes far beyond income and wealth. There is also great inequality in power. From way back, the Thai government has been highly centralized. Power is concentrated in the capital city. Only recently and very partially has that concentration been reduced by decentralization. The less well off have less access to the legal system, and to government officials. Partly that is a matter of money — access is available for a fee — but partly it is a function of social attitudes. This differential access results in great inequities in the distribution of public goods and services. In Bangkok, there is one doctor for every 850 people; in Loei Province in the northeast, there is one per 14,000.

There is also inequality in the distribution of respect. To put it bluntly, many Bangkokians look down on rural people as lazy, uneducated, and

Figure 18.4
Distribution of Wealth, 2006

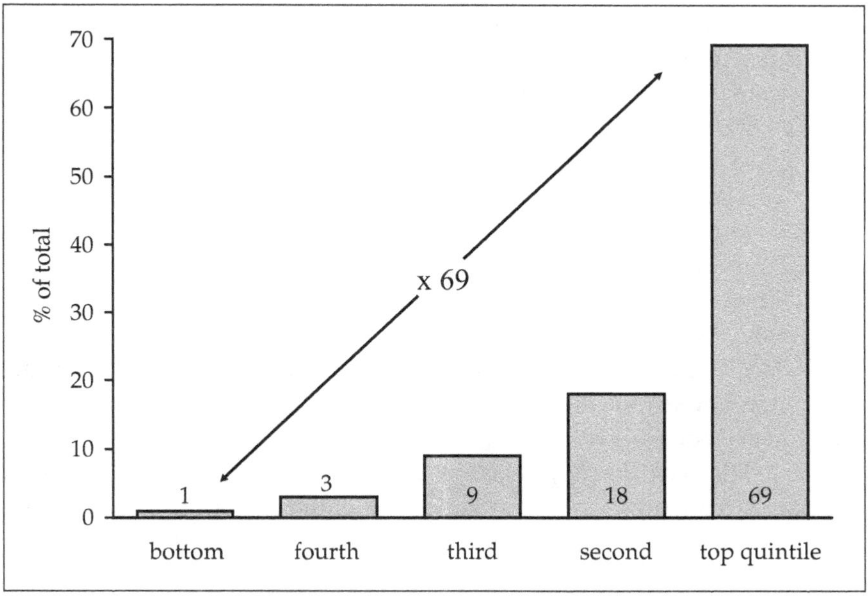

Source: Kiatpong, Wilatluk and Nalin (2008).

stupid. They are especially rude about people from areas once described as "Lao". Not uncoincidentally, these are the areas in the North and Northeast that supply much of the support for the Red Shirts. During the protests of March–May 2010, some Bangkokians went down to the protest site, held up signs and shouted abuse, calling the protestors "buffaloes"—very rude in Thai.

Finally, inequality is not only getting worse, it is also becoming more obvious, especially to those at the lower end of the scale. Twenty-five years ago, Bangkok still looked like an overgrown village. Since then, it has expanded massively in size, soared upwards into high-rises, and taken on the look-and-feel of an international city, very different from the village. Twenty-five years ago, rather few villagers travelled to the city. Now many do, often circulating back and forth in search of work to supplement a declining income from agriculture. These migrants experience Thailand's inequalities as a daily reality. It is no surprise that migrants working as taxi and motorcycle drivers have become one of the core bases of Red Shirt support. Even those rural-dwellers who do not actually visit the city in person can see it daily on the television screen. TV programming is all produced in Bangkok, with the Bangkok audience primarily in mind. Soap operas in particular love to dwell on the affluence of the urban newly rich.

In a recent national survey, over three-quarters of the sample said they believed the income gap is too wide. A third thought it "intolerably wide". Among the poorest fifth of the sample, that proportion goes up to almost half.[3] Inequality is not just about statistics. It is perceived and resented.

So, rising aspirations, and growing resentment of widening inequalities. But such conditions do not inevitably lead to a political movement. Why here? Why now?

In fact, the demand for change has been developing for a long time. During and after the Cold War, the Army branded any form of popular movement "communist", and suppressed it. But this repression eased by the 1990s. The disaffected tried to make themselves heard through campaigns and protests. In the early 1990s, there were only a handful. By the later part of the decade, there were a thousand demonstrations recorded per year, around three per day. The peaks come after economic crises, when much of the pain is passed down onto farmers and workers.

In 1998–99, after the Asian Financial Crisis, the capital was besieged by groups of protesting farmers, and also racked by labour strikes. The recent sub-prime crisis depressed agrarian prices, and caused unemployment among casual workers.

A major political shift occurred when the aggrieved began to seek redress through the electoral process, rather than protest. This change came about between 1997 and 2005. Thailand has had an elective parliament on and off for many decades, but for reasons discussed below, parliament was a cozy club for the rich, and ordinary people did not feel much benefit from it. Two things changed that. First, in the late 1990s, decentralization and related reforms increased the number of elections. Whereas people had earlier gone to the polls once every few years for a parliamentary election, they now elected their village headman, local mayor, local councillors, and senators. While the actions of their members of parliament were remote from sight, those of their local government representatives were very close at hand. In a very short time, people learned that the vote was a powerful tool for self-improvement.

The second reason that electoral politics became more important lies in the career of Thaksin Shinawatra, who broke the mould of Thai politics by making a direct deal with the voters.

ELITE CONFLICT, MASS MOBILIZATIONS, IDEOLOGICAL WARFARE

Key to understanding the present crisis is the fact that, in Thailand's modern political history, there has been no decisive break or disjuncture involving mass mobilization. There was no nationalist movement against colonial rule, no war defeat discrediting the elite. The revolution against the absolute monarchy in 1932 enjoyed wide support but required no mass mobilization. The communist insurgency of the 1960s and 1970s was located deep in the forests and hills and never swelled into a mass uprising. Peasant movements and labour agitation have been localized.

The modern Thai political system is best viewed as an oligarchy which has never been radically threatened from below. This oligarchy has constantly evolved, incorporating new groups and power centres, and building internal bonds through networks, patronage ties, and deals. Under the absolute monarchy, a bureaucratic elite developed in the early twentieth century, and has since been entrenched. From the 1930s to the 1980s, a military elite became absolutely dominant. As the urban economy grew in the post-war era of development, new business groups were accommodated. As prosperity spread up-country, and better communications tied the provincial areas more tightly to the capital, a provincial business elite was also incorporated. More recently, the senior judiciary and parts of civil society have also been included.

Although noble families and old money figure strongly in this oligarchy, this has never been a closed elite. Indeed its resilience has come partly from its openness and flexibility.

Until recently, the advent of parliament and electoral politics resulted in no major challenge to this order. People invested heavily to ensure that money was critical to electoral success, excluding all those who did not have enough. In the 1990s, around 70 per cent of MPs were drawn from the ranks of male business owners who make up less than 3 per cent of the population. Parliament was a highly unrepresentative rich men's club, and one of the key institutions of oligarchic networking.

The financial crisis of 1997 created the conditions for a challenge to this oligarchic structure. Thailand had not experienced a shrinkage of the economy since GDP figures were first collected, and the savage downturn of almost 20 per cent undermined the prestige and credibility of those in power. Against this background, a series of political reforms were pushed through, including a new constitution and decentralization. And the economic distress intensified the upsurge of pressure from below.

The full consequences of these developments, however, took time to emerge. Thaksin Shinawatra positioned himself at the head of a challenge to the old system. But initially he challenged only the excessive power of the central bureaucracy and the old political guard of the Democrat Party, which he pictured as bureaucratic in style. Thaksin promised to rescue the economy from the crisis and take Thailand into the ranks of First World countries by shouldering aside the bureaucracy and running the country like a business. At the start, he was enthusiastically supported by the business community and most of the middle class.

But a challenge to one part of the oligarchy gradually came to be seen as a threat to all of it. The bureaucrats resented and resisted Thaksin's efforts at reform. Because history showed that reformers in Thailand risk being ejected by coup, Thaksin tried to exert control over the military. But his efforts were clumsy, and he ended up antagonizing powerful factions in the military elite. Business initially cheered Thaksin's efforts, but then turned sour when it became obvious that most of the benefits accrued to a small coterie of families clustered around Thaksin, and especially Thaksin's own family businesses. The palace also showed its displeasure. This was shaping up as a classic inter-elite battle, of which there are many examples in Thailand's recent past. But the scene was totally changed by the new element in the political context — the upsurge of a demand from below for better access to power, better treatment, and more public goods.

Thaksin flirted with this new force from 2000, when his political organizers, recruited from among old student radicals, crafted an electoral platform including a universal health scheme, agrarian debt relief, and micro-finance. As the first signs of elite opposition to his project emerged, he implemented this programme rapidly, and was rewarded with an upsurge in popularity. He responded with more programmes, including a promise to end poverty and generous agricultural subsidies. Then in 2004–05, as opposition from the oligarchy and many of his early supporters swelled, he went much farther — presenting himself as a classic populist who drew his authority directly from the popular vote, who was dedicated to working "for the people" and who was openly disdainful of the old guard, including bureaucrats, bankers, academics, newspaper editors, and judges.

Thaksin had shown no sign of such radicalism in his early career. He had been changed from below, by the upsurge of demand for a better deal. In 2005, he won a landslide victory at the polls, and promised his supporters he would rule for a quarter-century, rather in the model of Mahathir Mohamad or Lee Kuan Yew.

The old oligarchy now closed ranks against Thaksin. But something else happened which broadened this confrontation beyond a narrow elite struggle. Much of the Bangkok middle class, which had earlier been generally supportive of Thaksin's project, reacted fearfully against his lurch towards populism. Conscious of their minority status in the electorate, and of their privileged position, they felt especially vulnerable to Thaksin's new populist crusade. The Yellow Shirt movement was launched in 2005 as an explicit campaign to defend the interests of the middle class.

To bind together the opponents to Thaksin, and raise the emotional temperature, Yellow Shirt leaders alleged that Thaksin was a threat to the monarchy. In fact, Thaksin had been careful not to attack the monarchy, or be seen as a threat. But the Yellow Shirts made up a story about Thaksin plotting the overthrow of the monarchy during an excursion to Finland. They dressed themselves in tee-shirts announcing that they were the monarchy's defenders.

In Thailand's old politics of oligarchy, the classic strategy at such times of conflict was a military coup. Indeed, that was what occurred on 19 September 2006. But the old politics no longer prevailed. So the coup did not really work. The Army was out of practice at this manoeuvre, and the post-coup government was a disaster, quickly losing all popularity. Because Thailand with its globalized economy needed to be politically acceptable in the world, parliament had to be restored quickly. Despite a massive attempt to rig the election using public funds and public servants, the pro-Thaksin forces won another victory, and could not be prevented from forming the government.

The attack on Thaksin and his populism now became a wider and deeper attack on electoral democracy. The post-coup government made a start with a new constitution which undid many of the gains of the 1990s reforms, diminished the power of parliament, and elevated the military and judiciary. The Yellow Shirts now became a military-godfathered mob that harassed ministers and besieged parliament. The judiciary handed down a series of judgements that overthrew two governments, sacked several individual ministers, disbanded three political parties, and banned 220 MPs from politics for five years.

In parallel, the Yellow Shirts developed an ideological justification for this attack. They argued that most politicians were corrupt, and that elections were won with money, and hence the results held no legitimacy. They proposed moving away from "one person, one vote" by bringing back appointed MPs, basing representation on occupational groups, or transferring power away to the monarchy, bureaucracy and judiciary.

The Red Shirt movement or the National United Front for Democracy against Dictatorship (UDD) emerged as counter to the Yellow Shirts. Its core is among the supporters of Thaksin, largely in the far North, the Northeast, and the migrant population of the capital. The movement has also gathered support from many in the intelligentsia and middle class who have no love for Thaksin but who believe that democracy is under threat. The movement was structured through media channels, with local groups clustered around community radio stations, and national communication achieved through a satellite TV channel. From late 2009, the leaders conducted political schools. Local groups regularly ran fund-raisers, and campaign meetings.

From mid-2008, Red Shirt and Yellow Shirt groups have occasionally clashed. In a moment of terrible clarity, Yellow Shirts claiming to be defenders of the monarchy clashed with Red Shirts claiming to be defenders of democracy.

At the end of 2008, the second pro-Thaksin government after the 2007 election was forced out of power by military pressure, judicial rulings, and a parliamentary manoeuvre. After that, the main demand of the Red Shirt movement was for an election to reinstate the popular mandate. They also wanted to change the constitution, perhaps back to the 1997 version. In their rhetoric, they called themselves *phrai*, an old word for serf in Thailand's version of a feudal system; described their enemies as *ammat*, an old word for a senior noble or official; and railed against "double standards". In this vocabulary, they clearly showed the resentment against the inequities of wealth, power, and opportunity.

After December 2008, the Democrat Party headed a coalition government. The party has a royalist heritage, and for the last two decades it has positioned itself as the party of the urban middle class. The government that came to power in 2008 relied heavily on military support. The prime minister lived inside an Army camp for a long period in 2010. In April 2009 and again in May 2010, large military operations dispersed protests demanding a new election. The government engaged in suppression of the media on a scale not seen since the military era, with pro-Red-Shirt newspapers closed, radio stations threatened, the Red TV occasionally disrupted, thousands of websites blocked, and an unprecedented number of cases under the *lèse majesté* law.

So, to sum up, there is an elite conflict in progress in Thailand, but there is also a widening of the political nation, which is challenging the political structure. Thaksin and his coterie set out to displace the bureaucracy and the old political establishment, represented especially by the Democrat Party. At the beginning, this was an elite conflict, and it is still in progress. The Democrats now hold power, and are desperate to prevent Thaksin returning.

But the conflict then flowed beyond the elites. Thaksin, despite everything in his background, became the instrument of a demand, bubbling up from below, for a fairer society. Thaksin was transformed by this force into a kind of politician common in most countries, but very new in Thailand — a stump populist who claims the direct support of the people. He thus became a trigger for the mass of people to find meaning in the vote as a means to better themselves.

Thaksin's lurch to populism, combined with his extraordinary wealth, then made many in the middle class feel insecure. They looked to the old institutions, the military and the monarchy, to make up for their weakness in numbers. Many were mobilized to join the Yellow Shirt movement of sustained street protests. The conflict within the elite thus broadened into two antagonistic mass mobilizations.

These two movements have then sparked a fierce ideological debate over how Thailand's democracy should develop. The Red Shirt side wants to restore the electoral system to something like the 1997 constitution as a precondition for reducing the "double standards", which of course means the entrenched power of the old oligarchy.

In response, the Yellow side argues that a democracy without checks and balances will be dangerous and unstable. They want a stronger framework of law, and a higher sense of morality, to restrain the patent corruption and rent-seeking by politicians.

The elite conflict and the social movement are joined through the person of Thaksin. This adds complication because he is a paradoxical figure — a modernist and business advocate who became a populist; a man with contempt for democracy who became its defendant; a corrupt moneybags who profited from the "double standards" and then railed against them. But history is strewn with such complications.

CONCLUSION: IN PERSPECTIVE

The turmoil in Bangkok during March–May 2010 needs to be placed in some perspective. It was dramatic, but not so very different from events in many other cities. In the same months, there were riots in Greece, battles with the police in Turkey, an occupation of the capital by the dispossessed in Egypt, Maoist demonstrations in Nepal, and a riot in the capital of Kyrgyzstan that physically drove the president out of his house and job. Many of these outbreaks, like those in Thailand, were revolts of the dispossessed against an old political establishment.

The widening of the political nation and challenge to old oligarchy are processes that most countries experience, especially as they become more prosperous. Thailand's transition is especially turbulent because, for certain historical reasons, it has come rather late and faces fierce opposition, strengthened by old institutions.

Over the past several years, a handful of reliable surveys have asked a representative sample of the Thai population about political matters. The overwhelming majority state that they have faith in electoral democracy, are happy with constitutional monarchy, have no problem with peaceful demonstrations, and would like the Army and members of the Privy Council to keep out of politics.[4]

At the same time, the most recent of these surveys shows that both Red Shirts and Yellow Shirts have significant bases of support.[5] The challenge for Thailand lies in getting these movements off the streets and into representative institutions so that their clashing views on reform can be debated with words and ideas, not crude weaponry.

The Red Shirt movement is an attack on Thailand's power structure. It is not an attack on business, or on the capitalist system. Although its support is based largely in certain classes, it has no enemy class that it wants to tear down.[6]

Although this turmoil has dragged on for more than five years now, its impact on the economy so far has been muted. In the first quarter of 2010, the Thai economy rebounded from the global slump by growing at a rate of 12 per cent; that rate seemed unsustainable. Tourism in particular was put a serious risk. But manufacturing was not directly disrupted, and exports are doing fine. Predictions for the full year's growth remained around 6 per cent.

The killing and burning at the end of the May 2010 outburst are the most searing images left in our minds. But it is worth recalling what had happened in the prior weeks. Tens of thousands of people poured into the capital. They were very good-natured, had very reasonable demands, and mostly had no interest in violence. They were welcomed by many Bangkok people — not only their brothers and cousins among the rural-urban migrants, but also typical Bangkok salarymen and salarywomen. Even when the city became badly disrupted by the demonstration, and when a minority vented their abuse in counter-demos and in cyberspace, an opinion poll showed massive opposition against the government using violence to clear the protest.

One positive outcome of the turmoil is that people in power are at last aware of the inequality problem. For the first time, the government has allotted a budget specifically for this issue. The peak business associations asked to meet with government to discuss inequality. The Thai Chamber of Commerce have come up with a "road map" to reduce inequality. One of the panels appointed in the wake of the May 2010 violence has been tasked to address this issue. But addressing economic inequality in top-down, paternalistic style will not work. Politics has to lead economics. Thailand's battered democracy needs to be rescued. In the wake of the 3 July 2011 polls, that means reforming the constitution to return towards the 1997 model; removing the multiplying restrictions on freedom of expression; reinstating the processes of bureaucratic reform and democratic decentralization; and providing a route for the Army to withdraw from the political front line.

We continue to believe that Thailand is engaged in a historic transition which will ultimately be positive. Yet it will take time.

Notes

1. Total industrial employment is around 12 per cent, but only 8 per cent are employed in establishments with ten or more people.
2. Research by Duangmani Laowakun.
3. Survey by Somchai Jitsuchon of the Thailand Development Research Institute.
4. The Thai Health Foundation commissioned a nationwide survey with a sample of over 5,000 respondents in July 2009. Among respondents, 93 per cent believed that the constitutional monarchy was the most appropriate system of government for Thailand; 85 per cent wanted to retain the right to peaceful demonstration; 79 per cent believed that the government should not attack a peaceful demonstration; 56 per cent believed the Army should have no right to stage a coup, rip up the constitution, or overthrow a government;

and 75 per cent thought that members of the Privy Council should not get involved in supporting or opposing political movements. The survey has never been presented or published.

5. In the same survey, 6 per cent of respondents said they had participated in Yellow Shirt demonstrations, and 6 per cent in Red Shirt demonstrations. In all, 18 per cent agreed with the Yellow Shirts, and another 23 per cent could accept them in part, while 26 per cent opposed them and a third declined to answer. For the Red Shirts, 20 per cent were supportive, another 18 per cent partially supportive, and a third were strongly opposed. Farmers and manual labourers are somewhat under-represented in the sample, which probably biases these results a bit.
6. The Red Shirt movement is a coalition of various groups. Some hold socialist or republican ideas, but probably these are in a minority.

19

FROM RED TO RED
An Auto-ethnography of Economic and Political Transitions in a Northeastern Thai Village

Pattana Kitiarsa

INTRODUCTION

The principal goal of this essay is to provide some vernacular explanations of Thailand's political crisis. Most scholars of Thai politics focus their attention on what has happened at the heart of the power game. This focus underlies their characterization of the current crisis as the country's most polarized political conflict ever. McCargo's powerful conception of "network monarchy"[1] and work on the rise and fall of Thaksin Shinawatra, on the power struggle among members of the Thai elite, and on the role of the middle class in Thailand's problematic democratization have made significant contributions.[2] The powerful elite and urban middle class, with much greater access to capital, the media, bureaucratic support, and electoral resources, are the perennial driving force of the Thai political economy. However, a focus on the elite and on political bargaining in Thai core offers only one side of a complex story. Ordinary people from the countryside and of urban working class backgrounds also have a very important part to play in Thailand's crisis. My concern is that the production of scholarly knowledge on the changing political and economic life of small people at the grass-roots level seems inadequate and of insufficient depth. Thailand's crisis cannot be explained without some understanding of what has actually happened in the political and economic microcosms of the countryside.

During a trip to my home village in early June 2010, I was astonished by a number of profound transformations of the village economy, of lifestyles, and of people's level of active participation in both local and national politics. The place that I forever call home is situated on the bank of the Mekong and in the farthest corner of Nong Khai Province, northeastern Thailand. Its marginal location is not far from the Laotian capital of Vientiane on the opposite river-bank. I have gradually realized that the geopolitical and socioeconomic landscapes of my birthplace are no longer the same. Walking through acres of young rubber plantations and observing village folks' busy everyday lives, my inner sense is that the village in which I grew up in the 1970s and early 1980s has come to exist only in my distant, nostalgic memory.

In this essay, I build on an auto-ethnographic account in order to reflect on the complex forces behind the radical changes in my own birthplace and to set them against the backdrop of Thailand's ongoing political crisis. From the margin, I look into the country's disturbing political polarization, which was most apparently manifested at the Thai core. I use stories from my recent homeward-bound journey to think through the questions of how and why villagers from the Thai countryside have become die-hard supporters of the pro-Thaksin Red Shirt movement. I seek to ask what the foundations of their current political thought and ambitions are.

I argue that rural villagers' unprecedented level of active participation in national politics, as demonstrated in anti-government protests in Bangkok between March and May 2010, is driven by changing civic consciousness and rights-oriented political sensitivity. This transformation is spurred by radical changes in the political economy and lifestyle of villages like my own native village, especially since the 1997 Asian economic crisis and the landmark promulgation of Thailand's 1997 constitution. The village world is ever expanding, and so are the geopolitical boundaries of its people's economic and political activities. Not only has the political world of rural Thai villagers been closely intertwined with both the national and global economies, but new-found agency and identity have also been accentuated in ways that help frame political actions beyond villagers' immediate localities. I suggest that one way in which to understand the rural villagers as well as some immigrants from the countryside to the city, who make up the urban working class and constitute the largest segment of the Red Shirt movement, is to capture the emergence of a new political consciousness and sensibility among village people, who have come increasingly to earn their living as mobile members of the global economy. The rise of a new political consciousness and sensibility has its ideological and material foundations in the changing village economy and in increasing socio-cultural mobility. Villagers' lives and the village community are fully integrated into the global economy in ways that Bangkok's elites and the Thai urban middle class often misjudge or misunderstand.

WAVES OF AGRARIAN CHANGE

Most northeastern Thai provinces — that is, the provinces of Isan — are strongholds of support for Thaksin Shinawatra and for people in his electoral networks, which are organized in the name of the Red Shirt movement. The villagers in the electoral constituencies of Nong Khai are no exception. They adored the ex-premier and felt that his being forced to leave office through a military coup in 2006 was a political injustice. Thaksin was their idol because of his business success, his populist style of leadership, and the massive outlays from the national budget that his administration channelled straight to people like them at the grass roots. Fewer than three weeks after the deadly political crackdown of 19 May 2010 in Bangkok, I made a short trip to visit my home village. My father, who is a retired local school-master and has twice been elected chairman of the local sub-district-level *tambon* administrative organization — *ongkan borihan suan tambon* or *O. Bo. To.* — since 2005, told me that scores of villagers, some our own relatives, went to Bangkok to support the Red Shirt movement's rallies between mid-March and May 2010. Observed my father, "Villagers nowadays are very politically passionate. There were at least two truckloads of people from our area, travelling to Bangkok to render their support to Thaksin and their Red Shirt fellows. They did not fear the military's crackdown. They were ready to risk their lives."

The proposition that rural villagers are passive participants in national politics now deserves to be put in the past tense. My father's observation connotes that the people of my native village were historically neither deeply engaged in politics, particularly at the national level, nor mobile enough to take part in socio-economic activities outside the local vicinity. They are today different people, compared to the members of earlier generations, who always had great respect for government officials and who had little experience of travelling or making a living away from their home turf. Bangkok and overseas countries were synonymous with alien planets in their minds. In my childhood memories, my village was very small, comprising fewer than fifty households in the mid-1970s. My father moved there and married my late mother in 1965, when he became the sole school-teacher in that remote setting. He came from another district near the provincial town of Nong Khai. But my mother's side of the family made up the majority of early settlers in the village. My mother was born at a village on Laotian soil in 1947 and grew up in the new village on the Thai side of the Mekong River. My maternal great-grandfather was among the village's founders who migrated from the Laotian side of the river. They were forced to flee Laos because of the invasion of the Japanese army during the Second World War. In the past eighty years of the village's history, all of the elected headmen of my native village have been members of my maternal clan.

In the decades after the settlement of the village, its people who were traditional peasants relied on the natural fertility of land, forest, and the Mekong for their survival. They cultivated both lowland and upland rice for subsistence. They also enjoyed an abundance of fish from the Mekong, wild game from the forest, and vegetation in the nearby mountains for their food. Timber, bamboo, fish, and wild produce were goods that the people of my village carried downstream on the Mekong by the bamboo raft to market towns such as Vientiane, Si Chiang Mai, Tha Bo, and Nong Khai. Feeder road networks were not extended to the remote mountainous areas until the late 1960s. My village later benefited from U.S. aid to Thailand during the Indochinese War and from the Thai national policy to suppress communists in the region. It was then classified as lying in a "Red Zone" by the Thai government's security forces. It sat on the edge of areas under the influence of the Communist Party of Thailand (CPT) and its allies from Vietnam and Laos.

My home village was gradually pulled into the market economy. Kenaf, cotton, maize, and soybean were among the first wave of cash crops that arrived in the 1970s. They had an instant impact on the local economy. More forest was cut down as the population significantly increased. Household economic activities were diversified, and people were now occupied with farm activities during both the wet and dry seasons. Cassava and banana became the most important cash crops, with the strongest impact on both deforestation and villagers' intensified involvement with the world market. My family, relatives, and neighbours relied heavily on the production and sale of both of these crops to local traders. One of my latest visits to my home village in June 2010 was the moment I returned to one of my grandfather's plots of farmland, which has been converted into young rubber tree plantations in the last decade. Observing a worker processing the latex collected from rubber trees into blocks and sheets of rubber, I realized that I was standing on the same plot of land on which I had learned how to plough the soil for our traditional wet rice cultivation and how to ride water buffaloes with friends when I studied in primary school in the mid-1970s. The same plot of land was converted into a large concrete pad to dry shredded cassava in the late 1970s and 1980s. Dry, shredded cassava was sold to the factories in nearby market towns. It was utilized as raw material for the production of tapioca flour or animal feed, which was exported to many countries in Asia and Europe.

Cash crops have penetrated into the texture of my village's economy and social life in successive waves. In the late 1980s Thailand's export of cassava was halted because of a drastic drop in demand from overseas markets; people in my village had to search for new sources of income. They found answers in two income-generating activities that now occupy the majority of villagers throughout the region: labour migration and Pará rubber plantation. During most of the 1990s, the cemented concrete pads and godowns for dry, shredded cassava on my grandfather's farmland were left empty. The land was filled with natural grass and weeds. With most of his grandchildren (myself included) in school and working in cities, my grandfather raised cattle on the grassland. My uncle and aunt, who inherited the land, have now turned parts of the grassland and other surrounding plots into one of the largest rubber plantations in the village. Capital for their investment in the rubber plantation came straight from their profitable retailing of bananas in the market town of Satuk District, Buriram Province, in the lower Northeast. They had to leave behind my grandparents for years in order to earn enough money to finance their children's education in Bangkok.

Through its colonial roots and route of transmission, the Pará rubber tree is a widely planted exotic commercial plant. If European imperialism is credited with efforts to introduce the rubber tree as well as methods of plantation management from Brazil to the tropical territories of Asia, its regional spread from southern Thailand or the northern part of the Malay peninsula to the northeastern Khorat Plateau of Thailand is the outcome of regional labour migration as well as agricultural extension work on the part of a number of Thai government agencies. In the mid-1990s, Saen, who is my childhood friend and a distant relative, and his younger brother Sommai joined the flow of migrant workers from the Isan high plateau for the first time. They were young, unmarried men in their early 20s in search of jobs. With their multiple skills in agricultural labour, they were hired by a family that owned rubber plantations and fruit orchards in Surat Thani Province, southern Thailand. They spent more than a year building up cash savings and, most importantly, acquiring first-hand knowledge and skills relating to the cultivation of rubber. The two brothers then returned to my village and started a rubber tree nursery business. With further training and technical support from local agricultural extension officials, both were informally recognized as the pioneers who introduced rubber plantations to my village. Since the mid-2000s, rubber plantations have expanded rapidly throughout the northeastern region. This expansion is in part a consequence of the healthy demand for natural rubber on the world market. A large number of rubber plantation owners from southern Thailand, who have experienced the low production of ageing rubber trees and sky-rocketing prices of land at home, have moved to buy cheaper land and to invest heavily in villages across many provinces in Isan.

The economic transformation of life in my village has magnified as well as intensified people's political awareness. It is my observation that the dynamics of agricultural livelihood in my village do not fit well with the mode of self-sufficient economy as described and emphasized by groups of Thai scholars, NGO workers, and officials. Villagers are no longer rice-growing peasants; village economic and social lives are remarkably complex and dynamic. The diversification of cash-crop farming has been very intensive over the past several decades. Villagers have engaged in both subsistence and market-oriented agricultural production. They either cultivate enough rice and other food for their home consumption, or buy them from neighbours with the money earned from other income-generating activities, which yield far higher cash revenues. Like their urban working-class counterparts and other people in modern Thai society, they have been involved in a series of different economic ventures. Their social world and political thinking have been reshaped as the bases of their economic activities have passed through radical transitions.

BECOMING POLITICAL ENTREPRENEURS

A common misconception among scholars and political analysts writing on modern Thai politics lies in the assumption that rural villagers are politically naïve. Villagers are expected to be passive or faithful voters, influenced by aggressive money politics. In reality, rural villagers and members of Thailand's urban working class are as politically sophisticated as its educated urban middle class. They have become active political entrepreneurs who have adopted a view that electoral politics is an emerging field of bargaining for power, connections, immediate benefits, and other resources. They have realized that they can be important actors in the country's multi-level electoral politics. Rural villagers and migrant members of the urban working class have developed their own political reasoning and sensibility. Villagers have perceived and embraced electoral politics via their immediate small-scale kin-based relationships and possible immediate reciprocal interests. Instead of the honour of filling public office, the chance to influence some public policies or to gain a share of the pie from graft in some big-budget schemes, and the logic of "who gets what, why, and how" are particularly noticeable in the village-level politics.

The Thai village was always inseparable from national and international political affairs. In the 1970s, my home village was an ideological battleground during the height of the war in Indochina. Channels of information were very limited for us villagers. The village then had neither electricity nor tap water. We listened to news items about the massacre of Thammasat University students, the suppression of communist insurgents, and the care-taker military government on the radio. Our favourite newspaper was the mass-circulation *Thai Rat*, which came to the village headman once in a while through a government-sponsored programme of newspaper subscriptions for rural villages nationwide. After the fall of neighbouring Vietnam, Laos, and Cambodia to communist forces in 1975, news concerning international and national politics from the government's radio station was rather intense and cautious. Patriotic songs were frequently played on the air. We were warned of threats from communism. The grown-ups in my village had to take part in training courses for Village Scouts or National Defense Volunteers. They were taught about the love of "nation, religion and king" as part of their civic duty. They were also trained in the use of basic weapons and the organization of self-defence units. My father's status as the village school-master meant that my family usually hosted the visit of the military psychological warfare unit. The presence of an influx of Hmong and other Laotian refugees in Nong Khai and Nakhon Phanom Provinces was often cited as an example of how dangerous the communists were and how a nation could come to an end due to a lack of unity among its people and to the military attacks from outside. It was ironic that many Laotian refugees who were forced to flee their homeland after the communists took over in late 1975 were our own blood relatives. Increasing emphasis on Thai national identity kept reminding us, however, that we were citizens of the democratic and Buddhist kingdom of Thailand, while they were foreigners from war-torn and disintegrating Laos.

Much the most exciting element of my childhood memories of growing up in a border village during the height of the Cold War era was open-air action cinema, brought to the villages in the Red Zone by the Thai military's CIA-sponsored psychological warfare unit. We loved to watch old American cowboy shoot-outs and B-grade Thai action films. My friends and I even imitated our action heroes on the school playground or in the rice fields, while tending to our families' water buffaloes after school.

Vote buying figured centrally in local and national elections in my village. When I was young, village voters had two things in mind: the number of their preferred candidate and the money that was usually paid through the headmen, local leaders, and vote canvassers (*hua khanaen*) who served as mediators between candidates and eligible voters. Voters, especially the elderly, were committed to the candidate who had bought their vote. They learned that their identification card was marketable paper during election season. The candidate who paid most usually won. However, events also sometimes proved that money might not be the sole decisive factor in electoral success. In one general election prior to the tragic events of 6 October 1976, the winning parliamentary candidate in Nong Khai's first electoral district was the late Mr Nitinai Nakhonthap from the pro-socialist New Force Party (*Phak Phalang Mai*). I was at the time a Primary Four pupil in the village school. My friends and I went around the village to help distribute flyers for this candidate. We schoolchildren did not see this task as part of a political campaign, but as kind of fun activity with which some grown-ups in the village had encouraged us to help out.

The elections of village headmen (*phuyai ban*) and sub-district chiefs (*kamnan*) were the most important political events in my village when I was a boy. Elections of members of the now-defunct sub-district-level *tambon* council (*sapha tambon*) or of the national parliament were not very important to the people of my village until the introduction of *tambon* administration organizations in the wave of decentralization that came to Thailand in the mid-1990s. When one of my maternal relatives ran for the village headman position in the late 1970s, people from the kin networks of my mother were united behind him. They voted for him. They saw it as their duty and honour to render support to their own man since he represented our extended kin group against a rival from other groups in the village. As my mother's family commands the largest kin network in my village, no one apart from my relatives has been able to win election as our village headman until today. The election of the *tambon* head presents a similar scenario, except that it includes a larger number of voters from several kin groups and different villages. In the old days, the candidate from a big extended family with strong kin support across village clusters always had the advantage. However, the wealthy candidate who promises handsome monetary and other material returns has often emerged as the winner in such contests. The replacement of *tambon* councils by newly formed *tambon* administrative organizations in the late 1990s streamlined grass-roots electoral politics into the same pattern that characterizes general elections. It has intensified the epidemic power of wealth and influence among local big men and their networks. It has highlighted the political business of vote-buying as a form of investment. Election to public office is seen by candidates and voters alike as an automatic route to reaping handsome profits after the assumption of that office.

Money defeated ties of kinship and relegated them to the backstage. However, both money and kinship networks continue to carry weight, as important qualifications for garnering villagers' votes. They are necessary, fundamental factors, more significant than a candidate's professional merit or reputation. The experience of waging two campaigns for his position in the *tambon* administrative organization has left my father a firm believer in the thesis that money can buy one's way into the heart of Thai politics. He carefully organized his team. He chose team members from different villages. He preferred to fill positions in the team with candidates coming from wealthy backgrounds and enjoying plenty of support from kin. Credit, merit, and reputation alone can never deliver success to anyone in modern-day electoral politics. "Everybody buys votes", my father and his team once revealed to me, sharing the open secret of Thailand's electoral politics. His strategy was that the team pooled money, manpower, and other resources. "To start with, we need plenty of bullets (*krasun*) in order to shoot and score. If you do not have money, forget about winning anything in the electoral game", he once described his campaign strategy to me, referring to the use of money for vote buying in the violent language reserved mainly for influential big men, godfathers, and politicians. "The wealthier a candidate is, the greater chance of winning he would have." He assigned team members to take charge of gathering votes. The team calculated and determined how much per head they needed to pay vote canvassers and how many votes from each village they would be able to buy in order to win. The team also analysed the strengths and weaknesses of their opponents, while planning day-to-day campaign activities in detail. Despite his professional reputation as a career school-teacher and later as an educational administrator, and as an adopted son of our village, my father only beat a wealthy candidate from a larger village by a whisker in both rounds of his local political campaigns in 2005 and 2008.

JOINING THE RED SHIRT MOVEMENT WITH HEART

Northeastern Thai constituencies have been infamously known for epidemic vote buying ever since former Prime Minister General Kriangsak

Chomanan and his party bought a parliamentary seat in Roi-et Province in the late 1970s. Vote buying in Thailand's electoral politics is well documented. However, the arrival of Thaksin Shinawatra and his Thai Rak Thai Party in the 2001 general election seemed to write an entirely new chapter in the story of Thai money politics. Armed with massive funds and experienced policy planners focusing on populist mega projects, such as village development funds and the 30-baht health-care scheme, Thaksin intensified political vote-buying. He elevated it to a very different kind of art by channelling taxpayers' money into mass programmes directed straight at villagers/voters through people in his electoral networks such as vote canvassers, local big men, officials, and local politicians.

One late afternoon back in my home village, my father recommended that I speak to Aunt Khamthong, aged sixty-one and our next-door neighbour. He noted, "she just came back from Bangkok." I went to talk to her. Aunt Khamthong smiled, and her eyes were sparkling as she recollected her experience supporting the Red Shirt's political outcry in Bangkok in March and May of 2010.

"How was your trip to Bangkok, Auntie?" I started our conversation.

Aunt Khamthong proudly told her story. "I went to Bangkok twice. I took pick-up trucks with other neighbours. The drivers were also from our village. I was in Bangkok for 10 days during the first trip, but stayed almost 14 days during the second one. Before the trip, I was nervous as I had never been to the event like this before. Bangkok is so much different from our village. To my relief, I was quite comfortable when I joined fellow Red Shirts. There were so many of us, coming from everywhere. We were divided by province of origin and assigned to stay in tents in the Ratchaprasong area. I made friends with many people from different provinces. Everybody was so friendly and shared similar ideas."

"Why did you go there? What did you and your friends have in mind?" I probed further, and her answer was straight and clear.

"We all adored Thaksin and wanted him back as our prime minister. The government and the military drove him out of power. With this government, the economy has not been good."

"How did you like the trips?"

"I truly enjoyed my time in Bangkok. We listened to series of rally talks by our leaders every day. Talks were usually sandwiched by musical performances. Food and drink were abundant. We had both packed meals and cooked food. Coffee and tea were also available. We were invited to join dancing and singing activities, particularly at night. Bonds with fellow villagers from different places were very strong. I still miss the friends from Khon Kaen and Mukdahan whom I met during our time in Bangkok."

"What did you think about the government's crackdown?" I was curious to learn about her true reaction. Aunt Khamthong's answer was no surprise.

"I thought the government treated us badly. They had strong biases against us. Many Bangkok people looked down on us as poor and stupid villagers coming from the countryside. I was crying for my friends during the crackdown. The military shot us down like vegetables and fish. I was so angry and sad."

"Did Uncle and your children worry about your safety during your time in Bangkok?"

Aunt Khamthong smiled and said, "They did, but not much. We talked on the phone almost every day. People in my family knew my whereabouts. But I knew I was safe because our tents were located far from the hot-spots. Besides, I am an old woman with no weapon."

I always wonder whether the widely circulated allegation that the Red Shirt villagers were paid by Thaksin and his allies is true or not. I visited two other returning Red Shirt movement participants in my village, Som and Chai. The couple are my old friends. We attended the village school together in the mid-1970s. They own a pick-up truck and sell bananas and vegetables to the markets in Nong Khai and other market towns around the region. The couple took a truck-load of villagers, including Aunt Khamthong, to Bangkok. When I asked about the financial side of the trips, Chai said: "I do not think we were demonstrators for hire. We were reimbursed for our fuel bill by people connected to the member of parliament for our area. Yes, they were organized by Thaksin and his network. If we wanted to make money, why wouldn't we stay home and earn our living as usual? We lost a lot of our income because we joined the protest in Bangkok for weeks. It was also dangerous for us to travel back and forth between Nong Khai and Bangkok.

But we wanted to help [the Red Shirt movement] with our heart. What the government did to Thaksin and to us was not fair."

Talking to a few people in my village, I learned something about their recent political activism. Village folk are more actively involved in both local and national politics, as my father noted. I am not so certain about some conventional descriptions of the political life of the Thai countryside. For example, in the dry season of March, April, and May, villagers in the countryside are generally unemployed or unoccupied with farm work. That is why they are likely to join the rallies away from home. Or rural villagers fall prey to money politics and the power bargaining game among the elites. The narratives of rural political activism that I heard from my fellow villagers seem to point to something else. For the first time ever in the history of my village, people have had a chance for direct participation in national political events, and they have embraced it. My guess is that a strong sense of political consciousness and sensibility concerning voicing and claiming their rights in electoral politics are in the air. For these villagers, the message is clear: elections mean democracy. Once the cycle of electoral politics is interrupted, there must be something wrong. They have demanded convincing explanations for this situation, even as they have asserted their side of the story.

A JOURNEY FROM RED TO RED

My efforts to explain the interconnections between the political and economic transformations of my home village and the political crisis at the national level are grounded in some conceptual understandings of the village. Recent works by Andrew Walker advance the criticism that scholarship on the Thai village political economy and central concepts like "community" (*chumchon*) and "village" (*muban*) either reflect romanticized visions of the distant past or are out of touch with the dynamic reality of the present. In the introduction to the edited volume on *Tai Lands and Thailand: Community and State in Southeast Asia,* Walker challenges the widely held thesis that traditional community is "being undermined by the modern forces of state incorporation, market penetration, globalization and population mobility". What I learned from my own short visit back to my home village seems to corroborate his observation that "community emerges as a thoroughly modern phenomenon, constructed in dialogue with both the state and the market".[3] It would be a grave mistake to view my village as a self-sufficient moral-economic unit, embedded in traditional ways of economic and political life. Although my grandparents have continued to make merit to monks at the village temple and kinship and filial ties are strong manifestations of old-time social relations, the social and economic life of my home village has taken on a different rhythm and sense.

The village world is complicated and sophisticated. Anthropologist Eric Thompson argues in the case of rural urbanization in Malaysia that "sociologically and culturally urbanism thrives in the *kampong*". The rural village has become "a site of living transformation" because of the widespread forms of urbanism in once geopolitically isolated rural areas, which include urban work patterns, urban forms of social interaction, and urban ideas.[4] Like rural villages throughout Malaysia, Thailand, and elsewhere in Southeast Asia's countryside, my home village is well connected to the national capital and the world through networks of transportation, satellite television, telephones, and other channels of communication. The flows of people and goods in and out of the village proper are very intensive. These conditions make it difficult to sustain the generalization that villagers are overwhelmingly passive, ignorant, or naive prey for participants in the country's money politics.

The people of my village have adjusted their lives to the globalizing world. Adopting Cindi Katz's terminology, Charles Keyes suggests that villagers supporting Thaksin and joining the Red Shirt movement have become "cosmopolitan villagers." He further suggests that "Northeastern families today have become increasingly 'cosmopolitan' because they are linked to a global labour force, have sophisticated understandings of Bangkok society, and yet still retain long-standing resentment for being looked down as country bumpkins".[5] Keyes traces a half-century-long stretch of time during which Isan villagers marched towards cosmopolitanism, exploring the pervasive impact of modernization, economic development, compulsory education, and labour migration. Elsewhere, I propose the term "village transnationalism" as a descriptive and analytical concept for understanding the social life of the Thai migrant community in Singapore, consisting mainly of village men and women from the countryside of northern and northeastern Thailand.[6] I suggest that the everyday life experience of the Thai migrant population in Singapore has been modelled on or refashioned on the basis of the transcendent identities of the cultural worlds back home in the Thai countryside. Thai migrants use cultural capital brought with them from home as a foundation to help them learn about, adjust to, and make sense of their work and life experiences as displaced foreign workers far away from home. With transnational identities grounded in the village, Thai workmen and women in the labour and marriage diaspora are able to survive and to serve as the emerging backbone of the country's politics and economy.

The folks of my village have travelled from being labelled "red" four decades ago to being labelled "Red" today. In the 1960s and 1970s, the anti-communist policy of the Thai state and the politics of the Cold War painted the colour red over the map and reality of my birthplace. However, in the 2000s and 2010s, a combination of forces of political and economic polarization turned the people of my village into supporters of the Red Shirt movement. Two points can be drawn from the red-coded journey of my village. First, both shades of red are labels attached by outside forces, especially the state and the Bangkok elite and media. The agency of the people of my village is apparently overlooked in this process of labelling. Second, as throughout the history of my village, its people remain today at the geopolitical and socioeconomic margins of the country.

The difference between life in Thailand's core and periphery seems to have widened over the years. Despite the widespread process of rural urbanization or globalization in the village setting, urban-rural disparities remain a significant feature of Thailand's economic-development failure. Poor income distribution and other features of social inequality are apparent. A recent survey pertinent to the comparison of incomes and occupations among participants in the urban-based PAD-Yellow Shirt movement and the rural-based UDD-Red Shirt movement undertaken by the Faculty of Economics, Thammasat University, confirms that socioeconomic differences divide the two groups. Its findings show that "members of the PAD have an average [monthly] income of 30,000 baht, while their UDD counterparts earn only 17,000 baht. Only 35% of PAD members are farmers, while 53% of UDD people are either farmers or wage labourers."[7] The question is, how could people from the Thai countryside, especially Red Shirt sympathizers, match the political and economic status of those living in the core of power and privilege? With limited means of bargaining made available to them, it explains why village folks and other less privileged people tend to pin their hopes so strongly on electoral politics and direct participation in elections and other forms of political activism.

CONCLUSION

In the aftermath of the 19 May 2010 crackdown, Pasuk Phongpaichit and Chris Baker suggested that "Thailand needs to bring its politics into line with its economy".[8] The country's democratization is deeply problematic and its body politic polarized. Divisive and self-destructive politics has hindered progress in all areas, especially the economy and education. Red Shirts argue that the ruling elite and establishment are behind the country's politics of inequality, injustice, and double standards, whereas the Yellow Shirt camp places the blame squarely on Thaksin and his networks and focuses its political activism on the need to fight for the monarchy to preserve the nation's unity. The reconciliation efforts undertaken by Prime Minister Abhisit Vejjajiva and his administration face daunting challenges.

As this essay suggests, any attempt to "bring politics into line with the economy" in Thailand must begin with a careful understanding of the political and economic agency of the people on the ground. The growing agency of the rural villagers and members of urban working class is a powerful force in contemporary Thailand's democratization process. These groups are the present and the future of democracy in the country.

Located at the margins of the Thai nation-state, my home village has marched from being labelled as one shade of "red" to being labelled another share of the same colour during the course of the past four decades. Along the way, the people in my village have developed a political identity and sensitivity as the economic base of the village and their lifestyle have radically changed. I suggest that the most significant message that the folk of my village learned from their brief time participating in the Red Shirt movement and their years of taking part in multi-level electoral politics is loud and clear. It says: Thailand's democratization and nation-building projects have reached a critical turning point, and the Bangkok-centred and elitist monopolization of power needs to be fundamentally reformed. These folk have criticized economic and political inequality and called for open and transparent political system. Many of them have stood up and demanded an inclusive form of democratization.

Currently active generations of villagers in the Thai countryside are very different from the members of older generations. They are new villagers with greater political awareness and sensitivity. There are certain characteristics resulting from their intensive participation in modernization and globalization at both the national and transnational levels. Observing my own people at home and conducting fieldwork among Thai migrant workers in Singapore since 2004, I suggest the following emerging identities of the villagers, many of which have contributed to their vocal and radical participation in the recent political crisis in Thailand.

First, the current generation of villagers from the Thai countryside are predominantly mobile subjects. Social and economic mobility has become a hallmark of village life throughout the region. Second, the current generation of villagers are cash-income generators or wage-earners. My fellow villagers passed from the stage of being described as peasants or rural cultivators many decades ago. Cash income is the most crucial impulse of the villager's life. Third, the current generation of villagers are consumers, no different to urban dwellers. Loyalty between villagers and Thaksin through his political networks is strong. Such loyalty may not be accurately characterized as the traditional patron-client relationship of the old Thai society. It looks more like the relationship between service providers and consumers in the modern political market. Finally, the current generation of villagers are sophisticated political entrepreneurs. As electoral politics is contagious at all level in Thailand, villagers from the Thai countryside have gained greater awareness of their rights as active citizens as well. They have come to take electoral politics very seriously. Unlike Thailand's elite or urban middle class, elections are real for them.

Notes

1. Duncan McCargo, "Network Monarchy and Legitimacy Crises in Thailand", *Pacific Review* 18, no. 4 (December 2005): 499–519.
2. See, for example, Kasian Tejapira, "Toppling Thaksin", *New Left Review*, 39 (2006): 5–37; Pasuk Phongpaichit and Chris Baker, *Thaksin* (Chiang Mai: Silkworm Books, 2009); and Thongchai Winichakul, "Toppling Democracy", *Journal of Contemporary Asia* 38, no. 1 (February 2008): 11–37.

3. Andrew Walker, "Introduction: Towards a Modern Tai Community", in *Tai Lands and Thailand: Community and State in Southeast Asia*, edited by Andrew Walker (Copenhagen and Singapore: NIAS Press and NUS Press, 2009), p. 10.
4. Eric C. Thompson, *Unsettling Absenses: Urbanism in Rural Malaysia*. (Singapore: NUS Press, 2007), p. 5.
5. See Charles Keyes, "The Colour of Politics: Thailand's Deep Crisis of Authority", in this volume.
6. Pattana Kitiarsa, "Village Transnationalism: Transborder Identities among Thai-Isan Migrant Workers in Singapore", ARI Working Paper No. 71, August 2006 <www.ari.nus.edu/pub/wps.htm>.
7. *Thai Post*, 19 July 2010, pp. 1 and 10.
8. Pasuk Phongpaichit and Chris Baker, "Sacrifices in Bangkok", *Wall Street Journal Asia*, 21 May 2010.

20

THE RICH, THE POWERFUL AND THE BANANA MAN
The United States' Position in the Thai Crisis

Pavin Chachavalpongpun

This short essay analyses the position of the United States vis-à-vis political developments in Thailand, its long established relations with traditional Thai elites, and Washington's views on the May crisis of 2010. It argues that the American perception of the current power struggle in Thailand is strictly constrained by an old, obsolete structure in which the Thai-U.S. relations have been shaped and dominated by the effective military-monarchy partnership in Thailand and the various American interests in the maintenance of such a partnership. As J. L. S. Girling once said, "The Thai-US relationship has remained an outgrowth of Thailand's patronage political system."[1] As a result, the United States has appeared to adopt a stance of support for establishment forces at the expense of serious advocacy of the pro-democracy agenda of the Red Shirt movement, known principally as the United Front for Democracy against Dictatorship or UDD.

Self-interest alone does not sufficiently explain unfailing American support for Thailand's traditional elites and its seeming disapproval of the Red Shirts' political activities. Based on extensive interviews with a number of Thai and American diplomats, this essay concludes that the obstinate attitude of the United States derives fundamentally from a lack of understanding of and genuine interest in Thai political development on the part of the Department of State and the American Embassy in Bangkok. The end of the Cold War and the gradual American disengagement with Southeast Asia, including Thailand, during the 1990s and into the period of former Prime Minister Thaksin Shinawatra's administration (2001–06) created a huge "vacuum of information" on political evolution in the country. This vacuum has conveniently prevented the United States from modifying its policy towards Thailand even when the Thai domestic and international environments have significantly changed. Washington continues to operate in its relationship with Bangkok on the basis of its conventional perception of Thailand, even as it endlessly pays lip service to the promotion of Thai democracy. The American policy of safeguarding the Thai political status quo, which has benefited the rich and powerful elites in the kingdom, has severely narrowed the perspective of the United States, and indeed its policy options, as it tries to keep up with Thailand's unfolding political situation. What has transpired has been the crude construction of a binary image of Thailand's leading political actors; whereas the ruling elites are "trusted friends", the Red Shirt demonstrators, along with Thaksin Shinawatra, are "threats" to the traditional form of Thai democracy.

The "banana man" is my own term. It refers to the *farang*, or Caucasian, and in this case the United States, which is supposedly a supporter of the pro-elite faction distinguished by the colour "yellow". It is an *en vogue* metaphor for a white man who wraps himself in yellow, just like a banana. This analogy, despite carrying undesirable racist tones, stands alongside earlier descriptions of some in the Thai military who were sympathetic towards the Red Shirts and thus called "watermelon soldiers".

OLD POLITICS, POWER, AND MONEY

In 2008, on the eve of the 175th anniversary of the establishment of the Thai-U.S. diplomatic relations, Krit Garnjana-goonchorn, the Thai ambassador to Washington, wrote an article for an American research institute emphasizing that as the oldest friend of the United States in Asia, Thailand valued its affinity and alliance and was committed to a long-term, mutually beneficial relationship.[2] In actuality, this relationship has always been confidently cordial. At the end of the Second World War, the U.S. government came to Thailand's rescue at the time when former military strongman Field Marshal Plaek Phibunsongkhram (1938–44 and 1948–57) was about to be put on trial on charges of having committed war crimes. The United States successfully persuaded Britain and France not to punish Thailand for collaborating with the Japanese imperial army. Bilateral ties became even more intimate during the Cold War, in which both Thailand and the United States shared a common enemy: the communists. During this period, the United States knitted a close alliance with the Thai military and the palace, compelling them to craft a pro-American and anti-communist policy. International circumstances offered Thailand's ruling elites an opportunity to take full control of domestic politics. With American support, they were able to overcome challenges to their political legitimacy and their lack of a broad political base. The Thai-American alliance was indeed built on the rock of repressive Thai military governments, and the military's success in establishing its authoritarian regime depended in part on that same alliance.[3]

Thailand participated in a myriad of U.S.-led security agreements, including the Southeast Asia Treaty Organization (SEATO) and the related Manila Pact from 1954 onward. In 1962, security relations were consolidated in the Rusk-Thanat Communiqué, which remains operative in contemporary thinking.[4] Undeniably, this bilateral relationship was predominantly security-oriented. Thailand's successive military regimes, backed by the traditional elites, the palace and senior bureaucrats, unswervingly responded to U.S. policy imperatives. Meanwhile, Washington realized that an alliance with traditional elites served its long-term interests both within the kingdom and in the Southeast Asian region as a whole, especially in the period leading up to the Vietnam War. It was therefore crucial for Washington to nurture its ties with those elites, even if in doing so it helped nourish their despotic rule. At the same time, the United States, together with traditional Thai elites, embarked on a re-glorification of the monarchical institution, casting it as some sort of inviolable unifying force that guaranteed political stability.

The United States has regarded King Bhumibol Adulyadej, the only monarch to be born on the American soil, as the ultimate moral authority in the political realm. It believed that aligning itself with him would automatically mean standing with the winning side in Thailand.

In the domain of foreign affairs, Thailand's military and foreign ministry continued to formulate a foreign policy centred on national security. Such a policy in turn legitimized the close connection between Thai security agencies and their American counterparts through which the generous U.S. military aid was offered to Thailand.[5] Wide-ranging military aid programmes opened doors for the Americans to forge a cosy relationship with top Thai leaders. Because the Thai political system was so highly personalized, American intimacy with these elites added weight to U.S. pronouncements and requests.[6] This pattern explained the entanglement of the United States in Thailand's patronage political network. The primary agenda on the part of the United States may have been to transform Thailand into one of its client states. But reconstructing Thailand in this way could be highly problematic. For it strongly encouraged the culture of corruption and reinforced the political position of the Thai elites. The United States, throughout the tumultuous years of the Cold War, did not even pretend to be interested in promoting Thailand's democratization. This reality has persisted into the current period of Thai politics.

For the United States, the benefits of preserving a pro-establishment stance have been manifest. It effectively made the bilateral relationship more predictable, less prone to disruption, because of the American-friendly Thai elites' continued domination of political power and foreign policy. Governments might come and go, but the traditional elites represented a permanent feature of Thai politics. During the past few decades, the Thai elites have actively and fiercely protected the status quo and resisted change in the Thai political consensus. For Washington to modify its long-held stance would be perceived as an unnecessary move, one that could shake the core of its relations with Bangkok. Besides, it could jeopardize the United State's interests in the region. For example, a close alliance with the old power-holders might assist in the maintenance of American influence over Thailand and Southeast Asia during a period in which the rise of China and its growing power in the region are increasingly threatening to the United States.

VACUUM OF INFORMATION

The United States has never been fond of former Prime Minister Thaksin Shinawatra. A sense of frustration over Thaksin's weak commitment to good governance, as displayed in episodes ranging from his hard-nosed measures against Thai Muslims in the South to the widespread extra-judicial killings of drug suspects in 2003, has been evident in Washington. Yet, ironically, the United States has never applied the same moral criteria to countless attempts on the part of traditional Thai elites to undermine popular confidence in the electoral process. Many in the current Obama administration might still remember when Thaksin called Washington a "useless friend" after a State Department report criticized his government's human rights record.[7] To put it crudely, for the first time since the Cold War, both the traditional Thai elite and the American government seemed to have found a common threat; this time it was not the communists, but Thaksin. At a deeper level, Washington perceived Thaksin's rise to power and his determination to alter the political consensus as a threat to its own power and interests in the kingdom. This perception explained the remarkable silence of the United States in the aftermath of the military coup of 2006 that ousted Thaksin's elected government. Although all aid offered to the Thai military was suspended, the annual Cobra Gold military exercise between the United States and Thailand continued. In fact, the coup was staged while Thaksin was attending the UN General Assembly in New York. Upon learning about the coup, the State Department released a brief statement saying, "We hope the people of Thailand resolve political differences by peaceful means."[8] The United States did not offer Thaksin political sanctuary. He left New York for London on 20 September, one day after the coup.

Then-U.S. ambassador Ralph Boyce was the first Bangkok-based diplomat or high-ranking American official to meet with military-appointed Prime Minister General Surayut Chulanon, a former Army commander. It was therefore unsurprising that the Department of State on 4 October 2006 issued a statement acknowledging the appointment of General Surayut and the promulgation of an interim constitution, while urging caution about restrictions on civil liberties.[9] But this and earlier statements were regarded as "gentle" in comparison with the harsher American responses to the emergence of military regimes elsewhere in the world. Bilateral ties continued as though the military coup had not occurred. The Cobra Gold kicked off in Pattaya on 8 May 2007. This annual military exercise is the core platform that strengthens relations between the American and Thai armed forces. The deputy chief of mission at the U.S. Embassy in Bangkok, Alexander Arvizu, said at the opening ceremony of Cobra Gold 2007, "For a quarter century, Cobra Gold has been the most visible symbol of US and Thai military cooperation."[10] The uninterrupted military exercise acted to symbolize the ongoing U.S. support for the Thai military and Bangkok's powerful elites in spite of the fact that they had staged a military coup eight months before.

From the military coup of 2006 to the May crisis of 2010, the United States released a handful of statements, most of which voiced typical disquiet about the rise of violence on the part of the Red Shirt UDD. The United States may have disapproved of the actions of the Yellow Shirt People's Alliance for Democracy (PAD) in occupying Bangkok's two airports. Its statement may have indicated that seizing airports was not an appropriate means of protest. But the United States also said that it respected the right to freedom of expression.[11] The Red Shirt movement thus came to feel that the United States had done nothing to support Thailand's democracy or to condemn the existence of double standards and social injustice. In March 2010, Red Shirt protestors submitted a letter to the U.S. Embassy requesting the United States to clarify the report that U.S. intelligence officials had eavesdropped on Thaksin and then warned the government of Prime Minister Abhisit Vejjajiva against possible sabotage during the Red Shirts' rally, supposedly on the orders of Thaksin. It was reported that American diplomats even accused UDD leaders of stockpiling arms at their protest sites, even as the latter insisted that their movement was pro-democracy and peaceful.[12] "If the United States interpreted events more carefully, it would see the true evidence", said Weng Tojirakan, a UDD co-leader later held on potential terrorism charges.[13] The Red Shirts were convinced that the United States was working with the military and traditional elites to isolate Thaksin and discredit the UDD. On 12 April 2010, Secretary of State Hillary Clinton called for a peaceful dialogue in Thailand following the first clashes between the Red Shirt protestors and the security forces, which had resulted in eleven dead — nine UDD supporters and two soldiers. She sent a video message, which was essentially banal and diplomatic, urging all sides to seek agreement on a way forward that solidified Thailand's democracy and the rule of law. She also stressed, "While you continue on the path to resolve your political differences, we remain confident in the strong, enduring bonds between the United States and Thailand."[14] But in the aftermath of the arson attacks against public property, allegedly by some members of the Red Shirt movement, on 19 May 2010, the State Department spokesman launched what was deemed as the strongest denunciation against the UDD so far:

> I would like to say that the United States deeply deplores the violence and loss of life that has resulted from clashes between security forces and protests from the United Front for Democracy against Dictatorship (UDD) ... We are deeply concerned that Red Shirt supporters have engaged in arson targeting the electricity infrastructure and media outlets and have attacked individual journalists ... We condemn such behaviour and call on UDD leaders and affiliated opposition politicians to urge their supporters to stop such acts. We remain very concerned about the situation in Thailand and we will continue to monitor those events closely.[15]

The disinclination of the United States to shift from its pro-establishment stance raises the crucial question of whether Washington has simply aimed to pursue its interests or whether it has indeed failed fully to comprehend Thailand's political development over the course of the past decade. In interviews with a group of Thai and American diplomats, it was clear that since the end of the Cold War and the consequent decrease in American influence in this region, the U.S. government has not adequately invested in training experts on Southeast Asia, including Thailand.[16] As the American role in Southeast Asia diminished, a series of U.S. governments have taken their ties with countries in the region for granted. The lack of experts has led to misjudgement of the evolving political process in Thailand. The United States has tended to rely on its old connections with traditional elites, while shoring up their argument that the Red Shirt movement is antithetical to Thai democracy and even a menace to the monarchical institution — an argument that aligns with the pro-monarchy position of the United States. A former American diplomat revealed that the United States was "freaking out" about the fact that there was a gap in its understanding of the Thai situation. The vacuum of information compelled the U.S. government to interpret its relations with Thailand on the basis of its constricted perception in favour of maintaining the political status quo even as new players in the Thai political landscape were emerging. United States ambassador Eric John has been criticized by some American expatriates for being out of touch with Thailand's complex politics and cultural mores.[17] The periodic Congressional Research Service (CRS) reports for Congress continue to paint a demonic image of Thaksin, while reiterating the importance of security relations between Thailand and the United States. Focus has been on unflagging Thai support for U.S. military operations, American security assistance for Thailand, U.S. military exercises with the Thai Army, and bilateral cooperation in the field of intelligence and law enforcement; all these resonated with the traditional security-centric relations between Washington and Bangkok. When it comes to describing the Thai situation, the 2009 CRS report asserts:

> The coup itself raised obvious concerns about the democratic process in Thailand. Much of the Thai press and some long-time Thai watchers embraced the notion that the coup was necessary for Thailand to move forward; that is, that the military coup represented less of a threat to Thai democracy than Thaksin's perceived systematic dismantling of the democratic system. In addition, much of the state's apparatus, including the key institutions of the parliament, the judicial branch, and watchdog agencies, reportedly has been undermined in the past several years.[18]

In one account, the CRS said, "Many military and diplomatic officials, wary of some aspects of Thaksin's leadership style and more familiar with the old establishment in Bangkok, appeared to want to maintain strong relations with the elite despite the interruption of democratic practices."[19] This statement sums up the persistent pro-elite standpoint of the United States. The CRS released its Thailand reports in 2005 and 2009 but did not discuss the root causes of the country's crisis in any depth. Although issues of democracy and human rights were examined, the reports said nothing about the Red Shirt movement and its pro-democracy objective. In looking closely, one would find that the contents of these two reports are strikingly similar; only a few updated statements were added, statements that remained superficial and indicative of American misinterpretation.

A diplomat who served at the Thai Embassy in Washington in 2006 explicated the origin of a possible American misperception. In the East Asian and Pacific Affairs Bureau of the United States Department of State, only one junior diplomat, possibly with the rank of a second secretary, was at the time in charge of all issues related to Thailand. She worked under the supervision of a director who lacked expertise on the country. "Thailand" was under-represented in the State Department despite the fact that it remained a principal American strategic ally and was awarded major non-NATO ally status in 2003. Other, more powerful countries in Asia, such as China and Japan, as well as the Muslim world received more attention. It was also revealed that there was nobody in the East Asian and Pacific Affairs Bureau able to speak Thai, in contrast to the Chinese Ministry of Foreign Affairs, all of whose Thai desk officers spoke Thai fluently.[20] The State Department seemed not to consider as important the background knowledge of a desk officer. Obviously, the Thai desk officer had no prior knowledge about Thailand and its ongoing political development.

This situation has not changed. Interviews with two Singapore-based American diplomats offered a rather more detailed understanding of the structure of the State Department's Bureau of East Asian and Pacific Affairs. At the so-called Thai desk, there is still one full-time mid-level official covering Thailand. In addition, there are a deputy director and a director supervising the Thai desk officer, in addition to the deputy assistant secretary and assistant secretary — currently Kurt Campbell — who have Thailand in their portfolios. But this total does not include other officers who work directly on Thailand, such as those in the public affairs, economic and consular bureaus; the population, refugee and migration offices; the Defence, Commerce and Agriculture Departments.[21] One of the American diplomats defended his government's position when asked if there was a lack of Thai expertise and consequent policy ignorance in regards to Thailand. The diplomat said that on many occasions, the real decision-makers in Washington do not rely on information provided by the Thai desk officer or sources from the U.S. Embassy in Bangkok since they do not represent the sole sources of information on the political situation in Thailand. "Campbell may just pick up the phone and request specific information from other offices, like from the National Security Council", said the diplomat.[22] But this does not answer the earlier question of whether other offices understand the complexity of the Thai situation better than the State Department. The American diplomat confirmed that Campbell had a keen interest in what had happened in Thailand, but he wanted to adopt a wait-and-see attitude and in doing so did not fully support the Red Shirts' pro-democracy campaign. More importantly, the diplomat asked, "If the Red Shirts formed the next government, would they change the country's policy toward Washington?"[23] Such a question seemed to imply that the United States would gain little if it lent its support to the Red Shirt movement.

Back in Bangkok, there has been no indication that the U.S. Embassy officials have actually established channels of communication with the Red Shirt movement or that they have visited the Red Shirts' power bases — the northern and northeastern regions, which are still Thaksin's strongholds — in order to conduct thorough interviews or research on the political ideology of these so-called Thaksin's supporters. The inability to access the Red Shirt movement or closely to monitor the situation on the ground could perhaps play an important role in explaining the fixed American mind-set on the political situation in Thailand. So far, the U.S. government, like other countries in ASEAN, repeatedly said that it strictly upheld the principle of non-interference in Thai domestic politics — an excuse for Washington and its mission in Bangkok for not making any contact with the Red Shirts, even when in reality it worked closely with the traditional elites. Scot Marciel, former deputy assistant secretary of state for Southeast Asia and currently ambassador to Indonesia, while testifying in the Congress on 10 June 2010, was careful not to veer off the non-interference track. Moral support from the United States, yes. Interference, no.[24] Marciel's position was reconfirmed when United States Under-Secretary of State William Burns visited Thailand on 17 July 2010. Meeting with Prime Minister Abhisit, Burns stated, "Thais will serve their own interests best via the peaceful reconciliation of their political differences."[25]

THE *FARANG* YELLOW AND THE EVIL RED

The Obama administration made a failed attempt to balance between its support for the traditional elites and its sympathy towards the Red Shirts. On his way to the Myanmar capital of Naypyidaw, U.S. Assistant Secretary of State Kurt Campbell had a brief visit with members of the Red Shirt camp in Bangkok on 9 May 2010, exactly ten days before the deadly crackdown. Campbell met with the former acting leader of the now defunct Thai Rak Thai Party, Chaturon Chaisaeng, and former Foreign Minister Nopphadon Patthama, who has also been Thaksin's personal lawyer. Later, Campbell revealed that, in his discussion with the leaders of the Red Shirts, he told them that the United States hoped that they would seize the opportunity responsibly and expeditiously to lead Thailand out of its current predicament.[26] Foreign Minister Kasit Piromya, a known anti-Thaksin figure and a People's Alliance for Democracy (PAD) sympathizer, immediately called in U.S. Ambassador John and criticized his role in arranging the meeting between Campbell and leaders of the Red Shirts.

This was not the first time that John was reprimanded by the Democrat-led government. In June 2010, the Thai government expressed its extreme disappointment to the United States for including Thailand on its human trafficking watch list. Accordingly, the United States could cut some civilian aid to Thailand. The U.S. Embassy was blamed for supposedly feeding incorrect information to Washington.[27] At almost the same time, the State Department announced the replacement of John with Kristie Kenney, who would be taking over the ambassadorial post in Bangkok later in 2010. The *Asia Times Online* reported that John's tour was cut short by four months for unclear reasons, although his name has been floated as special representative and policy coordinator for Myanmar. Moreover, the State Department recently conducted a probe into the personal activities of his wife, Sophia John.[28] Shawn Crispin wrote, "A petition circulated among influential Americans in Bangkok opposing his nomination [for the new position dealing with Myanmar], reasoning that his interventions in Thailand's political troubles have been indiscreet, ill-advised and counter-productive and that he lacks the cultural sensitivity or interpersonal skills for negotiations in Southeast Asia."[29] The U.S. Embassy denied that there was pressure or anything out of the ordinary regarding Ambassador John's replacement. But political observers interpreted the the State Department's decision to replace John as a reflection of Washington's affinity with the Abhisit regime and the traditional elites. As for those influential American expatriates, they characterize the non-state banana men whose private interests align with those of the traditional elites.

A month after Campbell's botched intervention in Thai politics, Prime Minister Abhisit sent his special envoy Kiat Sitthi-amon to Washington to encourage the United States to refrain from future mediation in the conflict. Kiat said to reporters, "We are long-time friends and allies for 177 years and that means a lot. The position of the United States has always been if we call for help and support, they will extend a helping hand. But it is up to us to request and we have not asked."[30] Back in October 2009, Campbell told me in Washington that the Obama administration was more anxious about the rising violence in Thailand than the political repression in Burma. This was because the United States possessed a real stake in the kingdom's political well-being. Campbell's intention to reach out to the Red Shirts seemed to reflect more his goals attempt, rather than any policy at the national level. In reality, the tactic of painting an image of "evil red" is continuing both in the old establishment camp and in the United States; it is exacerbated by the government's allegation that radical elements within the Red Shirt movement are terrorists (with Thaksin alleged to be the chief operator of that terrorist network). On 10 June 2010, a hearing on Thailand's political crisis before the House Foreign Affairs Committee's Subcommittee on Asia, the Pacific and the Global Environment took place on the Capitol Hill. It preceded the House's almost unanimous vote in favour of a peaceful resolution of the Thai crisis and Prime Minister Abhisit's reconciliation road map. According to *The Nation*, Congressman Eni F. H. Faleomavaega, the subcommittee chairman, set the tone for the hearing by emphasizing the long-term solid relationship between the United States and its close friend and ally, and every panellist stuck with the tone throughout the session. The newspaper reported:

> One [of the panellists] said that Abhisit's road map should receive backing. Dr Richard Cronin, who heads the Southeast Asia programme at the Henry L Stimson Centre, was apparently not a Thaksin fan, and at one point he described the former prime minister as a crook who had a poor human-rights record. According to Cronin, giving moral support to the Abhisit government in regard to its reconciliation efforts would not compromise US democratic values, and what was "very important" as far as the United States was concerned was that "oversimplification" of the Thai crisis must be rejected ... The chairman ended the hearing by saying ... that Thailand's problems were far more complex than a fight between the rich and the poor or lovers of democracy against the military. "I don't even know whether Thaksin can visit our country," Faleomavaega said.[31]

Defending his government's policy once again, an American diplomat stressed in an interview that 435 of the total 535 members of the United States Congress serve only a two-year term and that most of them lack a sense of international politics, let alone an in-depth knowledge of the American policy towards Thailand.[32]

The move to shame Thaksin also continued in Bangkok. Kasit personally recommended known anti-Thaksin diplomat, Kittiphong Na Ranong, to assume the ambassadorial post in Washington. Kittiphong, a former Director-General of the East Asian Department of the Foreign Ministry, replaced Ambassador Don Pramutwinai, who retired in October 2010. Kittiphong is a well-respected figure in the Foreign Ministry. The fifty-three-year-old diplomat has been recognized for his no-nonsense and straightforward style of management. While many younger diplomats admire his work ethic, some perceive him to be an intimidating figure. Additionally, some consider him to be relatively junior in terms of experience. Therefore, the perception remains that his ascent to the position of ambassador to Washington may not have been based purely on merit, but politics instead. The arrival of Kittiphong in Washington was indeed timely. After the May 2010 crisis, the Thaksin camp has been aggressive in its search for a connection with certain administrative and legislative figures in the United States. Nopphadon Patthama travelled to Washington, D.C. in late June 2010; he claimed that he was invited by academics, thinkers and members of the media to give his views on the Thai situation. He exploited this opportunity to launch an anti-government campaign drawing international attention to the suppression of the Red Shirt protestors at the hands of the security forces. His visit to the United States was not accidental; he arrived only a few days before the U.S. Congress voted on whether to back Abhisit's reconciliation road map. Noppadon tried hard to push for the introduction of a section in Congress's resolution that encouraged the Thai government to negotiate with Thaksin. But no such language was included in the final version; for the text, see the annex to this essay.[33]

On 1 July 2010, the United States Congress voted 411–4 to support a motion calling on all parties involved in the Thai political crisis to renounce the use of violence and pledge to resolve the country's political problems peacefully and through democratic means. It also urged everyone concerned to work hard to settle their differences on the basis of the national reconciliation plan proposed by Prime Minister Abhisit on 3 May 2010, which encompassed upholding the monarchy, reforming politics, and ending injustice.[34] Immediately, Abhisit claimed that the motion showed that the United States regarded his government positively, another indication of the banana man being on his side.[35] In the meantime, the U.S. Embassy in Bangkok refused to accept a letter issued by the June 24 Democracy Group, an affiliate of the UDD, and the Red Sunday Group, calling for the U.S. House of Representatives to review its resolution to support the government's road map to reconciliation. American diplomats said that they refused the letter because members of the two groups raised protest banners and staged a mock military suppression of the protestors in front of the embassy in breach of conditions agreed earlier between them.[36]

The battle between the traditional Thai elite and the Thaksin network is no longer confined within Thailand's borders. The United States has become directly involved in this power game.[37] Kittiphong would be tasked to beseech the United States for support in the continued effort to deligitimise the political activities of Thaksin and the Red Shirt movement. Unfortunately for Thaksin, he is not Aung San Suu Kyi, a figure who has long dictated U.S. policy and swayed Congress because of her struggle for democracy. Thaksin has too much baggage and is a threat to the old power structure. Nopphadon has an uphill task not only to change the American attitude towards the traditional Thai elites but also to refashion Thaksin into a figure more acceptable to the U.S. government. As for the Red Shirt movement, its fight for democracy is still a "boutique issue", one that appeals to a relatively small clientele in the American capital, compared to the major foreign and domestic issues facing the Obama administration. The terrorist acts allegedly committed by some of the Red Shirt members and rumours about their "underground" network and plot to subvert the Abhisit government have further deepened America's suspicion of the Reds and cemented its favourable position towards the old elites. After all, it is easy and convenient for Washington policy-makers to look at the Thai situation from their archaic perspective, and not seriously take into account new factors which have emerged in a changed environment. The election victory of the pro-Thaksin Phuea Thai Party in July 2011 should once again remind the United States of the emergence of a new political landscape in Thailand.

ANNEX

H. Res. 1321

In the House of Representatives, United States of America
1 July 2010.

Whereas Thailand became the first treaty ally of the United States in the Asia-Pacific region with the Treaty of Amity and Commerce, signed at Sia-Yut'hia (Bangkok) March 20, 1833, between the United States and Siam, during the administration of President Andrew Jackson and the reign of King Rama III;

Whereas the United States and Thailand furthered their alliance with the Southeast Asia Collective Defense Treaty, (commonly known as the "Manila Pact of 1954") signed at Manila 8 September 1954, and the United States designated Thailand as a major non-North Atlantic Treaty Organization (NATO) ally in December 2003;

Whereas, through the Treaty of Amity and Economic Relations, signed at Bangkok 26 May 1966, along with a diverse and growing trading relationship, the United States and Thailand have developed critical economic ties;

Whereas Thailand is a key partner of the United States in Southeast Asia and has supported closer relations between the United States and the Association of Southeast Asian Nations (ASEAN);

Whereas Thailand has the longest-serving monarch in the world, His Majesty King Bhumibol Adulyadej, who is loved and respected for his dedication to the people of Thailand;

Whereas Prime Minister Abhisit Vejjajiva has issued a 5-point roadmap designed to promote the peaceful resolution of the current political crisis in Thailand;

Whereas approximately 500,000 people of Thai descent live in the United States and foster strong cultural ties between the 2 countries; and

Whereas Thailand remains a steadfast friend with shared values of freedom, democracy, and liberty: Now, therefore, be it

Resolved, That the House of Representatives —

(1) affirms the support of the people and the Government of the United States for a strong and vital alliance with Thailand;
(2) calls for the restoration of peace and stability throughout Thailand;
(3) urges all parties involved in the political crisis in Thailand to renounce the use of violence and to resolve their differences peacefully through dialogue;
(4) supports the goals of the 5-point roadmap of the Government of Thailand for national reconciliation, which seeks to —

   (A) uphold, protect, and respect the institution of the constitutional monarchy;
   (B) resolve fundamental problems of social justice systematically and with participation by all sectors of society;
   (C) ensure that the media can operate freely and constructively;
   (D) establish facts about the recent violence through investigation by an independent committee; and
   (E) establish mutually acceptable political rules through the solicitation of views from all sides; and

(5) promotes the timely implementation of an agreed plan for national reconciliation in Thailand so that free and fair elections can be held.

Attest:

Clerk.

Notes

1. J.L.S Girling once described the U.S.-Thai relationship as an outgrowth of Thailand's patronage political system, especially in the context of the Cold War. In Girling's view, Thailand's involvement with the United States was based on its own political circumstances, with the military dominating political power and choosing its own international allies. See J. L. S. Girling, *Thailand: Society and Politics* (Ithaca, New York: Cornell University Press, 1981), p. 92, quoted in Daniel Fineman, *A Special Relationship: The United States and Military Government in Thailand, 1947–1958* (Honolulu: University of Hawaii Press, 1997), p. 5.

2. Krit Garnjana-Goonchorn, "Thai-US Relations in the Regional Context", *Southeast Asia Bulletin* (Washington: Centre for Strategic and International Studies, March 2008), p. 2.
3. Fineman, *A Special Relationship*, p. 3.
4. Michael K. Connors, *Thailand and the United States of America: Beyond Hegemony*, paper presented at a symposium on "Bush and Asia: America's Evolving Relations in East Asia", the University of Queensland, 26 November 2004 <www.latrobe.edu.au/socsci/staff/connors/connors-Thai-US.doc> (accessed 11 July 2010). In March 1962, the State Department publicly issued a communiqué on the occasion of a visit to Washington by Thai Foreign Minister Thanat Khoman. This communiqué reaffirmed American determination to maintain the preservation of the independence and integrity of Thailand as vital to the national interests of the United States and to world peace. Also see, Arne Kislenko, "The Vietnam War, Thailand, and the United States", in *Trans-Pacific Relations: America, Europe, and Asia in the Twentieth Century*, edited by Richard Jensen, Jon Davidann and Yoneyuki Sugita (Connecticut: Praeger Publishers, 2003), p. 224.
5. See Pavin Chachavalpongpun, *Reinventing Thailand: Thaksin and His Foreign Policy*, (Singapore: Institute of Southeast Asian Studies, 2010), p. 69.
6. Fineman, *A Special Relationship*, p. 136.
7. "Thai PM: US a Useless Friend", *China Daily*, 27 February 2004 <http://www.chinadaily.com.cn/english/doc/2004-02/27/content_310123.htm> (accessed 13 July 2010).
8. Cited in "Thailand's Military Coup in 2006", in Asia's Finest Discussion Forum <http://www.asiafinest.com/forum/index.php?showtopic=226503> (accessed 13 July 2010).
9. Press Release No. 038/06, 4 October 2006, Office of the White House Press Secretary available at <http://bangkok.usembassy.gov/news/press/2006/nrot038.html> (accessed 13 July 2010).
10. United States Embassy, Bangkok, Press Release No. 009/07, 8 May 2007, on "Cobra Gold 2007 Kicks Off in Pattaya, Chon Buri", <http://bangkok.usembassy.gov/news/press/2007/nrot009.html> (accessed 13 July 2010).
11. See "Thailand: U.S. Calls for End to Airport Seizure", <http://bangkok.usembassy.gov/news/press/2008/nrot063.html> (accessed 13 July 2010).
12. Shawn W. Crispin, "US Slips, China Glides in Thai Crisis", *Asia Times Online*, 20 July 2010 <http://www.atimes.com/atimes/Southeast_Asia/LG20Ae01.html> (accessed 29 July 2010).
13. Ibid.
14. "Call for Peaceful Dialogue in Thailand", statement by Secretary of State Hillary Clinton <http://bangkok.usembassy.gov/041210secstate_thailand.

html> (accessed 13 July 2010), available in video format at <http://www.youtube.com/watch?v=LPGYKvoDma8>.

15. United States Department of State, Daily Press Briefing, 19 May 2010 <http://bangkok.usembassy.gov/051910statement_thailand.html> (accessed 3 July 2010).
16. The interviews were conducted during June–July 2010 with three Thai diplomats who had been involved in relations with the United States and three American diplomats, two of whom were working in Washington and one in Southeast Asia. Because of the sensitive nature of the issues in question, the interviewees asked not to be cited by name.
17. Crispin, "US Slips, China Glides in Thai Crisis".
18. Emma Chanlett-Avery, "Thailand: Background and US Relations", Congressional Research Service, 8 June 2009, pp. 16–17 available at <www.fas.org/sgp/crs/row/RL32593.pdf> (accessed 13 July 2010).
19. Quoted in Crispin, "US Slips, China Glides in Thai Crisis".
20. Telephone interview with a Thai diplomat who formerly served at the Royal Thai Embassy in Washington, 9 July 2010.
21. Interviews with two American diplomats posted to Singapore, on 22 and 28 July 2010; the latter interview was conducted by e-mail.
22. Interview with American diplomat, Singapore, 22 July 2010.
23. Ibid.
24. Tulsathit Taptim, "The Americans Debate Thaksin", *The Nation*, 27 July 2010.
25. "PM Hints at Early 2011 Election", *Bangkok Post*, 17 July 2010.
26. Statement of US Assistant Secretary of State Kurt M. Campbell, 9 May 2010 <http://bangkok.usembassy.gov/050410statement_campbell.html> (accessed 13 July 2001).
27. US Watch List Disappoints Thailand", *Bangkok Post*, 17 June 2010.
28. Crispin, "US Slips, China Glides in Thai Crisis".
29. Ibid.
30. Ibid.
31. Tulsathit, "The Americans Debate Thaksin".
32. Interview with American diplomat, Singapore, 22 July 2010. Members of the American House of Representatives, the lower house of its federal congress, serve two-year terms, while members of the Senate, its upper house, serve six-year terms. Members of both houses are directly elected.
33. Crispin, "US Slips, China Glides in Thai Crisis".
34. For the full text of this motion, see the annex to this essay.
35. "PM Lauds US Congress Resolution on Road Map", *The Bangkok Post*, 3 July 2010.

36. "Reds' Letter Rejected by US Embassy", *Bangkok Post*, 17 July 2010.
37. Catharin E. Dalpino, visiting associate professor and director of the Thai Studies Program at the Edmund A. Walsh School of Foreign Service, Georgetown University, suggested at the hearing before the House Committee of Foreign Affairs Subcommittee on Asia, the Pacific and the Global Environment on 10 July 2010 that the United States should take pains to maintain a non-partisan approach to assisting democracy in Thailand. The perception that a foreign power was playing favourites in the Thai political arena would damage a fragile peace. See http://foreignaffairs.house.gov/111/dal061010.pdf (accessed 14 July 2010).

21

THE SOCIAL BASES OF AUTOCRATIC RULE IN THAILAND

Craig J. Reynolds

During the political disturbances in Thailand in March–May 2010, media attention was naturally focused on the legitimacy of the Abhisit government and the rights and expectations of disappointed voters. Over many decades democracy has been regularly thwarted by the military establishment and by business interests working hand-in-hand with the bureaucracy and regime of the day. Elected officials as well as military officers and bureaucrats have business interests, often managed through members of their immediate families. When a new constitution was promulgated in 1997, "good governance", translated into Thai as *thammarat*, became the catch-cry of advocates of political reform. Alas, the moral force signalled in that formulation by the Buddhist keyword Dhamma (*thamma*), best understood in this context as "righteousness", has been inadequate to the task of transforming the political system in

---

An earlier version of this essay appeared in e-IR online at <http://www.e-ir.info/?p=4372>. The current version was prepared for this volume.

ways envisioned by those who drafted the new constitution. Authoritarian, liberal, and communitarian strands of *thammarat*/good governance have stubbornly competed with one another in a way that was visible in the speeches, negotiations and media commentary in early 2010.[1]

What was missing from media and academic commentary on the 2010 round of the Thai political crisis, apart from the occasional comparison between Thailand and military despotism in Myanmar, was the regional context.[2] Since decolonization after the Second World War, democracy, however conjured by voters, academics, protestors, or ruling elites, has been a problem in mainland Southeast Asia. Despite the prevalence of one-party governments put in office by the popular vote, the distinction between democracy and elections is often not made. Governments, especially authoritarian ones, favour elections, because political leaders can claim popular legitimacy from the electoral process. But participatory democracy is undermined if elections are not free and competitive. Vote-buying — candidates handing out cash and other inducements to voters — is a recurrent issue, leading to the widespread belief that elections are fixed.[3] Most importantly, whereas the ambient ethos of the political culture in a participatory democracy needs to be tolerant of dissent, in the region those already in power strive to limit dissent and manipulate democracy to ensure not just their longevity in office, but permanency of rule.

In Myanmar the armed forces have governed for nearly fifty years with no end in sight to military rule even on the most distant horizon. In Cambodia a strongman is still in power some two decades after he was installed as prime minister by the Vietnamese during their military occupation of the country. In socialist Laos and communist Vietnam only one party is allowed to field candidates in national elections. In Malaysia there is more multi-party activity, but the United Malays National Organisation (UMNO), the dominant party in ruling coalitions since independence, expertly gerrymanders to preserve its electoral advantage and alters the constitution in its favour. In Singapore the People's Action Party (PAP) hobbles other parties if they exhibit meaningful opposition and thus maintains its one-party dominance. This, a region of autocratic political systems, is the immediate neighbourhood in which Thai democracy is expected to put down its roots and flourish.

The conflict of March–May 2010 generated prolific comment in the blogosphere in which the term "fascist" was used to describe both sides

— the government as well as the protestors, most of whom were rural people from the North and Northeast. In this usage, fascism is a lazy, sensationalist synonym for autocracy. Thai writers and academics have been known to hurl the fascist epithet at Field Marshal Po. Phibun Songkhram, Thailand's first military premier from 1938 to 1944. The Phibun government, which continued unscathed through the Japanese occupation, was much taken by Japanese militarism. Popular patriotic literature during the 1930s drew on the Japanese martial code of *bushido*, and Japanese journalists and ministers were received hospitably on visits to Bangkok where they were invited to view plays with pan-Asian themes celebrating the solidarity of Asian civilizations against the West.

Although a fascist party never took root in Thailand, Thai ideologues quickly latched onto Mussolini's fascism for its anti-communist ideology. The term was used approvingly in the Bangkok press in the late 1920s and early 1930s.[4] A Thai biography of Mussolini, adapted from *Le facisme c'est Mussolini* by Louis Roya, was published in 1932, the year that a civilian-military group deposed the absolute monarch.[5] But rather than the ideology of fascism, it was the personal style of the strongman, or a softer variant marked by heroic leadership, that attracted Thai leaders and political thinkers. World leaders such as Eamon De Valera, Stalin, Hitler, Gandhi, Nehru, Chiang Kai-Shek, Mao Zedong, and Zhou Enlai also commanded attention, a seemingly bizarre list of nationalists, communists and pacifists as well as fascists. In *Strategies for Creating Greatness*, published in 1952 by Luang Wichit Wathakan, the list of exemplary figures included several heroic women — Florence Nightingale, Sarah Bernhardt, and Helen Keller. In this success literature, such people were admired for their strength of mind, powers of concentration, self-confidence, and will power.

Throughout the decade before the Second World War, the Great Man Theory of History was popular elsewhere in the region as an inspiration for nationalists struggling for independence. Vietnamese nationalists, for example, were captivated by the exceptional lives of powerful Asian and Western leaders.[6] Subscribing to the Great Man Theory, President Sukarno wrote with admiration in 1939 and 1940 about Adolf Hitler as a masterly and exemplary orator. Sukarno saw Hitler's arrogant and superior manner as compensation for the dictator's many failures in life; at the same time, he regarded Hitler as a model teacher for moving masses with oratory.[7] Sidney Hook, who trumpeted "event-making men" in his

The Hero in History, first published in 1943, identified a leadership ideal that had currency in many parts of the world, especially in Southeast Asia. This ideal of the event-making man has had a very long half-life in Thailand. Spotted by a journalist in a Chiang Mai cafe during the recent disturbances were portraits of Mahatma Gandhi, Nelson Mandela, and Che Guevara. Next to them was Thaksin Shinawatra, the electorally successful Thai ex-prime minister and the *éminence grise* behind the protests in Bangkok who resides in Montenegro and Dubai as a fugitive from Thai law. The gallery of photos indicates that, while these men have power over others, it is an amoral power to be admired irrespective of the ideologies for which these people stand. Do those who possess this amoral power also have charisma, that strange yet compelling alchemic compound that makes a person a natural leader?

The juxtaposition of democracy and autocracy runs deep in the Thai elite psyche. Just days before the 1932 "revolution", which brought an end to the absolute monarchy, the seventh Bangkok king mulled over the possibility of granting a constitution, all the while clinging to the hope that the Thai people could be encouraged to support an absolute monarch. "Our country uses a 'dictatorship' system of government", he wrote, "but our system is not like other 'dictator' systems. On the contrary, it has many characteristics of a 'democracy'. Thus it is a sort of half-and-half, and we haven't really decided which system we will follow."[8] Political scientists both Thai and Western have written volumes on "semi-democracy" in Thailand ever since. Even as history has reversed the formulation, as if to say "our country uses a democratic system of government, but it has many characteristics of a dictatorship," there is not much improvement. The figures of the benevolent dictator and enlightened despot still loom large in the minds of Thai political thinkers as they puzzle over the real significance of the 1932 event.[9] Was it a bourgeois-democratic revolution? An oligarchic change of government, with one clique displacing another? A failed revolution?[10] In light of what happened in Bangkok in March–May 2010, the king's remarks in May 1932 about dictatorship and democracy were prophetic.

Looking at the socio-political landscape in Southeast Asia more broadly, I do not think that the charge of fascism, which had little resonance with nationalist aspirations during the 1930s apart from the personal style of the strong ruler, comes close to identifying the social bases of autocratic rule or militaristic leadership in Thailand. Instead, the personal style of leadership that one is inclined to label fascist is better understood in other terms. For one thing, there is a definite Buddhist element in this leadership style. The strongman, with or without a background in the military or security services, is sometimes of ascetic demeanour, and much admired for his personal discipline and powers of self-control. Several prime ministers, and some would-be prime ministers, fit this description. A Thailand-based columnist has described this variant of leadership as an amalgam of monk and gangster, the ascetic and the strongman in the one individual — always, of course, male. The current president of the Thailand's Privy Council, General Prem Tinsulanon, was mentioned as a case in point.[11] Major General Chamlong Srimuang, a core leader of the Yellow Shirts, is another.[12]

It is also possible to characterize this type of personalized leadership by drawing on the concept of "big men" familiar in other parts of the world, including the Pacific nation-states. The "big man" — or "man of prowess", as the type has been glossed in Southeast Asian contexts — rested his claim to authority not on lineage but on performance.[13] In pre-modern Southeast Asian kingdoms there was no law of primogeniture. Usurpations happened often enough, with half-brothers in these polygamous societies eager to advance their claims to the throne on the basis of paternity and maternal lines that strengthened those claims. The man of prowess rewarded supporters with land grants or suzerainty over subjugated populations. He was generous with these rewards, and ruthless in excluding latecomers who had dallied in declaring their loyalty. Like the big men of Melanesia, rulers widened their spheres of influence and created supra-local networks by means of a calculated generosity. They redistributed bounty acquired by trade or plunder to their personal retinues or entourages — read "political parties" in today's world — as well as to wider external sectors — read "constituencies" cultivated by means of "vote-buying" in national elections. In this way rulers accumulated social capital and extended their hegemony.

Everywhere there were "little big men," striving to increase their own prowess in competition with one other, ultimately to challenge the "big man" who had already achieved success. In the late colonial period in mainland Southeast Asia, revolts led by men of merit (*phu mi bun* in Thai) were early forms of redistributive populisms led by men of prowess who had been pushed aside by the colonizing state, be it Western or indigenous. Charms, amulets, and a reputation for supernatural powers helped to mobilise supporters. In modern times in Thailand, the man of prowess may be a high-ranking general who has risen through the ranks, become prime minister, and served the monarchy with distinction. Or he may be a successful businessman who has made a fortune selling telecommunications equipment to the security services. Whatever the modality of its transformation in the modern age, autocratic rule in Thailand today has its roots in earlier forms of a political economy of leadership that valorised a man who could be at once generous and ruthless, who would reward his supporters and punish his rivals and competitors. The enduring popularity of this kind of leadership in the region should never be underestimated.

Notes

1. The term, with all its bright promises and contradictions, is unpacked by Kasian Tejapira, "*Thammarat*/Good Governance", in *Words in Motion: Toward a Global Lexicon*, edited by Carol Gluck and Anna Lowenhaupt Tsing (Durham and London: Duke University Press, 2009), pp. 306–26.
2. In 2010, Freedom House ranked Thailand among "thuggish regimes like Burma for political rights"; Joshua Kurlantzick, "The End of Brand Thailand", *Newsweek*, 14 June 2010.
3. Benedict Anderson makes much of the distinction between elections and democracy in his comparison of Thailand, Indonesia and the Philippines in "Elections and Participation in Three Southeast Asian Countries", in *The Politics of Elections in Southeast Asia*, edited by R. H. Taylor (Washington: Woodrow Wilson Center Press, 1996), pp. 12–33. For discussion of vote-buying in Thailand, see Somchai Phatharathananunth, "The Thai Rak Thai Party and Elections in North-eastern Thailand", *Journal of Contemporary Asia* 38, no. 1 (February 2008): 106–23. Andrew Walker, "The Rural Constitution and the Everyday Politics of Elections in Northern Thailand", *Journal of Contemporary Asia* 38, no. 1 (February 2008): 84–105, argues against the common view that rural voters are gullibly seduced by money politics.
4. Benjamin Batson, *The End of the Absolute Monarchy in Siam* (Singapore: Oxford University Press, 1984), p. 164, n102.
5. Scot Barmé, *Luang Wichit Wathakan and the Creation of a Thai Identity* (Singapore: Institute of Southeast Asian Studies, 1993), p. 98, n101.
6. David G. Marr, *Vietnamese Tradition on Trial, 1920–1945* (Berkeley: University of California Press, 1981), Chapter 6.

7. Angus McIntyre, "Marx versus Carlyle: Sukarno's View of Hitler's Role in History", *RIMA: Review of Indonesian and Malaysian Affairs* 43, no. 2 (2009): 131–63.
8. Benjamin A. Batson, comp. and ed., *Siam's Political Future: Documents from the End of the Absolute Monarchy* (Ithaca: Southeast Asia Program, Cornell University, 1974), p. 96. See also Batson, *The End of the Absolute Monarchy*, pp. 141–42.
9. See, for example, Sombat Chantornvong and Chai-anan Samudavanija, *Khwamkhit thang kanmueang thai* [Thai Political Thought] (Bangkok: Bannakit, 1980), p. 23, published as General Prem began his eight years as prime minister; and Nidhi Eeoseewong, "Playing the Last Card in the Deadly Embrace", *Matichon*, 14 June 2010.
10. Craig J. Reynolds, "Thai Revolution," in *The Encyclopedia of Political Revolutions*, edited by Jack A. Goldstone (Washington: Congressional Quarterly Inc., 1998), pp. 479–80.
11. Chang Noi (pseud.), *Jungle Book: Thailand"s Politics, Moral Panic, and Plunder, 1996–2008* (Chiang Mai: Silkworm Books, 2009); see Chapter 4, "Monks and Gangsters in Thai Politics".
12. Duncan McCargo, *Chamlong Srimuang and the New Thai Politics* (London: Hurst & Company, 1997).
13. In Chapter 1 of O. W. Wolters, *History, Culture, and Region in Southeast Asian Perspectives*, rev. ed. (Ithaca: Southeast Asia Program Cornell University, 1999), Wolters develops the idea of the "man of prowess" in relation to early Southeast Asian kingship. The *locus classicus* of the big man type is Marshall Sahlins, "Poor Man, Rich Man, Big-man, Chief: Political Types in Melanesia and Polynesia", *Comparative Studies in Society and History* 5, no. 3 (April 1963): 285–303.

22

THE STRATEGY OF THE UNITED FRONT FOR DEMOCRACY AGAINST DICTATORSHIP ON "DOUBLE STANDARDS"

A Grand Gesture to History, Justice, and Accountability

David Streckfuss

The day 10 May 2010 may come to stand out as one of the most significant dates in Thailand's legal history. It was the day that the National United Front for Democracy against Dictatorship (UDD) issued its defiant demand: no amnesties. An amnesty would forgive the perpetrators of the violence of a month earlier, 10 April, when twenty-one UDD protestors — largely unarmed, according to their leaders — were killed in a government crackdown on their protest. On that latter date, then, the UDD made a clear choice: to risk going down on terrorism charges in exchange for the possibility that Prime Minister Abhisit Vejjajiva and Deputy Prime Minister Suthep Thaugsuban would go down for murder.

Historically speaking, such a call for government accountability is quite rare in Thailand. But it does echo a long-lost past challenge issued by a young member of a Thai parliament that had been abolished by a military dictatorship, a spirit who for the sake of justice and truth called a coup by its real name: rebellion, an illegal overthrow of a popularly constituted government. That man was Uthai Phimjaichon. He was, with two of his colleagues, sentenced in 1972 to ten years in prison for the insolence of speaking the truth.[1] His actions forced those in power to justify their actions. Uthai thus opened the logic of dictatorship for public scrutiny. It was only after fifteen months that the full import of his heroic deed became clear, as the diminishing legitimacy of the dictators, the exposure of their machinations, finally led to their great tumble from power in the face of the popular uprising of October 1973.

10 May marked the turning point of what might have started as a struggle for former Prime Minister Thaksin Shinawatra and a call for new elections that was transformed instead into a call for justice and equality under the law.

10 May was the one-month mark, at which finding legal recourse to the perceived brutality of the government became the rallying call. 10 April had redirected the protest's main aim from a call for new elections to a demand for government accountability. UDD protestors up-country distributed CDs portraying the bloodshed of that night, and huge posters of gruesome scenes of the dead hung silently over the continuing protest in Bangkok. The nightly announcement on the Ratchaprasong stage on 10 May made fully clear the transition in the UDD leadership's strategy. "Justice for more than 20 of our people who lost their lives is most important", UDD leader Natthawut Saikuea proclaimed, "while dissolution and election are a very small issue".[2] When asked whether the UDD was ready to end its protest, Jatuporn Phomphan, another core UDD leader, said no, "if authorities still are not pursuing these cases [against Abhisit and Suthep]. For me, I would prefer death."[3]

10 May saw the UDD accept "unconditionally" the five points of the "reconciliation road map" proposed by Prime Minister Abhisit Vejjajiva one week earlier. But it added two of its own demands, the first of which was to unblock access to the UDD's PTV channel (or to block the ASTV channel of the People's Alliance for Democracy, or PAD). The principle: all media should be governed by a single standard.

The second demand was curious and historically atypical: a demand that there be no amnesty for either the government or for its opponents. As part of this demand, the UDD leadership called on Deputy Prime Minister Suthep Thaugsuban, responsible for security forces on 10 April, to respond officially to the many complaints filed with the police by relatives of those who had died or been injured in the government crackdown. The UDD wanted Suthep to turn himself in to the authorities for processing on charges of murder and inflicting injury on 10 April.

The UDD leadership apparently pictured Suthep being treated like any other murder suspect: turning himself in to hear charges, being indicted, and brought before the court in a bail hearing. The picture would have been dramatic and historically unprecedented: a humbled Suthep, a brutal, fallen government minister, brought to justice. However realistic or unrealistic this possibility, the UDD placed all its bets on this one scenario, and promised to end its protest at once if that scenario came to pass.

The question here is, why was the UDD leadership willing to put two months of struggle, injury, and death on the line in exchange for Suthep's submitting himself to the justice system? Suthep was not covered by parliamentary immunity. Was this single and final strategy the result of confusion and conflicts within the UDD leadership? Was it born of a desperate desire to see the demonstrations end with the climactic transformation of the government's most powerful minister into a common murder suspect?

My argument is that 10 April changed everything for the UDD leadership. If Abhisit Vejjajiva's rise to premiership had been seen as illegitimate — engineered through a back-room deal with military interference — then the government's handling of 10 April took the situation into another realm entirely.

THE UDD'S STRATEGY SHIFT TO "DOUBLE STANDARDS"

After the 10 April crackdown, the UDD reframed its struggle in terms of "double standards" — expressed in two ways. The first was through conspicuous emulation of and comparison with PAD's experiences in 2008. The second revolved around the question of amnesties.

By mid-April, the dissolution of parliament may have still been a goal, but the issue of double standards was ascendant. The UDD was clearly pushing the limits of the law to make apparent to society as a whole the inequalities of the justice system in Thailand. In doing so, the leadership copied parts of the PAD's 2008 game book. It sought to make clear the gaping difference between its movement and the PAD as a way of addressing the frequently heard criticisms of the UDD's ongoing rallies.

"UDD rallies have hurt the economy and infringed on the rights of others."

Correct. UDD members never denied this fact. But they were quick to point out that their actions were nothing compared to those of PAD. Although estimates vary, the National Economic and Social Development Board said in late May 2010 that the overall economic damage of the UDD rallies (including the arson at their end) was "less than half" of the 290 billion baht in losses resulting from the PAD rallies of 2008.[4]

What was different about the latter is that the newly installed Democrat-led government in late December 2008 provided little government assistance to businesses hurt by the PAD rallies. However, even before the UDD rallies ended, that same government had already lavished tax breaks and soft loans on affected businesses. It would later actively help organize groups to sue the UDD for damages.

"The protest at Ratchaprasong is illegal."

Correct. UDD members openly admitted that the continued protest at Ratchaprasong was illegal. But they averred that they had just as much right, so to speak, to protest illegally as had the PAD in 2008. Then, the civil court had issued two orders — one for the PAD to leave Government House in August, and another for it to leave Suvarnabhumi International Airport in November. The PAD's lawyers appealed the first of these orders, and the Appeals Court lifted the injunction, as emergency law had since been imposed. But when emergency law was lifted, the court did not reissue its order. It thus placed the PAD's occupation of Government House in something of a legal limbo. The order to vacate the airport was simply ignored. PAD lawyers also argued before the Supreme Administrative Court that the government had abused power by imposing emergency law in ways inconsistent with the law, and asked the court to revoke its imposition.[5]

The UDD also petitioned the Supreme Administrative Court to revoke the Emergency Decree imposed by the Abhisit government on 7 April 2010. The UDD was, however, not so much making the argument that its protest was legal, but rather that the government had already shown that it eschewed international standards in dispersing demonstrators. The disastrous events of 10 April offered clear evidence. The UDD asked for a "temporary injunction" against the government that would prevent its use of excessive force to break up the demonstration at Ratchaprasong. Both attempts failed, and the illegal rally continued.[6]

"UDD leaders are charged with terrorism and serious violations of criminal law."

True. But the PAD's leaders also faced several criminal charges, including obstructing aviation and terrorism, for seizing Suvarnabhumi Airport.[7] In the PAD's case, leaders initiated a sort of court-preemptive strategy by appealing the charges themselves. After occupying Government House, PAD leaders were charged with insurrection. An appeals court revoked the insurrection charges in October 2008. Nine PAD leaders were charged on 18 November 2008 with "illegal assembly and inciting unrest". For more than a year thereafter, the Prosecution Department claimed that it was unable to decide on whether to indict the nine leaders. PAD lawyers proved able to impede progress on the case, claiming that their clients "were busy in other provinces" and requesting "additional investigation reports" from the police. Adding much credence to UDD claims of double standards, prosecutors postponed the case for the ninth time on 23 April, and then again on 16 June. Unsurprisingly, the Phuea Thai Party requested that the National Counter-Corruption Commission take action against the national police chief for delaying the cases against the PAD even when the chief police investigator for the case was ready to seek warrants from the court against 126 PAD leaders. All were given bail; two had been held for a few days in October 2009 and then released.[8]

In contrast, UDD followers were denied bail, sentenced, and jailed with alarming efficiency. Even before events came to a head, 11 UDD followers were sentenced to fifteen days in jail for obstructing traffic in late April, and another twenty-seven sentenced to six months for participating in an illegal protest in mid-May.[9] On 18 April, the Department of Special Investigations (DSI) set up a "red-shirt terrorist probe" that established "investigation procedures for the current intimidation cases carried out by the red shirts." On 2 May, the Thai cabinet approved an $870,000 budgetary allocation for the DSI so that it could make progress on "the terrorism cases and security related cases linking groups of people."[10]

The UDD's strategy was clear. To offer society a clear contrast, the UDD matched many of the PAD's 2008 actions, but — at least in the minds of UDD leaders — its never did anything worse. After 10 April, the leadership was fully aware that its members would be going to jail when their protest ended. They might have tried to engineer an amnesty for themselves. Instead, they adopted a strategy of exposing "double standards". Jatuporn, as paraphrased in a news report, claimed that he "would like to ask society if they want to see cases relating to the UDD be treated as special cases, while cases against the government or anti-UDD groups are put on hold".[11]

THE AMNESTY

The only way for the UDD leadership to achieve its goal of exposing double standards was to refuse any amnesty. In taking this tack, the leaders showed an atypical appreciation of Thai history. The pro-military, pro-coup, and anti-democratic PAD had long lost any claim to the mantle of the progressive movements of the past. But the UDD could legitimately claim to be the true heirs to a long democratic struggle whose earlier rounds had ended in bloodshed: on 14 October 1973, on 6 October 1976, in May 1992, and now on 10 April 2010.

Accordingly, to lay claim to the tradition of progressive historical movements, UDD leaders had to reject any amnesty. Their reasoning was clear. Amnesties have been the crucial component of state impunity since the 1950s, when coup maker began the practice of granting themselves amnesties. When a coup was bloodless coup, amnesty was merely a naked justification for seizing power. But when state-sponsored crackdowns resulted in bloodshed, as in 1976 and 1992, amnesty became not a form of compassion or forgiveness (as it was often portrayed) but rather of institutionalized impunity. These amnesties, while "forgiving" the victims, at the same time celebrated impunity and exiled truth and justice. Amnesties came in the form of law, and no Thai court, over a

60-year period, has ever overturned one. As a result, no (successful) Thai coup maker or soldier has ever been tried for involvement in bloody suppressions. Amnesties, in these cases, have induced periodic historical amnesia.

After the events of 10 April, the UDD did not want 2010 to take its place as the latest chapter in a dreary history of exoneration of power holders who, either by volition or carelessness, chose to use deadly force against citizens. It quickly rejected any calls for an amnesty. On 21 April, for instance, Natthawut dismissed the suggestion of an amnesty made by a senator, saying, "What would the amnesty be for? More than 20 friends of mine have lost their lives in the war against the government."

In early May Abhisit made it seem as if the UDD leadership was banking on an eventual amnesty as part of reconciliation efforts. On 4 and 5 May, for instance, he denied rumors that the government might offer UDD leaders an amnesty, saying that none would be granted to true criminals or terrorists.[12] A news report on 13 May said that "one of the main sticking points" in talks between the government and the UDD was likely the question of a "possible amnesty" for the latter.[13]

But in fact, at least publicly, the UDD was insisting that there be no amnesty. From the day the reconciliation road map was announced, UDD leaders made clear that no one should be granted amnesty. On 4 May, Weera Musikaphong said that UDD leaders wanted to fight the terrorism and *lèse majesté* charges made against them. On 10 May, the *Bangkok Post* reported that UDD leaders did "not want amnesty for themselves," but instead insisted on "a single standard applied to all".

As of 15 June, when the Abhisit government was mulling over the question of extending an amnesty to those of the UDD rank and file "with pure hearts", their leaders were still insisting on no amnesty. Jatuporn said, "The planned amnesty is something like offering a small shrimp in exchange for a big sea bass. The small shrimp is the criminal case against the red-shirts and the big fish is the government, who were involved in the killing of the red-shirt protesters."[14]

This challenge is serious. Robert Amsterdam, an international lawyer representing many of the UDD leadership (as well as former Prime Minister Thaksin Shinawatra), has warned Red Shirts against accepting an amnesty, as implicit in the acceptance is an admission of guilt. There has been a world of change in the legal field since the 1990s, says Amsterdam, where courts in countries like Chile and Argentina have taken strong stands against impunity. Amsterdam feels that such change is imminent in Thailand as well.[15]

Beyond the apparent legal immunization granted by the emergency decree, a Red Shirt lawyer in the Northeast of Thailand has claimed that the 2006 interim constitution lays the groundwork for a limitless amnesty. According to his logic, the issue of "double standards" was created by the 2006 coup. The criminality of the coup was expunged by section 37 of the 2006 interim constitution, which made state officials "absolutely exempt from any wrongdoing, responsibility and liabilities" for any acts committed or ordered by the Council for National Security [Council for Democratic Reform] "whether done on such date or prior to such date or after such date". Just as interesting was section 36 which stated that "all announcements or orders" of the CNS were to be "considered lawful and constitutional" in perpetuity.[16] The legality of these two provisions was extended to section 309 of the 2007 constitution, which reads:

> All actions that have been endorsed by the Interim Constitution of the Kingdom of Thailand B.E. 2549 [2006] as being lawful and constitutional, including all subsequent actions and activities taken both before and after the promulgation of this Constitution shall be deemed lawful and constitutional under this Constitution.[17]

At least according to this lawyer, these 2006 and 2007 constitutional provisions gave legal force to all coup decrees and made possible a blanket amnesty that can be interpreted to cover the bloody events of April and May 2010.[18]

I have argued elsewhere that the Thai Supreme Court handed down a set of decisions in the 1950s that justified military coups.[19] These decisions laid the legal framework for the military dictatorship that coalesced under Sarit Thanarat in the early 1960s. A legal-ish term describing a temporary state of affairs — "abnormal times" — eventually became permanent. Thailand entered into a "state of the exception", during which everything was conditional and often left to the whims of those in power. The legal regime was debased, and constitutional and statutory law became subservient to coup decrees.

The 1997 constitution promised to expunge the vestiges of dictatorship in Thailand. Certainly, former Prime Minister Thaksin Shinawatra did his part to undermine many of the democratic safeguards embodied in that charter. But, whatever his excesses in weakening the constitution, nothing could compare with the legal debasement created by the 2006 coup.

The Thai judiciary has never played much of a role in placing limits on executive power. In the aftermath of the 2006 coup, though, Thailand's courts merely became an appendage of the executive branch. Witness the judiciary's take on "double standards" in the following example. In light of criticism of the way that the courts handled Thaksin's assets case in February 2010, the Office of the Judiciary made the rare move to defend the court's decision. Its spokesperson, Sitthisak Wannachakit, argued that the court was not "prejudiced" and its verdict not "pre-determined or arranged," as some critics had claimed. The spokesperson then made a surprising confession about the nature of law in Thailand:

> there are those who say that the Supreme Court typically accepts [laws created by coup-makers] [while] the courts should apply only laws passed through parliament. On this point I would like to point out that from 1973 to the present, many coups have been carried out. After seizing power, the coup-makers will issue laws in order to legitimize their taking of power in the form of Announcements which are still in use in the criminal code and various legal acts. The courts enforce the laws which the legislative branch [*fai nitthibanyat*] has drawn up. If the law has come about legally in principle, the court has the duty to enforce and interpret the law in an equal manner; otherwise the court will be accused of double standards.[20]

Coups always have the effect of skewing the regime of law. But they also lead to such a skewing of perceptions that even obvious truths become obscured. Uthai pointed out in 1972 that the military leaders had staged a coup. The coup leaders, in response, so twisted logic that they were convinced it was not a "coup" at all that they had carried out. Abhisit spoke often about upholding "the rule of law". When faced with "terrorism", his government could and did get swift judicial decisions. But when it came to prosecution of the PAD, he claimed that his government did not interfere with the Prosecution Department. And it is a bit mind-boggling to note the response of the PAD to the UDD's rallies. Obviously suffering from severe bout of selective amnesia, the PAD's spokesman urged the government to crack down on the illegal protest of UDD "terrorists" without, apparently, recalling his own words on the PAD's takeover of the airport in 2008: "The PAD will protect all locations because we are using our rights to demonstrate peacefully without causing damages to state properties or rioting."[21] This amnesia may also be explained by the PAD's tendency to see the world in black-and-white terms, as a great struggle between the angelic forces (the PAD) against those of pure evil (Thaksin and the UDD).[22]

THE END OF "DOUBLE STANDARDS"?

The PAD's response to the UDD's rallies exemplified perfectly the pervasive Thai political malady that we might call "partisan exceptionalism": the belief that one's acts are justified while a similar or identical act of an opponent is a crime. The PAD wanted the UDD suppressed, while claiming that it was not guilty of similar conduct itself. The coup group in 2006 wanted to re-establish the rule of law without itself being willing to submit its members to the justice system for prosecution on the charge of overthrowing the government.

This is exactly why the UDD's insistence on there being no amnesty in 2010 was so atypical and ahistorical for Thailand. The UDD's leaders were willing to suffer the consequences of their own actions, to submit themselves to a justice system of which they are highly suspicious, in order that those responsible for the deaths of April and May 2010 not be allowed the luxury of impunity. In this sense, 10 May 2010 brought one of the greatest challenges ever faced by the justice system in Thailand. It threw the police, prosecutors, and courts into an awkward and exposed position.

No matter how the justice system takes on the cases of the UDD, the PAD, and Abhisit and Suthep, the UDD leadership will have proven its point: with the world and Thai society as witness, either the justice system adjusts to make all parties equal before the law, or it maintains double standards. By refusing an amnesty, the UDD leadership chose the only road to truth, justice, and accountability. Regardless of whether one agrees or disagrees with the UDD, its leaders deserve our admiration for their decision to adopt this approach. What they set out to do ought be kept in mind by Kanit Na Nakorn, chairman of the Abhisit-government-appointed committee to investigate the violence of April and May 2010 in his rushing towards the goal of forgiveness rather than, as Thitinan Pongsudhirak has written, "culpability and accountability".

Thitinan is right to worry "whether truth without justice can be sufficient for reconciliation".[23]

I began this article by saying that 10 May 2010 might one day prove to be a legal milestone for Thailand. Just as Uthai Phimjaichon appeared to lose in the short run, Natthawut, Jatuporn, and the other core leaders of the UDD perhaps embarked that day on a hopeless venture. 10 May (and the 10 April deaths to which it called attention) can only become a milestone if its significance can somehow resonate throughout society and into the future. The greatest miscalculation of UDD leaders was the belief that no society could bear the death of twenty largely unarmed citizens at the hands of its own military. Surely, the leaders must have thought, the government automatically lost its legitimacy in that night of death. But the attention the next morning in Bangkok was on the question of the "men in black". The deaths somehow did not register, just as the slow-moving massacre from 14 to 19 May was somehow not seen in increments of human lives. And, certainly, Suthep took the challenge of 10 May as some sort of impish joke, as he brushed off the murder charges made by distant Thaksinite families from the Thai hinterland.

"Double standards" in contexts such as these are really just impunity packaged in another way. By striking against double standards and impunity, Thai society has the rare opportunity to make justice and accountability a rallying cry. If what the UDD's leaders started continues, one can easily envision a ripple effect that leads to a new kind of reckoning with history in Thailand. Such a reckoning could provoke a re-assessment of the bloodshed of October 1976 and May 1992, the base illegality of the 2006 coup, and even events like Thaksin's "war on drugs" of early 2003 and the Tak Bai incident of October 2004.

The UDD's leaders have shown a willingness personally to pay the price of ending the legal double standard in Thai society that has over the years resulted in persistent impunity. That double standard has also resulted in a directionless legal morass of coups and blanket amnesties for perpetrators of violence. It is up to Thai society whether to recognize this sacrifice and respond to the demands of justice and history or to acquiesce to the urging for "reconciliation" and forgetfulness. Acquiescence will allow Thailand to fall once again into a restless and traumatized state of historical amnesia.

Notes

1. "Uthai Phimjaichon 10 pi Anan kap Bunkoet khon lae 7 pi" [Uthai Phimjaichon gets 10 years, Anan and Bunkoet each get 7 years], *Chao Thai*, 24 June 1972.
2. "Thai Army Authorised to Use Live Ammunition to Seal off Bangkok Protest Site", AFP, 13 May 2010.
3. "UDD Unveils 'red map'", *Bangkok Post*, 10 May 2010.
4. *Bangkok Post*, 30 May 2010. The impact of the UDD rallies may have been disproportionately bad for tourism said the president of the Tourism Council of Thailand. But this may be as much due to the duration of the government's emergency decree, its poor handling of events on 10 April, or its insistent allegations of "terrorism"; *Bangkok Post*, 21 May 2010.
5. International Crisis Group, "Thailand: Calming the Political Turmoil," 22 September 2008 <http://www.crisisgroup.org/~/media/Files/asia/south-east-asia/thailand/b82_thailand___calming_the_political_turmoil.ashx> (accessed 13 March 2011).
6. *Bangkok Post*, 20 and 24 April 2010.
7. "Kasit, PAD Leaders Charged", *Bangkok Post*, 5 July 2009. It seems that PAD leaders in the South who briefly closed down three airports in that region earlier in 2008 could have been similarly charged, although no arrests were apparently made in these incidents.
8. There seemed to be a little progress in the PAD cases in July as police made the lukewarm threat to issue arrest warrants against any of the PAD leaders who failed to report to police for investigation before 6 September (see *Bangkok Post*, 13 July 2010).
9. *Bangkok Post*, 27 April and 15 May 2010.
10. *Bangkok Post*, 18 April and 2 May 2010, respectively.
11. "UDD Unveils 'red map", *Bangkok Post*, 10 May 2010.
12. Abhisit himself in early May dismissed the idea of the need for any grant of amnesty to government forces, saying, "The army was confident that it had complied with the law in using force to crackdown on the red-shirts" (*Bangkok Post*, 6 May 2010). It was unnecessary, certainly, because Provision 17 of the Emergency Administration Act of 2005 already legally ensures evasion of accountability for any "competent official" acting under the act. Officials — including military personnel — "shall not be subject to civil, criminal or disciplinary liabilities arising from the performance of functions for the termination or prevention of an illegal act if such act was performed in good faith, non-discriminatory, and was not unreasonable in the circumstances or exceed the extent of necessity..." In the case of Tak Bai, where gross military negligence led to the death of more than eighty

detainees, an inquest cleared security officials of any responsibility. A *Bangkok Post* editorial at the time said that "such laws and martial declarations are out of tune with democracy and public expectation. The government or security forces cannot credibly absolve themselves to avoid responsibility" (*Bangkok Post*, 2 June 2009). The definition of "competent official" may even include Suthep, as such an official is defined in section 5 as "a person appointed by the prime minister to perform an act under this Emergency Decree". *The Emergency Decree on Public Administration in Emergency Situation, B.E. 2548 (2005)* (available at <http://www.asianlii.org/th/legis/consol_act/edopaies2005582/> (accessed 13 March 2011).

13. *Bangkok Post*, breaking news, 13 May 2010.
14. *Bangkok Post*, 15 June 2010.
15. Robert Amsterdam, telephone interview, 17 July 2010.
16. Constitution of the Kingdom of Thailand (interim version), B.E. 2549 (2006), unofficial translation.
17. Constitution of the Kingdom of Thailand, approved by referendum 19 August 2007, unofficial translation.
18. Interview with undisclosed source, 4 July 2010.
19. David Streckfuss, "Thailand as the Endless State of the Exception", paper presented at the 2010 meeting of Association of Asian Studies, Philadelphia, 15–28 March 2010.
20. See <http://manager-online.myfri3nd.com/blog/2010/03/03/entry-175≥ (accessed 13 March 2011), and *Bangkok Post*, 4 March 2010.
21. *The Nation*, 27 November 2008.
22. Read, for instance, Foreign Minister Kasit Piromya's interview with *Spiegel Online*, 15 July 2010, in which he rules out any similarity between PAD and UDD rallies on the level of causation (or intent) and compares Thaksin to Hitler (see <http://www.spiegel.de/international/world/0,1518,706552,00.html> (accessed 14 March 2011).
23. *Bangkok Post*, 12 and 16 June 2010.

23

NO WAY FORWARD BUT BACK? Re-emergent Thai Falangism, Democracy, and the New "Red Shirt" Social Movement

Jim Taylor

The conflict in Thailand following the coup of September 2006 concerns contested social, cultural and economic interests that are articulated through domestic politics from the summit downwards and extend to the base; it concerns essentially the enduring dominance of the centre and more recent structural changes in the social field at the periphery. In the case of the cultural, political and economic city-centre/summit, this has been seen in its dual function of protector and exploiter of the countryside/base. The last two decades started to bring change in the order of material relations, but not in the dominant social arrangements. The problem, which we saw tragically acted out on the streets of Bangkok in April and May 2010, concerns an attempt by the conservative "bureaucratic elite networks" (*ammat*, or *ammatayathippatai*) as part of the *ancien régime* ruthlessly to recapture control of emergent grass-roots democracy and reinsert their power, interests and influence. As an overview this paper can only touch on some of the issues that have led to the current crisis over democracy in Thailand and the new Red Shirt social movement (the UDD, or National United Front for Democracy against Dictatorship). I would argue that there is no middle ground remaining as lines are drawn and entrenched and bitter conflict persists, and as resistance to an emergent new state fascism becomes focused as much in the margins as the centre/summit.

Field research with extensive interviews was undertaken in Thailand following the crackdown 19 May 2010 to better understand the Red Shirt social movement and its argument for seeking social justice, the end of double standards in Thailand, and the return of cultural, political and economic inclusion at the margins which started during the premiership of Thaksin Shinawatra (2001–2006). This essay outlines the Red Shirt movement as it emerged in response to the jettisoning of the democratic process since the last coup, which ousted Prime Minister Thaksin in 2006, and the rewriting the following year of the 1997 People's Constitution. It also concerns the confrontational problematic embedded in the post-December 2008 authoritarian state, which I term new "Thai *Falangism*" — an authoritarian national leadership based on the aspirations of an organic, hierarchical state.

Thai does not have a word for "fascist"/"fascism". Instead, it uses (rarely) the foreign loan word *latthi-fasit*. Many Thais consider "fascism" as a particular historical moment in Thai history, which has now passed. I take Falangism from the name of a right-wing Spanish movement that imitated elements of German and Italian fascism and emerged in the early 1930s under the leadership of José Antonio Primo de Rivera. The movement was opposed to the Republican regime and supported Francisco Franco's Nationalist coup of 1936, but only as a minor element. It reappeared later in European history in the post-war years, but only momentarily.

The characteristics of Falangism with close affinity to the current Thai experience are a less ideological (softer, but no less insidious) form of *new fascism*, including an endogenous organic corporatism, ethnic-(Thai)-based ultra-nationalism, conservative anti-democratic trade unionism, conservative modalities of state Buddhism (through elements in the administrative royalist line of the Thammayut-nikai), a dislike for separatism of any kind; anti-communism, anti-anarchism and anti-(new) capitalism where it is seen as working outside elite networks;

anti-democratic sentiments, paternalistic pastoral values (communal ethnic-Thaiism), dislike of welfare-based neo-liberal economic (efficient) management (as in the case of Thaksin); and the union of non-competitive, traditional conservative units seeking to maintain their monopolies and ensuing privilege through a *nationalist* syndicated consensus. Finally, this also includes modalities of para-militarism including the ideological arm of the summit-state, the Yellow Shirts/PAD (rather misnamed "People's Alliance for Democracy") — although since 2010 self-named "multi-coloured shirts". The territorial issue on the border with Cambodia involves Yellow hardliners or the anti-democratic PAD remnants now calling themselves *khon Thai huachai rak chat* (the Thai whose heart that loves the nation). This also includes the dissenting Santi Asok Buddhist sect and shows the extent to which certain fascist tendencies can be articulated.

This complex social and political arrangement is controlled by an alliance of central bureaucratic elites, political representatives of the middle class, civil society, traditional network mafias, and ultra-conservative military factions with close ties to the royalist establishment. Thai elites are opportunistic; every time a new structure of governance is in place they try to control it. The 19 September 2006 coup was the last chance for bureaucratic elites to regain control over the nation-state. It was provoked not least by the fear that an election and continued runaway democracy, engendered at the grass roots, would undermine traditional interests.

Although order might seem to prevail after May 2010, as the despotic state tightened its grip, this order was illusory. Great disorder may well lie around the corner for Thailand. The weapons of war used against Red Shirt demonstrators and the Thai elites' hunting down of Red Shirt leaders and followers in the wake of the events of 19 May 2010 led many Red Shirts involved in that event to lie low. Nonetheless, more bloodshed is inevitable for Thailand where "reform" (*patirup*) of existing structures is not possible.

There was during the second half of 2010 a palpable sense of fear, anger and frustration among Red Shirt pro-democracy groups, following the military crackdown and subsequent purge against political dissidents everywhere, in towns, cities and villages. Many informants, those in prison such as core leaders interviewed[1], or those on the outside and on the run, could not hide their emotions and on a number of occasions cried when discussing the situation and their experience at the protest sites during the crackdown. These folk lay blame at the summit or the ritual centre, and at what they considered to be the "illegitimately installed regime" of Prime Minister Abhisit Vejjajiva's Democrat Party. Red Shirts had begun to meet where they could during a time of emergency law — in temples for commemoration of those killed by the state, at homes, restaurants or at country fairs. Military factions that are not aligned with Privy Council President General Prem Tinsulanon's so-called *thewan* (from the Hindu-Buddhist "Deva" or "higher celestial beings") lineage had begun to stir behind the scenes; alternative Red media sought ways of make their voices heard in the face of continued harassment, intimidation and closure; and radical monks at a number of Bangkok temples remained agitated, conducted seminars and produced for discreet distribution audio visual records of the crackdown from materials censored by the state. It seemed to be only a matter of time: The margins had been shaking at the roots for the past five years and preparing for action.

ACTIVIST MONKS, PROTEST, AND THE STATE

It was arguably the presence of some fifty monks that prevented an even greater massacre at Ratchaprasong intersection in Bangkok on 18–19 May 2010. In total during the protest around 400–500 monks had come to participate and offer support, from the countryside, from provincial towns and from within Bangkok.

Activist monks come from both the Thammayut and Mahanikai ordination branches of Thai Buddhism and were dismayed at the ease with which the Yellow Shirts' seized Government House in 2008, destroying important state records and security files, and occupying Bangkok's airports. A number of monks also said that they were worried that their earlier association with the Yellow Shirt movement would legitimize the heterodox right-wing Santi Asok monks who were participating in the anti-democratic protests. They noted also injustice and double standards: Yellow Shirts, for example, did considerable damage to state property without facing punishment, while Red Shirts were treated quite differently during their own demonstrations. As explained to me, the monks felt that these unarmed protestors, unlike the hot-headed and abusive Yellow Shirts, needed their protection.

Monks expressed their bitter disappointment at the handling of the protest and specifically the treatment of monks. At least five monks were arrested after the crackdown on 19 May. Three of these — monks with more than ten years' seniority — were forcibly disrobed. Two other monks were pressured to recite the Pali recitation for disrobing, but they refused. Pictures showed them with their hands bound tightly with plastic wire and abused verbally by soldiers. One monk who was forced to disrobe at a military camp later re-ordained, though of course losing his monastic seniority. These monks were forced to do this simply because they were offering their support through pastoral care to Red Shirt protestors. Informant "Maha X", a highly qualified Bangkok teaching monk, said that after he returned from the demonstration site, he received abusive phone calls from elite patrons of his royal monastery, located in the centre of Bangkok.

At the protest sites in 2010 there were three categories of monks: (a) real monks with proper identity papers and deportment in accordance with monastic rules; (b) real monks who were at times over-zealous and passionate (wearing headbands and carrying red flags); and (c) disguised monks who were special police agents and military intelligence officers infiltrating the protest site trying to discredit the Reds. When the fake monks were discovered by protestors, they were handed over to the police. But no further action seems to have been taken. Indeed, these individuals are reported to have returned to their previous activities. At least eleven monks were black-listed by the regime and placed under constant surveillance for their charismatic ability to mobilize the masses. There may have been a concern by the regime with parallels in neighbouring Burma's militant Buddhism, despite dissimilar social and historical conditions. These activists included highly qualified teaching monks from a number of Bangkok monasteries, including Wat Samphanthawong, Wat Saket, Wat Sam Phraya, Wat Mahathat, Wat Ratcha, Wat Chanasongkhram and the Thammayut Wat Bowonniwet.

"Maha X", who had in fact been watched by Internal Security Operations Command since 2007, faced illicit phone-tapping. He had to change his mobile "SIM" card regularly. In terms of their involvement in social and political issues, monastic informants said they saw events in Thailand as akin to the Dhammic "politics of life" — something into which we are all born and by which we are all affected — and therefore indeed a real concern to the monks. The killing of unarmed protestors in April and May 2010 was considered to be a breach of the boundaries of acceptable Buddhist ethics and morality in a predominantly Buddhist country. The regime had reason to be concerned, as it was clear that these monks had enormous influence in their constituencies, and many were clearly not afraid to speak out.

POLARIZATION OF THAI SOCIETY

The oppositional viewpoints of today's Thailand are sociologically rooted in early bureaucratic notions of ruling elites/aristocracy. These notions inform a perspective that traditionally sees the nation-state as an organic social hierarchy: a functional division between the nobility or lords (*nai*) and the commoners (*phrai*). The latter are constituted as subalterns, represented today by both the urban proletariat and small farmers. The elites are masters of cultural, and not necessarily financial, capital. Both of these forms of capital are connected to emergent middle-class interests and to the start in the 1980s of impressive economic growth concentrated in the metropolis and especially benefiting conservative urban Sino-Thai (ex-compradore Chinese) families. This was also a period of uneven development. The elites are a more complex social arrangement, one that goes back to the reforms to the feudal (*sakdina*) system during the modernizing Fifth Reign reforms of the period after 1890. This latter group is the nexus of the so called *ammat* system.

Elite and urban middle-class attitudes towards the Thai peasantry are entrenched in "an arrogance of modernity" that takes the country's poor majority as ignorant, uninformed (or misinformed), backward and uneducated. This arrogance partially explains why rural folk are not to be taken seriously in their social, political and economic aspirations and in their demand for the equitable redistribution of the fruits of late modernity. It also explains how small farmers are rendered voiceless, unworthy to cast a vote, and fit at best to be absorbed eventually into the modern (post-) industrial economy. In terms of continuing symbolic dominance, a quandary is inherent in social production and reproduction of existing stratified social structures in Thailand. In other words, a class system that is inimical to the very interests of the majority, who unconsciously carry on in their subordinate class position, is perpetuated. In Thailand the trans-historical functions are important in the ritual and symbolic centre as a dispersed arrangement of pervasive elite patronages or networks, linked to the symbolic capital of the royal institution. The system of a "network monarchy" is of course crucial to perpetuating the interests of the elites, as indeed it is in every subsidiary function of elite (civil and military) interests in Thailand.

THE IRASCIBLE POLITICS OF COLOUR

The current acute polarization in Thai society was symbolized earlier by colours: yellow and red. Yellow is King Bhumibol Adulyadej's personal colour. The claims by the ultra-nationalist minority group PAD to defend the monarchy were weak after the alliance of ruling Democrat Party-*ammat*-Army came to power. PAD see rule as coming from the ruling elites, as it has done for over a hundred years, and have no sympathy for the idea of effective grass-roots participation. If the masses are allowed to vote for the government that they want, it would not be in the interests of the self-seeking aspirations of the elite minority. The elites do not want to share the political, social and economic decision-making space with the Thai majority.

Interestingly, the epithet "terrorist" was cunningly used by the regime on the unarmed Red Shirt protest movement, though admitting later it was only referring to "elements" (unspecified) within the movement. It was a reason for the regime to seek support for its Falangist parastatal programme of annihilating all opposition and linking it back to single "terrorist" mastermind — Thaksin. The post-9/11 "terrorist" label was also a means of ensuring international support for the massacres of unarmed Thai citizens as some Western governments in mimicry of the regime, even praised the military for its "restraint" against the protestors. A foreign academic, disregarding the killing of protestors and use of snipers,[2] even went so far as to say that the Red Shirt casualties could have been higher had it not been for Thailand's "well trained" soldiers![3]

The so-called "third hand" element among Red Shirts in the 2010 demonstrations came in fact from factions contesting for power within the Army and opposed to dominant elements close to General Prem. As one Red Shirt leader told me, Prem was behind everything; his network power has been established over many years and extends across all sectors. It suited the state to have a so-called "third hand" because, the more chaos, the better for propaganda purposes. The regime freely used *agents provocateurs* to ensure this outcome and show to the world that the Red Shirts consisted of a violent hard-core element. In reality protestors had no access to military weapons but rather only to catapults, fireworks, Molotov cocktails and bamboo staves. Countless video clips and independent international media and informant accounts confirm this. After the crackdown the state showed reporters a cache of sophisticated weapons neatly laid out on a table, until it was discovered by a Thai reporter that these weapons were in fact unused and brought in for the spectacle.

The Yellow Shirts have claimed to be concerned above all with the defence of the monarchy. But relations between unelected Prime Minister Abhisit and the PAD leadership started to break down in mid-2009, after the PAD formed its own New Politics Party. Political life in Thailand is characterized by short-term and long-term allegiances: the PAD served its purpose in ousting elected governments in 2006–07, and its leaders were to be duly rewarded. Many felt that they were not and turned against the Abhisit regime. It may be recalled that before gaining power Abhisit showed unambiguous support for the Yellow Shirt protestors and their core leaders, even visiting them to offer support after they occupied Government House in 2008. Although promises of reconciliation were made after the May 2010 crackdown, which left some 90 dead, more than 1,900 injured and many missing, it was clear that Abhisit had no intention of reconciling with the Reds in a manner that would entail his relinquishing or sharing power.

For a time in 2009, the Yellow Shirts actually became blue shirts, wearing the Thai queen's personal colour. Probably acting on ill-informed advice, Queen Sirikit made a ritual display of support for the Yellow Shirts by attending at least one funeral of a member of that movement, but not attending the funerals of Red Shirt citizens killed by reactionary parastatal forces. This was unsettling for the rural masses that were (or are, though less so now) by and large dedicated monarchists. Bitter resentment of the Thai monarchy for inaction (in the case of the sick King Bhumibol) and inappropriate action (in the case of Queen Sirikit) has started to be felt widely in Thailand for the first time. Reverberations have been felt as never before throughout the countryside, as some folk even speak openly of their new-felt disdain for the institution of monarchy.

This development has been coupled with a noticeably increased use of *lèse majesté* as a political weapon to impose fear among opposition and to incarcerate individuals at the whim of the Thai Falange.

It may be recalled that the Yellow Shirts used references to the monarchy frequently in speeches; media leader of the Falange Sonthi Limthongkun wore a blue scarf allegedly given to him by the queen and members used shields with a picture of King Bhumibol on the front; they blocked vehicular access during the funeral of the king's sister; and Sonthi even went so far as to rub used tampons on the base of the statue of Rama V to "get rid of a spell". The ruling elites and PAD followers claimed to be acting for King Bhumibol. But it is evident that they were acting for themselves.

THE RED SHIRT SOCIAL MOVEMENT

The Red Shirts began as the Democratic Alliance against Dictatorship (DAAD) with the objectives of supporting Thaksin and opposing the illegal 2006 coup and the appointment of General Surayut Chulanon as prime minister under the Council for National Security (CNS). Then, after the December 2007 election victory of of the pro-Thaksin People's Power Party and a series of Yellow Shirt demonstrations, the movement became the UDD or National United Front for Democracy against Dictatorship (known as "Red for the Land"). Its motto is "Truth Today", shown in both Thai and English on scarves and displayed on posters, intended to show that certain institutionalized truths have been distorted in the past half-decade to serve class interests. The UDD also published a twice-weekly "Truth Today" newspaper, banned after May 2010. It used a symbolic plastic foot clapper, mocking the Yellow Shirts who earlier rattled plastic hand-clappers loudly at meetings to show approval of speakers. The nominal policies of the UDD (translated) are:

1. To achieve democracy with the king as the head of the state (a concession to the status quo) and with sovereignty constitutionally belonging to the *people of Thailand*.
2. To unify Thai people with the grass roots/masses as the main social and cultural force together with all people who seek democracy and justice resisting the domination by "aristocratic" forces (the *ancien régime*) that obstructs equitable national development.

3. To promote non-violence as *the only acceptable* means to achieve policy objectives.
4. To unite to overcome economic inequalities and to reduce poverty though a political action strategy that privileges the needs and legitimate aspirations of the majority of the Thai people.
5. To reinstate the "Rule of Law" and ensure transparent, equitable and accountable judicial process and the end of "double standards" under the control of aristocratic interests and elite networks.
6. To revoke the anti-democratic 2007 Constitution of Thailand, written hastily post-coup to favour certain military and elite interests, and to reinstate the 1997 "People's Constitution" of Thailand.

Red is a universal colour of resistance: heat, energy, blood, passion, sacrifice. It is a primary colour and one to be noticed. It is the colour of revolution. The ritual Brahmanic act of pouring donated blood on the front steps of parliament on 16 March 2010 expressed well these sentiments — loss, remorse and sacrifice. But, importantly, the colour red was first worn on 5 August 2007 to express disapproval of the military's draft constitution. It symbolized a "red light", to stop and not accept the conditions of the referendum on that charter called by ruling Falangists.

The Red Shirts come from a diverse cross-section of society. They have been brought together by a common sense of injustice and double standards. They are mostly constituted by culturally specific subaltern groups, especially landed ethnic-Lao peasantry who constitute around 70 per cent of the total population of Thailand and of whom most are in fact Red Shirt supporters. The North may show a more diverse pattern of political allegiance than the Northeast, because of the settlement and direct influence through migration of Bangkok Thai over the last hundred years. A number of scholars have noted that, in Theravada Buddhist societies, the most deprived folk often accept their kammic lot and only take to the barricades in exceptional circumstances.[4] The Red Shirts have tested the limits of this conservative thesis. Their taking to the protest sites over two months in 2010 indicated that people were no longer prepared to accept piecemeal efforts to address long-standing grievances. The time had come to demand radical structural changes that went directly to the heart, even the summit, of the modern Thai nation-state: to its ritual center, to the homes of the elite and places of hyper-consumption and to the commercial and business centre of the country.

The Red Shirts include many people who directly experienced the benefits of reforms undertaken during the premiership of Thaksin Shinawatra, or who were, as Phuea Thai spokesperson Phromphong Noppharit has said, "addicted" in a positive way to his policies. Red Shirts interviewed were from diverse backgrounds, including not only richer farmers but also urban and Bangkok business people. Although mega-rich, Thaksin has become a symbol of real possibility for the masses, pointing the way towards a shared set of values, practices and aspirations. These values have no place in the elite-dominated social and political system that resurfaced after the September 2006 coup. Thai subalterns had no voice after that coup; they were, once again, seen as having little value other than in a particular dependent mode of production in the context of late modernity. The call for Thaksin by the masses is a call for justice, equity, social and economic inclusion and political participation. The shouts at rallies of "Thaksin!", "Thaksin, come back!" were more than anything else calls for the return of these now lost values, a return to the political space engendered in the 1997 People's Constitution. Ironically, academics and intellectuals responsible for drafting the 1997 constitution were among those who helped bring it down in 2007. Thaksin made them realize that it was in fact too successful a template for inclusive democracy and thus worked against the economic, cultural and political interests of the ruling elites.

Although Thaksin was a focal point of the protests of 2010, many protestors claim to have moved beyond him. All would nevertheless agree on the need for popular democracy, good governance and public accountability. The elite's propaganda machinery worked hard in trying to discredit Thaksin, in the hope that the masses would turn back to them. This clearly did not happen. It is fair to say that the majority Thais do not see the oligarchy as having the ability to bring about participative and representative government for all people. Thus, the Red Shirts, although divided into a number of groups, uniformly called for a firm commitment to holding democratic elections.

In view of their composition, it is not surprising that some dissension appeared among the Red Shirts on matters of strategy and ideology. In July 2009 the UDD mass movement split when ex-Communist Party of Thailand member Surachai "Sae Dan" Danwatthananuson called for revolutionary action, rather than the prolonged and negotiated reform strategy favoured by the UDD leadership. Behind the scenes of the mass Red movement was the outspoken and charismatic Major General Khattiya Sawatdiphon, known as "Se Daeng" or the "Red Commander", providing support for the street protestors. Se Daeng had a massive and dedicated following in his own right. He was shot in the head by a sniper assumed to be sent by the Abhisit regime or perhaps its backers to silence him once and for all, as he was giving an interview to international media on 16 May 2010. Se Daeng was extremely well informed, maintaining considerable support among elements both inside and outside of the Army. But he had his power curtailed for some time within the Army because of an outspoken manner that was not to the liking of military elites close to the palace.

The slogan worn on red headbands in earlier stages of the 2010 conflict saying, "we were not hired to come here", showed Red Shirts' earnest passion for the cause and responded to accusations by the state and media that the luckless Thaksin had paid the tens of thousands of mostly rural folk to attend the demonstrations. Another slogan was "Whatever you do is correct; whatever I do is incorrect", a response to clear double standards favouring the Yellow Shirts. (Slogans became more provocative in 2011, indicating awareness among the masses as to who was actually backing the despotic regime). Red Shirt speakers inspired the listeners at Ratchaprasong to stand firm in their concerns and commitment to collective social action in a "dare to win, dare to lose" approach that reflected a desperate, last-stand mentality.

RED SHIRT ORGANIZATIONAL STRUCTURE

The Red Shirts maintain a dispersed horizontal organizational structure[5] so that, if one leader is killed at a protest site, the movement can continue. This structure encourages the masses to seek their own action in relation to the situation at hand. In other words, they should not be dependent on the leaders, as the masses at this time would understand what needed to be done when the time came. It was clear from 10 April 2010, after the first killings undertaken by the state, that the leaders could not order the masses or constrain their passion, as the protest took shape as a real movement of the people. Speakers and core leaders simply provided inspiration and information and strategic recommendations. The high level of awareness concerning issues and the individualistic nature of the masses was noticeable and ludicrously underplayed by a state that accused the masses of being manipulated and misled by a core element, and in particular by one involuntary expatriate (or, as the media calls him, "fugitive" — but from whose justice?), Thaksin Shinawatra. Henceforth the masses were known to become *"ta sawang"* or "awakened", an inclusive process that was first initiated under Thaksin's empowering grass-roots policies and programmes. They were now starting to be fully aware of institutional realities from the summit downwards and the structural limitations and related conditions of their own fate.

It is important to keep in mind that the mass Red Shirt organizational structure is the inverse of most centre-dominated systems. The rural masses through local-level leaders determine to a large extent the direction of the movement in consultation with provincial and regional leaders. The centre then provides the platform for the articulation of the movement's needs. This was emphasized to me many times in discussion with various second- and third-level leaders outside prison. The post-May 2010 movement had twenty-three committee members, and five sub-committees in the following regions: northern region (three persons), northeastern region (two persons), eastern region (three persons), central region (three persons), including Bangkok (four persons), and southern region (two persons).

All elements in the movement were allowed to act separately, autonomously, but peacefully. Collective action required consultation at all levels of the social movement. Importantly, the movement focused on engendering grass-roots empowerment for political participation and democracy. Until the state of emergency was declared, there was a mobile unit used for holding one- or two-day community-level field workshops on "democracy".

Because of the presence of *agents provocateurs* among the Red Shirts, it was quite dangerous to pass on messages or relay information for strategic purposes through communication systems or at public venues. During the 2010 protests, no one could know who and where state informants were among the masses, or when electronic messages would be tapped. The use of discreet systems of signalling one another in SMS or Twitter texts and displayed on web-boards were deployed early on, though many had been hacked by the state's computer technicians working around the clock.

THE CONCERNS OF THE ELITES, DELEGITIMIZING THE MOVEMENT

The state's use of delegitimizing epithets against the Red Shirt movement, such as "terrorists" corresponded to the hysteria generated thirty years ago by the label "communists". Red has an unfortunate colour association in this regard. As the UDD is a broad-based movement members may not necessarily share the same ideology, even though they were drawn together by marginality, increasingly critical worldviews, and an overarching need to restore justice, democracy and social equity. There is no unambiguous consciousness of class so much as a shared sense of suffering, but class must surely arise from the collective struggle framed by historical social hierarchies. As one poster displayed at the protest site stated: this is new "class war" (*songkhram chonchan*), under a picture of Democracy Monument with commoners as farmers fighting with lords. The Red Shirt protests in Bangkok that started on 12 March 2010 gave the masses a theoretical consciousness of being creators of new kinds of Siamese historical and institutional values. But can these values be reinserted into the structures of modern Thai society? The last five years would indicate that this is unlikely to happen without considerable conflict. Something has to give way.

Many middle-class Bangkokians are notoriously aloof when it comes to rural folk, to whom they refer to with the disparaging adjective "low class", "*ban nok*" (country-bumpkin), implying rustic, uncultivated, uneducated and uncouth. At one anti-Red Shirt demonstration in the city a placard read: "Rural Folks Get Out!"

In their struggle, Red Shirts articulate a counter-hegemonic discourse around the notion of an inclusive democracy. However, reactionary forces are more concerned with the maintenance of established cultural capital and in preventing the likelihood of losing their network power/privileges. When the present king dies there will be changes in the redistribution of power at the symbolic and ritual centre of the nation-state. But this is, at best, only conjecture.

Not conjectural is the fact that the post-coup constitution of 2007 was written to serve the purpose of the dictators, as in granting amnesty to the junta for executing the coup (Article 37). No previous permanent Thai constitution contained clauses giving amnesty for rebellion. The military junta was concerned about being prosecuted when an elected government came to power, if that day ever came. This is why it established a political compact with the Democrat Party and the bureaucratic elites. In the meantime, all the elites could do after May 2010 was further denigrate Thaksin at every opportunity, increase the hunt for Red Shirts around the country and even outside the country, close down and block as many websites and alternative media sources as possible. The media in Thailand have been, in fact, the state elites' main instrument in maintaining their hegemony.

MEDIA-DRIVEN ISSUES AND THE FAILURE OF CIVIL SOCIETY

A number of activists, including Somyot Prueksakasemsuk and Chulalongkorn University historian Dr Suthachai Yimprasert, held in detention from 24 May to 13 June and 31 May 2010 respectively, noted that the police used accusations made on reactionary Sonthi Limthongkun's propagandist ASTV as "evidence" against them. This is not the first time: the use of the elite's media against opposition to the state has been evident since at least 2005. Media worked in partnership with military interests in the run-up to the coup of 2006.

Thai society is now profoundly divided as a consequence of the production of mass propaganda in the state-compliant print and electronic media. No one, except those who had directly experienced the benefits of grass-roots democracy and opportunity opened up earlier under Thaksin's government or who could separate out truths from untruths, was immune to the forces and influence of this propaganda. As the late Se Daeng noted, "it was the media, ASTV, *Manager*, *The Nation*, *The Bangkok Post*, *Naew Na*, *Thai Post* [*sic*], *Khom Chat Luek*, that were all instigating the problem."[6] Se Daeng further noted, attacking the accusation that Red Shirts were paid to demonstrate, that "the Reds never actually received money from Thaksin, but the media started to make a [fictitious] link and in fact 'massaged' the situation".

In Thailand, the monopolistic control over the media, often supplemented by official censorship, makes it clear that the media serve the ends of the dominant elite.[7] In relation to Thaksin, a story is spun in

Manager daily newspaper by Sonthi, another media interests in a political compact to discredit Thaksin follow on in similar vein, and the matter quickly becomes familiar news. Accuracy or whether there is any real evidence matters little. Value lies in propaganda; there is no room for dissenting views, as they would conflict with already established truisms. This in turn opens up further opportunities for still more inflated claims, as these can be made without fear of serious repercussions. Lies in the service of the state have become a well organized affair; telling such lies has now become a habit.

The media as an integral element of civil society has failed Thailand. Pick up any copy of the English-language dailies and most of the Thai broadsheets to see the one-sidedness of their reporting. Dutch Journalist Michel Maas,[8] shot and wounded by the Army on 19 May, noted that "Thai media were almost all under the control of the government, including 'independent' newspapers *The Nation* and *The Bangkok Post*". He noted further that reporting especially "by *The Nation* was nothing better than 'anti-Reds-propaganda'", which "made the task of international reporters much more important — and difficult".

The conflicts of recent years were depicted in consistently distorted representations directed into the homes of influential members of the middle class and business elites. The media had a leading role in events leading up to the coup of 2006, softening the public for the inevitability that was to come, and then in covering the results of the December 2007 elections. As a complicit instrument of the *ammat*, the media in Thailand was rewarded for its anti-Thaksin coverage since at least early 2004 and in the post-coup redistribution of benefits. For example, along with other coup friends, representatives of the media were placed on so-called independent state bodies like the Election Commission of Thailand and the National Anti-Corruption Commission of Thailand. They were included among members of the now defunct Assets Scrutiny Committee, the State Audit Commission, and the National Human Rights Commission (NHRC). This was all in the cause of justifying the coup, protecting the interests of the coup-makers (as the coup was illegal under the terms of the 1997 People's Constitution), and making Thaksin and those who supported him into the state's most notorious villains.

The mass media has long been seen as an instrument of cultural domination. Its potential for use as a counter-hegemonic tool by subordinate groups has also been recognized. This is why the state attempted to regulate and control all media opposition after the 2006 coup and, failing this, to crush alternative voices, as it did with local community radio, People's Television, and then the People's Channel. The alternative Red Shirt media gathered in Bangkok at a discreet location on 3 July 2010 to plan a new counter-hegemonic strategy and to raise funds; their assets had been frozen and their equipment seized by the state.

The post-coup oligarchy set aside a massive amount of funds for spreading misinformation, and exerting discipline and control over anti-state elements. It imposed the draconian Internal Security Act when protests began in March 2010 and the Emergency Decree on 7 April 2010. Both conferred enormous powers on the military; the latter was extended to cover nearly half of Thailand. Neither could protestors expect any support from human rights groups aligned with the elites. The NHRC has been clearly partial, which is not surprising as the executive were handpicked by the post-coup ruling alliance. Dr Tajing Siriphanit, a commissioner of the NHRC, stated on NBT television on 4 April 2010 that the military-backed government "would be justified in using force" against the peaceful pro-democracy Red Shirt protestors "because they were disrupting shopping" in the centre of Bangkok. Even more depressingly, Chulalongkorn University's Professor Amara Phongsaphit, selected by the 2006–07 military junta as NHRC chairperson, encouraged people in Bangkok to sue the Red Shirts for disruption and violation of their (shopping?) rights. There was no mention of the rights of the unarmed Reds to demonstrate against a dictatorial regime or of the violence done to so many by the well armed thugs among Yellow Shirts supported by the military since 2006.[9] This epitomized the lopsided debate engineered by the regime and its supporters.

Thai civil society — including the media, NGOs, and public-sector unions — has failed to remain non-aligned and independent or to take a responsible and objective stance towards the country's subalterns. Although space limits discussion, the problem stems from the division among ex- and continuing members of the Communist Party of Thailand since amnesty was declared in 1980. Many have aligned with the Falange because of continuing patronage through state or civil society. Others have sided with the pro-democracy Red Shirt movement. In some sense the problem is also a function of the unfettered forces of globalization and neo-liberalism evident in the 1990s, especially during the time of

Thaksin's government. This period saw an oppositional compact among elitist/royalist interests articulated in the self-sufficiency/self-reliance model inspired by King Bhumibol. This modern elite vernacularism joined forces with new bourgeois elements to form a nationalist coalition based on conservative politico-religious patronage, embodied in modern traditionalism and in persisting corporatist views of society.

This social contract included powerful conservative state trade unions (in, for example, the railway sector, the electricity/utilities sector, and other branches of public sector) and reactionary elements of the new civil society, including the media. It is all about protecting networks. Take NGOs for instance: these started to proliferate in the mid-1980s and included many former student activists who had only recently returned from the *maquis*. Many of the NGO leaders in Thailand are concerned more with a woolly ideology of combating forces of global capitalism and maintaining self-interest and ties to influential patrons in order to retain access to state benefits and continuing financial support. This was particularly evident after monies from international donors started to dwindle in the late 1990s. Few, if any, Thai NGOs have an interest in promoting the underlying democratic processes of grass-roots empowerment, which happened under Thaksin's auspices. Indeed, this would have clearly challenged the existing power arrangements and patterns of patronage from the center.

International civil society organizations reported the conflict in Thailand as one based on assumptions of equal distribution of power such that, as *Human Rights Watch* noted: "*both sides* need to step back, de-escalate the violence, and negotiate in good faith for a political solution".[10] Inequalities of power do not equate to equal rights to be granted to both parties at the negotiating table. In any case, it was far from ever being a level playing field. The millions of protestors travelling back and forth to the capital could not overcome the might of the well equipped Thai Army, unless the Army itself split into competing factions.

CYBER-POLICING AND THE MINISTRY OF MASS MISINFORMATION

Information produced by the state-Army-*ammat* alliance under the management of the Ministry of Information and Communication Technology engendered continuing cultural hegemony through flows of innuendo, rumour-mongering and groundless accusation. The regime's media machinery would not let the public forget about Thaksin, or let it not be known that he was, as they say, behind every anti-statist action.

More recently, and worrying from a Gramscian point of view, was state cyber-policing, censorship and blocking of dozens of even remotely counter-hegemonic social and political websites, and even Facebook pages. The state's cyber-security intelligence team kept an eye on oppositional voices. It is clear that the despotic alliance under Abhisit's unelected government was the most repressive regime ever in the country.

Perniciously, the state also established a massive apparatus to regulate the consumption of information through strategies of fear and intimidation; tracking, blocking and tapping mobile networks; raiding local radio stations and wrecking or confiscating broadcasting equipment and computers, and countering oppositional voices through the production and distribution of cyber-viruses, hacking, and random attacks on opposition network servers.

How could the abuse of human rights (and the right to information) in Thailand after 2006 have been overlooked by outsiders? Article 19 of the Universal Declaration of Human Rights, of which Thailand is a signatory, states: "Everyone has the right to freedom of opinion and expression; this right includes freedom to hold opinions without interference and to seek, receive and impart information and ideas through any media and regardless of frontiers"[11]. National security and stability were framed as an excuse simply for maintaining the status quo. But the state had to justify itself in the eyes of citizens by claiming, as it did after coup, to be acting in a moral, loyal (to the monarch) and just cause.

CIVIL SOCIETY AND DEMOCRACY IN THAILAND

The attitude of ruling elites and their servants in Thai civil society is that farmers and the urban poor are passive and subject to the immoral forces of money politics and therefore need guidance or "directed democracy" (*prachathipatai baep mi kanchinam*). They have no real understanding of "democracy", and it is necessary to maintain a moral force which parallels politics to keep the politicians honest. Liberal royalists such as the prominent Dr Prawet Wasi and former Prime Minister Anan

Panyarachun, considered by ruling elites to be morally above politics, were after 19 May 2010 once again to take a community leadership role and vet resource allocations downwards. This "directed democracy" was presented as a local alternative to representative neo-liberal democracy. However, it assumed arrogantly that voters were not active agents and that they did not know what was best for their own interests. Even in situations of widespread rural vote buying involving all parties, farmers will take what is offered but in the end still vote for the political representative that they want. This is true empowerment at the ballot box; an electoral mechanism supported by the 1997 People's Constitution, which ensures consensual politics. It is a democratic process desired by the majority of the Thai people. Much to the dismay of the elites, Thaksin enabled the grass roots to have a voice; to be able to make choices about the future through fiscal devolution strategies after some four decades of "community development" programmes that "talked the talk", but in the end did little actually to empower communities to represent themselves. They instead simply increased rural dependence on the centre and continuing royal beneficence, which regulated the flow of resources downwards. In this context it is little wonder on one hand that the elites were starting to worry that, if liberal democracy continued to develop, they would lose the benefits accrued through continuing patronage networks. On the other hand, the subalterns started to experience inclusive democracy and increased local autonomy talked about since the 1980s. There is, for the villagers, no going back.

IS THERE NO WAY FORWARD BUT BACK?

The world of Thailand was after May 2010 an illusion of a certain kind of reality crafted in the imagining of the *ammat* and their urban middle-class lackeys. New Marxists may argue that urban-centred bourgeois values represent normalizing social values opposed to rural values and that this situation may attract the oppressed and intellectual classes to the cause of a proletarian movement. Whether the Red Shirt social movement will materialize in this way or lead to class revolution is uncertain. At this point concerns among the pro-democracy movement are closer to the heart than to the head/intellect. In this line of thinking, as a sustained social movement, it would need to develop a cultural orientation and consciousness as a class-based movement in which to overthrow the alliance consisting of the royalist-supported Democrat Party, the military, and the *ammat* bureaucratic and economic elites.

Thaksin, though no socialist, believed in the power of the subaltern to transform the social order and worked to empower and support the masses through the process of efficient government while (problematically) frequently bypassing traditional elite networks. This involved the disbursement of education scholarships for the poor, financial devolution down to the village through investment and development funds, universal and accessible health care, a people's bank, the promotion of entrepreneurial initiatives, asset capitalization and small and medium enterprise loans and more. Many in the Red Shirt movement claim to have moved beyond his charismatic authority and embraced a broader consensus for achieving democracy in Thailand. However, Red Shirts are also divided on how to achieve this outcome, either through a "reform" (*patirup*) of existing institutions, or as more radical elements believe, in a democratic revolution (*patiwat*) in order completely to "uproot" (*thon rak thon khon*) the persisting problem of hegemony and power invested in the *ammat* regime.

How is it then that the death of so many people over two months in an era in which communications technology allowed the whole world to see what the Thai military and its parastatal mercenaries were doing could be rendered invisible, insignificant, even worthless? None among the demonstrators initially thought that they would be so ruthlessly killed by the state apparatus in a context in which the actions of the state could be seen by the world. It was the mobile phone "heroes" who brought the success of the May 1992 middle-class uprising in Bangkok.[12] During 14 October 1973 (seventy-seven officially killed) and 6 October 1976 (forty-five officially killed), students and intellectuals lost their lives for much the same thing: popular democracy and the overthrow of the authoritarian state. In the period of 10 April–20 May 2010 there were formally some ninety persons killed, though informal estimates taking into account those still missing place this figure in the hundreds; so why no outcry? The reason, I would suggest, is that most of these folk are small farmers, and their brown sun-baked bodies are rendered valueless in the elite/middle-class discourse on the interpretation of directed democracy[13]. This discourse echoes colonial attitudes that associated "natives" with nature, which was not highly regarded, and took them as objects to be acted upon through the domination of a specific techno-scientific knowledge-power.[14] The modern Siamese nobility imitated this approach, even while retaining the traditional hierarchical order of nobility and servants. In the past officials saw their authority as based on moral authority; these days, they regard themselves as modernizers, leaders and teachers of the masses. The universe was ordered around a simplistic binary opposition of high and low, progress and backwardness, knowledge and ignorance. Urban *ammat* see themselves as moving along a continuum ordered by the clustering of these opposites, with the new middle-class technocrats working in their interests.

The attribution of knowledge-power to nobility, and later to members of the middle classes, meant that the Thai masses were seen as lacking knowledge, viewed as superstitious, backward, and concerned only with local issues rather than the affairs of the modern nation-state. Derogatory comments referred to the Red Shirts as "buffaloes", relegated not just to the lowest level of the human order but to the animal world. Sonthi Limthongkun's ASTV-*Manager* daily newspaper's 29 March 2010 edition included a pair of cartoons. The first showed a typical traffic jam in Bangkok with a caption reading, "Monday–Friday for car traffic." The second depicted a herd of water buffaloes led by Thaksin, with the caption reading, "Saturday–Sunday for walking water buffaloes", where Red Shirts were being "herded" to the rally. The protest was simply discredited by the urban elites concerned with their own power and interests to reflect the fact that, as Nakan Laohawilai (editor of the online right-wing Thai-language *Post Today*) said: "many people have yet to attain maturity when it comes to a real democratic system", and the solution was for Thailand to have "higher quality people". The implication is clear.

The events in the metropolis during March–May 2010 showed that the subaltern can act out of a shared or collective set of values, a sense of loss of benefits and life concerns. They can act in ways that override any sense of personal risk and disregard selective incentives. They placed their own lives at risk, unconcerned at the time about the loss of income.[15] When one of the core UDD Red Shirt leaders was asked by a foreign reporter if the masses were paid to join in the collective action, he retorted: "Everyone (here) is facing death! How much money do you have to pay for the people to die?"

The Red Shirts' 24-hour coverage of activities on the stage mounted at the front of their rally during the two months of demonstrations on their satellite People's Television (PTV) showed the final moments when the Army was advancing in the afternoon of 19 May 2010. It was clear that people were prepared to die and had taken the decision to act according to their own feelings. But core leader and Phuea Thai member of parliament Jatuporn Phromphan in a tearful finale wanted to prevent any more killing of the Red Shirts: "I know you are all beyond the fear of death. Today is surrender day, and I cannot stand to see people being killed anymore. Now we [core leaders] will go to the police headquarters and surrender ... [shouts from the people: "no, no, no"] ... It is painful for me to see you falling one by one in front of me ... There will be more killed before the Army reaches the stage ... [tears falling from Jatuporn's eyes, protestors shouting "no, don't cry!"]) ... We know that you are bitter ... People are dying ... "[16]

My post-crackdown fieldwork in Thailand confirmed that indeed, much to the surprise of the rank and file Army, many Red Shirts were prepared to die and had put their last foot forward fearing the failure of living more than liberation through death. Accounts were told of people bleeding from gunshot wounds, blinded by tear gas, refusing to stay down and standing their ground during the military onslaught. This was not a sentimental claim to an emotional moment but a calculation made by the people about continuing suffering, injustice and oppression under the Abhisit regime. The only question remaining in retrospect is why the masses were not successful in removing the regime when it appeared that they were so close to achieving their goal in April 2010?

Even many persons involved in earlier pro-democracy revolutions, notably reactionary Major General Chamlong Srimuang, lay leader of Santi Asok, had seen their real interests as lying with elites and their civil society friends over the past twenty to thirty years. All were united against Thaksin for various reasons, mostly personal jealousies and the obstruction of access to personal benefits. Few had any sympathy for the Red Shirt movement. They were visibly irritated by the determination of millions of small farmers coming to and going from the demonstration sites in Bangkok and creating a "mess" in high-society shopping precincts and the glamorous arcades of the Thai bourgeoisie. These are the sites of the urban elite, a place of the *ammat*, and as such clearly dangerous for anyone contesting this space and its dominant ideology and privileged social order.

In the view of Gramsci, any class that wishes to dominate in these modern conditions has to move beyond its own narrow "economic-corporate" interests, to exert intellectual and moral leadership, and to form alliances and compromises with a variety of cultural forces. In Thailand, cultural capital importantly includes religion, which is not tied to bourgeois cultural values and thus cannot be assumed to be hegemonic or allied with class. Counter-hegemony as forms of alternative or activist religion has been important cultural capital for the masses. The elites need to establish a mask of social compact with which to rule. But first they must clear away any resistance. After 19 May 2010 they worked to emasculate the pro-democracy movement, capturing its material bases and its means of social and cultural reproduction. Hegemonic dominance relies ultimately on modalities of coercion, and in a "crisis of authority" when the pretense of social consent or compact slips away there remains the fist of force: the Thai Army, although factionalized, always in the wings ready to take control.

In Thailand after the crackdown on the mass protest movement of 2010, a new Thai Falange sought to organize a nation once again on corporatist principles, traditional values and systems. The regime drew the forces of nationalist cultural capital among interests such as business, public sector labour, the military, and the ever-important elite patronage ties into a collective national body, But, importantly (and some say ironically), this body was articulated in the need to maintain the institution of the Thai monarchy.

Thaksin, who had a direct channel to the king bypassing the real power located in the conservative aristocracy close to the monarch and military elites, challenged many of these institutional circuits of power. This led to his downfall. The Thai Falangists have, one assumes, as much distrust for autonomous new mega-rich capitalists such as Thaksin as for Marxists/Socialists and autonomous social movements rooted in ethnic difference. Essential questions that scholars of Thailand were asking more than twenty years ago, about whether Thailand would become a more developed liberal democracy or an authoritarian state dominated by elite and military interests, were answered for the world on 19 May 2010. That answer came in the form of the emergence of a distinctive new endogenous falangism offering no way forward but back.

Notes

1. On 22 February 2011, seven of the core leaders were released on bail, under strict conditions.
2. See Amsterdam & Peroff LLP, "Application to Investigate the Situation of the Kingdom of Thailand with Regard to the Commission of Crimes against Humanity," filed with the International Criminal Court, 31 January 2011. Many of this document's comments concerning various incidents match the author's own research findings.
3. See the comments of Desmond Ball, in New Mandala, "Thailand in crisis — Episode 2", 4 June 2010 <http://asiapacific.anu.edu.au/newmandala/2010/06/04/thailand-in-crisis-episode-2/> (accessed 13 March 2011).
4. See Barrington Moore, *Injustice: The Social Bases of Obedience and Revolt* (Boston: Beacon Press, 1993 reprint ed.), p. 202.
5. Known as "Rhizomatics" following Gilles Deleuze and Felix Guattari, *A Thousand Plateaus: Capitalism and Schizophrenia* (Minneapolis: University of Minnesota Press, 1987); the rhizome metaphor was first used by Carl Jung to indicate a subversive and imperceptible nature of human life, is always generating linear connections and new possibilities.
6. "'Red' Army Major General Khattiya Sawatdiphon", *ThaiPost* <www.thaipost.net>, 8 June 2010.
7. This point was made lucidly by Herman and Chomsky; see Edward S. Herman and Noam Chomsky, *Manufacturing Consent: The Political Economy of the Mass Media* (New York: Pantheon Books, 2002.
8. "Q&A: Dutch Journalist Michel Maas Talks to IPI about Being Shot in Thailand Clashes", International Press Institute, 8 July 2010 <www.freemedia.at/singleview/5032/> (accessed 13 March 2011).
9. "NHRC Chair Urges People to Sue Reds for Rights Violations", *The Nation*, 26 April 2010.
10. Human Rights Watch, "Thailand: Revoke 'Live Fire Zones' in Bangkok", 15 May 2010 <http://www.hrw.org/en/news/2010/05/15/thailand-revoke-live-fire-zones-bangkok> (accessed 14 March 2011).
11. The text is available at <www.un.org/en/documents/udhr/> (accessed 14 March 2011).
12. See Alan Klima, *The Funeral casino: Meditation, Massacre, and Exchange with the Dead in Thailand* (Princeton: Princeton University Press, 2002), p. 148.
13. For a useful discussion in Thai, Yukti Mukdawijit, "The Politics of Massacre" [Kanmueang khong kankattakam ruam mu], 27 May 2010

<http://downmerngnews.blogspot.com/2010/04/blog-post_1557.html> (accessed 14 March 2011).

14. See Ann Laura Stoler, "Rethinking Colonial Categories: European Communities and the Boundaries of Rule", *Comparative Studies in Society and History* 31, no. 1 (January 1989): 134–61.
15. See James C. Scott, *The Moral Economy of the Peasant: Rebellion and Subsistence in Southeast Asia* (New Haven: Yale University Press, 1976).
16. Interview on "60 Minutes", Channel Nine, Australia, 22 May 2010.

24

FLYING BLIND

Danny Unger

Many Thais sympathetic to the government of Prime Minister Abhisit Vejjajiva were angry about what they saw as distorted reporting of the conflict of April and May 2010 by the foreign press and, in particular, by international television networks. This disgruntlement often failed to register the idiosyncratic nature of reporting on the conflict by the Thai media itself, although Red Shirts criticized the Thai mainstream media's coverage as well. More generally, debates about how the mass media covered the crisis and what animated the Red Shirt movement were particularly prominent. Once there was a pause in Bangkok's political violence, mass media reform held a prominent place in the Abhisit government's reconciliation schemes. In this essay, I use an analysis of how these events were reported to speculate more broadly on Thai political reporting and how political information is handled in Thailand.

A central part of this story concerns the advent of new mass media outlets, new communications technologies, and the proliferation and polarization of voices that surely contribute to divergent perceptions and preferences among Thais today. Not all these issues are specific to

Thailand. Clearly, changing communications technologies are having an impact on politics in many settings, including among followers of the insurgent Tea Party movement in the United States. There are reports from around the world that the blogosphere is pressuring the conventional media to produce its news more rapidly and with stronger judgements, even invective. The particular features of Thailand's information regime, however, can be explained neither simply in terms of technological changes nor by sweeping reference to state regulation and sham democracy.

Quality political information often has qualities of a public good. It can be invaluable to citizens, yet costly to acquire, and low-quality information often fares as well or better in media markets, reducing incentives to invest in the provision of the good stuff. Where quality political information is scarce, resource-poor citizens, lacking the means to ferret it out on their own, are penalized especially severely. It is likely that the scarcity of quality political information in Thailand impedes Thais intent on participating meaningfully in their country's politics. And, because Thais have only modest deliberative capacities (on which more below), once political division grows pronounced, as it is now, it may be unusually difficult to manage.

Below I first very briefly characterize some of the more puzzling features of political reporting in Thailand and speculate on reasons for its low quality. The second section of this essay considers information as a source of power and the ways in which the government and the protestors tried to shape it during Thailand's political confrontation of March–May 2010. I conclude by describing the obstacles that hinder political deliberations in Thailand.

THAILAND'S INFORMATION REGIME

Political news as reported on television or newspapers in Thailand can often be distressingly vague, desultory, and opaque while leaving many issues unresolved. It is easy to come away from reading news articles with the unsettled sense that you have missed something. More generally, one scholar argues that "Thailand is still a society where the capacity of the political system to transmit and circulate information is limited … [and] the ability of the people to gather, perceive and digest knowledge is low."[1] Little quality information flows to Thai citizens. In turn, Thailand's weak political institutions, low-quality reporting, and uneven public opinion polling ensure that representatives are handicapped in doing their jobs.

Presumably in part because of the impunity enjoyed in Thai security circles, Thai political reporting leaves many celebrated mysteries unexplained; think of the 1989 theft and subsequent fencing of Saudi gems, or the attempted assassination of Sonthi Limthongkun in 2009. The street clashes in Bangkok and Pattaya in 2009 and in Bangkok in 2010 generated enigmas that are unlikely ever to be resolved. With the contours of these cases never clearly traced, they live on in the realm of rumour and innuendo. And they remain subject to manipulation.

While puzzles often are left in the murk, political reporting leaves critical questions unasked. Where was the in-depth reporting, for example, on decision-making procedures within the National United Front for Democracy against Dictatorship (UDD) in April and May of 2010; on how different groups were linked to one another; and on whether they were differentiated in terms of ideologies, strategies, or tactics? In other settings, it is not unusual for the battlefield to be confused, but when the smoke has cleared, one fairly complete version of events generally emerges and gains widespread adherence. In Thailand, however, neither complete nor consensus versions of some very significant events seem to emerge with much regularity. We get instead media reports that refer to "swirling rumours" or events "clouded in controversy".

ACCOUNTING FOR THAILAND'S INFORMATION REGIME

So how might we account for the ways in which Thais handle information and in which the Thai mass media reports politics? My answers become increasingly speculative, but I start on relatively safe ground, referring to the major inhibiting effects on political reporting of *lèse majesté* and defamation laws. These laws are written and enforced in ways that ramify their inhibiting effects. We can get a sense of this effect in the case of defamation law by citing a statement by former Army commander General Anuphong Paochinda, speaking after the April 2009 attempt to kill Sonthi Limthongkun: "Sonthi will be held responsible for what he says, as will the media that publishes articles reporting what he did not say."[2]

State ownership of Thailand's electronic mass media also of course shapes Thai political reporting. Overwhelmingly, television is Thais' principal source of political information. Only recently have cable and satellite offered competition to established broadcast stations. Education levels in Thailand are not high, most people rely on television news to keep themselves politically informed, and the quality of television news reporting is low. It is likely therefore that many Thais have little political knowledge.

I suspect, however, that much about the ways in which Thais manage information has little to do with state ownership of media outlets or regulation of media. Several possibilities suggest themselves. One is that Thais are exposed to large doses of political ritual — ritual that tends to compact political information and reduce its substantive detail even as it lends greater emotional impact. Maurice Bloch suggested that rituals tend to have little information content, are easily manipulated, and are common in societies characterized by sharp political differentiation.[3] Ritual may be particularly powerful in cognitive contexts relatively uncluttered by masses of information or competing interpretations. And habituation to ritual forms may foster a didactic style of rhetoric and a Manichean worldview. Once you take part in collecting hundreds of litres of blood and splashing it about, are you then less open to reasoned debate?

Also potentially significant for this discussion is the Thai propensity to attend to surface qualities, even at the expense of underlying ones. Knowledge and truth may be less powerful than the prestige associated with images. If in the West there exists an "intellectual ethic of truth", in Thailand the "prestige value of an image may be independent of its truth value".[4] It is also possible that Thais' taste for avoiding confrontations encourages them, in a defensive spirit, to eschew precision because it makes attack easier.

Another factor that surely shapes to a significant degree the ways in which Thais process political information is the realm of magic. Many Thais invest time and money in efforts to manipulate or elude forces associated with numbers, heavenly bodies, and spirits. Think of former Prime Minister Thaksin Shinwatra in early 2006, as the challenges to his government were gaining traction. Dissuaded by senior Thai Rak Thai Party figures from busing in large numbers of his supporters to confront PAD demonstrators, he instead set off with Newin Chidchob, then a prominent member of his party and the grandson of a Cambodian mahout, to ride the neck of an elephant and walk under its belly to ward off bad luck and to boost his power.

In late April 2010, a Red Shirt leader claimed the government had set an imminent deadline for removing the Red Shirts from Ratchaprasong. The deadline allegedly was based on an alignment of the stars comparable to that which was obtained when Ayutthaya fell some two and a half centuries earlier. Such reporting and the way of understanding politics that it represents is not limited to a few marginal cases. One prominent example involves the notion that the current titanic political struggle is merely the latest manifestation of an epic reverberating through time and linked to the rise of Thailand's Chakri Dynasty over two hundred years ago. The first of the Chakri kings assumed the throne after he and other generals assassinated King Taksin. One variant of the story has it that Thaksin-the-present is the reincarnation of one of King-Taksin-the-past's faithful retainers. Given finite resources in money and time, the significant investment in trying to influence — or predict — the actions of other-worldly actors suggests fewer resources available to examine closely the voting records of members of parliament, the political platforms of different political parties, or other more profane political concerns. And if political fates are in the hands of spirits, that leaves little scope for participation or accountability.

Information is potentially a valuable asset, but it is less likely to be so in information-rich (high-supply, low-cost) than information-poor contexts. In the latter, a "cryptocracy", in which hidden and protected information constitutes an important and valued resource to which the poor in particular have little access, may result.[5] As a result, once established, low-information environments may tend to be self-sustaining, as people and organizations become information misers.

INFORMATION AS POWER

Machiavelli believed that hoodwinking citizens was easy. Emmanuel Kant argued that we escape self-incurred immaturity when we have the will to use our own understanding without others' guidance.[6] Of course neither Machiavelli nor Kant confronted television, the Internet, or Facebook. New communications technologies may not foster critical thinking or deliberative engagements. However, they certainly are potential instruments of political power.

Under what conditions is information empowering? John Stuart Mill believed that, once workers were able to read and had access to political information and competing opinions, they quickly would clamour for the vote (as, essentially, Thailand's Red Shirts have done). The French Revolution had a chastening impact in Great Britain, helping to convince most of its vested citizens of the wisdom of a very cautious expansion of the franchise. But rather than try to limit access to information, many concluded that greater information access had the potential to domesticate the masses. During this period the popularity of the Bell and Lancaster methods for spreading literacy was linked to the belief that only education could "draw the fangs of the mob".[7]

Many of his critics believed that Thaksin deluded the great unwashed while in power, in part through skilful control over information. Certainly Thaksin made effective use of the state-controlled mass media. In exile, he has broadened his technological repertoire. And the experience of pitched street and media battles in 2009 helped focus Red Shirt and government attention on the next round of information war in 2010.

I ONCE WAS ... BLIND, BUT NOW I SEE

These battles in fact began earlier, with the Thaksin government's determined efforts to control electronic and print media. The struggle then intensified with the onset of serious challenges to Thaksin's rule. As opposition to Thaksin grew early in 2006, observers devoted increasing attention to the impact of Sonthi's ASTV. The *Bangkok Post* quoted a couple of Northeasterners saying, "We used to be Thai Rak Thai supporters. But after watching ASTV programmes, we have become suspicious about state policies, particularly privatization and the adverse impact of free trade agreements."[8] One scholar argued that Thai society was no longer divided by class so much as by access to information. The PAD made extensive use not only of ASTV, but also of community radio stations, newspapers, and the Internet. The UDD eventually would mimic and improve on the exploitation of these information sources. As a result, some Red Shirts told reporters in essence, "We once were blind to society's injustices, but now we see." Analysts argued that the poor and less educated were demanding a voice because they had become more urban and because better education, more media access, and better political organization had made them more aware of their interests. This view suggests that, at least for some Thais, shifting patterns of information access were proving empowering. Other observers wondered if they were not observing the effects of a concerted programme of disinformation.

Media campaigns were a big part of preparations for the 2010 round of Thailand's political conflict. Early in 2010, the Thai Journalists Association, in its annual media situation report, noted the rise of new media outlets such as ASTV, *Manager*'s website,[9] the PAD's newspaper, the UDD's People Station (PTV), and the magazines *Red News* and *Truth Today*. These new media outlets were established by political groups and served up propaganda while instigating rifts and hatred, opined the association.

In recognition of the new media's growing power, political antagonists made major investments in media weapons as they prepared for further conflict. As the Red Shirt demonstrations intensified during April and May of 2010, the combatants worked assiduously to construct and disseminate lies, including frequent and flagrant doctoring of audio and video tape. Demonstrators attempted to intimidate broadcasters, newspapers, and individual reporters. After the government invoked the Emergency Decree on 7 April, it used its enhanced powers to shut down opposition voices. One close aide to Prime Minister Abhisit drew on American military analogies to describe the state's campaign to block and scramble signals, and to use diplomatic communications to contact Internet service providers and to request that they close down sites.

Thailand now has more media outlets and perhaps a rising sense of equal rights to participate in public space than in the past. Establishment information gatekeepers are weaker. Public arenas are proliferating and growing specialized. Barriers to participation are tumbling, and different groups are increasingly liberated from the need to communicate with others of different political views. Presumably, one result of this changed context is a premium on radical or outlandish voices that seek to command attention amid the cacophony and in the absence of any need to reach shared understandings with others. The picture looks more democratic, but it may not lend itself to deliberations.

QUALITY OF DELIBERATIONS

Deliberation involves public discussions that afford all stakeholders opportunities to participate. Participants should be reasonably well, or at least reasonably equally, informed. Discussions should be rational and civil. If higher-quality deliberations (those that are more inclusive and consequential) are associated with higher-quality democracies, this indicator does not reflect well on Thailand's democracy.

Most Thais have inadequate access to information, status still tends to trump arguments, and the state regulates information flows aggressively. Many political groups are intolerant and prone to efforts to intimidate their opponents. Effigy burning is a popular form of political communication. Some political leaders lie with alacrity. It is not always clear whether the liars acknowledge the lies to themselves, how widely these lies are recognized, and under what circumstances lies count against the liars. And the roles accorded to unaccountable spirits also raise questions about the place of deliberations among politically divided Thais.

Characterizing deliberations in Italy, Diego Gambetta suggests that the minority who follow public affairs tend to be bullying and opinionated. In public debate, it is not easy to distinguish arguments based on pride from those based on reason. Tough bargaining coincides with inspirational rhetoric, and together these drive "serious discussion on principles out of public life". He claims that he "cannot recall a political fight that was ever fought by the Italian political class on principled grounds". And he laments that television fits this style of deliberation as politicians can be "entertaining, make exalted statements, avoid subtle distinctions, and squabble with one another theatrically".[10] In broad outlines, this picture will be recognizable to those familiar with political debates in Thailand. As the April 2006 elections approached, one academic called for a televised debate among the contestants, suggesting that such an event might serve to cool temperatures and increase information, while making leaders accountable. He hoped to curb a situation in which "Neither the government nor the protestors have any belief in the power of reason and dialogue."[11] There was, however, no televised debate, not even much of an election, and there has not been much of reason or dialogue since.

CONCLUSION

Media reform occupied a central part of the Abhisit government's post-May 2010 reconciliation plans. Much of the mainstream media responded enthusiastically to proposals for media reform, though subsequently many grew chary. Natthawut Saikuea of the UDD, in the spirit of arms reduction talks, suggested his willingness to buy into curbs on what can only be called PTV hate-mongering, but only so long as ASTV would make comparable commitments.

The increasingly central role of media may retard any forces that might otherwise work to foster more deliberative political discussions in Thailand. Waisbord notes that the mass media everywhere now occupy the centre of the political stage, displacing political parties and other institutions of civil and political society. The mass media are implicated in the manufacture of the "political spectacles" of our time.[12] In Thailand and elsewhere, those spectacles are increasingly pitched to niche audiences. The increasing segmentation of information markets that results will have important political consequences. More broadly, the ways in which Thais apprehend, report, and debate political issues offer little scope for negotiating principled political differences.

Notes

1. Siripan Nogsuan Sawasdee, *Thai Political Parties in the Age of Reform* (Bangkok: Institute of Public Policy Studies, 2006), p. 134.
2. *The Nation*, 7 May 2009.
3. Katherine A. Bowie, *Rituals of National Loyalty. An Anthropology of the State and the Village Scout Movement in Thailand* (New York: Columbia University Press, 1997), pp. 34–35.
4. Peter A. Jackson, "The Thai Regime of Images", *Sojourn* 19, no. 2 (October 2004): 1–39; see pp. 204–205.
5. Donatella della Porta, "Social Capital, Beliefs in Government, and Political Corruption", in *Disaffected Democrats: What's Troubling the Trilateral Countries?*", edited by Susan J. Pharr and Robert D. Putnam (Princeton: Princeton University Press, 2000), pp. 202–29; see pp. 22–25.
6. Richard Sennett, *Respect in a World of Inequality* (New York: W. W. Norton and Co., 2003), p. 103.
7. Paul Johnson, *The Birth of the Modern, World Society 1815–1830* (New York: Harper Perennial, 1991), p. 424.

8. *Bangkok Post*, 31 March 2006.
9. That is, <http://www.manager.co.th>
10. Diego Gambetta, "'Claro!' An Essay on Discursive Machismo", in *Deliberative Democracy*, edited by Jon Elster (Cambridge: Cambridge University Press, 1998), pp. 19–43; see pp. 35, 40.
11. *Bangkok Post*, 9 April 2006.
12. Silvio R. Waisbord, "Reading Scandals: Scandals, Media, and Citizenship in Contemporary Argentina", in *Enforcing the Rule of Law. Social Accountability in the New Latin American Democracies*, edited by Enrique Peruzzotti and Catalina Smulovitz (Pittsburgh: University of Pittsburgh Press, 2006), pp. 272–303; see pp. 278–79.

25

THE POLITICAL ECONOMY OF THAILAND'S MIDDLE-INCOME PEASANTS

Andrew Walker

Military force, mass arrests and emergency rule succeeded in crushing the Red Shirt protests that paralysed parts of Bangkok in 2010, but the government of Prime Minister Abhisit Vejjajiva was nevertheless destined to fail in its attempt to hold back the course of Thailand's history. Over the past five decades, as Thailand has developed into a middle-income country, economic and social aspirations have outrun the nation's elite-focused political institutions. The pressures from this seismic mismatch have been building for some time, erupting in murderous confrontations between protestors and security forces in 1973, 1976, 1992 and now 2010. When units of the Thai Army closed in on the Red Shirt protest site in the heart of Bangkok on 19 May 2010, the Thai government easily won another bloody battle, but it had already lost the war. In order to understand the social transformations that gave rise to the country's crisis of April and May 2010 it is necessary to turn away from Bangkok and towards Thailand's rural hinterland, where about two-thirds of the population live and where support for the Red Shirts is strongest.

Many of the changes that have occurred in rural Thailand during recent decades have been very positive indeed. Half a century ago, 96 per cent of Thailand's farmers were living in poverty. This figure has now plummeted to only 13 per cent. Life expectancy has increased, infant mortality is close to First World standards, and primary schooling is near universal.[1] Thailand has achieved most of the United Nations' Millennium Development Goals well ahead of target. The rural population in Thailand can now be described as a "middle-income peasantry" in which subsistence rice farming, commercial agriculture and extensive off-farm employment are combined to produce levels of household income and consumption unthinkable a few decades ago. In the northern Thai village where I have been undertaking ethnographic research for the past eight years, 130 households own a total of 134 televisions, 129 refrigerators, 169 motor-bikes, 134 mobile phones, 75 fixed phone lines, 81 tape or compact disk players, 26 cars or pick-up trucks and 29 computers. For most people in rural Thailand, economic growth has meant that absolute poverty is no longer a predominant concern.

This rural prosperity has been seized upon by some critics of the Red Shirt protestors to undermine their claims of disadvantage, as if only abject poverty is a legitimate basis for political mobilization. But the rise in rural living standards is only part of the story. Thailand's rural transformation has two very important weaknesses. One of them is economic; the other is cultural. Both are political.

The economic weakness is inequality. Thailand has been very successful in managing absolute poverty, but it has failed to deal with relative poverty. Many developing countries face the challenge of a widening gap between rich and poor, but Thailand's performance is particularly bad and shows little sign of improving. Since the mid-1980s, Thailand has been significantly more unequal than its main regional neighbours. National statistics, which understate the affluence of the survey-avoiding rich, show that Thailand's inequality has grown steadily worse, dipping only temporarily after the Asian economic crisis of the late 1990s. In the mid-1970s the richest 20 per cent of the population earned about eight times as much as the poorest 20 per cent, whereas in the 2000s this ratio has climbed to between twelve and fourteen.[2] The recent *Human Development Report* for Thailand highlights the regional dimensions of inequality. According to a range of human development indicators of income, health, education and housing, Bangkok and its hinterland perform very strongly whereas the worst performers are predominantly rural provinces in the Northeast, North and far South. Gross provincial product per capita in Bangkok is eight times higher than in the Northeast and five times higher than in the North. Average household income in Bangkok is about three times higher than in the rural North and Northeast.

One very important reason for this persistent inequality is that workers in the agricultural sector are much less productive than workers in industry. There has certainly been impressive productivity growth in the agricultural sector — with real GDP per worker more than double what it was in 1980 — and this has made an important contribution to Thailand's dramatic reduction in rural poverty.[3] But productivity in industry not only started from a higher base, but increased more rapidly, especially during the economic boom from the mid-1980s to the mid-1990s. In 1980 labour in industry was about 9 times as productive as labour in agriculture. By 1993 this figure had increased to 16 times. The gap has closed to 8.5 times in recent years, as a result of the economic crisis of the late 1990s and unusually healthy agricultural prices, but it is still larger than the gap in Indonesia (7.5 times), the Philippines (5.3 times) and Malaysia (2.4 times).

This productivity differential lies at the heart of what agricultural economist Yujiro Hayami calls the "disparity problem" faced by some middle-income countries.[4] Hayami argues that as countries industrialize and move into a middle-income position, productivity growth in the manufacturing sector tends to outstrip productivity growth in agriculture. Manufacturing benefits from technology transfer, whereas the biological and environmental specificities of agricultural make it less amenable to technological innovation. Industry is also more likely than agriculture to benefit from economies of scale, especially in countries like Thailand where small-holder farming dominates. Hayami suggests that the widening gap between urban and rural areas creates an important axis of political tension: "farmers become envious and eventually develop [a] grudge against the social system". The political potency of disparity in middle-income countries is compounded by the fact that it emerges at the same time as rural education, communication and mobility improve. This circumstance means that rural residents are only too aware of their comparative disadvantage as a result of their wide exposure to national media and direct experience of urban areas, where many members of rural households work and study. Countries' attainment of middle-income status also often involves a decrease in authoritarian controls over rural political organization, meaning that concerns about relative poverty can be freely expressed by farmers' organizations, NGOs, and voters at the ballot box. The forces of socio-economic modernization that increase disparity also amplify the force and eloquence of rural political opinion.

Thailand's governments have been only too aware of the disparity problem, and attempts to address rural disadvantage have become the central dynamic of the relationship between the Thai state and the middle-income peasantry. These attempts certainly did not start with the "populism" of former Prime Minister Thaksin Shinawatra. His policy initiatives were consistent with a long-term trend — one in evidence since the mid-1970s, when newly assertive farmer's organisations moved onto the national stage.

In simple terms the Thai government, like many other middle-income countries, has moved from taxing the rural economy to subsidizing it. From the 1950s to the early 1970s the government levied a heavy tax on Thailand's rice producers via the "rice premium". This generated a generous proportion of government revenue and provided cheap rice for urban consumers by artificially lowering the price paid to farmers for their harvest. The premium fell rapidly in the latter years of the 1970s and was abolished in 1986.[5] Shortly afterwards the government shifted direction, introducing a series of crop price support schemes which, to this day, use government funds to boost farm-gate prices. These crop pricing measures have been accompanied by an explosion in more direct forms of support: government spending on agriculture increased fifteen-fold between 1960 and 2008; state-provided agricultural credit increased more than a hundred-fold between 1975 and 2008; rural road length increased nine-fold in the 1980s and 1990s; hospitals and secondary schools were established in virtually every rural district; and villages benefited from an array of rural development, social welfare and poverty alleviation schemes.[6] The Thai government now puts considerably more into the rural economy than it takes out, and government funding has become an integral part of the complex livelihood mix pursued by households throughout rural Thailand.

Thailand's current political tension owes much to the dilemmas of this transformed fiscal relationship. State investment, combined with wide-ranging support for the tenure of small-holders, has enhanced agricultural incomes and created numerous sources of non-farm employment in the construction sector, local development projects, and government agencies themselves. However, and this is the nub of Thailand's middle-income problem, the overall impact of this state support for rural Thailand has been to help develop and maintain a middle-income peasantry rather than fundamentally transform it. State investment in agricultural research and development has been lacklustre, and productivity gains in Thai agriculture are much less impressive than those achieved by many of its regional neighbours. More importantly, the Thai state has done little to develop the non-farm sector in rural areas apart from some high profile schemes that support the production of local handicrafts for niche markets. The expansion of secondary education in rural areas has been an important investment in human capital but there are persistent doubts about its quality and its ability adequately to prepare rural people for higher paid employment in the modern urban economy. The overall result is that the Thai state has helped to maintain a large rural population that, despite significant livelihood improvements, is insufficiently productive fully to meet the aspirations that economic growth has aroused.

The economic distance between the city and the countryside has a disturbing cultural counterpart which leaves Thailand very poorly equipped to deal with this modern dilemma of development. Scratch the surface of urban Thailand's corporate imagery of loyal and cheerful farmers in verdant paddy fields and it is not hard to find a rich store of contempt for the peasantry. Farmers are rough, ignorant, parochial, and easily led. "Buffaloes" has become a popular term of contempt for the supporters of the Red Shirts. In particular, urban Thailand has a very limited understanding of the modern forms of subsidy and exchange that characterize the middle-income peasant economy. Increasingly, rural social and economic development schemes have come to be condemned as the populist diversion of middle and upper class taxes to an insatiable countryside. When rural Thailand flexes its political muscle to support such schemes, farmers are all too readily dismissed as self-interested country bumpkins who happily sell their votes to the highest bidder. Of course, not all contempt is malicious and some of it draws on sympathetic, but outdated, stereotypes of impoverished peasants living under the yoke of merchants, tycoons, and strongmen. Some in urban Thailand see King Bhumibol Adulyadej's "sufficiency economy" approach as an antidote to the hazards of modernity and its distasteful money politics. According to the king's "new agricultural theory" farmers should turn away from the corrupting allure of money politics and the market. Instead they should focus on local capabilities, subsistence production and limited exchange with neighbouring areas. This anachronistic royal vision provides a moral template for those who feel uneasy about the integration of rural people into both the national economy and the national political system.

For a time in the 1980s and 1990s, there was hope that civil society advocates might be able to present a more sympathetic and realistic image of rural life. Thai NGOs became very active in defending the rights of farmers where they were threatened by large-scale infrastructure projects, conservation programmes, and the private appropriation of forest, land, and water. They had an important influence on the 1997 constitution, which granted rural communities rights to be involved in the management of natural resources. However, many players in this NGO movement were side-tracked by an old-fashioned localist and anti-capitalist agenda. They too constructed an anachronistic stereotype of communal lifestyles and subsistence-oriented farming that compounded the middle-income peasantry's cultural marginalisation.

Former Prime Minister Thaksin Shinawatra capitalized on these economic and cultural flaws in Thailand's modernization. His unprecedented political success owes much to the fact that he shaped his policies around rural aspirations for economic, cultural and political inclusion. He recognized that decades of rural economic growth and diversification had produced a very different type of peasantry. There was nothing particularly new about Thaksin's emphasis on grass-roots development, but he packaged it in a way that was very attractive for an economically sophisticated electorate: rural households can turn their assets into capital; villagers can manage agricultural credit; farmers can implement infrastructure projects; local hospitals can provide universal health cover. Yes they can! He cashed in on what has been described as a "new social contract" that embodied the notion that the state would play a direct and active role in supporting the rural economy.[7] This social contract had been developing since the 1970s, but it took Thaksin to turn it into a core political asset. Some of Thaksin's policies smacked of tokenism, others were much more substantial, but all of them underlined a shift towards engagement with the rural economy and respect for its middle-income values. Thaksin also had timing on his side; he governed during Thailand's rapid recovery from the financial crisis of the late 1990s. With a solid increase in the price of Thailand's most important crops and with the proportion of GDP contributed by agriculture increasing from 9 per cent to 11 per cent during Thaksin's term, farmers were certainly not cut off from Thailand's rising economic tide.[8]

So why did the Red Shirts come to Bangkok in March 2010? This was not an uprising of Thailand's rural poor, despite the mobilizing language of oppression and deprivation. The Red Shirts were, as one astute commentator put it, the "aggrieved with assets" arriving in convoys of pick-up trucks.[9] On specific policy issues they had little dispute with Prime Minister Abhisit's government. Abhisit maintained the long-term legacy of state support for the rural economy, keeping most of Thaksin's populist schemes in one form or another, though often repackaged to display "sufficiency economy" credentials. The agricultural budget continued to grow; a nationwide scheme of free education has been introduced; and the "Strong Thailand" programme allocated hundreds of billions of baht for nationwide investment in infrastructure and economic development. Of course, Abhisit did not have Thaksin's luck with timing. Just when Abhisit came into power, the global financial crisis sent Thailand's economy into reverse, hurting the labour-intensive export sectors where many rural people sought urban employment.[10] There was plenty of potential for economic anger.

But it would be a mistake to think that the Red Shirt movement was simply a political reaction to economic setbacks. In the midst of Thailand's current political complexity, it is important not to lose sight of one core issue: many rural people were angry because their electoral wishes were overturned. They are angry about the 2006 coup, about the dissolution of the parties they supported, and about the Yellow Shirt campaign to bring down the Thaksin-aligned government that was elected in December 2007. They are angry that Abhisit was manoeuvred into power despite the fact that his party has not come close to winning an election in more than a decade.

Rural Thailand cares about election results. It was once an anthropological truism that Thai villagers saw the government as a remote and rather threatening force that was best avoided. This is no longer the case. Rural economic growth, livelihood diversification and administrative expansion have bought rural people into regular contact with agents of the state. The massive increases in government spending in rural areas mean that the activities of government are now woven into the economic and social fabric of village life. The recent history of decentralization has resulted in a proliferation of points of productive contact between community and bureaucracy. Elections at the village, sub-district, provincial and national levels provide opportunities for rural people to guide this process of engagement. Some commentators like to dismiss elections as a meaningless few minutes spent marking a ballot paper, but this dismissal ignores the vigorous electoral culture that has developed in rural Thailand, through which voters evaluate, applaud, and critique the various ways in which government representatives implement the middle-income peasantry's new social contract.[11] The Red Shirts came to Bangkok to defend the direct relationship that they have established with the Thai state over the past forty years. This is not the old-style Southeast Asian peasantry of rebellion, revolution, or resistance. This is a middle-income peasantry with a thoroughly modern political logic that seeks to bind itself to the state, not oppose it.

In Thailand, iconic images of national unity often feature King Bhumibol dispensing royal wisdom and benevolence to crouching peasants. These images celebrate a model of elite patronage, with livelihood support wisely granted by the king and his loyal bureaucracy. This is an old model, an ideological template that may have suited earlier phases of Thailand's movement out of rural poverty. These old ideas are certainly enduring, especially in Abhisit's staunchly royalist governing party, but they have much less potency in the modern rural world of contract farming, off-farm employment, and mobile phones. Thaksin's populism capitalized on new ways of thinking about the rural economy, local power and political participation. Abhisit has succeeded in sweeping the Red Shirts out of Bangkok, but with Thailand's middle-income peasantry now a player of great significance in the economic and political life of the nation, they will certainly be back.

Notes

1. The data on poverty rates come from Peter G. Warr, "Boom, bust and beyond", in *Thailand Beyond the Crisis*, edited by Peter G. Warr (Abingdon, England: RoutledgeCurzon, 2004), pp. 3–65; see pp. 49–50. Information on other indicators comes from the World Bank's World Development Indicators Online <data.worldbank.org/data-catalog/world-development-indicators>.

Information on Human Development Goals comes from from Peter G. Warr, "Thailand's crisis overload", in *Southeast Asian Affairs 2009*, (Singapore: Institute of Southeast Asian Studies, 2009), pp. 334–54.

2. United Nations Development Program, *Human Security, Today and Tomorrow: Thailand Human Development Report 2009* (Bangkok: UNDP, 2010); Bowonsak Uwanno, "The Thai Political Situation: Wherefrom and Whereto?", paper presented at a panel discussion co-hosted by the Royal Thai Embassy, London, and the SOAS Thai Society, 29 January 2010, School of Oriental and African Studies, London.
3. Data on productivity are derived from sectoral GDP and labour force data from the World Bank's Development Indicators Online <data.worldbank.org/data-catalog/world-development-indicators>.
4. Hayami Yujiro, "An Emerging Agricultural Problem in High-Performing Asian Economies", Policy Research Working Paper 4312, World Bank Development Research Group, Trade Team, Washington, 2007.
5. W. M. Corden, "The Exchange Rate System and the Taxation of Trade", in *Thailand: Social and Economic Studies in Development*, edited by T. H. Silcock, (Canberra: Australian National University Press, 1967), pp. 151–69; and Kym Anderson and Will Martin, "Distortions to Agricultural Incentives in China and Southeast Asia", Agricultural Distortions Working Paper 69, The World Bank, Washington, 2008.
6. National Statistical Office, Thailand, *Statistical Yearbook of Thailand*, various years (Bangkok:National Statistical Office); Alpha Research, *Thailand in Figures*, various years (Bangkok: Alpha Research); Somsak Wongpanyathawon, Rawidprapha Rakphaophan, and Siriphon Siripanyawat, "Botbat sinchuea chonnabot to kancharoentoepto khong phak kankaset thai bot thotsop choengprachak khong khomun rawang pi 2527–2539" [The role of rural credit provision in the growth of Thailand's agricultural sector: an empirical test on the data between 1984–1996] (Bangkok: Bank of Thailand, 2000); Sorarit Sunthonket, *Botbat khong sinchuea chonnabot to kancharoentoepto khong phak kaset thai nai phuenthi phak nuea phaktawanokchiangnuea doi priapthiap kap thang prathet* [The role of rural credit provision in the growth of Thailand's agricultural sector: Northern and Northeastern regions compared with the whole country], Master's thesis, Thammasat University, 2000; Bank for Agriculture and Agricultural Cooperatives, *Annual Report*, various years (Bangkok: BAAC); and Fan Shenggen, Somchai Jitsuchon, and Nuntaporn Methakunnavut, "The Importance of Public Investment for Reducing Poverty in Middle-Income Countries: The Case of Thailand", DSGD Discussion Paper No. 7, International Food Policy Research Institute, Development Strategy and Governance Division, Washington, 2004.

7. Kevin Hewison, "Neo-Liberalism and Domestic Capital: The Political Outcome of the Economic Crisis in Thailand", *Journal of Development Studies* 41, no. 2 (February 2005): 310–30.
8. Data on agricultural share of GDP are from the World Bank's World Development Indicators Online <data.worldbank.org/data-catalog/world-development-indicators>. Data on crop prices come from from the United Nations Food and Agriculture Organization's FAOSTAT site <faostat.fao.org/>.
9. Chang Noi (pseud.), "Witness the Death of Deference", *The Nation*, 22 March 2010.
10. Peter Warr in *Thailand in Crisis, Episode 5*, New Mandala <asiapacific.anu.edu.au/newmandala/2010/06/25/thailand-in-crisis-episode-5/> (accessed 14 March 2011).
11. Andrew Walker, "The Rural Constitution and the Everyday Politics of Elections in Northern Thailand", *The Journal of Contemporary Asia* 38, no. 1 (February 2008): 84–105.

26

ROYAL SUCCESSION AND THE EVOLUTION OF THAI DEMOCRACY

Andrew Walker

In the northern Thai village where I have been doing fieldwork for several years, there is a carpenter, Uncle Phaibun, who became a fan of the September 2006 military coup. In the wake of the coup, as part of the military government's propaganda offensive, numerous photos of King Bhumibol Adulyadej were distributed in the village. Uncle Phaibun's positive feelings about the coup did not result from royalist sentiment, but from the windfall income he earned from making wooden frames for the royal portraits. Given the sacred power of the king's image, it was only natural that the villagers would treat it with respect and reverence. Duly framed, the pictures were hung in village living rooms along with other images of the king and his family, fading photos of long-deceased grandparents, posters of famous monks, out-of-date calendars featuring Thaksin and local politicians, images of the Buddha and other deities, university degrees, business advertisements, and elaborate clocks mounted on posters of artificially natural scenes featuring waterfalls and flower gardens.

These mini-galleries of power and auspiciousness are very revealing of a political world-view that motivates many of the grass-roots actors in Thailand's ongoing political crisis. This is a world-view in which power comes in many forms, and in which modern commercialization and administrative expansion have resulted in a proliferation of pathways to power. In this world-view, the king is one source of power, but the popular Thai cosmos is full of all sorts of power and influence, and Thais are adept at hedging their bets in maintaining a diverse network of relationships with potential sources of prosperity and protection. This is not a zero-sum game. Despite much speculation to the contrary, for most Thais there was no inconsistency in supporting both Thaksin Shinawatra and the king. Thailand's masses readily accept that two, or more, styles of leadership and benevolence can exist side by side. The contemporary challenge for rural politics is to draw these various types of power into local networks than can support safe and prosperous livelihoods.

Some members of Thailand's elite have much more rigid views about power, and they are not particularly adept at grasping the nuances of Thai popular culture. Whereas the villagers in northern Thailand pursue *human* security through cultivating connections with power in many different forms, the official Thai position is that the king's symbolic potency lies at the centre of *national* security. This selective and elite narrative of security asserts that the king is the pre-eminent paradigm of virtuous and disinterested power, rather than accepting that he represents one of the many ways in which leadership can be expressed. As the Royal Thai Embassy in Canberra wrote in an April 2010 protest to the Australian government about the national broadcaster's unflattering coverage of the royal family "We consider this an issue of national security… because the royal family, the monarchy, in our constitution is above politics."[1] The monarch, in other words, is not located in the crowded sphere of popular power, but floats above it, defined as sacred by constitutional fiat, backed by draconian law.

Of course it has not always been like that, and when King Bhumibol first came to the throne there were figures in the Thai government that welcomed his apparent weakness and malleability. Hardline princes fumed about the prospect of a young, inexperienced and, in many respects, un-Thai king who faced the swirling rumours surrounding his older brother's death. It was an inauspicious start to a long reign. But powerful military men, politicians and international allies found it useful to cultivate the royal charisma. The current assertions of King Bhumibol's central role in national security are the product of a sixty-year process that has been very effectively documented in Paul Handley's *The King Never Smiles*.[2] Royal goodness has come to represent the gold-standard of legitimate power, overshadowing grass-roots visions of legitimacy based on the pragmatic evaluation of benefits. Tangled and cross-cutting networks of patronage have been ideologically recast to place the king at the head of a nationwide hierarchy of meritorious power. As part of this reconfiguration, the king has come to be regarded as a champion of Thailand's farmers through his support for infrastructure projects, welfare services, high-profile rural development projects and, most supernaturally potent of all, rain making. I have no doubt that most villagers believe that the king deserves his prominent place within the galleries of power that they create in their homes.

However, the attempts of some royalists to maintain the position of the king at the symbolic apex of Thailand's power have met with real difficulties in recent years. Changing impressions of the potency of the monarchy are a direct consequence of Thailand's current political conflict. When soldiers staging the 2006 coup tied royal yellow ribbons around the barrels of their guns, they were very publicly drawing the king back into a very messy political realm. Of course, in the eyes of an anthropologist, their actions were not so different to those of the many other Thais who adorn themselves with various forms of supernatural protection before undertaking potentially hazardous enterprises, such as driving a car. But the soldiers' public acknowledgement of this aspect of Thai popular culture highlighted that, far from being a neutral force for stability, the king was a source of quite specific power that could be called upon to support partial and pragmatic objectives. This embedding of the king back into the political sphere became all the more evident in the months that followed the coup. The post-coup government promoted the king's back-to-basics sufficiency economy principles even while lavishing considerable largesse on the military. The government also wrapped the 2007 constitution in conspicuously yellow covers, offering the electorate a take-it-or-leave-it referendum that would constrain electoral power. After the election of a pro-Thaksin government in the post-coup election of December 2007, it was not long until the Yellow-Shirt People's Alliance for Democracy was on the streets of Bangkok, and in the airport, campaigning — under what it claimed was the king's banner — for the overthrow of an elected government. Nobody knows how the king himself felt about this expenditure of his carefully cultivated symbolic capital. But neither he nor his advisors appeared to do anything about it. There seemed to be a willingness to stake all on a high-risk campaign to destroy Thaksin's political influence. When the queen publicly supported the Yellow Shirt protestors, the genie of a deeply political monarchy was well and truly out of the bottle.

For a robust monarchy, these developments might be short-term symbolic setbacks that could be addressed by a sustained public-relations campaign. But this is no longer possible for the current king. With the king hospitalized since September 2009, the royal succession now looms large.

The succession issue has come to concern the Thai public at a time in which the rise of alternative forms of media means that that there is plenty of potential for free-wheeling and even mischievous discussion of such matters. Internet discussion boards have come to serve as home for a modern culture of dissent that builds on a rich popular tradition of gossip, rumour and slander. To some extent, popular interest in the succession is fed by the notion that at least some leaks and rumours originate from within the palace itself. Rivalry within elite families is an enduring source of fascination, not just in Thailand. Some of the seditious culture of innuendo may also be influenced by a tradition in Thai radical politics of royal vilification.

The international press — which is widely translated and read in Thailand via the Internet — has gradually picked up on this culture of dissent. However, commentary has in recent years become markedly more pointed. The ill-advised *lèse majesté* case against Australian writer Harry Nicolaides focused international media attention, and some anger. As Thai political tensions heightened, and as speculation about the king's health increased, things got even worse. In March 2010, the *Economist* published a noticeably blunt piece about the anxiety surrounding the royal succession.

For those accustomed to the tabloid coverage of European royals, the reports about Thailand's royal family may seem rather unremarkable and perhaps even a little childish. But, in cultural and political terms, there is something very significant going on. In today's Thailand, discussion of the royal succession offers an opening for alternative ways of talking about power. Rumour, gossip, and irreverence are part of a subaltern approach to evaluating the many forms that power and authority can take. In Thai popular culture, power is capricious; it can manifest itself in good deeds or ill; it can provide protection or retribution. Power is not based on intrinsic goodness or moral virtue. Rather, it needs to be domesticated and channelled in order to produce beneficial outcomes. Thailand's crowded spirit world provides an excellent guide to understanding this flexible and pragmatic orientation. Spirits are volatile entities. They can provide great benefits, but they are also potentially very troublesome. Some of them need to be encouraged towards appropriate behaviour with attractive inducements. Spirits, like children, are malleable. Even very powerful spirits can be placated if they are treated like lords — with feasts, liquor and dancing. Power is made desirable not just by those who possess it, but by the actions of those who can skilfully direct it to propitious ends.

Thai democracy can benefit from royal succession. The persona of the next monarch will be different to that of King Bhumibol. This difference will serve as a reminder that power comes in many diverse forms. In its diversity, power is routinely subject to people's pragmatic judgements about potency, efficacy and probity. The image of virtuous and disinterested royal power is the result of decades of domestication and ritual reinforcement. Whatever unfolds in Thailand over the next few years, one thing is clear: the symbolic potency of the royal institution has been affected in the past few years, not as a result of Red republicanism but because the royalists have undermined their own imagery.

Given the capriciousness of power, King Bhumibol's successor will not automatically occupy his pre-eminent position at the pinnacle of the Thai polity. Even if it were possible in this day and age, another long round of royal myth-making would be very different to the enterprise that established King Bhumibol's sacred potency. Among various factors relating to the succession, then, the markedly different persona of Thailand's next monarch is a virtue: the new reign will bring the prospect of a more culturally open orientation to power in Thailand. For the Thai embassy in Canberra, the prospect of a nation in which power and security are defined in much more inclusive terms seems to be an issue of national security. But is it such a threat? Or will that prospect in fact be good for Thailand and for the evolution of Thai democracy?

Notes

1. "The Embassy and the ABC", New Mandala, 16 April 2010 <asiapacific.anu.edu.au/newmandala/2010/04/16/the-embassy-and-the-abc/> (accessed 14 March 2011).
2. Paul M. Handley, *The King Never Smiles: A Biography of Thailand's Bhumibol Adulyadej* (New Haven: Yale University Press, 2006).

INDEX

A

Abhisit Vejjajiva, 5, 7–8, 20, 25, 27, 30–31, 38–40, 43–45, 47, 72, 77–80, 100, 120, 123–5, 132, 135, 144, 165–66, 168, 173, 178, 182, 186, 194, 200–201, 245, 253, 257–62, 274–76, 282–83, 285, 290, 294, 298, 313, 319, 321, 323
  background of, 35
  government under, 32–36, 42, 44, 74, 76, 82, 102, 111, 115, 138, 158, 169, 179, 183, 185, 195, 203, 205–207, 209–10, 267, 278, 280, 305, 309, 329
  reform package proposed by, 89, 95
absolute monarchy, 22, 192, 221–22, 269–70
  see also constitutional monarchy; monarchy
absolute poverty, 27, 156, 324
Academy Fantasia, reality show, 93
activist monks, 290–92
agents provocateurs, 294, 299
agrarian change, waves of, 232–36
"ai mong", 78
Allende, Salvador, 50
Amara Phongsaphit, 303
American Embassy, *see* U.S. Embassy
ammat (establishment), 21–22, 27, 29, 38, 93, 99, 135, 137–38, 140, 144, 179, 225, 287, 292–93, 302, 304, 306–309
  see also elite governance
amnesty, 279–83, 285, 301, 303
Amnuay Virawan, 17
Amsterdam, Robert, 280–81
Anan Panyarachun, 44, 104, 169, 305–306
Ananda Mahidol, King, 73, 180
ancien régime, 287, 295
Angkor Sentinel, military exercise, 208
anti-monarchical conspiracy theory, 74, 80
  see also "lom chao"
"anti-system" forces, 129
anti-Thaksin media, 79
Anuman Ratchathon, Phraya, 2
Anuphong Paochinda, 25, 33, 315
Apichatphong Weerasethakun, 184–85
Appeals Court, 277
"aristocratic liberalism", 105
Army, Thai, 21–22, 25, 35, 43–44, 76–78, 87, 133, 139, 165, 220, 224, 227, 293, 298, 302, 304, 307, 309–10, 323
  psychological warfare unit, 237
  restructured, 128
Arvizu, Alexander, 253
ASEAN (Association of Southeast Asian Nations), 166, 202, 204–205, 210–11, 257, 262
ASEAN Charter, 202
ASEAN Plus Three, 4, 202
ASEAN Secretariat, 202

ASEAN Summit, 178, 200–202
"Asia for Asians", 208
Asia Times Online, 258
Asian financial crisis, 2, 15, 100, 110, 113, 146, 148, 150, 162, 215, 221–22, 231, 232, 329
"assembly of slaves", 163
Assembly of the Poor, 113
Assets Scrutiny Committee, 302
Associated Press, 182
ASTV channel, 77, 79, 184, 193, 275, 301, 308, 318–19, 321
Atthasit Vejjajiva, 115
Aung San Suu Kyi, 261
Australian Broadcasting Corporation, 182
authoritarianism, 97–99, 101, 105, 164, 190
autocracy, 267–68, 270
Aylwin, Patricio, 51

B

Baker, Chris, 27, 245
Ban Ki Moon, 209
"banana man", 249
Bangkok Commune, 133
Bangkok Post, The, 24, 36, 94–95, 173, 183, 185, 280, 286, 301–302, 318
Banharn Silpa-archa, 16, 166
BBC, 32, 36
"beacon of democracy", 161–62
Bhumibol Adulyadej, King, 2, 109–10, 177, 180, 182, 262, 293–95, 304, 327, 330, 333–37
  born, 251
  see also Chakri dynasty
Bhumjaithai Party, 33
"big men", leadership concept, 271
"biopower", 91
black-clad gunmen, 77–78, 82, 112, 206, 284
Black May, public uprising, 162
Bloch, Maurice, 316
"blue shirt" militia, 79, 294
bomb attacks, 112, 122, 131, 133
Border Patrol Police, 44
Bottomore, Tom, 145
Boyce, Ralph, 252
"brainwashing", 26–27
BSI (Business Sentiment Index), 58–59, 61, 63
Buddhism, 30, 288, 290–91
Bumrungrad Hospital, 115
Bunchu Rotchanasathian, 2, 16
Burmese-style junta, 102, 105, 268
Burns, William, 257
bushido, code of, 269

C

Cambodia
  confrontation with, 186, 203–204, 208
  Thaksin as economic advisor to, 204, 212
Campaign for Popular Democracy, *see* CPD
Campbell, Kurt, 82, 256–59
capitalism, 2, 89, 101, 113, 146, 288, 304
cash crops, 234, 236
censorhip, 184–85, 305
Central World Plaza, 134, 172
Centre for the Resolution of the Emergency Situation, *see* CRES
CFD (Confederation for Democracy), 193
Chai-anan Samudavanija, 192
Chakri dynasty, 3, 317
  see also Bhumibol Adulyadej
Chalat Worachat, 194
Chamlong Srimuang, 79, 176, 191–92, 195, 271, 309
"Chang Noi", 186
Chatchai Choonhavan, 125
Chatrichaloem Yukol, Prince, 185
Chaturon Chaisaeng, 82, 258
Chavalit Yongchaiyut, 31, 194–95
China's Communist Party: Atrophy and Adaptation, 37
China, influence of, 208–209

Chirmsak Pinthong, 77
Chuan Leekphai, 7, 18, 117, 166, 195
Chulachomklao Military Academy, 195
Chulalongkorn Hospital, 28, 133
Chulalongkorn, King, 199
see also Rama V, King
Chulalongkorn University, 301, 303
civil disobedience, 24
civil society, 328
democracy, and, 305–306
failure of, 301–304
class warfare, 29, 143, 144–45, 157, 166, 300
Clinton, Hillary, 253
CNN, 36
CNS (Council for National Security), 281, 295
Cobra Gold, military exercise, 252–53
Cold War, 73, 87, 117, 167, 220, 237, 244, 249–52, 254, 263
colonialism, 199
communism, 16, 30, 237, 250
communist insurgency, 221, 237
Communist Party of Thailand, *see* CPT
communist resistance, 28
Confederation for Democracy, *see* CFD
Congressional Research Service, *see* CRS
Connors, Michael, 3
conservatism, 99
"Constituent Assembly", 128
"Constitutional Convention", 128
Constitutional Court, 165, 204
constitutional monarchy, 22, 180–81, 227
see also absolute monarchy; monarchy
contract labour, 114
corporate interest, 101
corruption, 100, 103, 111, 164–65, 251
"cosmopolitan villagers", 243
Council for Democratic Reform, 281
Council for National Security, *see* CNS
coup d'état, 88, 100, 161, 165, 192
see also military coup; September 2006 coup
CPB (Crown Property Bureau), 109, 149–50
CPD (Campaign for Popular Democracy), 193–94
CPT (Communist Party of Thailand), 12, 144, 167, 168, 181, 234, 297–98, 303
CRES (Center for the Resolution of the Emergency Situation), 11, 44, 77–81, 85, 102, 124–25, 141
Criminal Code, 44, 167
Criminal Court, 167
"crisis of authority", 310
crisis of power, 180–83
Crispin, Shawn, 258
cronyism, 16
Crown Property Bureau, *see* CPB
CRS (Congressional Research Service), 255
"cryptocracy", 317
Cunningham, Philip, 112–13
cyber-policing, 304–305

D

DAAD (Democratic Alliance Against Dictatorship), 295
Daily News, newspaper, 83
Death and the Maiden, 50–51
decentralization, 238, 330
deglobalization, 57
Democracy Monument, 4, 76, 133, 300
Democrat Party, 7, 19–21, 27, 33–34, 38–40, 72–77, 79, 82, 84, 97, 100, 104, 115, 138, 145, 150–54, 156–57, 166, 178, 182, 187, 193–95, 204, 210, 222, 225–26, 290, 293, 301, 307
democratic rule, 22

demonstrators for hire (*mop rap chang*), 196
Deleuzeo-Guattarian, defining desire, 89–90, 95
Department of Special Investigation, *see* DSI
despotism, 268
Dhammic Power (*Phalang Tham*) Party, 176
dictatorial conservatism, 22
"directed democracy", 305–306
"disparity problem", 325–26
Doner, Richard, 114
Don Mueang Airport, 24
Don Pramutwinai, 260
Dorfman, Ariel, 50–52
"double standards", 88, 95, 108, 139, 144, 179, 206, 225–26, 245, 253, 281, 288, 296, 298
  UDD strategy on, 276–84
DSI (Department of Special Investigation), 81, 84, 138, 278–79
Dusit Thani Hotel, 25

E
EAS (East Asia Summit), 4, 202
East Asian and Pacific Affairs Bureau, United States Department of State, 255–56
Economist, The, 127, 182, 336
economy, of Thailand, 24, 34, 55–62, 137, 174, 181, 183, 215, 227
"EDSA", mass demonstration in the Philippines, 192
Election Commission, 163, 302
electoral fraud, 165
electoral politics, 239–40, 242
11th Infantry Regiment, 79
elite governance, 17–18, 24, 293
  see also ammat
elite liberalism, 99, 103, 105
elites, concerns of the, 300–301
Emergency Administrative Act, 285
Emergency Decree, 43–48, 77, 82, 89, 92, 100, 122, 278, 290, 303, 319
Emory University, 114
Emporium, shopping mall, 2
"e-san Discovery Channel", 79
EU (European Union), 57, 210
"event-making men", 269–70
executive decree, 163
executive power, 100–101, 282
extrajudicial killing, 30, 111, 126, 176, 210, 252

F
Fair Deal, 23
Faleomavaega, Eni F.H., 259
farang, 17–18
fascism, 105, 268, 270–71, 288
feudal system, 292
Fifth Reign, reforms during, 292
Fifth Republic, France, 191
financial crisis of 1997, *see* Asian financial crisis
Financial Times, The, 182
First World, 222, 324
First World War, *see* World War I
fiscal policy, 2, 326
five-point "compromise" (*prongdong*) plan, 81, 84–86, 262, 275
"flexible engagement", 210
Forbes, magazine, 110
foreign capital, 110
foreign policy, 199–200, 211, 251
  politicization of, 201–205
Fox News, 116
Franco, Francisco, 288
Free Aceh Movement, 211
"free speech", 93
Freedom House, 272
French republicanism, 191

G
G-20 Summit, 210–11
Gambetta, Diego, 320
GDP, of Thailand, 55–56, 59–62, 216, 222, 325, 329
Gini coefficient, 217–18
Girling, J.L.S., 248, 263

globalization, 114, 244, 246, 303
government accountability, 275
Government House, 3, 21, 23–24, 33, 79, 111, 178, 194, 196, 277–78, 290, 294
Graham, Bruce, 191
Gramsci, Antonio, 98, 310
"Grand Bargain", renegotiation of social compact, 126
Great East Asian War, 12
Great Man Theory of History, 269
Great Society, 23
grenade attack, 25
GST (Goods and Services Tax), 62

H

Handley, Paul, 335
Harrington, Michael, 23
Hayami, Yujiro, 325
health-care scheme, 92, 113, 115, 223, 240, 307, 328
Hero in History, The, 270
historical amnesia, 280, 284
Hitler, Adolf, 269
HLAC (Human Rights and Legal Assistance Centre), 49
Hook, Sidney, 269
House of Representatives, Thailand, 93, 127, 163
House of Representatives, United States, 261, 262-63, 265
HRW (Human Rights Watch), 44, 164, 304
Human Development Report, United Nations Development Program, 324
Hun Sen, 31, 204–205
"Hyde Park" movement, 196

I

"ideological state apparatus", 93
IMF (International Monetary Fund), 100, 110
income, in Thailand, 27, 147–48, 166–67, 217–18, 325
Independent, The, 182
Independent Truth and Reconciliation Commission, *see* ITRC
Indochinese War, 233
Indonesia, reforms in, 211
inequality, in Thailand, 148–50, 217, 219–20, 228, 324–25
information regime, 314–18
Internal Security Act, 122, 303
Internal Security Operations Command, 85, 291
International Court of Justice, 203
Interpol, 207
Irish Times, The, 145
Irrawady, The, magazine, 145
ITRC (Independent Truth and Reconciliation Commission), 45–50
  members of, 53

J

Jackson, Andrew, 262
Jakrapob Penkair, 116
Japanese militarism, 269
Jatuporn Phomphan, 114–16, 275, 279–80, 284, 309
Ji Ungpakon, 112–13
John, Eric, 255, 258
John, Sophia, 258
judiciary, 207, 224, 282
June 24 Democracy Group, 261

K

Kahan, Alan, 105
Kanit Na Nakorn, 5, 44–46, 283
Kanngoen thanakhan, magazine, 150
karma, concept of, 92
Kasit Piromya, 78, 82, 84, 139, 144, 182, 203–205, 207, 258, 260
Katz, Cindi, 243
Kenney, Kristie, 258
Keyes, Charles, 29, 243
Khattiya "Se Daeng" Sawatdiphon, 76, 112, 298, 301

Khom Chat Luek, newspaper, 301
Kiat Sitthi-amon, 208, 210, 258–59
King Never Smiles, The, 335
Kinokuniya, 2
kinship network, 238–39
Kittiphong Na Ranong, 260–61
Kittiwutho, 30
Korn Chatikawanit, 34, 36
Klausner, Bill, 20
Kraisak Choonhavan, 179
Kriangsak Chomanan, 28, 30, 181, 239–40
Krit Garnjana-goonchorn, 249
Kukrit Pramoj, 2, 16
Kuznets, Simon, 217

L
labour migration, 235
Laos, communist takeover, 237
Le facisme c'est Mussolini, 269
Lee Kuan Yew, 223
lèse majesté, law, 3, 73, 76, 80–81, 88, 182, 225, 280, 295, 315, 336
liberal authoritarianism, 100–103
liberal-conservative pact, 99, 100–103
liberal democracy, 162
liberal-democratic polity, 100
liberalism, 3, 98–101, 103–105, 107
Lintner, Bertil, 114
"*lom chao*" (anti-monarchy views or conspiracy), 75, 80, 84
  list of suspected members, 81
  see also monarchy
Lumphini Park, 80, 133

M
Ma Nakhon, film, 174, 187
Maas, Michael, 302
Mahathir Mohamad, 223
"Maha X", monk, 291
Malaysia, rural urbanization in, 243
Manager (*Phu chatkan*), media group, 301–302, 308, 319
Manila Pact, 250, 262
"manufactured crisis", 193
"many-coloured" group, demonstration, 79–80
Marciel, Scot, 257
Marcos, Ferdinand, 192
market economy, 234
Marxism, 144
mass media, 175, 313, 315–16, 318, 321
mass rally, 190, 221
Matichon, weekly, 4
May 2010, crackdown, 4–6, 38–39, 43–50, 52, 58, 65, 72, 75, 82–83, 87–89, 93, 97, 102, 104, 11–12, 115, 117, 124–28, 131, 133, 139–40, 144, 157, 161, 168–69, 185, 191, 206–207, 209–10, 220, 226–28, 231–32, 240, 245, 248, 253, 260, 267–68, 270, 274–75, 283–84, 288–90, 292, 295, 299, 301, 306, 308–10, 314, 319, 321, 329
  casualties, 14, 43, 171–72
McCargo, Duncan, 115–16, 230
McChrystal, Stanley, 94
media control, and Thaksin, 163–64, 176
media-driven issues, 301–304
"men in black", 112, 133, 284
  see also black-clad gunmen
micro-finance, 223
middle class, 22–23, 28, 109, 111, 157, 166, 173, 175, 177, 181–83, 216, 222–24, 226, 230, 236, 292, 300, 307
"middle-income peasantry", 324, 327, 330
militant Buddhism, 291
military coup, 20–22, 27, 73, 108, 124, 127, 132, 152, 165, 173, 181, 206, 224, 252–53, 282, 333
  see also coup d'état; September 2006 coup
military role, 88, 180
military rule, 22, 181

military, use of force, 25, 74
Mill, John Stuart, 318
Millennium Development Goals, 324
Ministry of Culture, 185
Ministry of Foreign Affairs, 203, 256, 260
Ministry of Information and Communication Technology, 304
Ministry of Public Health, 14
"mobilized crisis", 193
monarchy, 2, 73–74, 101, 104, 109, 125, 157, 168, 173, 180, 182, 223, 225–26, 251, 254, 261, 272, 293–95, 310, 334–36
  landholdings, 149–50
  overthrow of, 12, 72, 75, 78–80, 83, 88, 123
  politics, and, 3, 250
  relationship with military, 181
  see also absolute monarchy; constitutional monarchy; *"lom chao"*; CPB
money politics, 236, 240, 242, 303, 328
Montenegro, Thaksin in, 31, 203, 270
mop rap chang (demonstrators for hire), 196
"multi-coloured shirts", 289
Muslims, in Southern Thailand, 30, 34, 94, 112, 127, 177, 252
Mussolini, Benito, 269

N
Naew Na, newspaper, 301
Nakan Laohawilai, 308
Naresuan, King, 185
Nation, The, newspaper, 79, 102, 186, 174, 259, 301–302
National Anti-Corruption Commission, 163, 278, 302
National Commission for Truth and Reconciliation, 51
National Defense Volunteers, 237
National Economic and Social Development Board, 277
National Human Rights Commission, *see* NHRC
national identity, 237
National Police Office, 44
"national reconciliation", 92
national referendum, 165, 177
National Security Council, 256
National Statistical Office, *see* NSO
National United Front for Democracy against Dictatorship, *see* UDD
nationalism, 11, 73
NATO (North Atlantic Treaty Organization), 256, 262
Natthawut Saikuea, 115–16, 275, 280, 284, 321
NBT television, 77, 84, 303
neo-liberalism, 303
nepotism, 164
"network monarchy", 230, 293
"new agricultural theory", 328
New Aspiration Party, 150, 194
New Deal, 23
New Force Party, 238
New Mandala, blog, 106
"new politics", 195
New Politics Party, 79, 294
"New State", 80, 85
Newin Chidchob, 21, 31, 33, 317
NGOs (Non-Governmental Organizations), 34, 99, 163, 177, 192, 194, 209, 235, 303–304, 328
NHRC (National Human Rights Commission), 302–303
Nidhi Eowseewong, 157
Nitinai Nakhonthap, 238
Nopphadon Patthama, 203–204, 206, 210, 258, 260–61
North Atlantic Treaty Organization, *see* NATO
NSO (National Statistical Office), 65, 147

O
Obama, Barack, 94, 252, 257, 259, 261

October 1976 generation, 28
Office of the Judiciary, 282
old money, 222
oligarchy, 221–24, 227, 270, 297, 303
Operation Ratchaprasong, 133, 139
Osama Bin Laden, 83
OTOP ("One *Tambon*, One Product") programme, 19, 176

P
PAD (People's Alliance for Democracy), 3, 24, 34, 43, 73, 75, 77, 79–80, 84, 92, 110–12, 116, 127–29, 144, 157, 164, 177–79, 182–84, 193–97, 204, 244, 253, 258, 275–80, 282–83, 285, 289, 293–95, 317–19, 336
PAP (People's Action Party, Singapore), 268
parliament, members of, 222
"partisan exceptionalism", 283
party drive, national politics, 191
party politics, 192
Pasuk Phongpaichit, 27, 245
"people power", 190
People's Action Party, Singapore, *see* PAP
People's Alliance for Democracy, *see* PAD
People's Channel, 77, 303
"People's Constitution", 100, 162, 177, 288, 296–97, 302, 306
People's Power Party, *see* PPP
People's Television, *see* PTV
Phalang Tham (Dhammic Power), political party, 176
Phan Fa Bridge, 76, 109, 132, 143
Phansak Winyarat, 117, 119
Philippines, "EDSA", mass demonstration in the, 192
Phiphop Thongchai, 193
phrai (commoner), 98, 111, 144, 179, 196, 225, 292
Phrommin Lertsuridet, 117
Phromphong Noppharit, 297
Phuea Phaendin Party, 33
Phuea Thai Party, 83, 109, 114, 165, 178, 182, 186, 193, 261, 278, 297, 309
Pinochet, Augusto, 50–52
Plaek Phibunsongkhram, 180, 250, 269
politics of colour, 293–95
politics of desire, 90–91
populist politics, 34, 92–93, 102, 113–14, 164, 176, 223–24, 226, 326, 330
Post Today, newspaper, 308
poverty level, 146, 156, 159, 324
PPP (People's Power Party), 20, 33, 92, 97, 116, 153–54, 165–66, 178, 207, 295
Prachatai, online newspaper, 49, 54
Prajadhipok, King, 180
Praphat Charusathian, 124
Prawet Wasi, 44, 104, 169, 305
Preah Vihear, temple, 203
"Premocracy", 124–25
Prem Tinsulanon, 7, 21, 24, 28, 30, 73, 85, 125, 181, 271, 290, 293
Pridi Phanomyong, 73
"Primary Conspiracy Theory", 72–73, 75
Primo de Rivera, José Antonio, 288
Privy Council, 21, 73, 85, 110, 227, 271, 290
problem state, Thailand as, 205–209
profiteering, 164
prongdong (five-point "compromise" plan), 81, 84–86, 262, 275
Prosecution Department, 278, 282
PTV (People's Television), 275, 303, 309, 319, 321

Q
Queen's Guard, 73

R
rally drive, 191, 194
rally politics, 191–93, 196–97

Rama III, King, 262
Rama V, King, 295
see also Chulalongkorn, King
Ramon Magsaysay Award, 169
Ratchaprasong, shopping district, 4–5, 26, 43–44, 55, 58, 62, 77–78, 95, 109, 132–34, 139, 171, 240, 275, 277–78, 290, 298, 317
Ravenhill, John, 148
regime change, 194
reconciliation, 38–41, 123–24, 126–29, 172, 212, 259, 275, 280, 284
reconciliation plan, 168, 183, 186, 206
Red, symbolic meaning of, 296
Red Gaurs, 30
Red News, magazine, 319
Red Shirts, 4–6, 8, 21, 24–39, 42–43, 49, 55, 64–65, 72–75, 87–88, 92–94, 98–99, 102, 108–109, 111, 115, 122–23, 126–27, 138, 143–45, 155, 157, 166, 171–73, 177, 179, 180, 183–87, 190, 197, 200, 202, 205–206, 208, 210, 220, 224–27, 229, 231–33, 240–45, 248–49, 253–54, 257–61, 280, 288–91, 294, 296, 303, 307, 309, 313, 317–19, 323–24, 327, 329–30
delegitimizing the, 300–301
discredited, 76, 79, 89
grievances, 82, 169
impact on economy, 55–63
"Marxists-Lenninists", as, 208
motivations, 26–27
organizational structure, 298–300
origins of the movement, 135–36
profile of, 135, 141, 196, 215, 296–98
social movement, as, 295–98
statistical analysis of, 66–67
terrorists, branded as, 77–84, 89, 139, 259, 261, 278–79, 293, 300
TV channel, 77, 319
use of force against, 87, 91, 97, 100
see also UDD and *Siam Daeng*
Red Sunday Group, 261
Red TV, 225
"Red Zone", 233, 237
Rettig Commission, 51
Reuters, 144
revolution of 1932, 180–81, 270
"rice premium", 2, 326
right-wing groups, 30
"road map to national reconciliation", 7
Roya, Louise, 269
royal family, 337
royal institution, 3, 293, 337
"royal liberalism", 104
royal succession, 182, 193, 336–37
rule of law, 164, 165, 169, 210, 253, 282, 283, 296
rural people, *see* villagers
rural poverty, 325
rural transformations, weaknesses of, 324–27
Rusk-Thanat Communiqué, 250, 264

S
Samak Sundaravej, 20, 33, 178, 202–204
Sansern Kaewkamnerd, 102
Santi Asok, Buddhist movement, 176, 289–90, 309
Santi Prachatham Network, 43, 49
Sarit Thanarat, 2, 120, 124, 180, 281
Sean Boonracong, 119
Second World War, *see* World War II
Senate, Thailand, 163, 265
September 2006 coup, 3, 9, 20, 22, 92, 97, 100, 105, 109, 132, 134–35, 137, 140, 152, 157, 165, 177, 192, 199, 224, 284, 287, 289, 295, 297, 301–303, 333, 335
see also coup d'état; military coup
SEATO (Southeast Asia Treaty Organization), 250
"semi-democracy", 270
SES (Socio-Economic Survey), 65
Shambaugh, David, 37
Shin Corporation, 3, 201

Siam Daeng (Red Siam), 135, 141
Siam Paragon, shopping mall, 2
Siam Square, 134
Singapore, Thai migrants in, 243, 246
Sinocentric Greater East Asia, 1
Sirikit, Queen, 294–95
Sitthiphon Kridikon, Prince, 2
Sitthisak Wannachakit, 282
sniper attack, 25, 133, 293, 298
social contract, 304, 328
Social Investment Fund, 100
social liberalism, 99
Socio-Economic Survey, *see* SES
Soeharto, 211
"soft coup", 100
soldiers, and risks, 10–14
Sombat Bunngamanong, 52
Somchai Homlaor, 47–48
Somchai Jitsuchon-Viroj Na Ranong paper, 67
Somchai Wongsawat, 20, 33, 178, 204
Somkiat Phongphaibun, 193
Somsak Kosaisuk, 193
Somyot Prueksakasemsuk, 301
Songkran events, 2009, 24, 34, 65, 178–79
Sonthi Limthongkun, 3, 111, 176, 192, 195, 295, 301–302, 308, 315, 318
Sophon Ongkara, 79
Southeast Asia Collective Defense Treaty, 262
Southeast Asia Treaty Organization, *see* SEATO
southern separatists, 88
Southern Thailand, Muslims in, 30, 34, 94, 112, 127, 177, 252
"stable subsistence", 121
State Audit Commission, 302
state propaganda, 83, 124, 139, 301
stimulus measure, 34, 57
Strategies for Creating Greatness, 269
street politics, 195
"Strong Thailand" programme, 329
student activists, 88
Suchinda Kraprayun, 125, 190, 194–95
"sufficiency democracy", 91–92, 121
"sufficiency economy", 91, 235, 327, 329, 335
Sukarno, 269
Supreme Administrative Court, 277–78
Supreme Court, 108, 112, 164, 166, 281–82
Surachai "Sae Dan" Danwatthananuson, 298
Surayut Chulanon, 203, 252, 295
Surin Pitsuwan, 209–10
Susilo Bambang Yudhoyono, 210
Suthachai Yimprasert, 301
Suthep Thueaksuban, 78, 85, 173, 274, 276, 283–84
Suvarnabhumi International Airport, 4, 24, 64, 200, 277, 285
Sydney Morning Herald, The, 144

T

Tajing Siriphanit, 303
Tak Bai incident, 285–86
Taksin, King, 317
TAN, cable TV station, 79
TDRI (Thailand Development Research Institute), 64–65
Temasek Holdings, Singapore, 3, 201
terrorism, 72, 74–75, 81, 83, 124, 157, 173, 207, 253, 274, 278, 280, 282
"terrorist acts", 29, 77–78
Thai Army, 21–22, 25, 35, 43–44, 76–78, 87, 133, 139, 165, 220, 224, 227, 293, 298, 302, 304, 307, 309–10, 323
  psychological warfare unit, 237
  restructured, 128
Thai Chamber of Commerce, 228
Thai Civil Code, 83, 86
Thai Embassy
  in Canberra, 334, 338
  in Washington, 255
Thai Falangism, 288, 295–96, 303, 310

Thai Health Foundation, 228
Thai Journalists Association, 319
Thai particularism, 23, 36–38
Thai penal code, 83
Thai Post, newspaper, 301
Thai Rak Thai Party, *see* TRT
Thai Rat, newspaper, 237
Thai society, polarization of, 292–93
"Thai-style democracy", 91, 121–22, 124–25
Thai-U.S. relations, 248–60, 262, 263
  see also U.S.-Thai relations
Thailand
  crisis of power, 180–83
  culture, 37
  distribution of wealth, 219
  economy, 24, 34, 55–62, 137, 174, 181, 183, 215, 227
  employment, 183, 189, 216, 228, 329
  FDI, 56
  fiscal policy, 2, 326
  foreign policy, 199–205, 211, 251
  GDP, 55–56, 59–62, 216, 222, 325, 329
  history of coups, 132
  income, 27, 147–48, 166–67, 217–18, 325
  inequality, 148–50, 217, 219–20, 228, 324–25
  judiciary, 207, 224, 282
  labour force, 217
  national referendum, 165, 177
  political activism in, 145
  political change in, 18
  political divide in, 93
  poverty level, 146, 156, 159, 324
  problem state, as, 205–209
  reserves, 58
  rural sector, 114
  social structure, 292
  tourism, 57, 59–62, 81, 205, 227
  United States, and, 208
  see also Thai-U.S. relations
Thailand Development Research Institute, *see* TDRI
Thaksin Shinawatra, 2–3, 8, 14, 18–24, 26–28, 30, 33, 36, 73–75, 77, 92–93, 98–99, 110–13, 126, 132, 134–37, 140, 145, 162, 167, 172–73, 177, 181, 187, 190, 199, 203, 205, 210, 214, 221–22, 224–26, 230, 233, 240, 243, 245, 249, 252–53, 255, 261, 270, 275, 280–81, 288, 295, 297, 299, 302, 304–305, 307, 309, 313, 317–18, 326, 328–29, 334
  as head of "New State", 80, 85
  as martyr, 40
  as Prime Minister, 101
  as terrorist, 78, 83–84, 173, 206–207, 259, 293
  criticism against, 165
  economic advisor to Cambodia, as, 204, 212
  family assets, 108, 150, 164, 166
  in Montenegro, 31, 203, 270
  military, control over, 223
  opposition to, 182, 223
  media control, 163–64, 176
  stronghold of, 232
  UDD, and, 195
thammarat (good governance), 267–68, 272
Thammasat, massacre, 30, 236
Thammasat University, 80, 124, 236, 244
Thanin Kraiwichian, 30, 124
Thanom Kittikhachon, 124
The Other America, 23
Theravada Buddhism, 296
"third-hand" element, 293
Third-Wave democracy, 117
Thitinan Pongsudhirak, 125, 283–84
Thompson, Eric, 243
Thongbai Thongbao, 24
tourism, 57, 59–62, 81, 205, 227
Tourism Council of Thailand, 59, 285
Treaty of Amity and Commerce, Siam-U.S., 1833, 262

Treaty of Amity and Economic Relations, Thai-U.S., 1966, 262
TRT (Thai Rak Thai Party), 19–21, 33, 82, 92, 97, 124, 126, 150–51, 153, 162–63, 165, 175–78, 181–82, 201, 240, 258, 316, 318
"Truth Today", as motto and as title of magazine, 295, 319

U
UDD (National United Front for Democracy against Dictatorship), 4, 42–44, 46, 49, 58, 61, 75, 78, 80, 85, 98, 108–19, 134–35, 141, 166–68, 177, 190, 193–94, 196, 206, 224, 244, 248, 253–54, 261, 274–75, 288, 300, 308, 315, 318–19, 321
  impact of rallies, 277, 285
  "national enemies", as, 179
  policies of the, 295–96
  principles of, 142
  "double standards", strategy on, 276–84
  Thaksin Shinawatra, and, 195
UMNO (United Malays National Organisation), 268
UN Security Council, 211
Uncle Boonmee Who Can Recall His Past Lives, film, 184
UNDP (United Nations Development Programme), 146, 148–49, 156, 167, 174
UNESCO (United Nations Educational, Scientific and Cultural Organization), 203–205
United Nations, 204, 209
United States Congress, 260
United States,
  anti-communist efforts, 18
  Tea Party, 314
  Thailand, and, 208
  see also Thai-U.S. relations
Universal Declaration of Human Rights, 305
urban-rural conflict, 29
U.S. Embassy 249, 256–58, 261
U.S. intelligence, 253
U.S.-Thai relations, *see* Thai-U.S. relations
Uthai Phimjaichon, 275, 282, 284

V
Vajiralongkorn, Crown Prince, 182
Valech Report, 54
"vicious circle", of Thai politics, 192
Victory Monument, 178
Vietnam, support for ASEAN statement of concern of, 210
Vietnam War, 250
"village development funds", 113
village economy, 231, 234
village-level politics, 236
village political economy, 242
villagers
  attitudes towards, 300, 307–308, 327
  politically conscious, 20–21, 27–28, 175, 231–33, 236, 242, 246
Village Scouts, 237
"village transnationalism", 243
vote-buying, 92, 237–40, 271
voting patterns, 150–55

W
Walker, Andrew, 91, 121, 242
Wall Street Journal, The, 127
war crime, 250
"war on drugs", under Thaksin, 111, 127, 284
Washington Post, The, 127, 144, 185
Wat Bowonniwet, 291
Wat Chanasongkhram, 291
Wat Mahathat, 291
Wat Pathumwanaram, 4, 12, 25, 39, 134, 171
Wat Ratcha, 291
Wat Saket, 291
Wat Samphanthawong, 291
Wat Samphraya, 291

"watermelon soldiers", 249
wealth distribution, 219
Weera Musikaphong, 115–16, 280
Weng Tojirakan, 144, 193, 253
Wichit Wathakan, Luang, 269
Wilson, David, 120
World Bank, 148, 150
World Economic Forum, 36
World Heritage status, for Phreah Vihear, 204
World War I, 12
World War II, 199, 233, 250, 268–69

Y

Yellow Shirts, 3, 5–6, 8, 21, 24, 27, 29, 31–32, 34, 39–40, 43, 64–65, 72, 92–93, 101, 110, 139, 177–79, 200, 202–204, 223–27, 229, 244–45, 253, 271, 289–90, 293–95, 298, 303, 329, 336
  statistical analysis, 66–67
  terrorists, branded as, 84
  TV channel, 77, 79
Yingluck Shinawatra, 186

www.ingramcontent.com/pod-product-compliance
Lightning Source LLC
Chambersburg PA
CBHW021808270326